D0706947

Unless Recalled Earlier

DATE DUE

MAY 8 2002

ARISTOCRACY, ANTIQUITY & HISTORY

RECEIVED

JUN 1 6 1998

MSU - LIBRARY

ARISTOCRACY, ANTIQUITY & HISTORY

Classicism in Political Thought

Andreas A.M. KINNEGING

TRANSACTION PUBLISHERS
New Brunswick (U.S.A.) and London (U.K.)

HT
647
.K55
1997

Copyright © 1997 by Transaction Publishers, New Brunswick, New Jersey 08903.

All rights reserved under International and Pan-American Copyright Conventions. No part of this book may be reproduced or transmitted in any form or by any means, electronic or mechanical, including photocopy, recording, or any information storage and retrieval system, without prior permission in writing from the publisher. All inquiries should be addressed to Transaction Publishers, Rutgers—The State University, New Brunswick, New Jersey 08903.

This book is printed on acid-free paper that meets the American National Standard for Permanence of Paper for Printed Library Materials.

Library of Congress Catalog Number: 96-5601
ISBN: 1-56000-222-0
Printed in the United States of America

Library of Congress Cataloging-in-Publication Data

Kinneging, A. A. M.
    Aristocracy, antiquity, and history : classicism in political thought / Andreas A.M. Kinneging.
        p.   cm.
    Includes bibliographical references and index.
    ISBN 1-56000-222-0 (alk. paper)
    1. Aristocracy (Political science)—History. 2. Aristocracy (Social class)—History. 3. Political science—History. 4. Classicism. I. Title
HT647.K55   1996
305.5'2—dc20   96-5601
                                                                    CIP

FOR MY PARENTS

CONTENTS

The writing of this book has taken me much longer than I had expected. The delay is due to a number of factors, the most important being that the subject of the book gradually changed. It is hard to say what caused this change. To some degree, it is undoubtedly due to a lack of discipline on my part to finish what I had begun. But mine is not a case of weakness of will pure and simple. For the path I eventually took was at least partially the outflow of the questions I had initially set out to answer.

Although I used different labels at that time, these original questions are most accurately rendered as dealing with the roots and rise of what goes by the name of 'modernity'. That is to say, I was interested in the great transformation that changed first the westernmost countries of Europe and the United States, later the rest of Europe, and at the moment the whole world from a society that is commonly called 'traditional' into one unlike any previously known to mankind: modern society. More specifically, I was interested in the genealogy of the tradition of social and political thought that is generally viewed as the theoretical vindication of modernity: the tradition of liberalism.

However, as I was trying to get a grip on the literature I ran into a seemingly insolvable difficulty. In the endeavor to point down the origins of modernity one almost inevitably winds up in a virtually infinite historical regress, terminating only with Socrates or the sophists. Whatever key feature of modernity one traces back through time -rationality, individuality, the market economy, and so on- one never encounters its 'spring' and 'fountainhead'. Each and every modern thinker seems to have had precursors who apparently knew 'everything' already. Each and every modern institution seems to have been 'foreshadowed' by yet another, earlier institution. The logic of this analysis has led many to seek the seeds of the modern age in the renaissance or even in the high middle ages, and some go so far as to discern the first signs of the present condition at the dawn of Western civilization. In effect, the history of modernity is history *tout court*. History is the genealogy of modern man and the modern mind. Admittedly, this is a deeply enticing philosophy of history, and there is a ring of truth to it. For history does of course lead up to us; we are in a sense the end of history.

But it does not follow that we are the 'star' actor in and of history. If we -that is, the moderns- were on stage at all in the past, until quite recently we at best played the part of an extra. This is the central insight of the present

book. The author has derived it from the work of J.G.A. Pocock, Quentin
Skinner, and -through them- Herbert Butterfield. These writers, more than
anyone else, have reminded their readers of the one-sidedness and unwarran-
tedness of the view of the past as 'leading up to' the present, as the present
'in aspiration'. In the chapters that follow we will go into this subject at
length. Here, it suffices to say that this insight enabled me to see that a
historiography of modernity that does not lose itself in a spiral of anachro-
nisms is possible only if one does *not* study the history of modernity.
Concentrating on the new in the old, as the historians of modernity do, one
is like the friends or the family of a minor actor in a stage play, who are
bound to overestimate the importance of his role in the plot. Only if one is
prepared to study the old on its own footing, as an entity *sui generis*, it is
possible to acquire an adequate understanding of the evolution of old into
new.

Having come to this point I decided to radically alter his plans, and
study the history of not-modernity, so to speak. More specifically, I decided
to concentrate not on the new in the old, but on what was clearly not new in
the old; that is, on the part of the story that is usually left out. This is the
story of those who are commonly regarded as the 'losers' in and of modern
history, those who went down as modernity acquired shape: the aristocracy
and its social and political thought. This book is the result of that investigation.

There is no lack of sweeping statements in the literature about the
aristocracy's fate. Politically domesticated by the crown, economically a
burden, and spiritually superficial the aristocracy supposedly was 'in crisis'
as of the sixteenth century. Its demise was the counterpart of the rise of the
middle classes, the hard-working, thrifty, and enterprising bourgeoisie, the
harbingers of the modern world. I quickly discovered that this picture depends
more on a preoccupation with the origins of modernity than on historical fact.
There is a wealth of literature on every aspect of 'the rising bourgeoisie',
there is hardly anything on 'the demising aristocracy'. That is largely taken
for granted. Yet, things seem to be changing. In the last decades a small but
significant number of monographs has appeared, which point in a direction
that is at variance with the established view. Instead of a weakly and lingering
aristocracy, these studies reveal a strong and thriving *noblesse*, not only in
East-European countries like Russia and Prussia, but also in countries like
France and Britain. Moreover, they suggest that the demise of the aristocracy
is a process that belongs to the history of the nineteenth and twentieth century
rather than to that of the period from the sixteenth to the eighteenth century.

These are still not more than indications that something is deeply wrong
with the standard account of the development of modernity. A new general

view has yet to emerge. At present, we need to chart the whole map, much of which is still *terra incognita*, and we must think through all the implications. This book is a modest attempt to sketch some of the outlines of this map, in particular with regard to the *Überbau*, the social and political thought of the aristocracy. It is in a sense an essay, in spite of its length, precisely because it remains an attempt, an exploration, arising out of a dissatisfaction with the established view, to see if and how a more acceptable account can be constructed. It is not intended as a replacement of that view, but as an effort to achieve a greater balance. For it seems clear that the standard account suffers from a blind spot, which is inherent in its analytical model. Removing that blind spot can only improve our vision.

If the hypotheses developed in this book make some sense, the established view of modernity is challenged in at least two fundamental ways. In the first place, the lineage of the modern turns out to be much less ancient and glorious than is usually suggested. Modernity is an upstart rather than a scion of an old and celebrated line. Just like any parvenu on his way to the top it has fabricated a grand genealogy, whereas in truth its ancestry is 'buried in the dirt'. But if the roots of modernity in the world are much less secure than we have long thought, that leads to the further question how deeply modern the modern really is. Concentrating, as the ruling approach does, on the new in the old, a blind spot for the old in the new is a priori built in. If the demise of the old, as the author believes, was a matter of rhetoric rather than reality, if the old was driven underground rather than extinguished, if the old represents something deeply engraved into our souls, the romantic suggestion that we have become estranged from ourselves needs to be taken much more seriously than most of us, who define ourselves as moderns, are prepared to admit.

In the writing of this book I have incurred many debts, not least to those with whom I disagree. After all, it is often not by the comrades in arms that the eye is sharpened. Nevertheless, the intellectual and moral support of people who are prepared to think along is indispensable. I want to express my gratitude to them. I am indebted in particular to professors H.R. van Gunsteren and U.Rosenthal, who acted as supervisors of an earlier version of this book, which was presented as a Ph.D.-dissertation at the University of Leyden in the fall of 1994, to professors E.H.Kossmann, H.Daalder and P.B.Cliteur, for their valuable comments on the semi-final manuscript, to my friends Brigitte Hermans and Timo Slootweg, sparring-partners in the life of the mind, and to my wife, who frequently -but secretly- believed that my labors would never end. The Netherlands Organization for Scientific Research (N.W.O.) gave me the opportunity to begin my research on what eventually became this book, and the department of political science of the University of Leyden let me finish it properly, even though it took much longer than anybody had expected. Of course, many other people have in some way or the other been helpful: friends, colleagues, and students. If they are not mentioned here by name, it is only because they are with so many. Needless to say, all remaining mistakes, errors, and lapses are due to my deafness, and not to the clarity of the voices that have so benevolently admonished me.

A.A.M.K.

The Hague
January 1996

PART I

THE MODERNS AND THE ANCIENTS

CHAPTER ONE

POLITICS, HISTORY, AND TELEOLOGY

> *If the whole era of the renaissance, from the middle of the 15th century, was essentially the product of the city, and hence of the* Bürgertum, *so was philosophy, which was reborn at the time; its gist was merely the philosophical expression of the thought that reflected the development of this petty and middling* Bürgertum *into a grand bourgeoisie.*

> *Engels*[1]

> *Everywhere I recognized the roots of today's society, deeply implanted in that ancient soil.*

> *Tocqueville*[2]

1. The issue

Just like the notion of 'the middle ages', which was coined in the renaissance, the notion of 'the ancien régime' was introduced when man began to believe that it was all over, and a new epoch had begun.[3] The first studies of the ancien régime as a society and a system of government that no longer existed, appeared in the 1850's. Ever since that time the term ancien régime has been applied to the social and political order of the period that lies between the middle ages and the so-called modern age, that supposedly began towards the end of the eighteenth century. It was originally employed with regard to France, but since most of the other European states have had very similar social and political arrangements, it has become common to think of the ancien régime as a European phenomenon. However, France still holds a special position: it is regarded as the 'paradigm' case, so to speak, of the category.

1.1. The Maîtres-Penseurs
Ever since its inception the idea of modernity has held the study of the ancien régime under its sway. Puzzled by their own age the historians have defined the ancien régime as the birthplace of modern society, and have accordingly concentrated on those aspects which seem to point forward to it. This point

of view and research-agenda was initiated by two men in particular: Alexis de Tocqueville and Karl Marx. They developed theories that have dominated the research on the ancien régime unto this day.

Both believed that modern society differed fundamentally from the society that had preceded it; both believed that it was the creation of the bourgeoisie, the class they thought had come to dominate society in their own day; both believed that modern society had roots that go back to the renaissance, and both accordingly regarded the ancien régime as a kind of embryonic modernity. But whereas Tocqueville saw the development of a centralized, bureaucratic state and the rise of democracy, grounded in an egalitarian and individualist philosophy, as the central features of modernity, Marx regarded the growth of an urbanized, industrialized market economy as its fundamental trait. Moreover, they disagreed on the delineation of the bourgeoisie. Tocqueville defined as a bourgeois virtually everyone who was neither a nobleman nor a manual worker, whereas Marx saw the bourgeoisie as the class of 'capitalists', involved in commerce and industry. Tocqueville emphasized political and intellectual factors, Marx emphasized social and economic factors. Hence, their analysis of the rise of the bourgeoisie differs substantially.

Yet, they do not explicitly contradict each other. Indeed, it is probably due to the fact that the two theories can and have been used in combination that it has become an orthodoxy to view the ancien régime as a hybrid entity, constituting at the same time a kind of postscript to the middle ages, when the aristocracy ruled supreme, and an overture to the modern age, dominated by the bourgeoisie. On this view, the most distinguishing feature of the ancien régime is the decline of the aristocracy and the rise of the bourgeoisie in all spheres of life: the political as well as the intellectual, the social as well as the economical. The ancien régime is conceived of as a society that is not yet modern, but 'aspiring' to modernity. Not surprisingly, given this perspective, much more time and effort has been put into research on the rise of the bourgeoisie in the ancien régime, than into research on its alleged counterpart, the decline of the aristocracy. The latter was largely taken for granted.

Tocqueville was mainly interested in the political role and the world view of the bourgeoisie, defined by him as the *classe moyenne*, that stands between the *peuple* and the *gentilshommes*, encompassing all *roturiers* living off a non-manual occupation.[4] The bourgeoisie mostly lived in villages or towns, according to Tocqueville, but did not have a 'capitalist' outlook or 'capitalist' goals of any kind. On the contrary, its only ideal and ambition was to acquire an office.[5] In the course of time the bourgeoisie succeeded in realizing this ambition and gradually came to dominate the administration in the ancien régime. The *philosophes* of the enlightenment prepared the way for this development intellectually. On Tocqueville's view therefore, the rise of the bourgeoisie is an utterly political and ideological phenomenon. Although his analysis is largely confined to the developments in France, he maintained that these had not been limited to France, but had taken place almost everywhere in Europe.[6]

In Marx's analysis the rise of the bourgeoisie in the ancien régime is interpreted as a consequence of the slow but steady transformation of the 'feudal' into a 'capitalist' economic system. The bourgeoisie is defined by him as the 'capitalist class', made up by people who own 'moveable' as opposed to 'landed' property. Marx was aware of the fact that large-scale industry was still absent and even manufacture was far from dominant in the ancien régime, but the rising influence of the 'profit-motive', inducing reinvestment of earnings, which distinguishes the bourgeoisie from the 'rent-seeking' and consuming aristocracy, was clearly visible according to him. Even in agriculture a growing part of the landowners started to view the augmentation of the productivity of the soil instead of raising the rents as the best way to increase the revenue of their property, Marx argued.[7] Like Tocqueville, he linked the enlightenment to these developments. The only difference is that in Marx' view the *philosophes* are an 'expression' of a material development, whereas for Tocqueville they were part of the cause of this development. Summarizing the above one might say that in the view of both Tocqueville and Marx the ancien régime cleared the way for modern society. It is a period that is marked principally by a gradual *Verbürger-lichung* or *embourgeoisement*. The main protagonists are the bourgeoisie and the aristocracy, conceived of as each other's adversaries.

Yet, the picture would not be complete if it were left unmentioned that both Tocqueville and Marx distinguish a third party on the stage of history, whose role is evaluated in much the same way by both of them. This party is the king. In essence, they regarded him as the proverbial man who is hoist with his own petard. Believing that he could use the bourgeoisie for his own purposes he forged the weapon that was eventually to destroy him. In Tocqueville's version of the story the king, aiming to centralize political power, progressively excluded the aristocracy from government, because it was too independent and stubborn, and ruled increasingly by means of a more pliable and loyal bourgeoisie. In doing so, however, the king destroyed the old order, to which he himself belonged. His removal in the revolution was therefore nothing but a logical culmination of a long process of modernization (i.e. political centralization and equalization) that had been inaugurated by royal absolutism.

Like Tocqueville, Marx considered the king a historical 'force of progress' in the ancien régime, but for a somewhat different reason. He agreed with the former that the king had promoted the bourgeoisie in order to strengthen his own position, and had thus set in motion the process of modernization that eventually led to his own fall. In contrast to Tocqueville on the other hand Marx believed that this process was basically economic, and not political. Pursuing higher tax revenues, to pay the ever rising expenses of the royal court and the army, the king promoted the destruction of the feudal mode of production and stimulated the more remunerative capitalist mode of production. Towards the end of the ancien régime economic power was firmly in the hands of the bourgeoisie, as a consequence of which political power was bound to change hands, Marx argued, because those who control the economy dominate the entire society. In other words, the ancien régime is interpreted by both Tocqueville and Marx as an alliance of some sort between the king and the bourgeoisie, which turned the aristocracy into a useless and powerless ornament. By destroying all the vestiges of aristocratic power and predominance, and setting up a system of royal absolutism, in which their authority was unlimited and their command was law, the kings unwittingly ruined the society to which they owed their own position.

Tocqueville's *Ancien Régime and the Revolution* appeared in 1856, Marx' early work, including the *Communist Manifesto*, in the 1840's, his magnum opus *Capital* (vol.I) in 1867. Surely, historians of the ancien régime have made new discoveries since then, which have changed our perspective of the age? Yes and no. On the fact-finding level, so to speak, our knowledge has increased substantially, as a result of which many old beliefs have become untenable and new ideas have been introduced. Yet, the general perspective on the ancien régime as established by Tocqueville and Marx still seems to prevail virtually unchallenged. Significantly, in what is perhaps the most authoritative and influential history of the ancien régime of our own day, Fernand Braudel's massive *Civilization and Capitalism*, this framework of the age as a period of impending modernity is unthinkingly adopted. And yet, it has become crystal clear by now that as an interpretation of the ancien régime this Tocquevillean-Marxian orthodoxy leaves much to be desired. The first doubts arose in the 1950's, and from that time onwards more and more elements of the orthodox interpretation have come under attack. As a result, a new picture of the ancien régime has gradually begun to emerge, which does not leave much intact of the traditional view.

1.2. The revisionist claim

Most importantly, it became increasingly clear that the idea of the rising bourgeoisie can hardly be considered the *Leitmotiv* of the ancien régime. Indeed, there does not seem to have been a rise of the bourgeoisie at all, at least not in the ways pictured by Tocqueville and Marx, bringing about a gradual *embourgeoisement* of society. Once this dogma was assailed, the complementary suppositions of a declining aristocracy and a system of royal absolutism also began to lose much of their plausibility. Once the linchpin of the traditional view had been removed, the whole edifice started to pulverize. And the doubts that have crept in only a few decades ago have in the mean time been corroborated by a substantial amount of research. The central assertion of the revisionist position is that until the very end of the ancien régime -and beyond- the aristocracy was politically, socially, economically, and ideologically the most powerful and influential group in society in all European countries.[8]

At first sight this probably seems an overstatement. But consider the following basic facts. Virtually all the senior offices in the judiciary, the church hierarchy and the royal administrations were firmly in the hands of the aristocracy. Economically too, the position of the aristocracy was unassailable. The great majority of the population -between eighty and ninety percent- lived in the countryside, which remained the main source of wealth and the largest 'employer' until well into the nineteenth century.[9] These people were mostly peasants, to whom bourgeois values were completely foreign. The aristocracy owned a large part of the land and had some kind of proprietary rights over much of the rest. This gave it such an immense economic power that, by comparison, even rich bankers looked like shopkeepers. It is true that gradually the weight of industry and trade -the economic 'base' of the bourgeoisie- increased, but in comparison to agriculture, industry and trade remained of secondary importance until well into the nineteenth century. Nor was there much of a 'rationalization' in agriculture, with the exception of Britain, which was a source of amazed admiration in France and the other countries on the continent. Much of the agriculture remained subsistence agriculture. Relatively little was produced for the market.[10]

It is no wonder then that throughout the ancien régime the aristocracy remained the frame of reference for social climbers. The aristocracy was the top of the social scale, towards which such people aspired. Every bourgeois wanted nothing more urgently than moving up that scale, in the hope that eventually his progeny would belong to the aristocracy. And this was no idle hope. There was quite some upward mobility, although it was not easy to enter the ranks of the nobility. It usually took several generations of gradually working one's way up, in the process of which such a family invariably dissociated itself altogether from its former background. By the time a family acquired nobility there was usually nothing about it anymore that still reminded of its humble ancestry, so completely had it assimilated to the standards, manners and ethics of the aristocracy.[11] So instead of *embourgeoisement* we find in the ancien régime a process of continuous *Feudalisierung* or *Aristokratisierung*.

There is now much evidence that the rise of the bourgeoisie and the corresponding decline of the aristocracy in the Tocquevillean and Marxian sense was a phenomenon of very limited extent and impact throughout the ancien régime. In reality, the bourgeoisie in the ancien régime was in all respects quite insignificant. Even if one uses the broadest possible definition of the bourgeoisie, including all those who were neither noblemen nor peasants, servants or wage earners in the manufacturing sector, it encompassed ten percent of the population at the most.[12] That might seem a significant percentage, especially as compared to the aristocracy, which on average made up no more than one or two percent of the population, but the wealth and the influence of the bourgeoisie were negligible, as compared to the wealth and the influence of the aristocracy. And most importantly perhaps, the bourgeoisie did not have its own ideology, let alone a 'capitalist' ideology. The bourgeoisie saw the world largely through the eyes of the aristocracy. Even to the section of the bourgeoisie that was singled out by Marx as the engine of modern history, viz. the section that was involved in commerce and industry, 'capitalism' was no more than a dangerous but swift way of getting rich, the purpose of which was to acquire as quickly as possible the means to become a gentleman.[13] Moreover, bourgeois aspirations remained traditional even as the eighteenth century drew towards its close, in France no less than in other European countries.[†14]

[†] The revisionist view does not deny that a decline of the aristocracy has taken place, but it asserts that this phenomenon is part of the history of the nineteenth century and particularly the first decades of the twentieth century. In a sense, the revisionist view does not even deny that a rise of the bourgeoisie has taken place. In fact, the notion of *Aristokratisierung* implies such a process. But it asserts that in working its way upward the bourgeoisie failed to reshape the world according to its image, because in the process it adopted another, well-established and ancient identity. Indeed, a strong case has been made for the idea that the whole idea of modernity as somehow bourgeois should be rejected. After all, it can hardly be maintained that the nineteenth century was the era of the bourgeoisie. This century brought the dissolution of the ancien régime and the development of mass democracy, and placed the bourgeoisie very insecurely in between opposing forces. Hence, the predominance of the bourgeoisie was as little the *Leitmotiv* of the nineteenth century as the rise of the bourgeoisie was the *Leitmotiv* of the ancien régime. The bourgeoisie never dominated the modern world to a degree that would make its position in the nineteenth and twentieth comparable to that of the aristocracy of the ancien régime. It would thus be hazardous to presume that the intellectual developments of this age must somehow be related to the *classe moyenne*. Contrary to what its proponents believe the class analysis of society, which has been so popular for a time, is pre-eminently suited for a study of the ancien régime, and quite useless as a tool to understand the modern world. The notion of a ruling class exploiting the rest of the population for its own purposes does fit the aristocracy of the ancien régime to some extent, but it is merely mystifying when applied to the bourgeoisie of the nineteenth and twentieth century. The idea that the modern age is the age of the bourgeoisie in the same sense as the ancien régime was the age of the aristocracy is an absurdity. There seems to be no *apriori* reason to single out a specific historical factor -the bourgeoisie- and bestow on it the metaphysical role of a prime mover. On the face of it, many things occurred in the nineteenth century which cannot be adequately explained by simply referring to the bourgeoisie's interests, objectives, outlook or whatever. Consider, as an example of the absurdities this idea

The orthodox view that the French kings were absolute monarchs with unbridled power, heading a slightly less efficient version of the modern, centralized, bureaucratic state, or even of a totalitarian state, has also turned out to be insupportable. Apart from the purely physical restrictions on royal authority due to the poor network of communications -it took a courier a week to travel from Nice to Paris-, and the traditional dependence of the French kings on the advice of their counselors -Louis XV constantly reiterated Louis XIV's advice to take counsel in all things-, there was a wide range of formidable checks upon the exercise of monarchical power. The many municipalities, law courts, guilds, provincial estates, and other corporate bodies, all with a different historical background, a different culture, and a different legal code, together formed a profound barrier against royal despotism. The kings could rule only because they enjoyed a large measure of support, which in its turn could only be sustained if the king by and large respected traditional rights and did not act in an arbitrary and illegal way.[15] The traditional view of French government as being absolute confuses theory with practice.[16] From the end of the fifteenth century onwards until the French Revolution there was a whole string of brilliant royalist ideologists, who pleaded for the centralization of authority, and demanded unqualified obedience to the king. Absolutism was above all an ideology, whose aims were never fully realized.

1.3. The Whig interpretation of history

If all this is true, one is of course tempted to ask how it is possible that the orthodox view could have become an orthodoxy at all, presuming that the older historians of the ancien régime were as interested in the truth as we are.

---

generates, the case of late-nineteenth century colonialism, or 'imperialism' as some prefer to call it. The preconception that everything is related to the bourgeoisie naturally invoked the thought that colonialism was essentially a worldwide bid of the bourgeoisie for markets, natural resources, and investment outlets, a view which became so widespread -just like the view that the bourgeoisie brought about the French revolution- that it eventually ended up in highschool and college textbooks. Careful investigation, however, has revealed that it is a myth, just like the allegedly bourgeois French revolution. The economic importance of the territory seized was marginal at the most, and some of it was in fact a liability. Moreover, there is little evidence that pressure was exerted by the bourgeoisie to acquire colonies. 'Imperialism' must be explained in different terms. Hence, the modern age is not the age of the bourgeoisie. The decline of the aristocracy took more than a century and reached its conclusion only in or after the first world war. This decline brought about not only a new society, but a whole new type of society. What disappeared was the type dominated by one specific, clearly identifiable class. Call it traditional society. What characterizes modernity is not that the ruling class of traditional society is replaced by a different ruling class, but that the concept of the ruling class has itself become inapplicable. See Schumpeter 1951; Mayer 1981, pp.275-329

The answer is that the orthodox view seems to be a species of what has been termed 'the Whig interpretation of history'.[17] This is something of a misnomer; a more accurate label would be 'the teleological interpretation of history'. In this interpretation, the society of the ancien régime is an embryonic, imperfect form of modern society, presumed to have already existed 'in aspiration' in those earlier days.[18] Such a conception of the ancien régime (and the past in general) is almost inescapable, if the questions the historian asks pertain to the present instead of the past. As was argued above, ever since its inception the idea of modernity has held the study of the ancien régime under its sway. Puzzled by their own age the historians have defined the ancien régime as the birthplace of modern society, and have accordingly concentrated on those aspects which seem to point forward to it, for instance 'the capitalist mode of production', bureaucracy, bourgeois values and the bourgeois way of life, democracy, and so on. This produces a unsatisfactory kind of historiography, however.

This is not to say that the 'genealogy of modernity' is an illegitimate question for the historian. Indeed, it is one of the most important he can ask: it is one of the main roads to the knowledge of ourselves. But the historian who interprets history teleologically can never arrive at such knowledge, for he has unwittingly begun where he should have ended. He starts with a definition of modern identity, and then traces it back through time, whereas he should have begun in the past and inquire what has remained and survived until today. The teleological interpretation of history incarcerates us in our present self-conception, because it looks for what we already know is there. This book intends to make a case for an non-teleological interpretation of history and, since the proof of the pudding is in the eating, purports to arrive at a different and better conception of modernity and hence of ourselves.

Our objection against the teleological interpretation of history is in essence very simple. Certainly, the origins of many features of modern society can be traced back to the ancien régime, but if one reads the past too much in the light of the present, one is bound to overestimate the importance of the new in the society of the past, and underestimate the old in the society of the present. Of course, many of the seeds from which the modern age grew were sown much earlier, but that does not warrant the conclusion that the ancien régime already exhibited many features of modernity, that it was, so to speak, an 'imperfect', not yet wholly developed form of modernity. Seeds, after having been sown, often lie virtually idle for a substantial time, covered by earth and concealed from sight. The fact that one can dig them out, does not prove that they have started to produce offshoot. But even if it did, such a proof would still be inconclusive. Seeds beginning to sprout and grow often pale into insignificance beside other, more common or more splendid species. It is only when one consciously starts to look for them, that they become visible, and that -after a while- they appear to be everywhere. Thus, the new perspective on the ancien régime does not deny that many of the features of modernity can be traced back to the ancien régime, but questions that these should apriori be taken as notable or even as its principle characteristics. In contrast with the older view, that focused on the signs of impending modernity in the ancien régime, the revisionist view suggests that one investigates the ancien régime without reference to its future, and subsequently trace its remnants in the modern age.

This shift entails more than a mere change in emphasis. It also entails a switch in our framework of thinking. When we study the new in the old we must concentrate on those features that might have appeared inconsequential at the time, and might have escaped the attention of the people living at the time, but have turned out to be the harbingers, the heralds of the new. This presupposes an analysis of the new. When we study the old in the new we must follow exactly the opposite course. We have to begin with an examination of the old, without using as a criterion of relevance the importance aspects of the old have acquired in the new, for if we did we would still be investigating the new in the old. We have to try to see the old on its own footing, i.e. comprehend its *essentialia* without reference to the new. We must see the old as a phenomenon *sui generis*, and realize that the fact that it fathered the new plays only a minor role in its own 'biography'. Having thus analyzed the old we can trace the imprint it has left on the new. If the former approach points out the new in the old, this approach draws attention to the old in the new, and helps us to recognize how much of the old has survived, and how much we are indebted to the old.

The question is of course whether such an approach is possible at all, and if so how the historian has to go about in encountering his material. These issues will be addressed in the following paragraph. But suppose for a moment that it is possible and that we have figured out how to do it, in which direction would that lead us? In virtually all the fields of historiography a substantial body of literature now exists that expounds and defends the revisionist view of the ancien régime, and more and more books appear that address the aristocracy's continuing predominance and supremacy in the nineteenth century.[19] In the field of the history of ideas however, the revisionist view on the ancien régime does not seem to have gained a foothold up till now. This is probably due to the fact that most historians of ideas ignore the *Unterbau* almost completely, and most other historians are very reluctant to set sail on the treacherous waters of the *Überbau*. Consequently, the ideas of the aristocracy, the aristocratic world view, the political and moral thought of the aristocracy have as yet received scant attention and have been largely passed over in silence. But if it is true that this class dominated the ancien régime across the board, and that it continued to play a significant role in society until much later, the question forces itself upon us what remains of the aristocratic ethos in the modern world. Would it not be worthwhile then to chart the aristocracy's outlook? This book is a modest attempt to do just that. It does not consider the aristocratic ideology in the various European states, but concentrates on France. The ideas that circulated in France seem to have been fairly representative of the aristocracies' ideas in the ancien régime as a whole though, if only because the aristocracies of the other countries tended to admire the refinement, the taste, and the ideas of their French counterpart and tried hard to emulate it. The conclusions obtained therefore have a wider application, including even the Republic of the Seven Provinces.[20]

The presupposition is of course that there was such a thing as an aristocratic ideology in the ancien régime. Since this is a controversial point a few words have to be said about it. After all: even if that social class had been very homogeneous -*quod non*-, and its contours could have been distinguished with complete clarity -*quod non*-, there seems to be no good apriori reason to believe that all noblemen shared a common outlook only because they shared a common social and legal status. Only if one held that ideas are mere epiphenomena, mere 'shadows' cast by the *Unterbau*, one could maintain that. But such a position gives too little credit to the inventiveness -or the fickleness and backwardness- of the human mind. Nevertheless, it is more than likely that there is a definite connection between the *Unterbau* and the *Überbau*, although it is sometimes rather enigmatic, and nothing can be said with assurance about the direction of causality. It is probably safest to assume that the two spheres exert a mutual influence on each other. This implies that if it makes sense at all to speak of an aristocracy in the ancien régime it is not apriori meaningless to speak of a concomitant ideology, unless the links between the two spheres are too indirect and unstable to enable us to draw any conclusions about their influence on each other. In that case, social history and the history of ideas cannot be meaningfully combined. But such utter skepticism seems unwarranted. As long as one keeps in mind the caveats named, much stands to be gained from an integrated approach; past ideas become more comprehensible when embedded in their social context, and vice versa.

2. Towards non-teleological hermeneutics

How does one study the world view, the ideology, of the aristocracy of the French ancien régime? Obviously, one has to begin with defining the aristocracy. Who belonged to it, and who did not? To decide this we need some accurate criteria, which are not always easy to obtain. Must we see nobility as a status recognized by law and granted by royal power, or should we rather take the possession of certain legal and honorific privileges as our criterion? Maybe the aristocracy has to be regarded as the governing elite of a state in the ancien régime, or as a group with a certain lifestyle and outlook?

2.1. A matter of definition

In Britain, for instance, there was a peerage and a gentry. The latter wasn't noble in a narrow sense, since it lacked either a title or noble privileges, or both. Also, unlike continental law, English law formally regarded the wives, the daughters and the younger sons of peers as commoners, as well as the eldest sons, until they inherited the title.[21] Younger sons of peers with the title of duke or marques were permitted to call themselves 'Lord', but this title was strictly personal and did not imply any noble privilege.[22] As a result, one of the most notable features of the English aristocracy was the continuous descent from the peerage into the gentry.[23] This group encompassed, in order of descending rank, all baronets, knights, esquires and simple gentlemen. By the eighteenth century, only the baronetcy, which was hereditary, and the knighthood were titles endowed by the crown, and recognized by law.[24] They did not convey any important special privileges, however.[25] The least prestigious ranks were those of esquire and gentleman, which implied a certain standing recognized by society, but were not recognized by law.[26] It should be noted, by the way, that the term 'gentleman' was also used in a wider sense in the eighteenth century, to denote all those belonging to the aristocracy, the peerage as well as gentry.[27]

The question is whether we should regard the gentry as a part of the aristocracy or not. Many older historians have presumed that, since the gentry consisted largely of commoners, it should not be counted as a part of the aristocracy, but rather as a part of the bourgeoisie. That leaves us with a British aristocracy of about 300 families in the eighteenth century -a trifling number indeed- and a society in which commoners occupied most of the leading positions.[†] But is it correct to conclude from these figures that Britain

---

[†] The lack of statistical information makes it impossible to give a very detailed account of the size of the British aristocracy in the eighteenth century. The highest ranking titles, the peers, the baronets and the knights, which were awarded by royal grant, are the easiest to enumerate. A total of 1,003 persons held English peerages during the whole of the century. Before the premiership of the younger Pitt the number of peerages was fairly constant. In 1700 there were 173 peers, in 1750 there were 187 peers and in 1780 there were 189 peers. Pitt's liberal grants of titles caused the number of peers to rise substantially after 1780. In 1800 there were 267 peers. In addition, there were Scottish peers -135 in 1700, 88 in 1800-, sixteen of which sat, since the Act of the Union of 1707, in the House of Lords as representatives of their equals. Finally there were Irish peers -88 in 1700, 208 in 1800-, who, until 1801, could not sit in the House of Lords, but were

was on its way to become a bourgeois -middle class or capitalist- society? A very strong case can be made for a view of the gentry as a part of the aristocracy. The *habitus*, the life style, and the outlook of the gentry and the peerage were quite comparable, and very unbourgeois.[28] Contemporaries believed that the peerage and the gentry were much alike, and regarded the gentry as a part of the aristocracy.[29] Together they ruled, on the land, in the state and in the church.[30]

The delineation of the aristocracy in France proves to be even more difficult, if only because in the ancien régime itself an endless discussion was going on as to the true nature of nobility, and the definition of a nobleman. Some insisted that true nobility was a matter of race. Nobility, they believed, was the mark of descent from the Franks, who conquered Gaul in the fifth century A.D. Others maintained that nobility was a legal status that depends on recognition by the king. And up to the revolution and beyond, the idea persisted that nobility was closely associated to the profession of arms. But there were also many according to whom the holders of high administrative or judicial office were equally noble.

---

eligible to the House of Commons. Excluding the sixty or more Catholics among them, who lived as a group apart and were barred from office, and the handful of indigent, lunatic or otherwise 'disabled' peers, these maybe 300 men, and their relatives, advisers and associates, constituted the top of the political elite in the eighteenth century. It is well established that the majority of the English peerages was of a relatively recent age. The medieval peerage had been largely extinguished in the War of the Roses, but natural factors, like infertility, also caused the decline of many ancient noble families over the years. As a result, the turnover of peerages was extensive. In the eighteenth century about sixty percent of the peerages had been granted less than twenty years previously, about eighty percent had been granted within the previous century, and about ninety-three percent dated from less than two centuries before. This appears to confirm the view that the English aristocracy was very open, but the appearance is deceptive. Investigation of the social background of the newly created peers, makes clear that by far the most of them had direct familial connections with the peerage, and the few that did not have these commonly belonged to the upper echelons of the gentry. A handful were lawyers and only one, Robert Smith, who became Lord Carrington, was a wealthy and distinguished banker, but even his family belonged to the gentry. It was not replenishment that took place, but recycling. The number of English, Scottish and Irish baronets declined from about 860 in 1700 to about 750 in 1800, the number of knights (bachelors) declined from 290 in 1700 to 160 in 1800. Any attempt to assess the size of the group of esquires and gentlemen must remain an informed guess. At the end of the seventeenth century the renowned statistician Gregory King estimated the number of esquires 3,000 and the number of gentlemen 12,000. A century later another statistician, Patrick Colquhoun counted 6,000 esquires and 20,000 gentlemen in England including Wales, and 11,000 esquires and 35,000 gentlemen in the whole of Britain. These estimations have proved to be quite good. If we add all of them together, the British aristocracy of the eighteenth century must have encompassed something between 20,000 and 50,000 families. Taking the average of these totals, and multiplying that average by five -the number of persons per family- we get an, albeit very speculative, figure of 175,000 aristocrats. See Beckett 1986; Cannon 1987

The older historians of the ancien régime employed a very narrow definition of nobility. In this they were following the lead of Tocqueville, who argued in the *Ancien Régime and the Revolution* that the aristocracy had gradually been displaced by commoners in the government of the state. 'At the heart of the realm, very near the throne, an administrative body with exceptional authority had taken form, combining in a new manner all the pre-existing powers, the *conseil du roi*. (..) This council was composed not of great lords, but of persons of mediocre or low extraction.'[31] The same goes for the provincial administration. 'One still finds great lords in the eighteenth century bearing the title of *gouverneurs de province*. (..) But though they still were treated with deference, they had ceased to have any power. All authority was now vested in the intendant. (..) Under him (..) came the sub-delegate. The intendant was usually a man who had recently been raised to noble rank, the sub-delegate was always a commoner.'[32] (author's emphasis)

Until the 1950's these ideas were not seriously disputed. Indeed, they are still widely held. In the meantime, however, a large quantity of evidence has been assembled, suggesting that Toqueville's 'persons of mediocre or low extraction' were bourgeois only by the standards of the most ancient nobility, which could prove that its lineage had been noble 'from time immemorial'. It is true that the French kings of the ancien régime did not generally choose their ministers and intendants from this group. That does not mean, however, that the kings chose *roturiers*. These men had a somewhat shorter noble lineage than the *noblesse de race*, but their plebeian origins usually lay generations behind them, they had completely adopted the standards and manners of the older nobility, they possessed the title and the legal status of a nobleman, and they were regarded as *gentilshommes* by the population at large. To all intents and purposes, these men were noble. It makes no sense to see them as bourgeois. And the *conseilers du roi* and *intendants* were no exception. Wherever one looks one finds that the upper reaches of a hierarchy are almost exclusively filled by men of comparable background: in the administration, the judiciary, the church, and the army. In chapter two of this study the picture of the contours and the social position of the French aristocracy of the ancien régime that has emerged from recent investigations is sketched in broad outlines. To demonstrate that there was little or no sign of a demise of the aristocracy even towards the end of the ancien régime its social position in the eighteenth century is particularly stressed.

2.2. The second rate

But with a definition of the aristocracy we are still only halfway. True, to be able to study the ideology of the aristocracy one has to know whose utterings are to be qualified as aristocratic, since the historian must know where to find this ideology. But it cannot be maintained that aristocratic views on politics and morality can be found only within the boundaries of this class, or that every nobleman necessarily had aristocratic views. On the other hand, it is unquestionably true that they deserve the epithet only when a substantial part, or at least the leading part of the aristocracy believed in them. Unfortunately, that is always difficult to verify. The majority within the aristocracy was 'silent', at least in the sense that it has left no written evidence of its convictions, which is hardly surprising of course, for the majority is 'silent' almost by definition. How to get round this difficulty?

The most common strategy is to link the great writers of an era to the spirit of that era, arguing either that these writers are opinion-leaders who set the tune, or that they express the predominant views most pointedly, because they have the best sense of what moves (a part of) the people of their age. Hence, the opinions expressed by these writers are taken to represent not only their own view, but that of a whole class, party, or nation. This strategy has an intuitive appeal, but as some reflection reveals, in this case our intuition is not a good guide. Usually, the link between the great writer and the spirit of the age is just taken for granted. Yet, no one will deny that, in principle, one should measure his influence rather then simply assume that it exists.

It is obviously no sinecure to measure the influence of a writer. The vagueness and abstractness of the concept of influence brings along a great 'distance' between its definition and any operationalization, necessitating an apprehensive epistemological long jump back to the concept, once we have measured the concrete variables that are supposed to represent influence. Also, the concept of influence points to a recipient: the influenced. It is clear that a writer who is influential in some circles, might well be ignored in many others. Therefore, in order to establish the relative influence of two writers, who are influential in different circles, one would have to establish the relative influence of these different circles, which in its turn can be done only by considering the relative influence of the environments of the two circles. Obviously, we are caught in an endless regress here.

Many historians of ideas recoil from such methodological complications, and concentrate on the influence of writers on other writers, or entirely avoid the question of influence and focus on exegesis, comparison, and criticism of specific writers or texts. However, the first of these approaches doesn't do away with any of the problems named, since it still has to measure influence, and the second tries to solve a pertinent question simply by not posing it anymore. Such withdrawals are to be rejected. The influence of ideas on society in the broadest sense is undeniably one of the most important issues the historian of ideas can raise. Ultimately, ideas are interesting only if they 'matter', if they have 'consequences' in the 'real world'. Even though it is difficult to positively pinpoint writers' influence, we are not completely at a loss, unless we stick to an overly rigid standard of proof derived from the natural sciences. We may safely assume that writers who are frequently quoted (or plagiarized), whose books are on many bookshelves, went through many editions, and are staple fare in school and university curricula, who are often praised (or condemned) in letters, newspapers, and magazines, and who move in the best circles, are influential. Moreover, indicators such as these also give us a clue as to why they were influential.

The most important thing to be learned from such an approach is that it cannot be taken for granted that those writers who from our perspective are the towering figures of an age, or the books which to us seem to incorporate their most essential insights, were similarly esteemed by contemporaries. Like some of the greatest painters, some illustrious political theorists have acquired fame and/or a following only *post mortem*. Sometimes they were known and admired for different works than we judge to be their principal works. And not infrequently a writer (or a book) that is now regarded as of secondary importance at most, was considered an intellectual master(piece) in his (its) own day, and exerted a considerable influence. The history of ideas abounds with telling examples of such shifting appraisals.

Hobbes, for instance, who is today regarded as a cardinal figure in the history of political theory, was in his lifetime and for quite some time afterwards generally seen as a disreputable and marginal writer, whose views did not fit into any of the existing traditions of reflection on the political. Although Hobbes emphatically defended royal absolutism, his ideas were odious even to the staunchest of royalists. It is probably not much exaggerated to say that Hobbes' views 'belong' more to the modern age than to the time when they were first published.

Locke and Hume provide us with two celebrated instances of writers who are at present admired for other books than during their lifetime. Since the nineteenth century Locke's renown is based to a large extent on his *Second Treatise on Government*. In the eighteenth century on the other hand his fame seems to have rested principally on the *Essay concerning Human Understanding*. Whatever may have been the influence of the *Second Treatise* before the nineteenth century, it is certain that, as compared to the *Essay*, it was modest. The pre-revolutionary Locke was essentially an epistemological sensationalist, not a political contractualist. The transvaluation of Hume's work in the course of time is even more remarkable. Until the middle of the nineteenth century his intellectual reputation was based primarily on the multi-volumed *History of England*, which appeared between 1754 and 1762. But eventually public interest in this work began to falter, and at present hardly anyone reads it anymore. The Hume we admire is the author of the *Treatise of Human Nature*, a tract that attracted little attention when it was first published -just enough to give him a certain notoriety and impede his academic career-, but is now widely regarded as one of the foremost philosophical publications of the eighteenth century.[33]

As long as one studies Hobbes, Locke and Hume consciously anachronistically, i.e. as masters of political theory whose views are relevant to the universal or present human condition, it is permissible to study them in isolation from their social and intellectual context, because in such an approach their historical influence or meaning is of no concern. In a 'genealogical' approach on the other hand that would obviously lead to grave interpretative mistakes. It is bad history of ideas to explain the rise of modernity as an effect of works that were in a sense discovered only in the modern age. From a 'genealogical' perspective Hobbes, Locke, and Hume, at least as we read them, are much less important than from an anachronistic viewpoint. Making them central to a history of the political theory of the ancien régime is a fine specimen of the mistakes a teleological interpretation of history is bound to produce. One always has to keep in mind that it may well be that the thinkers or writings we consider important, were not considered important in their own day. As these examples indicate we have to tread carefully; what seems significant and portentous to us may very well have seemed secondary and of minor importance, or even a *faux pas* in an earlier age. And what seemed pivotal and acute to our forebears frequently appears insignificant and irrelevant to us. Whether this is caused by a sharpening of our perception or by the fact that our interests have changed is of no concern to the historian of ideas. He must be aware of these shifting appraisals, he does not have to judge their merit.

More than anything else perhaps we should be on the lookout for what we would now call lesser figures, who do not belong to our pantheon of intellectual giants, who are accorded a minor place at best in the textbooks and anthologies, and are read only by a handful of specialists today, but were celebrities in their own day. Such men were frequently more widely esteemed and had a greater following than those Olympians whose ideas have survived time and escaped oblivion, suggesting that these lesser figures habitually reflect the spirit of an era better than those who are now recognized as the most outstanding writers, whose views were often considered idiosyncratic by their contemporaries. Here we have one important methodological difference between a teleological and an non-teleological approach. But there is more.

2.3. Interpretation and alienation

A study of the ideology of the aristocracy is to a large extent -although perhaps less than we are prepared to admit- a study of a world view that belongs to a different age. The concerns and categories that are central to it are, at least at first sight, unlike the concerns and categories central to any of the modern political and moral traditions. Although it has left us a considerable legacy, for all practical purposes the lineage of aristocratic political and moral theory seems to be extinct today. The writers (and writings) that most clearly and authoritatively expounded the ideology of the aristocracy seem to defend views that are antiquated, irrelevant, or utterly unintelligible, and therefore tend to be disregarded by everyone except the specialist. If at all, they are usually mentioned only in the footnotes of the textbooks and anthologies that are largely devoted to the works of those that do seem to have a more universal message, or simply speak to us with a clearer voice (for instance because they have a more democratic message). The few that have escaped this fate and are still perused, owe their continuing renown largely to the fact that they are seen, teleologically, as forerunners of modernity, who already perceived important ideas that were later more fully or more consistently elaborated.

Montesquieu is undoubtedly one of the most famous of this species. He is hailed as one of the founders of modern liberalism, modern conservatism, modern constitutionalism, modern sociology, modern historiography, modern pluralism, and so on. The number of honorary titles is vast. Anyone can apparently find something to his liking in Montesquieu's works, especially in the *Spirit of the Laws*. Yet, viewed from any of these perspectives his work seems to make no sense as a whole. Accordingly, he is frequently accused of lacking a clear purpose. His work gives the impression of being a potpourri.[34] It is not so much what he says, as what he wants to say with what he says -what is the point-, that escapes most of his modern readers. The question is to what extent this impression is the effect not of Montesquieu's sloppiness but of our reading the text in the light of today's concerns and categories. Without denying that Montesquieu can be profitably read as a founder of any of the traditions named -he manifestly inspired many later authors for many disparate reasons-, that certainly wasn't how his contemporaries read him or how he himself would have described what he was doing. The fact that it is impossible to discover what is the point of some of Montesquieu's utterances in relation to his other seemingly more comprehensible utterances, when we view him in the light of today's concerns and categories, should be taken as an indication that our interpretation misses the point Montesquieu wanted to make, not that he did not have a clear purpose with what he was saying.

It does not seem altogether unlikely that his (partial) unintelligibility is caused by taking him as an (early) participant in our own 'conversations' in the first place, sharing our concerns and categories. Since some of these conversations revolve around themes that are of long standing, and were debated in Montesquieu's time as well, there is no reason to entirely rule out such an approach. But there is no question that he also participated in conversations that have ended a long time ago and are sometimes quite foreign to us, because they hinge on concerns and categories that have little in common with our own. To understand this side of Montesquieu's work and hence acquire a more complete grasp of what he was getting at, the historian of ideas has to lay bare the concerns and categories that structured those now terminated conversations. The more he succeeds in discovering them, the more he will be able to make sense of Montesquieu's *oeuvre*. And the less 'pockets' of 'inexplicable' text remain, the more confidence he can have that his understanding of these conversations is probably quite substantial.

These considerations apply with even more force to less celebrated writers in this intellectual tradition, because these are in general still more engrossed by the conversations of their own time and have less to say to us as moderns, which frequently makes their works even harder to comprehend. It is important to recognize this, since they are arguably more representative of aristocratic thought than Montesquieu, who in some ways is a rather idiosyncratic figure and, like many of the other most outstanding political thinkers, stands somewhat apart from his contemporaries. Though greatly admired by them, some of his views were perplexing and others were considered outrageous. He clearly writes within an established tradition, but his employment of some of the key concepts of this tradition is out of the ordinary. For instance, his claim that 'virtue is not at all the principle of monarchical government', in which it is supposedly replaced by honor, was evidently idiosyncratic, since it suggested not only that in monarchies there could be no virtue, but also that virtue and honor were wholly foreign to each other.[35] To mollify his critics on this point Montesquieu felt obliged to preface the edition of 1757 with an *avertissement*, declaring that he had been misunderstood: the concept of virtue as he had used it was supposed to mean political virtue, i.e. 'love of the fatherland and of equality', and even that could be found in monarchies. He had merely wanted to argue that the ultimate spring -*ressort*- of monarchies is honor.[36] The necessity of this apologetic move is explained by the fact that traditionally virtue and honor were regarded as two sides of the same coin, and both were assumed to be of central importance in the life of a gentleman, whether he inhabited a republic or a monarchy.

As this example demonstrates, it is imperative that we understand the *langue*, the concerns and the categories basic to the discussion, before we can make sense of any *parole*, i.e. of what a particular writer is doing. This implies that we start by studying the first. Yet, this is impossible since *langues* exist only in and through *paroles*. It follows that we can only learn the first by studying the second. Clearly, we are mixed up in a circularity here.[37] How to proceed to emerge from it unscathed? There seems to be no precise method. The historian must learn to recognize and familiarize himself with these concerns and categories by reading a considerable number of texts from the period he is studying and from before that time.

While doing that he should keep in mind four things.[38] First of all, an anachronistic reading of a text must be avoided, for he does not want to invent, but to uncover the past. To succeed in that, he must endeavor to distance himself from present concerns and categories, and he must eliminate from consideration those interpretations of a text that could not have been conceived by the author and/or his readers.[39] Obviously, such a distancing can never be completely successful. Present concerns and categories will always to some extent 'contaminate' the historian's view of the past. Nevertheless, a mental effort can reduce one's unreflected immersion in the present.

Secondly, in order not to overemphasize the features that 'lead up to' the later era, he has to 'bracket' his knowledge of 'what happened in the end'. In this pursuit hindsight is not a benefit but a disadvantage. To give a rather provocative example: in studying the French ancien régime one should 'forget' that it ended in a revolution. Because this fact -the revolution- preoccupied the minds of the older historians of the ancien régime, they could think of this society only in terms of a conflict between a progressive and a reactionary party. The problem was to find the conflict, which theoretically had to exist. And when none worthy of the name could be discovered, they were obliged to revert to subsidiary hypotheses, proclaiming the situation was 'objectively contradictory', and therefore bound to lead to a clash, even though those concerned, due to their 'false consciousness' were not yet aware of the circumstances. But perhaps there weren't any major conflicts? Perhaps the revolution had no 'structural' causes, and was just an accident? In any case, there is no good reason to let the revolution dominate our view -and our research- of the ancien régime.

Strictly speaking, the prescription to 'bracket' our knowledge of 'what happened in the end' is rather impractical. For how can we forget what was the outcome? It is an entirely different soccer-game we are watching, when we already know the final score. However, the observation is somewhat beside the point. Of course, when studying the French ancien régime the historian cannot forget the fact that it was eventually displaced by the social and political order we call modern society. But in doing such a study he should not begin with an analysis of modernity, and then read (and reason) backwards in time. For if he does he will inevitably make modernity central to his analysis of the ancien régime. Departing from a contraposition of alleged 'forces of reaction', doomed to collapse, and 'forces of progress', with history on their side, he will produce the kind of teleological historiography that reduces an era to the status of overture to the subsequent era. This would be like making someone's death central to the study of his life. That is feasible and legitimate, as long as one is aware of the fact that one is not ultimately interested in that person's life, but merely in the question why and how he died. No one can claim, however, that to know the cause(s) of his death *eo ipso* provides us with much valuable information about his life. Chances are that all it tells us is that the person had a smoking habit or a weak heart, or that he was at the wrong place at the wrong time. Even if he died of a drug overdose, it would be premature to conclude that he must have led the life of an addict. In sum, the cause(s) of a person's death say little about his life, with the exception perhaps of his last months or years, in case his demise was heralded by a protracted disease. The methodological upshot of this is that, instead of reading backward in time, the historian should read forward in time -literally-.

Thirdly, he must compare the texts throughout, searching for identical or similar utterances, but also for shared presuppositions behind dissimilar or even contrary utterances. Initially, the consistency of every text should be assumed; if it appears to be inconsistent that should be taken as a sign that the historian does not yet grasp the exact nature of the author's utterances or presuppositions. Criticism pertaining to consistency or cogency comes in only at the very end, if at all. It is meaningless unless one has a thorough understanding of the text's basic categories, and it is of no concern to the historian of ideas unless he believes that inconsistency or incogency can to some extent explain subsequent intellectual development.

Finally, he should focus on the question what were ordinary utterances and presuppositions, and try to separate these from the extraordinary. Of course, Montesquieu's declaration that he had had 'new ideas: new words have had to be found or new meanings given to old ones', holds good for many if not all writers.[40] Every *parole* departs from a pre-existent *langue* and transforms it in and through its employment of this *langue*. It does not follow, however, that a distinction between the ordinary and the extraordinary is pointless. Every writer probably exhibits the two in his writings, but on the whole some writers possess a more traditional verbiage than others; they stay closer to ordinary language. Hence, they are the principal heralds of a *langue*. They receive their message from the immediate past, treat it with the respect due to a valuable legacy that should be preserved, and hand it over to posterity as little revarnished as possible.

Because of that and the fact that in the short run these writers are generally more influential than their more deviant colleagues (even though in the modern age the deviant has become rather fashionable, as long as it is innocent), it is clear that they are the main source of the historian who aims to discover the contours of a *langue*. As has been set out above, these ordinary writers are often men that were eminent during their lifetime, but are now regarded as lesser figures in the history of ideas. The historian should therefore devote at least as much attention to these men as to the happy few who have ended up in the textbooks and anthologies. If and only if all four of these guidelines are consistently followed, something like an non-teleological interpretation of history will emerge.

2.4. Inverted Cartesianism

Admittedly, all of this sounds fairly old-fashioned, and is reminiscent of the efforts that originated in the early nineteenth-century to establish a truly historical consciousness. Preoccupied with the ideas of deceptive appearance and incomplete explanation (i.e. not doing justice to complexity), these efforts aspired to tell *wie es eigentlich gewesen*, respecting difference and development. The author hastens to say therefore that, doubtlessly, the uncontaminated truth about the past is unattainable.

Every interpretation is necessarily imbued with present concerns and categories. The ambition to recount how things truly were, is a romantic ideal of authenticity, that can never be attained by the historian. But does it follow that anything goes, and every interpretation is as good as any other? Not everything that cannot be proved with certainty, is equally enshrouded by darkness. Certainty is not the only good reason for a belief. Indeed, certainty has little bearing on life at all. Everything we do involves interpretation, but not always with equal 'accuracy'. Sometimes we misinterpret, and are run over by a car. Hence, it is not only possible but necessary that we distinguish between good and bad interpretations. Therefore, theoretically there is no objection against a distinction between good and bad interpretations.

Of course, it is a somewhat different matter whether in the specific field of historiography we can legitimately say that some interpretations of a text are closer to its true historical meaning -whether we speak in terms of intention or in terms of reception- than others. In some realms interpretative problems are much greater than in others. Everybody 'knows' what the different colors of traffic-lights signify, except the occasional Martian who believes that 'red' means 'stop', 'green' means 'go', and 'yellow' (always) means 'accelerate'.[41] But he is clearly mistaken, and is bound quickly to correct himself or be forcefully corrected. Moreover, there is no debate about the question which is the right interpretation.

It is more exacting to make sense of a literary text, whether it is 'ancient' or 'modern', and there is usually no consensus as to its true historical meaning. This used to be taken as a sign that more research had to be done to acquire a better understanding, but in recent years many have become skeptic as to the feasibility of a justified reduction of interpretations. More and more different interpretations coexist and they are not likely to converge, it is argued, unless for some reason our epistemological reflexivity were to diminish. But this is not the end to it, for the question then shifts to a higher level. Instead of asking whether interpretation A is better than interpretation B, it now becomes crucial whether a cumulation of interpretations improves our understanding of the past. If even that cannot be maintained the conclusion must be that historiography is nothing but a kind of fiction. The present writer is not yet prepared to draw such a conclusion. It seems to him that those of us who have lost all faith in the possibility of an accurate understanding of the world, are in fact still Cartesians, who believe that certainty is the ultimate criterion of knowledge.

3. Ontology and political theory

Simplified to the utmost, the political discourse in the ancien régime was a discussion within the aristocracy about the political relation between the king and the nobility. Put in this way, it is immediately clear why today not many people are interested in this issue anymore. Both kings and nobilities have become relics of the past, whose political influence has all but vanished, at least in Europe. The issue deserves better, however. Not only is it interesting, but below the surface it deals with matters that are still highly relevant both in theory and in practice.

The aristocracy conceived of itself as an order of the greatest and the best, with a natural right (and duty) to rule the realm. Aristocratic political theory is basically a tradition of reflection on the nature and the limits, the rights and the duties of leadership, particularly public leadership. It is not difficult to comprehend that such a self-conception was bound to make of central concern to the aristocracy the question of the extent and the limits of the authority of the king, who -everyone agreed- was in some sense placed above all others. Whole libraries of books and pamphlets appeared on this subject in the ancien régime. Sadly, virtually nobody reads them today, but they were once avidly perused, and intensely discussed. Apart from the fact that the subject seems hopelessly irrelevant to the modern world, anybody who delves into this literature out of sheer curiosity, notwithstanding its apparent uselessness, will notice immediately how strange and impervious it is. Two good reasons not to study the subject, most historians must have figured; which would explain the lack of scholarly interest.

However, this judgement is unjustified. Once one has penetrated through the surface, the sense of irrelevance quickly disappears. Whether it has really become obsolete, or whether it still lingers on unacknowledged, studying this pre-modern discourse on politics and morals deepens our insight into modernity and into ourselves, if not by making us recognize what was there all the time but was driven in the underground, then by the sheer force of contrast, thus greatly enhancing our power of vision.

3.1. Classicism
A formidable hurdle must be taken, however, before this aristocratic discourse

opens itself up to us. We must break through its strangeness and imperviousness. And that is far from easy, because the impenetrability is not superficial but goes to the very core: the ontological presuppositions of being. It is quite impossible to make sense of the writings that make up the aristocratic discourse if one is not acquainted with this ontology, since it runs counter to the deepest convictions most of us hold about the nature of reality.

If *nomen est omen*, the aristocratic discourse must be called the classicist tradition in political and moral thought. On first consideration, this might seem a peculiar proposal. Classicism is a common designation in the historiography of literature and art, but in the historiography of political and moral thought the notion of classicism is, significantly, a neologism. It is usually suggested that classicism was principally a literary and artistic phenomenon. That it had an elaborate political and moral counterpart is mostly passed over in silence. It is not that one is not aware of the existence of such a pendant. That classicist principles were partially reflected in the political and moral thought of the age is common coin. But in the historiography of this field it gets little or no attention, because it is regarded as reactionary, superficial, outdated, and confused. In the contemporary, modern view of the political and moral thought of the seventeenth and eighteenth century the figures that stand out are Hobbes, Locke, and the *philosophes* of the enlightenment. Not surprisingly, these are all considered precursors of modernity, the harbingers of the new, bourgeois world. Here we have the teleological view of history at work. (Interestingly, as the above makes clear, this view seems to have less of a grip on the historiography of literature and the arts.)

The following facts about classicism are generally recognized. First, that it was the prevailing literary and artistic 'style' in seventeenth- and eighteenth-century Europe. Secondly, that it reflected aristocratic taste. Thirdly, that the ancients, particularly the Romans, furnished the models; hence the designation. And fourthly, that France was the epicenter of classicism. The aristocratic discourse of the ancien régime on politics and morality shared all of these characteristics with its counterparts in literature and the arts. That is why it makes sense to call it the classicist tradition in political and moral thought. That this tradition reflected aristocratic taste is obvious, and that France was its epicenter will be readily underwritten, but that the aristocratic discourse on politics and morality was the prevailing 'style' in social philosophy in seventeenth- and eighteenth-century Europe, and that the ancients, particularly the Romans, furnished its models, are claims that must clearly be documented. Because if they are true our historiographies of political and moral thought must be substantially revised. Indeed, the 'genealogy' and even the personality of modern man might then be different, viz. more 'ancient', than is generally presumed. Chapter two to five are devoted to a substantiation of these claims.

As has been set out, due to its ontology classicism is bound to appear strange and impervious to today's student. Our first concern must therefore be the delineation and explanation of the fundamental categories of its analysis of being. These, like most other elements of classicism, were derived from the ancients, especially the Romans. But because the classicist authors, like their Roman educators, were rather more interested in politics and ethics than in metaphysics, little can be found in their works on their ultimate assumptions as to the nature of reality. These have to be largely deducted from their writings on the former subjects. However, we do not have to grope in absolute darkness, for they are clearly of Platonic and Aristotelian descent, though perhaps in somewhat loose a fashion.

3.2. Being: permanence and hierarchy

Like all thinkers ancient and modern, classicist writers agree that the world as we perceive it is in a state of continuous change. Moreover, they agree that nothing is knowable unless it is to some extent unchanging. For pure change implies the impossibility of a localization of an entity in time and space, of knowing that 'it is there', or even that 'it has been there', however short. Knowledge presupposes stability, continuity, order. The question then becomes how and to what extent knowledge is linked up with the world, with being. The classical/classicist answer to this question is that knowledge is and must be knowledge of reality. But since knowledge is knowledge of the changeless, reality is changeless. Knowledge of the real is knowledge which abstracts from change, and seeks the permanent and universal. The permanent and universal is the real. It is called the essence or true nature of an entity. It is independent of time and space. And it is not directly perceptible, since perception in captivated in the flux of appearance. But it is intelligible. Concrete matter is part of reality to the degree that it transcends fluctuation, to the extent that it 'participates' or 'shares' in the essential characteristics of an entity. The more the concrete succeeds in imitating the essential, the more real -permanent and universal- it will be. Hence, the classical/classicist doctrine of *mimesis* or *imitatio*. To be sure, this is not a doctrine of resemblance. Concrete entities never resemble the essences, for they always contain much that is not essential. *Mimesis* thus allows for the apparent differences of the world of perception, as well as for change. What it demands is that the essential characteristics of an entity must be held on to if it is to continue to exist, to be a reality.

It follows that there are two kinds of change. On the one hand there is change that does not count ontologically, because it is limited to the ephemeral world of the phenomena. On the other hand there is change of the essence. This kind is ontologically of the greatest consequence, for it involves a qualitative jump. The entity acquires a wholly different identity, so to speak. It becomes something else entirely. Thus, apparently great changes may have no real effect whatsoever, and apparently minor changes can turn all things upside down. Consequently, it is of the utmost importance for an entity to remain essentially the same, i.e. to stick to what is permanent and universal, to what has always been the rule or the way of doing things; a position which obviously invokes a strong interest in history. For on this view studying the past of an entity is a good method to lay bare its essence, to find out what is constant in its make-up.

Classical/classicist ontology assumes that behind the flux of perceptions lies the real, eternal world of stability and order. This world is in all respects hierarchical. Each and every relation is by its very nature a relation between a superior and an inferior. The natural order is an order of ranks, reaching from the most perfect and excellent at the top to the most wanting and mean at the bottom. As a species man is superior to the animals, because he is endowed with reason. Within the species one man is superior to another, because one is more reasonable than the other.

This relation between the superior and the inferior man is not simply a relation between more and less. It has strong overtones of opposition, of polarity, of good and bad. The inferior is consistently associated with the perceptual world of the concrete phenomena, the superior with the *mundus intelligibilis* of abstract essences. Moreover, the perceptions are intimately related to the so-called passions; both are part of the sense-world, and thus belong together in the classical/classicist idiom. The link between the superior and reason entails not only the transcendence of the perceptions but also of the passions, i.e. of animal existence. Theoretical reason enables man to see the world as it really is, practical reason enables him to act reasonably and lead a reasonable life. If the perceptions were to rule instead of true knowledge, the passions instead of reason, the natural order would be subverted, the world put on its head, bringing about instability and chaos. Such an inversion is precisely what the classical/classicist notion of vice refers to. Conversely, the notion of virtue always implies rule of reason and true knowledge, conformity with the natural order, which effects permanence, stability, peace.

In a sense, vice, the rule of perception and passion, comes easier than virtue, the rule of reason and true knowledge. That is why the superior are with so few and the inferior with so many. Vice 'comes natural'; it is the weakness, the insufficiency that is there to begin with, it is that which must be transcended. Virtue on the other hand takes an effort. Reason and knowledge must be acquired and conserved; they can never be taken for granted. Before one is aware of it, degeneration and corruption, the change from good to bad, has set in. Nature easily jumps from virtue to vice. To jump back, however, is quite a different matter. Clearly, on this view, the good and the bad are closely related. They belong to the same family, so to speak, and have a distinct family-likeness. One always reminds you of the other. And yet, they are essentially each other's opposite. That is exactly why they look so much alike. They are each other's mirror-image. Change for both of them means becoming the other. Vice 'comes natural' to man. But at the same time, the transcendence of perception and passion is what makes man more than a beast. To know reality and to be virtuous is what makes him truly human, and is therefore his mission and purpose as man. To forsake that mission is to remain less than human, to linger on the level of the beast, driven by passion and perception. There are two options for man. Either he chooses the good, in which case he must refuse to obey his immediate impulses, and let reason be his sole guide. Or he lives according to the dictate of his perceptions and passions.

This may be called the classical/classicist doctrine of spiritual freedom, although the ancients would have spoken of it in terms of leadership or rulership. Only that man is a leader who is governed by the *telos* of man. All others are really slaves; they derive their principle of motion from the phenomenal world. Although they may still be said to choose, the choices they make have no significance. The natural order commands that these men obey. This 'logic' of virtue and vice is all-pervasive in life. It is effective at all levels of human existence; within the human breast, between different persons, within groups and states. Indeed, the whole human world is structured by it. With order, hierarchy, and polarity, analogy is a basic axiom of classic ontology. The peace of mind of an individual, for instance, does not, in principle, differ from the peace within a state, or between states. The nature of the one reflects that of the other. There is always a superior and an inferior partner.

3.3. Being and politics

Returning now to our point of departure, the central theme of the aristocratic political discourse of the ancien régime, viz. the political relation between the king and the nobility, it is obvious that in view of its ontological presuppositions this discourse revolved around the questions (1) what was the essence of kingship, of nobility, and of monarchy in general -the *maior*-, and (2) how the relevant French institutions fitted into this abstract, timeless pattern -the *minor*-.

As for the *maior*, what is necessary from this perspective is an abstract 'political and moral science', which enlists the essential properties of all relevant entities and the relations between them. How does one do that? How can one transcend the empirical multiplicity of the phenomenal world, climb out of the cave, and point down the essences? The main source of inspiration and guidance in these matters were the ancients, especially the Romans. From them the aristocratic writers derived their definition of kingship, nobility, monarchy, and all the other relevant concepts. And if they disagreed, their argument commonly took the shape of a discussion of the correct interpretation and message of the ancient sources. For instance, classicist political analysis consistently employs the classical scheme of regimes, which usually distinguishes seven forms of state. Monarchy, aristocracy, and democracy, and their respective corrupt counterparts, tyranny, oligarchy, and ochlocracy or mob-rule. And a mixed form of state which is generally considered the best of all. The debate was about the questions what could count as essential features of each of these forms of state, and how corruption came about and could be prevented. In looking for a solution to these questions Roman literature was regarded as the highest authority, and was accordingly studied with the utmost attention.

Understanding the French institutions -the *minor*- meant applying this general scheme to France. But such a categorization is feasible only if one knows the essence of its institutions. This essence is what has always been there, the timeless, the changeless. Only a study of the past can reveal it. Hence, we see a massive turn to history by virtually all the political and moral writers of the classicist age. History was at the heart of politics. It was felt first that an understanding of politics presupposed a thorough knowledge of the past, and secondly that all political claims must be historically founded. Of course, this concern with history seems strangely 'unhistorical' to us, because it sees identity where we see difference.

An example might be helpful at this point. Today it is taken for granted that the dissimilarities between the French monarchy of the fifteenth century and that of the eighteenth century are so considerable that they must be interpreted as different political systems in their own right, even though both are named 'the French monarchy'. To the *gentilshommes* of the ancien régime this view would have been incomprehensible. Not being fools generally, they did not deny that notable changes had taken place between the fifteenth and the eighteenth century, but instead of drawing the conclusion that this had changed the nature of the monarchy, many of them denied that these changes had altered the fundamental characteristics of the system as a whole, indeed that these could not be altered without turning the monarchy into a tyranny. It was admitted that the monarchy governed by Louis XII and that governed by Louis XV were in many ways distinct, but as long as certain fundamental characteristics of the political system were left intact, the French monarchy of the fifteenth century was considered to be essentially the same as that of the eighteenth century. Similarly, the threats to the survival of the monarchy might look different every time, but were conceived of as in essence the same, since they had identical effects on its nature, and must therefore be countered in a similar way.

If this sounds incomprehensible, it will probably become clearer in the following. For the discussion of the *maior* -the political and moral science- and the *minor* -the historiography- of classicist thought will take up the bulk of these pages. The former is the subject of part III, which is the centerpiece of the book, in a literal as well as in a figurative sense. The latter is the subject of part IV. Two important remarks should be made in advance, however, one of a methodological and another of a programmatic nature.

3.4. Studying the ancients and the moderns

First, for the sake of clarity and economy a short cut has been taken in the chapter that expounds classicist political and moral science. Instead of approaching the Romans via the aristocratic writers of the ancien régime, we turn to the first right away. Hence, the chapter is largely devoted to a review of Roman political and moral thought, although it purports to be something else (as well), a move which may seem rather precarious methodologically. It is allowable, strictly spoken, only if it can be proved that classicist thought and classical thought are very much alike, and that our picture of classical thought is similar to the classicist picture. To check that out would be beside the point however. The present author has no wish to defend either one of these two presuppositions. Many significant differences can surely be found in the various views and interpretations. But such a conclusion asserts what is obvious, at least to the modern mind. As will be shown in chapters three and four, the classicist mind perceived itself as stringently classical in orientation. In all fields, classical thought was its point of departure. It seems plausible therefore that the intellectual history of the ancien régime can most profitably be read on the basis of this fact. Amazingly, however, such a reading has not been provided yet. Of course, as always the proof of the pudding is in the eating. If we succeed, in this way, to get a firmer grip on the texts of the age, if they become more accessible and meaningful to us, if they make more sense than before, we will have obtained as much as we can hope for.

The second remark that must be made here is that the thesis of the predominance of classical/classicist political and moral thinking in the ancien régime opens up a much wider horizon of research than that covered in part IV of this book, which concentrates on the *Wirkungsgeschichte* of only one element of the classical political language, viz. the idea of mixed government, in the discourse of only one country, France. As has already been set out, there are very strong indications that the intellectual language was similar in all European countries, including Britain and the Seven Provinces, which are customarily regarded as oddities in the ancien régime. But further research is undoubtedly necessary. Moreover, the language as such deserves a much more comprehensive and thorough examination than it has obtained until now. For instance, it is clear that the notions of honor, pride, shame, reputation, renown, and the like are central to the aristocratic concept of morality and politics, and that these notions are largely derived from the ancients, but their exact meaning, interrelation, and working still have to be investigated *in extenso*. A history of ethics and politics thus conceived would look very different from the ones we are used to today. It would concentrate on figures like Castiglione, the chevalier de Méré, Lord Chesterfield, Lord Shaftesbury, La Bruyère, La Rochefoucault, Corneille, Racine, Madame de Sévigné, le Duc de Saint-Simon, to name only those that are still relatively well-known, although scarcely read, today. And such a history of ethics and politics would give an entirely different reading of celebrated authors like Montaigne, Hume, Smith, Montesquieu, Rousseau, Burke and many others. All of these men, the famous as well as the forgotten, were deeply concerned with the question of honor and pride.

That most contemporary commentators pass over this issue in silence, that it is evidently an intellectual blind spot, is also an effect of the predominance of the teleological approach in historiography. Viewing these men as precursors of modernity, the historian feels justified in stressing the aspects of their work that seem to provide the ideological foundation of his own world, and in disregarding the aspects that appear to him as remnants of a more dated style of thinking, which merely prove that the precursors were still confused in their thinking. This conception is mistaken, and very obviously so. Yet, probably no other mistake in historiography is made as frequent as this one. How to explain this? The answer may be simply that a teleological bias is almost inescapable when the roots of modernity are the historian's central concern. In such a framework the past is essentially a prelude to the present, and what counts in the past is what leads up to the present. The rest is conceived of as noise. This noise is what we have left behind us, what we once were but are no longer. It is our former self, the pluperfect, the not-modern. Hence, the framework is ultimately grounded in the idea of an antithesis between the ancient and the modern. The meaningfulness of theorizing about modernity depends on the viability of the belief that 'something has changed fundamentally', that we are worlds apart from our ancestors. Otherwise the desire to know what is new in the old, what points forward to 'us' and separates as from 'them', would not even have occurred to us.

So we are *homines novi*, on a quest to find our roots, presumably to understand ourselves better. The crucial point is that as long as we look for our roots in this way, this goal will never be reached, since the teleological approach to history begins where it should end: with a conception of modernity. Suppose a part of us is still ancient, so to speak. That will never occur to the historian, if he has apriori excluded the possibility of ever having to draw such a conclusion, because he has eyes only for what is not ancient. If he accidentally stumbles over something that is evidently ancient, he will dispose of it with the argument that this has really nothing to do with us, that it is at best a rudiment, and is bound to wither away. But what if the ancient is still a very important part of us, instead of a rudiment, and the modern is only a superficial layer of varnish? Aren't we then condemned to remain a riddle to ourselves, as long as we see ourselves as moderns? Perhaps not only the *history of* ethics and politics stand in need of a revaluation of the ancient. In the final chapter of this book we will return to this question how modern the modern really is.

NOTES

1. *Ludwig Feuerbach und der Ausgang der klassischen deutschen Philosophie* (1888), in: *Marx-Engels Werke*, vol.XXI, pp.302-303. 'Wie die ganze Renaissancezeit, seit Mitte des 15. Jahrhunderts, ein wesentliches Produkt der Städte, also des Bürgertums war, so auch die seitdem neuerwachte Philosophie; ihr Inhalt war wesenlich nur der philosophische Ausdruck der der Entwicklung des Klein- und Mittelbürgertums zur großen Bourgeoisie entsprechenden Gedanken.'

2. Tocqueville, *L'Ancien Régime et la Revolution*, Avant-propos, 'J'y rencontrais partout les racines de la société actuelle profondément implantées dans ce vieux sol.'

3. Campbell 1988, p.1

4. Tocqueville, *L'Ancien Régime*, II.9

5. Tocqueville, *L'Ancien Régime*, II.9

6. Except in Britain, where 'les anciennes familles nobles (..) étaient restées les premières en richesse aussi bien qu'en pouvoir. Les familles nouvelles qui s'étaient élevées à côté d'elles n'avaient fait qu'imiter leur opulence sans la surpasser'. Tocqueville, *L'Ancien Régime*, II.8

7. Like Tocqueville, Marx thought of Britain as an exceptionable country, but for a different reason. In his view the rise of the British bourgeoisie had not been less but more marked than on the continent.

8. This applies with equal force to countries like Britain and the United Provinces. The idea that these countries were more bourgeois than France is a misconception. On the situation in Britain there is a wealth of literature. See e.g. Beckett 1986, Bush 1984, Cannon 1987, Habbakkuk 1953, Mingay 1963, Ravitch 1966. On the United Provinces, see e.g. De Jong 1987, Van Nierop 1990, Aalbers and Prak (eds.) 1987.

9. Taylor (ed.) 1975, p.xlix

10. Behrens 1985, pp.128-133

11. Chaussinand-Nogaret 1984, p.52

12. Dakin 1972, p.36

13. Taylor 1973 , pp.288-328

14. Campbell 1988, p.72; Doyle 1978

15. Campbell 1988, pp.54-55; Doyle 1980, pp.54-55

16. It probably is the result of placing too great an emphasis on the institutional records of the central government. See Campbell 1988, p.54

17. Butterfield 1959

18. Butterfield 1988, pp.169-170

19. E.g. Cannadine 1990; Chaussinand-Nogaret (ed.) 1991; Lieven 1992

20. It is clear that the Dutch *patriciaat* of the seventeenth and eighteenth century was much more like the European nobility than older generations of historians were prepared to admit. See e.g. De Jong 1987. On the political theory of the Dutch ancien régime, see Kossmann 1960

21. Cannon 1987, p.10; Beckett 1986, p.24; Habbakkuk 1953, p.1

22. Beckett 1986, p.23

23. Beckett 1986, p.23

24. Beckett 1986, p.25

25. Beckett 1986, p.24; Bush 1984, pp.17-34

26. Palmer 1959, vol.I, p.73

27. Bush 1984, p.3 Later the term lost all meaning, because it was increasingly assumed by the bourgeoisie.

28. Mingay 1963, p.8

29. Bush 1984, p.3

30. The peerage and the gentry were only placed apart as to their respective parliamentary function. The peers were members of the House of Lords and the government, the gentry dominated the House of Commons and the numerous local offices.

31. Tocqueville, *L'Ancien Régime*, II.2

32. Tocqueville, *L'Ancien Régime*, II.2

33. More accurately, modern students of Hume concentrate on a single part of the *Treatise of Human Nature* 1739/40, viz. that called 'Of the understanding', which was republished separately in 1748 in a revised and watered-down version as *An Enquiry concerning Human Understanding*.

34. Compare Gay 1977, vol.II, p.324, who actually uses that word to describe (a part of) the *Esprit des Lois*.

35. Montesquieu, *L'Esprit des Lois*, III.5-6, 'la vertu n'est point le principe du gouvernement monarchique'

36. That is to say' 'false honor', a notion of honor, not tied to the service of one's *patria*, which was central to the 'true', classical notion of honor.

37. This is of course the so-called hermeneutical circle. See Gadamer 1990, pp.270-280

38. See Tully (ed.) 1988, Pocock 1989, Pocock 1985, Rorty et al. (eds.) 1984

39. Pocock 1985, p.5, Rorty et.al.(eds.) 1984

40. Montesquieu, *Esprit*, avertissement

41. This example is derived from the 1984 movie *Starman*, by John Carpenter

PART II

THE APPEAL OF THE ANCIENTS

CHAPTER TWO

ANATOMY OF THE ARISTOCRACY

> *He who wanted to paint with fidelity the order of the nobility, would be obliged to have recourse to various classifications (..). Nonetheless, one saw within the bosom of that great body the reign of a homogeneous spirit; it was wholly obedient to fixed rules, it was governed by invariable customs, and it cherished certain ideas, common to all its members.*
>
> Tocqueville[1]

> *The acquisition of nobility, which is attainable with money, greatly encourages traders to put themselves in a position* d'y parvenir. *I am not examining whether it is well done thus to give to riches the price of virtue: there are governments in which it may be very useful.*
>
> Montesquieu[2]

1. The noble condition

A great number of historians of the ancien régime, past and present, have been and still are engaged in the investigation of the history, the sociology, and the politics of the bourgeoisie. Much less effort has gone into the study of the nobility of the ancien régime. The cause of this asymmetry is obvious. Following Marx and Tocqueville, the left and the right were in agreement that the future belonged to the bourgeoisie, whereas the nobility was a mere remnant of the past, an anachronism. A bygone that should be let a bygone. As a result, well-researched information about the nobility is scarce and most of it lies scattered in monographs and articles. Much still needs to be done. The present chapter summarizes the state of the debate.

1.1. Size and structure

Learned opinion varies somewhat as to the numerical size of the French aristocracy of the ancien régime. One author gives a total of something over 190,000 individuals in 1715 on a population of almost 20,000,000.[3] Another author estimates the size of the aristocracy in the second half of the eighteenth century as something between 300,000 and 400,000 individuals on a total population of 30,000,000.[4]There are various other estimations, some as low as 80,000, others as high as 500,000.[5] The discrepancy between the different estimations is at least partly the consequence of the fact that the contours of the French aristocracy were confused. In the view of the royalist jurisconsults and genealogists of the ancien régime nobility was defined as a specific legal status granted by the king, conferring certain privileges.[6] However, this definition was controversial. The most ancient noble houses for instance often could show no document confirming such a royal grant. Yet, it would have been absurd to deny their nobility. Many other definitions were put forward, but all were equally contested. Even those who agreed on the definition often disagreed on its application to specific persons and families.

It is certainly not true, as is sometimes maintained, that tax-exemption is a sure sign of nobility in the ancien régime. Admittedly, noblemen were generally exempt from the most important direct tax, known as the *taille*, as well as a variety of other taxes.[7] But one should not attach too much weight to this exemption. First of all, all the major towns in France were exempt from the *taille* as well, as was every office-holder, however humble, at least to some extent.[8] Secondly, in some provinces, -Dauphiné, Provence, Languedoc-[9] the *taille* was *réelle*, i.e assessed on non-noble land, rather than *personelle*. Since many noblemen possessed few or no true feudal fiefs, but mainly an accumulation of *roturier* tenures assembled by successive purchases over the centuries, they were not exempt from the *taille* in these provinces.[10] And finally, from Louis XIV's reign onwards the government introduced many other taxes, in particular the *vingtième* on land, which had to be paid by nobles as well as commoners.[11]

If the question who belonged to the nobility, and what were its outer limits, baffled even the contemporaries, is it likely that we can come up with a definite answer? None of the estimates is outside the range of between one and two percent of the population. That gives a fair enough idea of the proportion of noblemen to the populace as a whole. One should perhaps not think too digitally about this matter. *De facto*, if not *de iure*, nobility was a matter of relative plausibility in the ancien régime. There were many 'borderline cases' whose claims were rather ill-founded or just nor very ancient and therefore not very respectable. To many, such men were noble, to some they were not.

More important to our purposes than the exact number of noblemen in the ancien régime is the structure of the aristocracy. Although it considered itself to some extent a unity, the aristocracy of the ancien régime in fact contained within itself a complex and elaborate hierarchy, in terms of wealth, profession, prestige, and even in terms of legal privilege.

Since money is the key to many a thing, let us take a look at the distribution of wealth within the aristocracy first. The French aristocracy of the ancien régime was a divergent lot in that respect. The nobles' circumstances varied from destitution[12] to the possession of enormous fortunes.[13] On one end of the scale one finds the indigent rural gentry, the *hobereaux*, on the other end one finds the *ducs et pairs de France*, the chief military officers, the top of the church hierarchy and the upper echelons of the judiciary.[14]

In his book *La Noblesse au XVIIIème Siècle* Chaussinand-Nogaret gives some interesting statistics. According to that writer there were 25,000 noble families in 1789, comprising 110,000 or 120,000 people.[15] He divides them into five groups, corresponding to their wealth.[16] The richest group, with an annual income of at least 50,000 *livres*, he calls the plutocratic nucleus of the second estate. It consisted of 160 to 200 families which made up the highest nobility -*les grands du royaume*- and fifty families belonging to the financial elite of the country. Most of these plutocrats lived in Paris or Versailles, in profitable proximity to the king. All in all this group included not more than one percent of the aristocracy. The second richest group consisted of about 3,500 families, about thirteen percent of the aristocracy, encompassing most of the highest magistrates and their families. Their annual income was somewhere between 10,000 and 50,000 *livres*, which still allowed them to lead a very luxurious life, one part of the year in their Parisian *hôtel*, and the other part at their *château* in the province. The next, third, group encompassed about 7,000 families, about a quarter of the aristocracy, consisting largely of provincial nobles, with an annual income of 4,000 to 10,000 *livres*, which allowed them to lead a comfortable life on their estate, with a few servants. More than forty percent, about 11,000 noble families, belonged to the fourth group, whose annual income, between 1,000 and 4,000 *livres*, permitted them to live a decent but frugal life, with two servants at the most. The fifth and last group of nobles, about 5,000 families or twenty percent of the aristocracy, had an income of less than 1,000 *livres* a year and sometimes as little as one hundred or fifty *livres*. These nobles could barely be distinguished from peasants. Too poor to enter the army, too poor and too ignorant to enter the judiciary and too proud to enter commerce, they were fated to lead a miserable life of poverty.

Although these statistics should be approached with some reservation, because they are based on fiscal sources that are probably not very reliable[17] and they pertain to the years just before the revolution, they do give an impression of the enormous differences of wealth within the aristocracy of the ancien régime. The question is, what does that tell us? Differences of wealth were obviously of considerable importance, but it seems rather exaggerated to assert, as some historians have done, that wealth was the only key to social status and political influence in the ancien régime.[18] Many other factors counted in the determination of the hierarchy within the nobility, and these have to be taken into account as well.

1.2. Classifications

Many a jurisconsult and genealogist of the ancien régime in his learned works classified the nobility according to the way noble status was achieved.[19] For instance, they distinguished between on the one hand a *noblesse de lettres*, which derived its nobility from royal letters patent, which ennobled directly, or from letters of provision, certifying that the king had repeatedly bestowed *grands offices* on the family,[20] and on the other hand a *noblesse de dignité*, conveyed by the holding of certain high financial, administrative and judicial offices of state. Alternatively, they classified on the basis of titular rank -*ducs*, *marquises*, *comtes*, and so on- or type of landholding and the rights associated with it -whether the land was a fief or not, whether the owner possessed certain seignorial rights or not, and so forth. Some of these writers were very ingenious indeed in devising different categories. A certain Gilles-André de la Roque for instance listed twenty types of nobility in his *Traité de la Noblesse*.[21] Yet, it is doubtful whether such intricacies reflect consequential social distinctions.

More important to the noble mind than these classifications was the seniority of a man's noble status.[22] Above all others ranked the *noblesse de race*, which supposedly consisted of the old aristocracy whose origins lay 'beyond the memory of man'. As a working rule, however, the jurists and genealogists included everyone who could prove at least three generations of male noble ancestors.[23] The *noblesse de race* owed its name to the fact that it allegedly consisted of the descendants of the Germanic Francs, who conquered Gaul in the fifth century and therefore belonged to a different -and superior- race than the rest of the population of France.[24] This was a myth of course -the nobility of virtually all *nobles de race* was of a much later date-[25] but it was a very forceful myth, which played a major part in the ideological debate of the ancien régime, and hence in the story that is told in this book.

Within this category the *nobles chevaleresques*, who could prove that their family had been noble in the year 1400 A.D., ranked highest, followed by the *nobles d'ancienne extraction*, who could prove the same with respect to the year 1500 A.D.[26] How important the antiquity of the lineage was is proved by the fact that in 1732 Louis XV introduced a rule restricting the *honneurs de la cour* -the presentation to and the personal association with the king and the queen at the royal court in Versailles- to the members of families of the *noblesse chevaleresque*, although the ultimate decision on this matter rested with the king, who could and did make many exceptions.[27] The privilege of presentation to the king and queen was no mean advantage. It was perhaps the greatest of all privileges, and divided the nobility in two distinct groups: the *présentés* and those that were not. The first were considered the *haute noblesse*. In the second half of the eighteenth century it consisted of perhaps 20,000 souls.[28] Having the best access to the king, they often managed to obtain considerable favors -offices, pensions, exemptions and so on- for themselves, their relatives, or their dependents, and could sometimes exert much influence over decisions of policy.[†]

There is yet another way contemporaries differentiated between nobles, which is particularly important to our purposes. This is the distinction between the *noblesse d'épée*, the aristocracy of the sword, and the *noblesse de robe*, a distinction which was widely but not unequivocally used. Some referred to *l'épée* and *la robe* in relation to its roots in respectively the military profession and high civilian office, others stressed present occupation as the defining gauge, or used the concepts ambiguously.[29]

The relationship between the sword and the robe was complex. Because the nobility had originally been a purely military order, the sword tended to pride itself on its origins and/or occupation and to look down upon the robe as consisting of parvenus and ignoble pen-pushers.[30] And it is true that, as a group, the historical credentials of the robe were less exalted than those of the sword. In the estates-general of 1614 -the last before the revolution- many *robins* had still sat with the third estate. But a century later matters had changed considerably. Most robins had enjoyed nobility for several generations, as a result of which the robe by then counted as a part of the old nobility.[31] In the eighteenth century the noble status of the robe was beyond doubt, although *épée* snobbery never died out completely. It is probably true that, to a certain degree, the robe and the sword remained recognizably different groups throughout the eighteenth century, but the differences became

---

[†] The old idea, going back to Tocqueville, that the *haute noblesse* had been 'domesticated' in the seventeenth century, and reduced to an idle and powerless existence at the Court of Versailles, can no longer be upheld. It is the mirror-image of the idea that the country was ruled by bourgeois parvenus. That idea was based on a mistaken notion of the concept of nobility, this idea is based on a mistaken notion of what constituted a powerful position in the ancien régime, anachronistically applying nineteenth-century realities to the centuries before. It is true that the *haute noblesse* did not assume high civilian office -at least before the second half of the eighteenth century- but that does not imply that it was powerless, or that it was ousted from such offices. To the first of these suggestions it must be objected that in the ancien régime regular personal intercourse with the king often carried much more weight than even a ministerial office. A first gentleman of the bedchamber might have more power than a secretary of state. The second suggestion neglects the fact that the *haute noblesse* tended to regard a civilian office as demeaning and ignoble. The first *duc et pair* to accept ministerial office was the Duc de Belle-Isle in 1757, and much argument was needed before he agreed. See Antoine 1970, I.3.; Campbell 1988, p.59, p.68; Mettam 1988

less and less clear-cut and tended to dissipate. Scions of robe families often opted for a military career, sword and robe intermarried frequently, and the life-style and culture of the two groups gradually assimilated. [32] Only the poor *hobereaux*, sometimes of very old lineage, who had nothing but the glorious past of their family, seem to have remained hostile to the nobility of the robe in the end. But, as they possessed virtually no wealth and had no influence, that hostility probably did not concern the nobility of the robe very much.

To sum up, it is clear that the structure of the French aristocracy of the ancien régime is a matter of some complexity, and that sweeping generalizations about the second estate are not very helpful, if we want to understand the role it played in the ancien régime. It certainly wasn't the monolithic order it is sometimes believed to have been. To shed more light on this structure, to understand how it came about and was perpetuated, we have to go deeper into the factors that lay behind it. In discussing these, the notions of (1) land (2) office and (3) education are of prime importance.

1.3. Landed property

In pre-industrial society land was by far the largest source of wealth. And it was also the most prestigious source of wealth. The French aristocracy had a major stake in the land. Less than two percent of the entire population of France, it possessed between a quarter and a third of the land, although considerable regional variations existed.[33] Around Toulouse, for example, forty percent of the land belonged to nobles, in Auvergne only eleven percent.[34] As compared to the English aristocracy, which owned perhaps eighty percent of the land,[35] the proportion of land owned by the French aristocracy was relatively small. The difference was probably due to a divergence in the law of inheritance. In England the rule of primogeniture kept most estates together over the years, whereas in France entails were relatively rare and most of the estates were divided among the children of the owner. This led to an increasing dispersion of the land, and a continuous flow of uneconomic portions being put up for sale, and available for purchase by bourgeois would-be nobles.[36]

But the domination of the French aristocracy over the land went further than the figures mentioned suggest. It possessed various rights of overlordship over maybe three-quarters of the land -and the people living on the land.[37] That is to say, the nobles had rights over lands that did not belong to their 'personal domain', but fell within their 'fief'. As the expression used makes clear, these rights were remnants of medieval feudalism. Although the obligation of military service justifying these rights was no longer effectuated, they had not been abolished or forgotten. On the contrary, a bewildering number of these rights of overlordship had survived. They included a wide variety of different dues, the right to administer justice, *péages* -tolls-, *droits de marché* -taxes on merchandise sold on markets within the seignory-, a *droit de chasse*, *banalités* -the obligation of the 'vassal' to use the lord's mill, oven, or wine-press to ground his corn, bake his flour, and pulp his grapes-, and so on.[38] Interestingly, these rights could also be bought and sold without the land to which they had originally been attached. Moreover, the king continued to create 'fiefs' by converting *roturier* landholdings.[39] These land holdings brought the aristocracy substantial returns. Although many of them were dependent on income from offices also, the rents and dues derived from these holdings constituted the mainstay of the annual income of most nobles. The French aristocracy was essentially a class of *rentiers*.[40]

Land was by far the largest source of wealth, but it was not only that. It would be a mistake to focus exclusively on the monetary value landed property represented. For land was regarded as the most honorable, preeminently aristocratic form of property. Property in land was an indispensable and essential precondition of noble dignity. Although higher rates of profit could be achieved in trade and industry, the aristocracy commonly preferred investment in land, because land was much more prestigious. Revenues from the land were the established means of living nobly, i.e. without the necessity of trade or manual work. These were regarded as base and degrading. The aristocracy saw itself as a social elite of soldiers and statesmen, as the ruling class of the country. It consisted of *bellatores* assigned to fight and lead the nation, not of *laboratores*, assigned to work and feed the nation. This view was reflected and reinforced by the *loi de dérogeance*, going back to Francis I, which decreed that a nobleman engaging in trade would be deprived of his noble status. Exceptions existed: the cultivation of one's own land and the sale of its products, glassmaking, and the exploitation of mines were not derogatory. Also, derogation did not involve loss of *noblesse de race*. This might lie 'dormant', in consequence of derogatory actions, but could be regained by the 'trespasser' himself or his posteriority, by obtaining a letter of rehabilitation from the king. All this, however, does not change the fact that the aristocracy generally regarded the involvement in manual labor and commerce as shameful activities.[41]

Ever since the days of Richelieu the crown had tried, through provisions in the relevant edicts, to encourage the aristocracy to turn to commercial activities, well aware of the fact that more commerce and industry would lead to higher tax revenues. In 1701 this policy was confirmed and extended by an edict of Louis XIV, permitting all nobles to enter trade without derogation, provided it was wholesale trade. Later government policy was also directed at encouraging the aristocracy to engage in trade. Yet, except for the little group of court nobles, who invested quite substantially in big commercial enterprises, the ancient aristocratic contempt of commerce was so strong that the lifting of legal obstacles by the government failed to have an effect on the behavior of most noblemen, who sticked to their traditional values and way of life.[42]

1.4. Office, military and ecclesiastical

The only occupations the French aristocracy of the ancien régime considered in accordance with its dignity, were serving the king as an officer (1) in the army, (2) in the church, (3) in the judiciary or (4) in the royal administration. There were two different kinds of office: the *charge* and the *benefice*. The first had to be purchased; it was venal. The second could not, at least not officially. There were two kinds of *charges*. Royal commissions, the holder of which could be discharged anytime, and *offices* which were in principle of infinite duration and more or less the property of the office-holder.[43] In the army and the administration, commissions were the rule, in the judiciary *offices*, and in the the the church *benefices*.[44]

To many nobles the occupation of arms was the aristocratic occupation *par excellence*.[45] Society, they believed, was a *societé d'ordres* in which three different but complementary functions had to be performed by three different estates. The clergy (*oratores*) must pray for the well-being of the realm, the third estate (*laboratores*) must provide the realm with the means of living, and the nobility (*bellatores*) must fight for the realm. This differentiation between three different estates had become axiomatic by the eleventh century and was fundamental to the noble mind of the ancien régime.[46] Although the correspondence between the medieval function assigned to the nobility and its actual occupations diminished considerably in the period from the middle ages to the nineteenth century, the conception of the nobility as the order of *bellatores* stayed very much alive. Much of what noblemen believed, said, and did can only be understood in the light of the grip these old ideas still had on the noble mind of the ancien régime.[47]

A strong ethos of warriorship governed the aristocracy. Many nobles looked upon themselves as born soldiers. Even the so-called 'military revolution' -the formation of large standing armies, which took place mainly in the seventeenth century- did not alter this. These standing armies consisted at least partially of professional, relatively well-armed, trained and drilled forces, and were kept in being in peacetime. They had been introduced with great success by the Dutch and the Swedes in the Thirty Years War, but the other states quickly followed their lead. Between 1640 and 1680 France built up its standing army. By 1666 it already numbered almost 100,000 men, and in the eighteenth century it sometimes counted more than 300,000 troops.[48] The upshot of this development was that the military profession could no longer remain the monopoly of the nobility. More and more *roturiers* joined the army on a more or less permanent basis, some voluntarily, other less so, to become professional soldiers.[49] But if the military revolution eroded the monopoly of the aristocracy on professional warriorship, it also found a new function for the noblemen, that resembled the one they had lost: that of a military officer. On the eve of the Revolution in 1789 most of the 35,000 officers the French army counted were noble. *Roturiers* could attain the rank of lieutenant, but it was very uncommon for them to reach any further. On the whole, the higher ranks were the privilege of the aristocracy.[50] That is to say: the wealthiest part of the aristocracy. Since the crown commissioned most of the military offices, the higher ranks were within the reach of the rich only, and effectively closed to the middling and petty nobles.

High ecclesiastical office was also very respectable in the eyes of the French aristocracy of the ancien régime. To understand why let us take a closer look at *ecclesia*. One could say that the church was a state within the state, but putting it that way seems to suggest that the relationship between church and state was predominantly antagonistic. In reality, the church was very much integrated within the state, although occasional batterings did occur.[51] Religion was generally regarded as an essential component of government, and the clergy as an indispensable part of the civil service, infusing the population with the virtues of trust and deference. There is a well-known anecdote about the *anoblis* Voltaire that once, when he was entertaining fellow-*philosophes* at Ferney and they frankly talked about atheism, he silenced them, sent the servants out of the room, and then justified his precaution with the words: 'Do you want your throats cut tonight?'[52] An interesting observation, particularly as it came from the mouth of a man who was known to be anti-clerical. It makes clear how far the mind of the ancien régime was still removed from the idea of a secular society. Even the radicals could not conceive of such a society. Of course, this is not to say that the French aristocracy was utterly cynical about religion. Most noblemen were faithful Christians. But they were well aware of the beneficial social effects of God's Word, as long as it was preached by the right men.

The church claimed the service of about 130,000 people, and had its own income from various revenues derived from its estates, covering about one tenth of the land.[53] It had an all-embracing influence. It registered practically all births, deaths and marriages, it administered all charitable assistance, it operated all hospitals and alms-houses, and it had virtually complete control over education.[54] And, last but not least, new royal edicts were made public from the pulpit.[55] In effect, it was an important part of the civil service. Indeed, many clerics conceived of themselves as a sort of civil servant. For once, the abbé de Saint-Pierre was not at all eccentric, when he expressed the opinion that 'priests are state officials with the task of rectifying morals, that is, causing the citizens to be just and beneficent in their everyday conduct, so as to please God'.[56] Such ideas were widely accepted, not only among the French clergy, but also by the population at large. Hence, high ecclesiastical office fitted nicely into the conception the aristocracy had of itself as the ruling class.[57]

All the offices within the church were *benefices*, with an income attached to it, in the form of tithes (tenths) and rents drawn from church property.[58] As has already been mentioned a *benefice* could not be purchased, like a *charge*. The idea of openly selling an ecclesiastical office was not acceptable, which set it apart from the other offices.[59] This does not imply, however, that the most pious and meritorious men had a good chance of being assigned to the highest ecclesiastical offices, regardless of their social background. On the contrary, these offices were almost completely monopolized by the aristocracy, more specifically by the members of the small group of noble lineages particularly trusted by the crown.[60] Although formally the pope had the complete right of disposal over all *benefices*, the king nominated all the senior appointees, such as those for bishoprics and abbacies, who in their turn controlled the lesser ecclesiastical offices.[61]

It has been calculated that of the 240 men who received bishoprics between 1700 and 1774, eighty-three percent (200 men) were nobles, four percent (nine men) were *roturiers*, and the remaining thirteen percent (thirty-one men) probably came from families not yet noble, but owning ennobling offices. For the period of 1774 to 1790 the numbers are respectively ninety percent (173 men), one percent (two men), and nine percent (seventeen men).[62] Most of the abbots and vicars-general, and many of the canons were nobles as well. Only at the level of parish priest we come to a different class: sons of petty merchants, shopkeepers, schoolmasters, craftsmen and small cultivators.[63] Hence, the church was neither a *Fremdkörper*, nor a countervailing power in a society dominated by the aristocracy. On the contrary, it was one of the pillars of this domination.[†]

[†] The revenues of bishoprics varied widely, some bringing in less than 10,000 *livres* a year, and some more than 75,000 *livres*. On average, however, the annual income of the bishops, derived from their *benefices* -often in addition to income from their own possessions- was little less than 40,000 *livres*. Abbots, vicars-general and canons too, except those belonging to the mendicant orders, earned thousands of *livres* a year. The benefice of a parish priest on the other hand was 300 livres a year until 1768, when it was increased to 500 *livres*. In 1786 finally the *portion congrue* of the parish priests became 700 *livres* a year. Curates earned even less. The inequality of income within the clergy was evidently enormous, and corresponded with the differences in wealth, status and power to be found in French society at large, the aristocracy securely standing at the top of every hierarchy. See Mousnier 1979, pp.331-337; Göhring 1947, p.11

2. The nobility of the robe

The third option open to the aristocracy of the ancien régime was a civil office -the robe. Ancient and enduring prejudice had it that such an office was not on a par with one in the army or the church, and although there was an increasing number of noblemen who disregarded this prejudice, it was a belief that continued to be professed and acted upon.[64] In terms of prestige a civil office seems to have remained somewhat inferior to a military or an ecclesiastical office. This belief is most likely explained by the fact that civil office was of old, to a much larger degree than the two other, tainted by *roturier* infiltration. In fact, civil office was the principle way of social ascent in the ancien régime, by means of which wealthy bourgeois entered the ranks of the nobility. It was the engine, so to speak, of the process of *Aristokratisierung*. Nowhere else in Europe was high civil office more easily accessible to commoners than in France. Behind this was a curious phenomenon, the so-called *venalité des charges* or *des offices*, which was a pan-European phenomenon, but reached proportions in France unknown to the neighboring countries.[65] Because it had such profound social and political repercussions, and the noble condition depended heavily on it, we will sketch in outlines the contours of this practice.

2.1. Venality of office

The venality of office was basically a financial expedient, prompted by the crown's unremitting shortage of funds. It was easier than increasing the tax-burden, which was sure to incite opposition, and cheaper than raising loans. In principle, the office-holders received a periodical *gage* from the crown, a small percentage of the official value of the *charge*, that was much below the interest on loans the government would otherwise have had to pay, which could be eight to ten percent.[66] Venality of some sort had existed for a long time in France. As early as the fourteenth century some appointments by the crown already required a payment to it. In the fifteenth and sixteenth century there was a steady increase in the number of offices sold by the crown, and a strengthening of the hold of the incumbents upon many of these offices. By the 1580's the crown was selling grants of heredity in numerous offices.[67] Some offices, however, were kept out of the reach of full-blown venality. They had to be purchased as well, but could not be alienated at will. Hence, we see the gradual development of two distinctive kinds of office in the ancien régime. In his *Cinq Livres du Droit des Offices* (1610) the celebrated jurist Loyseau named them 'vray offices formés' on the one hand and 'dignités avec fonction ordinaire en l'Estat' on the other; let us call them *offices formés* and royal commissions respectively.

In the early seventeenth century the venality of *offices formés* was fully institutionalized. It was ruled by the *paulette* edict of december 1604 that every holder of an *office formé* must pay the crown an annual sum of one sixtieth of the official capital value of the office, in return for which the office-holder was guaranteed the right to sell or endow his office at any time. The office thus became more or less the personal property of the office-holder.[68] It is true that, in principle, the crown could always suppress *offices formés* by refunding the official value of the office to the office-holders. In practice however, the crown's incessantly pressing financial needs made it impossible to substantially reduce the venality of office, although from its point of view the system of venality had clear shortcomings -primarily the office-holder's independence. However, the suppression of offices was too costly, and reduced their salability as well as the cooperativeness of the remaining office-holders. Hence, such suppressions hardly ever occurred. Even restricting the proliferation of offices proved to be quite infeasible. Every time that was tried, the crown undermined its own policy. Apparently the advantages of the practice outweighed the disadvantages, at least in the short run.[69] The age of Louis XIV brought an unprecedented expansion of venality, particularly in the last thirty years of his reign.[70] In the eighteenth century too the practice flourished, and the traffic in *charges* and *offices formés* continued to expand until the revolution.[71] It has been estimated that the total number of venal offices at the end of the ancien régime was about 51,000.[72] Their total value exceeded the whole annual revenue of the French government.[73]

If the crown had good reasons to sell *charges*, the purchasers had good reasons to buy them. As has been set out, every office, regardless how humble, conveyed some legal privileges such as tax-exemptions. Offices were relatively safe financial investments, and most of them provided the holder with a regular income in some form or another. But most important of all was that a part of these offices conferred hereditary nobility, though on terms which varied according to the hierarchical level of the office. Some conferred hereditary nobility on the moment of purchase, others after a period of service -usually twenty years-, still others only in the second or third generation.[74] According to Necker -whose *De l'Administration des Finances* (1784) was the first book to lay bare the structure of the French government- there were about 4,000 ennobling offices in the second half of the eighteenth century.[75] The 47,000 remaining offices which did not confer nobility were often a preliminary station on the way to those that did.[76]

When the ennoblement by office was permanent and hereditary, the office could be sold after the ennoblement. This assured a substantial circulation in ennobling offices and was probably the main reason why the aristocracy of the ancien régime never became the more or less closed caste of feudal remnants it was once believed to have been, but remained open to the aspirations of the bourgeoisie, whose most successful members it constantly absorbed into its ranks, thus renewing the wealth and vigor of the aristocracy, and enabling it to preserve its predominance in society. It has been calculated that the eighteenth century saw about 5,500 ennoblements by *charge*.[77] Including the families of the newly ennobled, this would give a total of perhaps 27,000 *ennoblis*, a significant proportion of the nobility as a whole. If ennoblements since 1600 are taken into account, the percentage of recent nobles becomes very substantial indeed; hence, only a minority of the nobility was of really ancient stock, going back more than a few generations.[†]

Some of the ennobling offices were sinecures, which had the advantage that they could be multiplied without inconvenience. A good example is the office of *secrétaire du roi*.[78] It conferred not just hereditary nobility, but fourth-generation nobility, the legal mark of *noblesse de race*.[79] Originally there were sixty *secrétaires de roi*, under Louis XIV there were two or three hundred, and under Louis XVI there were perhaps nine hundred men who held such an office.[80] The price of the most coveted of these offices -those formally attached to the *grand chancellerie* in Paris- was 70,000 *livres* in 1700, 100,000 *livres* in 1750, 200,000 *livres* in 1770 and about 300,000 in the 1780's, equalling the value of a luxurious and well-furnished *hôtel* in a provincial capital.[81] However, most ennobling offices were no sinecures, but real 'jobs'. Foremost among these were the offices in the so-called *cours souveraines*, numbering maybe 3,000 in all in the late eighteenth century.[82]

2.2. The sovereign courts

The sovereign courts were the highest royal courts of law. Each judged by direct delegation from the king and each could be overruled only by him.[83] Because many subordinate courts existed, the sovereign courts were mainly courts of appeal.[84] It would be a mistake, however, to presume that they were equivalent to modern courts of appeal. Like most of the other agencies of government in the ancien régime, the sovereign courts united administrative and judicial powers. A separation of powers as we know it had not yet materialized. The first sovereign court appeared in the late thirteenth century.[85] Gradually their number multiplied. In the second half of the eighteenth century there were thirty-four sovereign courts. These were far from equal, either in background, or in authority, in function, and even in

---

[†] Moreover, ennoblement by *charge* never was the only road to nobility. If one adds all the families ennobled by a *lettre d'anoblissement* and all usurpers, the percentage of recent nobles becomes even more impressive. According to Chaussinand 1984, p.46, at least 1,000 of such lettres were issued in the eighteenth century. As concerns the usurpers, Carré 1920, p.13, writes that it seems likely that noble status was still more often acquired by 'usurpation' of titles than by letters of ennoblement or by venal offices.

name. It is common to distinguish between *parlements, chambres des comptes, cours des aides, cours des monnaies*, and the *grand conseil*.

The *parlements* had jurisdiction over all civil and criminal cases. The first and most powerful among them was the *parlement* of Paris, whose statute goes back to 1302. Its jurisdiction covered a major part of France. Other *parlements* were set up in Toulouse in 1443 for the Languedoc, in Grenoble in 1456 for the Dauphiné, in Bordeaux in 1467 for Guyenne and Gascogne, in Dijon in 1476 for Burgundy, in Rouen in 1499 for Normandy, in Aix in 1501 for the Provence, in Rennes in 1553 for Brittany, in Pau in 1620 for Navarre, in Metz in 1633 for the three bishoprics of Metz, Toul, and Verdun, in Besançon in 1674 for Franche-Comté, and in Douai in 1686 for French Flanders, Hainault, and Cambrésis. Three *conseils souverains*, which were *parlements* in all but name, were established in Arras in 1530 for Artois, in Colmar in 1657 for Alsace, and in Perpignan in 1660 for Roussillon.[86] The *parlement* of Paris was an outgrowth of the ancient *curia regis* and had assumed separate existence and identity in the course of the thirteenth century: a historical fact of great importance to the political discourse in the ancien régime. The other *parlements* were newly created by the king as the territory of the kingdom expanded.[87] The administrative responsibilities of the *parlements* were quite extensive. To name only the most important: they possessed broad police powers, to execute their own judicial decisions and preserve law and order. They had obligations in matters of public hygiene, the upkeep of public places, and the provisionment of the cities. They played a supervisory role in education, and in the censorship of printed matter. And they could issue administrative rulings, so-called *arrêts de règlement*.[88]

The first *chambre des comptes* -the one in Paris- emerged in the early fourteenth century. It was also an offshoot of the *curia regis*. Subsequently more and more provincial *chambres des comptes* were created.[89] In the late eighteenth century they numbered eleven in all. There was one in Paris, and one in Aix, Blois, Dijon, Dôle, Grenoble, Montpellier, Nancy, Nantes, Pau, and Rouen.[90] In principle, the division of labor between a *chambre de compte* and a *parlement* was lucid. The latter administered justice in matters of civil and penal law, i.e. in all cases 'related to the tranquility of the citizens'. The former were established to supervise and exert justice in the last resort in all matters concerning the king's finances; that is to say the *finances ordinaires*, which consisted of the revenues from the royal domain.[91] It should not be forgotten that the ancient idea that 'le roi doit vivre de son domaine' never died in the ancien régime.[92] The royal domain was partly *corporel* and partly *incorporel*. The first consisted of the king's feudal and seignorial rights over his real estate, the second consisted of his rights over less tangible assets, like the right to create and sell offices, the right *d'anoblissement*, the *paulette*, and so on.[93]

The *cours de aides'* jurisdiction originated in the fourteenth century. Their responsibilities covered the second part of the king's finances, the *finances extraordinares*. Surprisingly perhaps, these consisted of the various direct and indirect taxes that together made up the bulk of the government's annual revenue in the seventeenth and eighteenth century: the *taille*, the *gabelle*, the *aides*, the *décimes*, the *traites* and a few more.[94] The paradox is explained by the fact that taxes 'were originally not normally levied, but only at certain occasions, for the extraordinary needs of the state', most notably wartime expenses.[95] Everybody knew this; and it was likewise common knowledge that originally, 'that sort of aid or subsidy was accorded, either by the estates-general of the kingdom, or by the particular provincial estates, and even by the towns, and did not last but for a limited time'.[96] Again, we encounter historical facts with a tremendous impact on the political discourse in the ancien régime. Thirteen *cours des aides* had once existed, but one after the other had been incorporated in a *parlement* or a *chambre des comptes* and in the eighteenth century only four were left as independent bodies, one in Paris, one in Bordeaux, one in Clermont, and one in Montauban.[97] All of them had been created by the crown except the most ancient *cour des aides*, the one in Paris, which -significantly- originated in the meeting of the estates-general of 1355.

The *cours des monnaies* decided in cases concerning counterfeiting and other disputes involving the royal coinage. They were sovereign only in civil matters. Their penal verdicts were subject to review by the *parlement* of Paris.[98] Obviously, the crown had a great interest in the currency, and it need therefore surprise no one that royal interference goes back a long time. The appearance of royal *magistri monetae* in the early thirteenth century is perhaps the first real token of its concern. Nonetheless, the first *cour de monnaie* with the status of a sovereign court was established relatively late: in 1570. Of course it was located in Paris. In 1704 a second *cour de monnaie* was created in Lyon, but that court did not persist. In 1771 it was merged with that of Paris.[99]

The *grand conseil* in Paris finally, although generally recognized as one of the sovereign courts, occupied an ambivalent place. It acquired identity in 1497, and did not have an independent, well-defined sphere and territory of jurisdiction, but judged in those cases the king considered the rulings of the other sovereign courts unacceptable.[100] Its tasks also included, among other things, taking the oaths of fealty of the bishops and judging in cases of litigation of the religious orders.[101] Because the *grand conseil* was used by the crown to limit the authority of the other sovereign courts, these often complained that it was a parasitic and harmful institution.[102] On the other hand, both in terms of policy and personnel, the *grand conseil* was an integrated part of the upper judiciary of the French ancien régime.

The prestige, influence and power of the sovereign courts were far from equal. The *parlement* of Paris was by far the most important court, followed by the *grand conseil*, the Paris *chambre des comptes* and the so-called *grands parlements* of Rouen, Rennes, Bordeaux, Toulouse and Dijon. The other sovereign courts were less significant.[103] 'Competitive' is perhaps the most accurate description of the relationship between the various sovereign courts. Their jurisdiction was ill-defined. Cases were frequently contested on the ground of the fact that it was often unclear what type of dispute and which area of judicial competence was involved. Consequently, hostility and conflict was not uncommon between the sovereign courts.[104] Particularly the relationship between the *parlement* of Paris and its counterparts in the provinces could be strained, because the first tended to claim jurisdiction over the whole kingdom, and resented the establishment of *parlements* with sovereign powers within their own areas.[105] Nevertheless, the sovereign courts did constitute a unity, which exhibited considerable and growing professional and social solidarity.[106] The existence of a high degree of intercourse among and interchange of personnel among the various sovereign courts is very significant in this respect.[107] The magistrates were members of a proud and powerful group that was well aware of its indispensability to the crown.

This indispensability was due largely to the judicial and administrative services provided by the sovereign courts, but also to their capability to interfere with most of the crown's resolutions, which stemmed from a third task accorded to the sovereign courts. In addition to their administrative and judicial responsibilities they acted as registration offices of new ordinances, edicts, declarations, orders, and letters-patent issued by the government. Every kind of ruling, from the most specific, such as letters of nobility, to the most general law covering the whole territory and the whole population, had to be registered by one or more of the sovereign courts. This was no minor assignment, since by this procedure the will of the sovereign was incorporated into the body of law.[108] No registration, no incorporation.

The sovereign courts were supposed to receive these royal decrees, record them in the court's registers, transmit their contents to the subordinate courts and enforce them.[109] Registration was no simple formality, however. The magistrates first examined the new enactments to detect possible conflicts with established law or other legal difficulties. This was an old custom, going back to the fourteenth century, but rooted in the even more ancient idea that the king should ask counsel. As such, there was nothing remarkable and anti-royalist about this. The kings themselves had contributed substantially to the emergence and the perpetuation of this custom. If irregularities were detected the sovereign courts delayed registration and presented their objections to the crown in what were called *remonstrances*. If the response did not satisfy the magistrates, and they decided to further delay registration, the crown could send royal *lettres de jussion*, ordering registration in its original form. If in spite of this the magistrates still refused to give in, the king had to appear in court in person to hold a *lit de justice*, a ceremony in which the sovereignty of the court was officially suspended, following the principle *adveniente principe, cessat magistratus*, to personally supervise the registration of the contested decree.[110]

All this was within the bounds of legal custom, as it had developed in the course of time, but that does not imply that *lits de justice* or even *lettres de jussion* were considered as ordinary, routine occurrences. It was generally accepted that the crown had the right to overrule his courts in these ways, but if it did so too frequently the incrimination of despotical intentions would sooner or later be made, which could easily lead to violent upheavals. If the crown had really set its mind on a decree, it could always have its way. In addition to his formal prerogative the king possessed a number of informal 'weapons' to break the resistance of the sovereign courts, such as threats and bribes.[111] But as a rule the most prudent course of action for the crown to take was to obtain the voluntary consent of the sovereign courts, hence granting them a *de facto* role in the process of legislation.

Most of the *charges* in the sovereign courts were *offices formés*, the holders of which could not be removed at will, and were quite independent.[†] As has been set out, the crown could theoretically suppress the office by refunding its official capital value to the holder, but in practice such an option was impracticable. One could perhaps get rid of a few magistrates in this way -although even that was considered an act of coercion and could incite opposition- but a large-scale suppression of offices was quite impossible. It

---

[†] Within each sovereign court there was a painstakingly defined and observed hierarchy, in which the status of each office-holder depended on his rank and his seniority in that rank. The names differed slightly among the various courts, but the same general levels of titular hierarchy existed in all of them. Everywhere, a first president stood at the top, whose office was a commission, which made him relatively susceptible to royal influence. Just below him stood the other presidents of the court, who in order of seniority replaced the first president in his absence. In some courts -the Paris *chambre des comptes* for example- there were as many as twelve presidents, but usually there were only five or six. After the presidents of the court came the *gens du roi*, whose charges were also commissions: the *procureur-général* and two to four *avocats-généraux*. These represented the king, supervised the criminal prosecutions and the police, and were responsible for the registration of all the king's edicts. After them came the counselors, including more than eighty percent of the high robe officers, and various other officers, like the *greffiers-en-chef*, who supervised the clerical staff, and the *premier huissier*, the master of the ceremonies.

was too expensive, it was widely perceived as despotical and would hence spawn social strife, and it was impossible to dispense with the magistrates' juridical and administrative expertise. In effect, the crown could not afford to stay on a collision course with the sovereign courts for a protracted time, and was obliged to seek their counsel and consent.

2.3. The royal government

As has already been said not all civil offices were completely venal. The most important *charges* remained royal appointments. Such commissions have to be clearly distinguished from the *offices formés*, which were more or less pieces of private property. They could not be sold or endowed at will although they too often had to be bought, and a number of them conferred hereditary nobility. Not surprisingly, those holding such positions usually identified much more with royal policy than the other *robin* office-holders. It is perhaps not exaggerated to call these men the governmental elite, the king's party. The apex of this elite was made up by those who were invited by the king to sit in what was named the *conseil d'état du roi*.[112] Originally this had been a single body of royal counselors, the *curia regis*, and officially it still was, but since the sixteenth century a division of the *conseil* into various subcouncils had taken place.[113]

The most important were the *conseil secret* and the *conseil des dépêches*. There, the main policy decisions were taken. The *conseil secret* consisted of the king and a handful of advisers carrying the prestigious title of minister of state. In this council the great affairs of state were discussed. It had been separated from the single medieval council in 1547. The *conseil des dépêches* was the place where the bulk of internal policy was determined. It included the heads of the departments of state, the so-called secretaries of state: the *contrôleur-général*, who headed the finance department, the *chancelier* or keeper of the seals, who headed the judiciary, and the men who headed the departments of foreign affairs, war, the navy, and the royal household. It existed as a separate body since 1630. It sometimes happened that the secretaries of state did not sit in the *conseil secret*. Everything depended on the king's wish. There were times when not even the *chancelier* and the *contrôleur-général* sat in the *conseil secret*.[114] The remaining councils were of less consequence. There was a *conseil privé* and a *grand conseil*, and for a longer or shorter period there were also separate *conseils de finance*, *de commerce*, and *de conscience*.[115]

The business of all the councils was prepared by eighty *maîtres des requêtes*.[116] The holders of this *charge*, which cost at least 100,000 *livres* and often twice that amount, were in a sense the heart of the royal government. Although the office itself did not confer any real power, the men holding it were those from whom the king preferred to choose the members of his council. And they were the men from which he preferred to chose his intendants.[117] The intendant was the direct royal representative of the crown in the *généralités*, the administrative districts of the realm, numbering about thirty in the eighteenth century. From the beginning of the sixteenth century the king had sent *maîtres des requêtes* out into the provinces to inspect the local situation, and from about the middle of the seventeenth century they were permanently stationed in the province, where they wielded wide powers over justice, police and finance.[118] The intendants, as they were called from then on, supervised all governmental activity in their respective *généralité*.[†]

All in all, this governmental elite consisted of not more then one or two hundred persons, assisted by a 'civil service' of something between 1,000 and 2,000 *commis* who prepared the dossiers.[119] Most of these men lived in Paris. Most of them were by marriage related to each other. 'Tout ce beau monde était cousin'.[120] Though their gages were moderate, and their pensions only a little less moderate, the governmental elite used the power inherent in their offices well, which generally resulted in rapid enrichment, and the building up of enormous fortunes, which in their turn formed the basis of the continuation of the families' influence in the following generations. Not just anyone with enough talent and stamina could rise to the ranks of this political elite. The king kept a close watch on who was admitted to it. It is true that anyone rich enough could purchase the charge of *maître des requêtes*, but if the king did not trust that man, he would stay a *maître des requêtes* for the rest of his life. A necessary qualification to rise further was *fidélité*, which depended to a large extent on the side a noble family had taken during the great crises of the monarchy: during the Ligue, the time of Henry IV, the Dupes, the time of Richelieu, and the Fronde, the youth of Louis XIV.[121]

3. The political class

The men who held office in the sovereign courts and the royal government together constituted the high robe. Evidently, they wielded tremendous political power. They made up the core of the *classe politique*. Who were these men? A quick look at their social background suffices to observe that,

---

[†] They were never the tremendously powerful spearheads of administrative centralization Tocqueville thought they were, if only because most intendancies were chronically understaffed. For example, in 1784 the intendant of the large *généralité* of Bretagne only had ten *commis* to assist him. But an even more important consideration is that the intendant had to share his power with other authorities -military, ecclesiastical and judiciary-, who often refused to accept his rule.

as compared to the *haute noblesse*, the historical antecedents of many robe families were rather modest. Legally they were all noble beyond a shadow of doubt. Individual grants of personal and hereditary nobility by the king to his magistrates had a very long history, going back to perhaps the early thirteenth century. Gradually, out of this practice of ennobling certain office-holders the notion of ennobling offices evolved. By the beginning of the seventeenth century it was an established rule that high office initiated nobility. The most exalted of these offices conferred 'perfect' i.e. hereditary nobility, the remainder only to the third generation in office -*patre et avo consilibus*- and carried mere personal nobility during the first two generations. Towards the end of the sixteenth century the offices within the sovereign courts and the royal government all conferred nobility, and from the early eighteenth century on all conferred perfect nobility.[122] *De iure* the high robe belonged to the nobility alright.

But legal recognition was the most superficial of criteria, at least in matters of nobility. Much more important was the length of the lineage. In general, the high robe's score in this respect was relatively mediocre. Some families were of very ancient nobility, like the Tocquevilles, the Turgots, and the d'Argensons, and some had been ennobled quite recently, but most of them were families that belonged to the *noblesse de robe* since one or two centuries, that had risen by way of a local office in the province, and a judiciary office in one of the lower courts. And up to the revolution there was a considerable number of office-holders whose nobility had begun with their own entrance into the office.[123] Following Tocqueville, former generations of historians have taken this as evidence that the nobility was effectively excluded from positions of power in the ancien régime, and that the Bourbons ruled the country by means of a *parvenu* bourgeoisie. This seems to confirm the theory that the ancien régime saw the rise of the bourgeoisie and the decline of the aristocracy. But such a conclusion is premature. What counts is not social background as such, but the extent to which this background still determines the thought, behavior and social status -the identity- of a person or group. The -crucial- question is to which degree the bourgeois can still be traced in the *noble de robe*.

Many have assumed that this must necessarily have been the case, and have given it no further thought. But such a judgment overlooks one of the most important facets of the society of the ancien régime: the fact that the ultimate goal of most bourgeois was to join the ranks of the aristocracy. In his own lifestyle he would try to imitate the nobility to the best of his ability, and having amassed sufficient wealth he would buy an estate and an office. In extraordinary cases, such a man -provided he was rich and talented enough- would cross the line between *roture* and *noblesse* himself, but usually the rise was more gradual, taking up a few generations. In this process of social ascension the families concerned devoted all their energies to separate themselves from their humble origins, and adopt as completely as possible the standards and deportment of the nobility. Hence the *robin* in the sovereign courts and the royal government had nothing in common with his bourgeois ancestors. He thought like, lived like, and was generally considered a nobleman. So remarkable was this assimilation that it is justified, as has been set out, to speak of a process of *Aristokratisierung*.[124]

But this is not the whole story, yet. Indeed, the most important part still has to come. For it would be erroneous to believe that the robe merely copied a pre-existing concept of nobility, that it merely aped the views and the lifestyle of the older nobility. In reality, the robe effected a transformation of the idea of nobility and thus brought about a considerable change in the lifestyle, thought and manners of the aristocracy. It is not that the robe introduced bourgeois values into the nobility, as has been asserted by many a historian. What it introduced was a humanist education, imbued with classical values, derived in particular from the Romans, and above all from Cicero. Eventually, such an education came to be regarded as synonymous with a good i.e aristocratic education and a *sine qua non* for public office. This radically changed the nobility's conception of what it meant to be noble, and accordingly turned this formerly ignorant, illiterate, rude, and violent order into a class, the like of which, in certain respects, the world never saw before or again.

3.1. Education

A good education was considered absolutely indispensable for a nobleman of substance in the ancien régime. It was of decisive importance first of all in 'rubbing off the rough corners and untoward affections'.[125] And without a good education a career, whether in the army, the church, the judiciary, or the administration, was out of the question.[126] Hence, it is not surprising that the aristocracy attached great importance to the education of its children. It was expected to prepare them for their leading role in society and their responsibilities in government.[†]

This connection between gentility and education was a *nouveauté*. It was incorporated into the aristocratic ethos only in the seventeenth century. Until that time the nobility had held learning in contempt. Books were regarded as the turf of pale and unwarlike clerks. It is largely due to the integration of the high robe in the nobility that this prejudice lost much of its force. True, the

---

[†] Of course, this applied much more to sons than to daughters, whose education was generally limited to the acquirement of the social graces, although this did not prevent some ladies to play a notable role in society, holding salons, and acting as a patron of the arts.

aristocracy never learned to appreciate real expertise. That was considered bookish and impertinent. A gentleman always remained a *dilettante*. It is easy to misunderstand this, however. What was held in contempt was specialization. A gentleman had to be a generalist, who knew something of everything.

However, a good education was costly. Major revenues were necessary to cover the expenses. As has been set out, the majority of noble families was not very wealthy, and could not afford an expensive education for its sons. Hence, most young provincial noblemen received no more than an elementary education, often together with the other children of the village, by the local *curé*, by their parents, or at best by some indigent tutor.[127] The finest educational institutions were within the financial possibilities of the wealthiest nobles only, since they cost something between 400 and 4,000 *livres* per person annually, boarding included.[128] Hence, in fact only the top-layer within the nobility was in the position to give its sons a good education.

After a few years of private education by an *instituteur public* -someone with a small, private school- or a tutor, these privileged youngsters were preferably sent to one of the great colleges attached to the universities. The Jesuit *collège de Clermont* in Paris, renamed *collège Louis-le-Grand* in 1682, which was opposite the Sorbonne, was perhaps the most famous of them, until in 1762 the society of Jesus was expelled from France and it had to be closed.[129] But the *collège d'Harcourt* and the Oratorian *collèges*, especially the one in Juilly, were no less distinguished. At these colleges the future ruling elite of the kingdom was educated.[130] Now the question is of course, what were these boys required to learn?

All of these colleges had more or less the same curriculum, which was overwhelmingly classical in orientation. Their education was almost entirely based on the study of the ancient Latin and Greek authors, the latter usually translated into Latin. Latin and, to a much lesser extent, Greek grammar and literature, especially poetry and plays, took up most of the pupils' time. The first four years[131] were mainly concerned with the teaching of ancient grammar in the wide sense of the word: phonetics, morphology, syntax, sentence construction etc. The fifth year was devoted to the study of the 'humanities', that is the explication of classical poetry and literature: Homer, Pindar, Aeschylus, Sophocles, Euripides, Virgil, Ovid, Lucian, Martial, Horace, and others. What was read was read thoroughly, was translated and often had to be learned by heart. In the end, many students could recite large pieces of Horace, Virgil and Homer.

Having completed their secondary education the pupils then went on to follow at least one year of higher i.e. university education, largely devoted to 'rhetoric', i.e. the study of the classical orators and historians: of the Greek authors primarily Herodotus, Thucydides, Xenophon, Demosthenes and Plutarch, and of the Roman authors primarily Caesar, Livy, Sallust, Tacitus,

Seneca, and above all Cicero. Most then left university, steeped in the ancient writers, and in little else.[†]

Some boys, however, mostly from the nobility of the robe, went on with their studies, because as future sovereign court officers or royal magistrates they needed a licentiate or a doctorate. An essential preliminary to such degrees were two years of instruction in 'philosophy'. In the first year logic and ethics was studied, and in the second year physics and metaphysics. Now the pupils could enter the specialized faculties of the university, i.e. divinity, law, and medicine. Most future *robins* went on to study law. It took two years to acquire a *baccalauréat*. The first year was devoted mainly to the study of Roman law, the second to Roman and canonical law. A *licence* required one more year, a *doctorat* two more years of study, mainly of French law.[132] Although this curriculum appears more formidable than it was in practice -the standards particularly at provincial universities were not always very high, nor were the examinations always very demanding-[133] many magistrates were relatively learned man.[‡]

The nature of and the differences in education are neatly reflected in the libraries of the various noble families.[134] The minor and middling nobility possessed hardly any books. Within the wealthy elite on the other hand,

---

[†] Interestingly, as criticism of the 'uselessness' of the classics increased, and more and more voices were raised in favor of a more comprehensive curriculum, including 'useful' subjects like modern languages, mathematics, modern history and science as well as the classics, an exclusively classical education increasingly became the revered symbol of the gentleman's education, because it underlined his gentility, his elevation above bigoted utility.

[‡] Sons of nobles aspiring to an ecclesiastical benefice went to a *séminaire*. These already existed in the sixteenth century, but the great rise of seminaries came with the so-called Catholic renaissance, in the second half of the seventeenth century. Between 1642 and 1715 one hundred and three seminaries were founded. At the same time many 'minor' seminaries were established, often attached to a college. Increasingly, future priests absolved both a 'minor' and a 'major' seminary. Of both there were two types. A 'minor' seminary either gave only a religious education and sent its pupils to the attached college to receive the normal college training, implying grammar, the humanities, rhetoric and philosophy, or it gave this 'profane' education itself, beside the religious education. More or less the same goes for the 'major' seminaries, in some of which one could only obtain practical instruction in composing homilies, plainsong, the liturgy, the catechism, the administering of the sacraments etc., necessary to carry out the priestly functions, whereas in others a theological training was added. In the seventeenth century practical subjects dominated, and the period of study therefore was relatively short. The curriculum became increasingly theoretical, however, and consequently more and more prolonged. For example, in the 1770's it took five years to absolve the 'major' seminary of the canons of Sainte-Geneviève in Rheims, two devoted to philosophy and three to theology. Other subjects, like the study of canonical law, Hebrew, and the history of the Bible, were introduced too. As a result, the priests of the eighteenth century generally were among the most erudite of men in France. See Mousnier 1979, pp.340-351

including perhaps ten percent of the *noblesse*, one finds impressive collections of several hundreds and sometimes thousands of volumes. Again, the high robe towers above all others. Here the really magnificent collections were amassed, some of which acquired a reputation throughout Europe, and attracted scholars from everywhere.[135] A considerable number of libraries has survived the passage of time more or less unscathed, and the contents of many others are known to us through records and catalogues. We hence have a good picture of what the lettered elite within the aristocracy was interested in intellectually.

History and *belles-lettres* were the most popular *genres*, each constituting on average perhaps a quarter of the total. The remainder consisted of books on jurisprudence, arts and science, and theology.[136] The historical works possessed by the nobility show that its main interest lay in the history of the French monarchy, and in ancient history.[137] The works of Thucydides, Herodotus, Tacitus, Sallust, Polybius, Livy, Xenophon, and the other Greek and Roman historians were always well represented, the Greek authors usually translated into Latin or French.[138] As to the collection of *belles-lettres*: Corneille, Racine, Molière, Montaigne, Fénélon, and -in the second half of the eighteenth century- Montesquieu were unfailingly popular. And here too the ancients are prominent. Virgil, Ovid, Horace, and Cicero, but also Homer, Demosthenes, and some other Greek writers, again in translation, crowd the bookshelves.[139] There were of course individual, regional, and social variations. The provincial nobility took a greater interest in religious works than the nobility in the capital.[140] And the libraries of the *haute noblesse* probably contained a more than average number of contemporary books.[141] But the general configuration is unmistakable.

What the substance of the nobility's education and the contents of its libraries manifest, is confirmed by many other signs. The classicism that pervaded the education and the literature of the nobility of the ancien régime was reflected in many other facets of its life as well. Noblemen adorned their houses with pilasters and porticoes, filled their rooms with urns and busts and placed temples, statues and satyrs in their gardens. Their minds were imbued with classical images and models, which deeply affected both their behavior and their lifestyle. In acting, they constantly compared themselves to the ancients, particularly the Romans. In writing they frequently used pseudonyms like Cato, Tribune, Lucius, Junius, or Atticus, and they never tired of quoting the ancient writers. In short, as even a short glance will reveal, aristocratic culture of the ancien régime was permeated by the ancients. *In fact, it is unmistakable that the concept of nobility as well as the process of* Aristokratisierung *is to a large degree based on the example set by antiquity.* Is it surprising then that aristocratic political and moral discourse also owed much to the ancients?

3.2. Aristocratic politics

This discourse was almost exclusively a matter of the most exalted circles within the nobility, the men with a *grande charge*, and the *haute noblesse*, who had had a classical education. Petty noblemen might be dissatisfied, but they were generally not capable of expressing a clear and consistent opinion on political matters. Besides, many of them were too busy eking out a living to give much attention to the great affairs of state. The middling nobility might have some say in the government of its home region and might appear to the villagers a very fine and elevated sort of people, but issues of national import were mostly out of its league. And even if such matters were discussed, the opinions that were expressed originated somewhere else. The upper layer of the aristocracy, where the ideas concerning the nature of the monarchy and the rightful place of the nobleman in its government were developed, consisted mainly of the high judicial magistracy of the sovereign courts, the higher clergy, the court nobility, and the nobles serving in the royal administration.

Most of the men belonging to this *crème de la crème* contended that the action of the king should be constrained by the nobility. They defended a 'conciliarist' position, so to speak, in which the king was but the *premier gentilhomme*, the *primus inter pares*. This position came to be known as the *thèse nobiliaire*. It was the dominant view within the nobility -naturally- but not everyone agreed with it. Throughout the ancien régime there was a 'faction' of noblemen, who defended the need of a strong and dominant royal authority, which was clearly superior to the nobility. This 'papist' view came to be called the *thèse royale*. Because the king had a greater say in their appointment, the higher clergy and the nobles serving in the royal administration not surprisingly tended to support this 'thesis', whereas the court nobility and the magistrates of the sovereign courts, who usually were more independent, more often vindicated the other.

As we shall see, this discourse depended heavily on the ancients. Their intellectual presence is perceptible everywhere. It comes to the fore most obviously in the importance attached to the *Corpus Iuris Civilis*, Tacitus' *Germania*, and Caesar's *De Bello Gallico*, as sources directly relevant to the question of the true nature of the French monarchy. But the influence of the ancients was much more deep and pervasive than that. If in this 'historical' debate they played a leading part, the ancients were by and large the sole authors and spiritual fathers of the theoretical and normative notions that lay behind it and structured the debate. The concepts of monarchy, mixed government, and tyranny, which played a central role in this debate, were of ancient stock. And so was the concept of the ancient constitution, the idea, central to the political and moral thought of the ancien régime, that in the past there had been a long period of purity and goodness in which all had been well, that society was now corrupted, and that only a return to the customs and practices of the ancestors would cure the present wrongs. This too had been one of the principle themes of the ancients. Moreover, not only the abstract scheme was adopted -purity, corruption, badness- but also the ancients' ideas of what these concepts meant. The good and the bad of the ancien régime's aristocracy were largely inspired by the classical notions of virtue and vice. Its notion of the good society, but also of the good life and the good man depended heavily on the ancients. The aristocratic political discourse represented classicism in morals and politics.

This is no small issue. Since this classicism emanated from the ruling class, dominating society not only politically, but also economically and ideologically, it provided the very conceptual framework that was generally employed to understand and legitimize the way of life of the aristocracy, and of the political institutions of the society of the ancien régime in general. A discussion of this classicism is therefore long overdue.

Analytically the subject has two different facets. It includes two different fields of investigation. The precise structure and content of this aristocratic classicism has to be determined. The ideas making up this view of man and society have to be set forth and explained. The question what aristocratic classicism meant, what exactly it stood for has to be answered. Chapters four to ten deal with this issue. But first, it must be shown how this classicism came to dominate the minds of the French aristocracy and became the main source of inspiration of their political and moral thought. Before going further into the exact meaning and content of aristocratic classicism, it is necessary to contemplate this second question a little longer, and examine how classicism came to dominate the minds of the French aristocracy, and hence their political and moral thought. That is the subject of the following chapter.

NOTES

1. Toqueville, *L'Ancien Régime et la Revolution*, État social et politique de la France, 'Celui qui aurait voulu peindre fidèlement l'ordre de la noblesse, eût donc été obligé de recourir à des classifications nombreuses (..). On voyait régner toutefois au sein de ce grand corps un certain esprit homogène; il obéissait tout entier à certaines règles fixes, se gouvernait d'après certains usages invariables, et entretenait certaines idées communes à tous ses membres.'

2. Montesquieu, *L'Esprit des Lois*, XX.22 'L'acquisition qu'on peut faire de la noblesse à prix d'argent encourage beaucoup les négociants à se mettre en état d'y parvenir. Je n'examine pas si l'on fait bien de donner ainsi aux richesses le prix de la vertu: il y a tel gouvernement où cela peut être très utile.'

3. Ford 1968, p.31

4. Weis 1971, p.29: 'Der französische Adel umfaßte in der zweiten Hälfte des 18.Jahrhunderts 300 000 bis 400 000 Personen, das waren maximal 1,5% der Bevölkerung.'

5. Chaussinand-Nogaret 1984, p.ii, p.11 and p.39; Behrens 1985, p.17; Campbell 1988, p.27; Goodwin 1965, p.356; Carré 1920, pp.14-18

6. Quite a number of such treatises appeared throughout the ancien régime. To name only a few: A.Tiraqueau, *Tractatus de Nobilitate*, Paris 1594; Ch.Loyseau, *Traité des Ordres et Simples Dignitez*, Paris 1613; G-A. de la Roque, *Traité de la Noblesse*, Paris 1678; A.Belleguise, *Traité de la Noblesse et de son Origine*, Paris 1700; Devyver 1973 contains a very good list of sources.

7. Ford 1968, pp.27-28; Behrens 1985, p.70

8. Behrens 1985, p.75

9. In general, the *taille réelle* was imposed in the more recently conquered provinces, known as the *pays d'états*.

10. According to Ford 1968, pp.27-28, even in the provinces where the *taille* was *réelle* every noble could claim exemption for an average of four *charrues* of his land, which practically freed the small country gentlemen from this tax.

11. Behrens 1985, p.70, p.166

12. Chaussinand 1984, p.89: 'Les plus heureux sont paysans, les plus à plaindre des pauvres honteux. Et il ne s'agit pas là d'une pauvreté sociologique, mais bien réelle, et dans certains cas d'une authentique misère.'

13. Behrens 1985, p.17

14. Ford 1968, pp.32-33; McManners 1953, p.36

15. Chaussinand 1984, p.48

16. Chaussinand 1984, pp.77-92

17. Chaussinand 1984, p.75

18. E.g. McManners 1953, p.26

19. McManners 1953, pp.22-23

20. Ford 1968, p.24

21. Ford 1968, p.23n6

22. Levantal 1987, p.36

23. Chausinnand 1984, p.70

24. Neumann 1949, pp.xxiv-xxv

25. Compare Chaussinand 1984, pp.39-50, who concludes that 'la noblesse à la fin de l'Ancien Régime, est un groupe social jeune et en pleine ascension. Elle est constituée par les élites sécrétées par le tiers état au cours des XVIIe et XVIIIe siècles.'

26. Behrens 1985, p.49 and 207n13

27. Behrens 1985, pp.49-50; McManners 1953, p.23; Chaussinand 1984, p.67; Carré 1920, p.23

28. Carré 1920, pp.22-23

29. Levantal 1987, p.35

30. Behrens 1985, p.49

31. Mousnier 1979, p.132

32. Chaussinand 1984, pp.73-74, p.170; Shennan 1968, pp.129-132

33. Doyle 1978, p.77 Other authors mention similar figures. Campbell 1988, p.27, speaks of twenty percent.

34. Campbell 1988, p.27

35. Doyle 1978, p.77

36. Doyle 1978, pp.77-78

37. Doyle 1978, 78-79

38. Mousnier 1979, pp.477-550; Mackrell 1973, pp.1-5

39. Ford 1968, pp.164-165

40. Goubert and Roche 1984, vol.I, pp.111

41. Doyle 1980, p.118; McManners 1953, p.37; Doyle 1978, pp.74-86; Mousnier 1979, pp.131-135

42. Chaussinand 1984, pp.119-131; Mousnier 1979, pp.190-193

43. Göhring 1965, p.7

44. Mousnier 1979

45. Mousnier 1979, pp.193-198

46. In fact, it is of very ancient Indo-European origin. Distinct versions of it can be found in Plato and Aristotle for instance. See Goubert and Roche 1984, vol I, p.117; Duby, 1980

47. Goubert and Roche 1984, vol.I, pp.117-118

48. Doyle 1978, p.242

49. It was common policy to press criminals and vagrants to sign up. Doyle 1978, p.243

50. Mousnier 1979, p.197

51. Doyle 1980, pp.68-69

52. Gay 1977, vol.II, p.526; In a similar vein Voltaire noted down in his *Dictionnaire Philosophique*, that 'I want my attorney, my tailor, my servants, even my wife to believe in God, and I think that then I shall be robbed and cuckolded less often'.

53. Cragg 1976, p.200; Doyle 1980, p.68

54. Cragg 1976, p.200

55. Göhring 1947, p.12

56. Mousnier 1979, p.318

57. The ecclesiastical hierarchy was a dual one. The 'secular' clergy has to be distinguished from the 'regular' clergy, which belonged to a religious order. The first consisted of priests, in charge of a parish, the second of monks, who had devoted their life to contemplation and usually did not preach to laymen. Politically the most significant was the 'secular' clergy. It had a much closer contact with the population at large, and it was not unusual for a bishop to become a minister of the crown. Mousnier 1979, pp.283-294; Göhring 1947, p.10; Campbell 1988, pp.52-53

58. Note that some historians call only the income attached to an ecclesiastical office a *benefice*. Mousnier 1979, p.304.

59. Mousnier 1979, p.281, pp.337-351

60. Göhring, 1947, p.10; Mousnier 1979, pp.322-325

61. That is after the Concordat of Bologna (1516). See Göhring 1947, p.10; Mousnier 1979, pp.305-307; Shennan 1968, p.193

62. Most of the noble bishops were younger sons, as the eldest son usually received a company or a regiment if he belonged to the nobility of the sword, and a judicial office if he belonged to the nobility of the robe. To an increasing extent the noble bishops came from the sword. Between 1700 and 1774 sixty-nine percent came from the nobility of the sword, between 1774 and 1790 seventy-five percent, whereas respectively sixteen and eight percent came from the nobility of the robe. Ravich 1966, pp.69-86

63. In general, the parish priest was not recruited from the lowest section of the people, the *laboureurs*. Mousnier 1979, pp.325-331

64. Behrens 1985, p.54-55

65. See especially Göhring 1965; Mousnier 1971; Swart 1949

66. Goubert and Roche 1984, vol.I, pp.340-341

67. Ford 1968, pp.108-109

68. Behrens 1985, p.50

69. Ford 1968, pp.110-111

70. Ford 1968, p.110

71. Behrens 1985, p.51 However, according to Doyle 1980, p.132, few venal offices were created after the 1730's.

72. Göhring 1965, p.262

73. Behrens 1985, p.51

74. Behrens 1985, p.50; Goubert and Roche 1984, vol.I, pp.141-143

75. Behrens 1985, pp.50-51; Chaussinand 1984, pp.42-46; Doyle 1980, p.119, asserts that there were perhaps 6,500 such offices in the eighteenth century, but it is not clear how this number is computed. Nevertheless, it is probably true that the number of 4,000 is somewhat low. See Ford 1968, pp.53-54

76. Behrens 1985, p.51; Goubert and Roche 1984, vol.I, p.147

77. Chaussinand 1984, p.46 This total includes a small number (110) of ennoblements by military *charge*, which was made a rule only in 1750 by the edict of Fontainebleau. See Carré 1920, pp.10-11

78. Behrens 1985, p.51

79. Behrens 1985, p.52

80. Goubert and Roche 1984, vol.I, p.141

81. Goubert and Roche 1984, vol.I, pp.141-143 The office of *secrétaire de roi* in one of the higher courts in the province was somewhat cheaper, but still expensive. It stood at about 120,000 *livres* in 1789.

82. Chaussinand 1984, p.42 The number is given by Necker. If it is accurate the total of ennobling offices in the sovereign courts expanded quite substantially in the eighteenth century, since, according to Ford 1968, p.54, it never exceeded 2,300 in the first half of that century.

83. Ford 1968, p.37

84. Goubert and Roche 1984, vol.I, pp.275-276

85. Parker 1983, p.6

86. The dates are taken from Shennan 1968, pp.74-85. Other authors sometimes mention slightly different dates of creation. See for instance Ford 1968, p.38; Parker 1983, pp.6-7

87. Furthermore, the creation of the *parlements* of Grenoble and Rouen was nothing but a confirmation of already existing and quite ancient courts as royal courts.

88. Campbell 1988, p.48

89. Parker 1983, p.10

90. Doyle 1980, p.224n16. Instead of Blois he erroneously speaks of Bar.

91. *Encyclopédie*, t.III, p.782 and the whole item 'Comptes, Chambres des', pp.782-795, 'L'un eut en partage l'exercice de la justice qui avoit rapport à la tranquilité des citoyens, & l'autre celui qui concernoit l'administration des finances'.

92. Goubert and Roche 1984, vol.I, p.337, suggest, albeit indirectly, that this idea withered away in the eighteenth century. But a reading of the *Encyclopédie*, t.V, 1755, p.21 shows that it was still up to date at that time.

93. Goubert and Roche 1984, vol.I, pp.337-338; See *Encyclopédie* t.V, pp.21-28, for an extensive overview of the concept of *Domain de la Couronne*.

94. Behrens 1985, pp.69-72, is far off the mark in her discussion of *finances ordinaires* and *extraordinaires*. She believes that the first category included all taxes, and the second principally loans.

95. *Encyclopédie*, t.IV, p.357, t.V, p.21, 'Dans leur origine ne se levoient point ordinairement, mais seulement dans certaines occasions, & pour les besoins extraordinaires de l'état.'

96. *Encyclopédie*, t.IV, p.357, 'Ses sortes d'aides ou subsides s'accordoient, soit par les états généraux du royaume, soit par les états particuliers des provences, & mêmes des villes, & ne dureoient qu'un tems limité.'

97. Ford 1968, p.39; Doyle 1980, p.224n16; In *Encyclopédie*, t.IV, pp.355-356 it is maintained that 'il y a actuellement en France cinq cours des aides'. But it is also admitted that the one in Montpellier has long been united with the *chambre des comptes* in that same town.

98. Ford 1968, p.40

99. Ford 1968, p.40; *Encyclopédie* t.X, pp.656-658

100. Ford 1968, p.40; Shennan 1968, p.80

101. Ford 1968, p.40-41

102. Shennan 1968, p.80

103. Ford 1968, pp.43-44

104. Ford 1968, p.41

105. Shennan 1968, pp.82-84

106. Ford 1968, p.52

107. Ford 1968, p.50

108. Ford 1968, p.80

109. Ford 1968, p.80

110. Shennan 1968, 159-161

111. Ford 1968, p.97

112. Antoine 1970; Goubert and Roche 1984, vol.I, pp.222-235

113. Mousnier 1979, p.247, p.340; Shennan 1968, p.80; Doyle 1980, p.58 incl.note 12; Dakin 1972, pp.149-150

114. Dakin 1972, p.149, p.331

115. Goubert and Roche 1984, vol.I, p.233; Dakin 1972, p.331n2. In 1787 Brienne created a *Conseil de Guerre*.

116. Goubert and Roche 1984, vol.I, p.235

117. Goubert and Roche 1984, vol.I, pp.235-236

118. Goubert and Roche 1984, vol.I, p.236

119. Goubert and Roche 1984, vol.I, p.234

120. Goubert and Roche 1984, vol.I, p.238

121. Goubert and Roche 1984, vol.I, pp.236-245

122. Ford 1968, pp.59-65

123. Ford 1968, pp.126-129

124. Behrens 1985, pp.47-56

125. Hume, *Treatise of Human Nature*, III.2.2, but he is talking about society, and not about education.

126. Chaussinand 1984, p.103

127. Chaussinand 1984, p.102

128. Chaussinand 1984, pp.96-102

129. Mousnier 1979, pp.713-714

130. Chaussinand 1984, p.98

131. Mousnier 1979, p.714 speaks of 'forms', each taking up one year.

132. Mousnier 1979, pp.713-722

133. Shennan 1968, p.136; An alternative to a college education became the *écoles militaires* that were set up in the second half of the eighteenth century. In 1751 the *École Royale Militaire* in Paris was created, in 1764 the former Jesuit college of La Flèche was converted into a military college, and in 1776 eleven other provincial military colleges were set up. Although all of these colleges had originally been intended only for indigent nobles of ancient lineage, they were quickly more or less monopolized by the sons of the court nobility and the high robe. A third, extremely expensive, possibility was an education in one of the *académies d'équitation*, three of which existed in Paris, one in Versailles, one in Angers and one in Bordeaux, where horsemanship, 'the art of warfare', and dancing was thought, but also languages, history and mathematics. See Mousnier 1979, pp.195-196; Chaussinand 1984, pp.98-102

134.Chaussinand 1984, p.104

135. Shennan 1984, 133; Roche 1988, p.93; Chaussinand 1984, p.109; Goubert and Roche 1984, vol.II, p.239

136. Roche 1988, p.96

137. Roche 1988, p.96

138. Shennan 1968, p.134

139. Shennan 1968, p.134

140. Roche 1988, p.97

141. Chaussinand 1984, pp.105-108

CHAPTER THREE

THE RISE OF CLASSICISM

The Thracians, the Scyths, the Persians, the Lydians, and almost all other barbarians, hold the citizens who practice trades, and their children, in less repute than the rest, while they esteem as noble those who keep aloof from handicrafts, and especially honor such as are given wholly to war

Herodotus[1]

1. The medieval heritage

Classicism was a child of the renaissance. At the time of its birth the French nobility was already very old, and had developed a distinctive way of life and intellectual outlook going back several centuries. Let us call it the warrior ethos. In consideration of this fact, it would have been surprising if classicism had conquered the mind of the nobility without effort and resistance, and had wholly superseded that older moral language. Eventually, classicism did to a substantial degree replace the warrior ethos as the outlook of the aristocracy, but this occurred only after a protracted period of upheaval, which has been aptly named a collective crisis of identity.[2] Moreover, the warrior ethos was neither entirely rejected nor forgotten. There was no need for that: its basic value -manly courage- was shared by the new classicism. This created a bond which, notwithstanding the much greater sophistication of the concept of courage in classicism, made it possible on the one hand to incorporate classicist ideas without utter loss of identity, and on the other hand to introduce some medieval ideas into the classicist framework. The duel is of course the most obvious example of the latter. As a consequence, the classicism of the renaissance-and-after acquired a special flavor, differentiating it somewhat from its ancient model and paradigm. However, the pagan original shines through everywhere.

1.1. The warrior ethos
'The proper, and only, and essential *forme* of the nobility in France, is a military occupation', writes Montaigne. It was a common judgement in the ancien régime. The main duty of the nobility was fighting. Its alleged ancestors, the Francs, it was argued, who had invaded Gaul in the fifth

century, had brought the warrior ethos along with them from the German forests, where it had flourished for ages. Tacitus' description of the Germans in the *Germania* supposedly bore witness to this: 'the Germans have no taste for peace; renown is more easily won among perils (..). A German is not so easily prevailed upon to plough the land and wait patiently for harvest as to challenge a foe and earn wounds for his reward. He thinks it tame and spiritless to accumulate slowly and by the sweat of his brow what can be got quickly by the loss of a little blood'.[3]

On closer consideration such reasoning seems spurious, however. For it does not explain the intimate bond between the warrior ethos and the aristocracy that was propagated in the ancien régime. The Francs regarded all free men as -potential- warriors. The warrior ethos was associated with masculinity rather than nobility.[4] It is not that this people did not have an aristocracy. But it was leadership -in war and peace- rather than warriorship that distinguished the nobility of the Francs from the commoners. The identification of the nobility with warriorship was a product of the middle ages, of the eleventh and the twelfth century in particular. It is tied up with the genesis of the trifunctional view of society, which became paradigmatic in the eleventh century, a view that distinguished three types of action: praying, fighting, and farming, and three concomitant orders of men: *oratores*, *bellatores*, and *laboratores*.[5]

Soon after the introduction of this tripartite conception the *bellatores* were identified with the mounted and aristocratic warriors, who came to have a virtual monopoly over the military art around the twelfth century, and whose principal occupation was to serve their lord and protect their retainers in battle.[6] This type of warriorship was new. Unknown during the whole Merovingian and Carolingian era, it was a product of the high middle ages.[7] Prior to the eighth century one did not think of horsemanship or nobility as qualities inherent in warriorship. There were many foot-soldiers, and armies included persons of a very varied social position -noblemen, free men and serfs-, most of whom were part-time soldiers, convoked only in emergencies.[8] In the eighth, ninth, and tenth century, however, these armies were gradually displaced by armies of 'professional', heavily armed horsemen, so-called *chevaliers*.[9]

Various explanations for the advancement of the mounted soldier have been suggested, such as the example set by the Saracens who invaded the south of France in the early eighth century, and the introduction of the stirrup and the horseshoe, which greatly enhanced the effectiveness of horsemen.[10] Whatever may have been the causes of the displacement of the foot-soldier, its consequences were tremendous. The equipment of a mounted soldier was much more expensive than that of a foot-soldier, and his training was much more time-consuming and extensive, and increasingly so, as in the course of time relatively light armor gave way to much heavier armor, for the horseman as well as for his horse.[11] Hence, wealth and leisure became indispensable prerequisites of military preparation, and warfare consequently an affair of elites. The military value of the overwhelming majority of men on the other hand diminished continuously, as a result of which they were less and less used in combat, and gradually began to regard themselves as peasants rather than soldiers.[12]

Initially, the name of *chevalier* was not very prestigious. A knight was just a mounted soldier in the service of the king or of some other leading personage. There was nothing aristocratic about him. Prior to the twelfth century a nobleman would not have appreciated being called a knight.[13] Significantly, the word is derived from the old English *cniht*, and is related to the German *Knecht*, both meaning servant. When referred to in Latin, knights were called *milites*, a name the ancient Romans had given to foot-soldiers -privates-, whereas *equites* would have seemed a more appropriate name, from a technical point of view; an apparent incongruity which is explained by the discrepancy between the social value of the notion of *equitus* and the status of the knights at that time. *Chevaliers* were soldiers who had 'commended' themselves to a lord, promising to serve him faithfully, in return for protection and assistance, thus becoming his *vassus*. This term is the Latinized version of the Celtic *gwas*. During the whole Merovingian era it meant slave. Hence, at first vassalage was anything but a mark of honor.[14] From the eighth century onwards it was also applied to free men, whether mounted or not, who were dependent on a lord, but even at this stage every man of some consequence still looked down upon it.[15] Being a *chevalier* did not make a difference in this respect.

It was only when the cavalry began to surpass the infantry in importance and became the decisive arm of war, that current views about knighthood began to alter. In order to create more *chevaliers* more and more vassals were given estates by their lords to enable them to provide themselves with the necessary military equipment, which had become much more costly than before.[16] This union[17] of vassalage and landed property[18] attracted people from the higher levels of society into the ranks of the knights.[19] As a steadily growing number of noblemen was prepared to become a knight, the status of knighthood, and vassalage in general, rose hugely. Hence evolved a new, feudal aristocracy, for which the *chevalier* was the incarnation of true nobility.[20]

For a considerable period of time this nobility ruled supreme. The noble warriors were the undisputed leaders of society. The king, who still stood on top of the hierarchy in theory, was in practice virtually impotent. The great mass of the people had been disarmed, and was utterly dependent on their lord, who could command and judge them with almost no interference from outside the manor. Hence, each lord was the sole ruler over his domain and *vilains*. Of course the feudal order imposed some structure on this fragmented society, but just like the king's authority it was to a large extent an imaginary rather than a real order. Frequently, a powerful nobleman was perfectly prepared to disobey, and even fight his formal overlord, an attitude reinforced by the appearance of castles all over Europe in the eleventh and twelfth century.

It is true that as of the opening of the twelfth century the position of the king began to improve, and a process of gradual consolidation of royal power was set in, marking the origin of the states that have persisted until the present. The royal domain was extended, a central administration was developed, the first efforts to establish a unified body of law were made, a royal system of local government was devised, etcetera. Socially and economically too, a new era began to dawn. Agricultural productivity expanded considerably, city life was revitalized as trade and manufacture grew, and a new social class was born: the bourgeoisie. However, it would be fundamentally mistaken to conclude from these developments that as of then the nobility was in decline. Such a conclusion is typical of a teleological approach to history. Eventually, these developments were of course material in that decline, but for centuries to come the political, social, and economic position of the nobility remained unassailable. In fact, the nobility was the first to profit from the improvement of things.

1.2. The chivalric ideal

It was in this context that the ideal of chivalry was born, which added certain new elements to the older concept of knighthood. Chivalry is not very well understood; opinion varies both as to its definite meaning and as to the degree to which is was actually practiced. What is clear, however, is that chivalry was essentially a noble -as opposed to a vulgar- attitude towards the enemy, towards the weak in general, and towards women in particular.[21] This implied quite a refinement of the previous notion of noble behavior, which had centered on prowess in warfare, and little else.

These earlier noblemen were crude and rough; their pursuits were limited to heavy eating, drinking, gambling, hunting, riding, dancing, wenching, and fighting. They were often illiterate and had to send for a cleric to learn the contents of a letter. Now the *chevaliers* were also expected to obey the laws of chivalry. These restrained their behavior. The nobleman was supposed to fight only enemies worthy of himself. The killing of an unarmed adversary came to be considered ignoble, and also the waging of war against the weak: women and children. It was shameful even to kill a knight thrown from his horse. One was supposed to dismount and continue to fight on foot.[22] These new rules of 'fair play' had nothing to do with the Christian notion of *misericordia*. It was rather that an easy victory was no source of pride and honor. One could show one's bravery and superiority only in a fair fight.

The most celebrated aspect of the ideal of chivalry is the new role accorded to women, known as the cult of courtly love. We come across it for the first time in the *chansons* of the twelfth-century troubadours.[23] (Remarkably, there is no trace of it in the preceding centuries. That was a world in which women still occupied a very subordinate position, and were of interest to the knight mainly in connection with dowries, family alliances, and the preservation of his lineage.) Courtly love had nothing to do with the romantic notion of the meeting of two kindred hearts.[24] It was a motive, a force urging man to test himself, to prove his virtue and nobility. Love was treated as a source of excellence for man. This may have been an exclusively martial excellence to begin with, but it soon called for standards of behavior beyond the ability to wage war, such as graciousness, gentleness, and courtesy. To what extent the ideal of chivalry was really practiced at the time is irrelevant to our story. What counts is that as an ideal it had a great importance for posteriority, for it civilized and refined the primitive medieval notion of nobility and thus prepared the way for the classicist conception of the gentleman.

That is not to say, of course, that the evolution from the chivalrous knight to the nobleman of the ancien régime merely involved a change of style, the assumption of a new, antique garb for something that basically remained the same. That would leave unexplained why the transition took so much time, and was paired with an unprecedented collective crisis of identity of the nobility. The crucial event was the radical change in the nature of warfare, which occurred in the next two centuries. The development of artillery in the fifteenth century provided the death-blow to the preeminence of the noble horsemen in warfare.[25] The invention of new weapons like the crossbow, the longbow, and the gun, which could easily pierce through a knight's plate armor, reversed the odds in favor of the infantry. This resulted in the birth of a new type of army, consisting mainly of foot-soldiers. Moreover, the relative cheapness of these new arms made it feasible to sign up commoners again. These by and by replaced the mounted nobleman in the armies, destroying the military monopoly of the aristocracy. The cavalry became a small elite corps within the army, of relatively little consequence from a military point of view. Is it surprising, in view of these developments, that the nobility was confused over its role?

2. The crises of identity

The renaissance, which brought a renewed interest in Greek and Roman antiquity, initially passed by the nobility unnoticed. Strongly committed to its warrior ethos, the nobility tended to look down upon *les lettres*. These belonged to the world of the *hommes de plume*, unworthy pen-pushers.[26] What a gentleman needed was practical training that prepared for warfare, the honorable service of one's lord, and for elegant courting. Bookish learning was seen as servile, and not proper for men of the world.[27] It would only make the young gentlemen effeminate and cowardly, and incapable of bearing arms.

This attitude began to change only at the very end of the sixteenth and early in the seventeenth century.[28] That is not surprising, for until about the 1560's the medieval view of the noble as a warrior remained quite tenable. Notwithstanding all the military innovations that had been introduced on a large scale in the fifteenth century -the *condottieri*, the cannon and the hand gun, and foot-soldiers[29]- the Italian wars, which began in 1494 and continued until 1559, were in many ways of an old-fashioned nature. Most importantly, they were wholly medieval in ideology and motivation. The *chevaliers* who took part in them saw themselves in the same light as the feudal warriors of a few centuries earlier. Although there was a rapid shift in emphasis from horse to foot -in 1525 only one fifth of the French army of 30,000 men was still mounted- noble horsemen, striving to excel in individual feats of prowess and courage, were still considered the backbone of the army.[30] The idea that the noble was a warrior and a warrior a noble went as yet more or less unchallenged in the first half of the sixteenth century.

In the second half of that same century, however, the nature of warfare changed dramatically. In this age of religious wars, as the period is often called, the involvement of *roturiers* in battle became so extensive that the traditional image of the noble as a warrior rapidly lost its persuasiveness and tenability. And not only did the infantry become the decisive section of the armed forces, but non-nobles also penetrated the cavalry on a large scale, and sometimes even reached positions of command.[31] If this had been all, it might not have effected the malaise and the consternation that it did. But as the noblemen returned home from the war, they discovered that there too their traditional authority lay under fire. The erosion of the role played by the nobility in the government of the realm had been going on for some time, as the king kept on creating new royal offices, and filling them with people of non-noble descent. But this process received an extra impetus by the striking proliferation of venality that occurred in the latter half of the sixteenth century, that was almost entirely to the advantage of non-nobles.[32]

These developments produced considerable malaise within the nobility, a kind of collective identity crisis, which invoked a prodigious outpouring of books, pamphlets and *cahiers* attempting to (re)define the quality of this class, and its specific role in society, both as a part of a more general argument concerning the religious and constitutional predicament of the country, and as a subject of its own.[33] This debate stands out in the history of French political thought, because it resulted in a reformulation of the meaning of the concept of nobility, that successfully transformed the self-image of (substantial and influential sections of) the aristocracy in a direction that was to remain dominant throughout the ancien régime.

This is not to say that the debate brought about a new *communis opinio* on the nature and function of the nobility. 'Conservative' nobles tended to cling to the medieval idea of the nobility as the warrior class, and never accepted the newfangled views. And in this case the passing of time did not soften the heart. In the second half of the eighteenth century, indeed on the very eve of the Revolution, one still hears the 'conservatives' muttering in discontent over present corruption, lamenting the disappearance of the good old days of the middle ages.[34] What these 'conservatives' thought is of limited interest, however, because most of them belonged to that group of poor country squires, the *hobereaux*, who possessed nothing but a proud and ancient lineage, and had little or no influence, either in everyday politics or in political theory. Their more flexible brethren came to perceive fairly quickly that the clock could not be turned back, and adaption of the idea of nobility to the changed circumstances was necessary in order to preserve the nobility's prominence within the realm.

2.1. The military revolution

In the period from roughly the Italian wars to the Thirty years' war the nature of warfare -and with it the nature of warriorship- was transformed beyond recognition. Some historians have thought it fit to speak of a military revolution that stands as a great divide separating the middle ages from the modern world.[35] Apart from the fact that using the concept of a revolution to cover a development taking up a century or more seems somewhat inappropriate, there is a great deal of truth in this contention.

In 1500 the 'archetypical' soldier was still a mounted and noble individualist, who strove for personal glory by acts of courage and heroism, and used his own personal equipment, typically consisting of a horse, a suit of armor, a lance, a battle-sword, and a shield. He served his feudal overlord in his wars, and fought his own wars, assisted by his vassals. By this time the new age in warfare was already dawning, but only the most astute -Machiavelli for one- were aware of that then, and even they had little idea what the future would bring. The extremely complex and erratic process that acquired momentum around 1500 resulted, by the second half of the seventeenth century, in royal standing armies largely made up of predominantly professional *roturier* foot-soldiers in uniform who were relatively well-disciplined and drilled. Ranks and orders had been introduced. The men marched in step and battled in linear formations. Hence, little scope was left for individual feats of prowess. The soldiers' motivation had changed as well. Personal glory had given way to money and fear of punishment -many criminals were given the choice: the legion or the dungeon- as the principal motives for joining the army, urging on to caution, cunning, and collective action rather than to a competition in outclassing others in individual excellence. On top of all this, the size of the armies, and the proliferation and technical potential of firearms had increased tremendously, and tactics and strategy had become complicated fields of study.

Is it surprising, in the light of this metamorphosis of the 'art of war', that the French nobility of this period felt confused and sometimes demoralized for lack of a recognized social function? If it was not the warrior class, what was it? Various suggestions were uttered, some feasible, others less so. The one that eventually became the new orthodoxy solved the identity problem brilliantly. It avoided a clear break with the past, but was nevertheless compatible with the new developments in warfare: the idea of the nobleman as a military officer. This permitted the nobility to continue thinking of itself as a *noblesse militaire*, and at the same time to reconcile itself to the fact that non-noble soldiers were there to stay. Inspired by this new self-image the nobility succeeded remarkably well in establishing a dominating position in the officer corps, both numerically and psychologically.[36] As a result, the notion that 'an officer and a gentleman' were, if not synonymous, than at least largely congruent, became one of the strongest and most unshakable convictions of the seventeenth- and eighteenth-century aristocracy, in France and elsewhere.

Significantly, important aspects of this military revolution were of classical parentage. The introduction of discipline and drill for instance was inspired by the military models of Greek and particularly Roman antiquity. They were initiated by Maurice of Orange and William-Louis of Nassau in their army reforms of the 1590's, and due to their manifest effectiveness,[37] within a few years copied by most other European countries.[†] And even more

---

[†] Why exactly a break-through was achieved in the Netherlands towards the end of the century is difficult to say. Undoubtedly specific factors played a role, like the personality of Maurice and William, the fact that the Dutch were in a precarious position, forcing them to be exceptionally inventive, and the fact that during the last third of the century the Netherlands were the principal center of the study of antiquity. More important are the factors explaining the causes of the general break-through. Two in particular should be mentioned here, in the first place the availability of classical literature, and in the second place the practicability of the ideas expressed in this literature. Although the largest part of the 'lost' classical literature had been rediscovered by the humanists and antiquaries much earlier, most of it became available in print, and thus accessible to a larger public, only towards the end of the sixteenth century. But even if it had become accessible earlier that would not have changed much, because the military ideas expressed in classical literature would presumably have been brushed aside as irrelevant, as the

significantly, for our purposes at least, the idea of the nobleman as a military officer, seems to have been largely derived from the example set by the ancients. That suggests that the ways of the ancients were known and valued by the nobility.

2.2. The educational revolution

In the high middle ages the warrior class was the governing class. And as long as governing consisted mainly of warfare, this was a stable situation. But when agricultural production began to grow, trade and manufacture were revived, city life expanded, and royal efforts at political centralization commenced, government gradually became more than warfare. Most importantly, perhaps, the legal needs of this new society were very different and more complex than before, and could not be satisfied within the context of existing feudal and manorial law and legal process. Hence, gradually legal expertise became essential to the government of the realm.

But the nobility possessed no such expertise, and had no intention of acquiring any. It conceived of itself as a class wholly committed to warfare, and looked down upon book-learning. As a consequence, the nobility obtained a reputation for illiteracy and backwardness. Hence, the nobles were utterly unequipped for governmental positions, an increasing number of which required extensive intellectual, particularly legal training, as the laws, the jurisprudence, and the commentaries were quickly growing in number and complexity.[38] Accordingly, a king who wanted to get things done hardly had a choice. Most nobles were out of the question; non-nobles were the only option. These men had had ten to fifteen years of education and possessed a university degree in law.[39] They were just right for these offices. Thus, the governmental rights and duties of the nobility suffered an increasing curtailment, as more and more offices went to commoners. Admittedly, there was at least one other reason for the king to prefer commoners to nobles: the loyalty of men of mediocre birth to their king, to whom they owed every-thing, was undoubtedly greater than that of the feudal nobles, who were

---

ancient armies were known to have consisted mainly of infantry, whereas contemporary armies were at that time still predominantly mounted. It was only with the military developments of the sixteenth century that this changed. The fundamental alteration in the relative weight of the cavalry and the infantry since the Italian wars made contemporary armies look more like their classical forbears. As in the days of antiquity, the infantry now became the decisive section of the armed forces. This remarkable development had the effect that the classical literature earlier discovered began to be studied eagerly even by those whose interest and purposes were wholly practical. By the beginning of the seventeenth century the classical armies were widely regarded as almost perfect models of military organization. The introduction of *disciplina* in the armies was an outflow of this. See Hahlweg 1941; Delbrück 1900/20

hardly prepared to be his mere servants. But due to their educational deficiency even those who were loyal usually could not be employed.

The first aristocratic complaints about *la douce France* being ruined go back as far as the thirteenth century.[40] But not until the second half of the sixteenth century, when several trends converged, did the erosion of the governmental functions of the nobility cause intense and widespread alarm. Most importantly, a sudden increase in the sale of offices came on top of the change in the nature of warfare. Desperately in need of money and lacking sufficient ways and means to collect enough taxes, the crown had long ago resorted to the sale of offices. This had begun as a little stream, but especially during the sixteenth century it swelled into a gigantic flood. The nobles were generally unable to purchase these offices. Their nominal seignorial income was often fixed by custom, whereas the American silver, that glutted the continent, produced an unprecedented inflation. Moreover, a frequent carelessness in the exploitation of one's estate, the heavy expense on military equipment, and a taste for 'Italian' luxuries were not very helpful either. Indeed, many families had to put up for sale pieces of the land of their forbears, and were in no position to buy royal offices.[41]

A heated discussion about the nature and significance of the nobility ensued. Complaints were common about the debasement of the nobility by the crown, that gave all the offices to *roturiers*, who were supposedly easier to manage. This ruined the nobility, it was argued, by taking away its income and making it useless.[42] Many a noble pamphleteer believed that all problems would be solved, once the system of venality was abolished. Virtue, which had been displaced by wealth, would then automatically return to prominence, the assumption being of course than only nobles were virtuous, and that this quality made them pre-eminently suitable for governmental functions. In an earlier age this would, perhaps, have been regarded as obvious and irrefutable, and put an end to the discussion, but not so in the second half of the sixteenth century, in which the traditional concept of government had lost its pertinence. As a consequence, difficult questions began to be raised about the extent and nature of the relationship between nobility and virtue, and between these two and the nature of the French government, forcing the nobility to explicitly ground many claims it had until then taken more or less for granted. And as is so often the case, these efforts led to a revision of those claims.

The crux of the matter was of course the educational deficiency of the nobility. The clash of opinions on this point eventually persuaded significant layers within the nobility that the traditional education of a noble needed modification and augmentation, that they had to lay aside their anti-intellectual ethos and qualify themselves intellectually, if they wanted to stay the governing class of the realm.[43] Slowly but surely, it began to dawn upon them that 'the non-nobles did not take the judicial offices from us; it is ignorance that deprives us of them', and 'the door is open to all those who see to the education of their children'.[44]

Admittedly, this revisionism was fiercely contested at the time, and remained somewhat controversial afterwards. The *hobereaux* in particular commonly adhered to the view that the education of young *gentilshommes* should be wholly geared to the life of a warrior and a *seigneur*. Bookish learning they continued to regard as useless, or even as positively menacing to the manliness of their sons. If the noble could not adequately render justice anymore, not he but the legal structure was to blame. That had become much too complex and extensive, and should be simplified and restricted. Theirs was a lost cause, however. By the seventeenth century this view was not much more than a subcurrent in aristocratic thought, doomed to a marginal, though long-lived, existence.

The future belonged to the revisionists, who concluded that the nobility must become educated to regain supremacy within the government of France.[45] Accordingly, more and more nobles sent their sons to school and to a university. This was such a striking ideological switch that some historians have called it a 'révolution scolaire: la noblesse d'épée renonce à l'ignorance'.[46] It is here that the roots of the subsequent classicism of the nobility are to be found.

3. The renouncement of ignorance

Interestingly, the sort of school that was needed already existed: the *collège*. At the beginning of the seventeenth century there were hundreds of them, in every part of the country.[47] Most of these schools had been founded in the previous century -although there were some older ones as well- in towns of almost any size. Everywhere, the founders were the municipal authorities, led by the wealthier citizens -the *gens de bien*-, who also endowed and administered the *collèges*, and controlled their staffing.[48] They were set up because dissatisfaction existed with regard to the functioning of the old schools under clerical governance, which were primarily meant to train future men of the church. The families in town sought another kind of education for their sons, adapted to the worldly careers they were destined for. For a long time proficiency in reading and writing, necessary to draw up contracts and handle all other business administration, had been common among the *gens de bien*. But once great wealth was acquired, ambitions inevitably rose beyond *marchandise*, to the honorable service of their city and eventually the crown, and for that more than these simple skills was required. Holding an elected office in the city council themselves, they dreamt of gaining for their sons an office in a *baillage*, for their grandsons one in a *parlement*, and for their great-grandsons perhaps an even more august office, close to the king himself.

3.1. The collèges

The historian George Huppert, who besides having done much to lay bare these facts, employs a wonderfully baroque style, writes that, 'beyond the walls of the cities where (the *gens de bien*) reigned supreme -secure in the possession of real estate, assured of their precedence in banquets and processions, owning the land as far as the eye could see, basking in the rich smells of dried fish, wine, and wool gloriously filling their houses- beyond this small world where they were known and feared, these men, alas, were mere bourgeois, tongue-tied in the presence of Latinizing prelates, awkward in the sight of arrogant noblemen. To overcome these debilities, the notable bourgeoisies of the good towns devised "the means of arriving": *le moyen de parvenir'*.[49]

The new schools that were founded by them everywhere in the country during the sixteenth century were central to this idea. To 'arrive' there where they wanted to, a university degree in law was needed; the *collèges* were devised as a preparation to further studies at the university.[50] The choice of subjects taught followed more or less logically from this. To pursue legal studies at the university a thorough knowledge of classical Latin was a prerequisite. Hence, Latin grammar and Roman literature and history were the core of the curriculum. Cicero was the main thing, but one also taught Cato, Terence, Virgil, Ovid, Horace, Quintilian, Caesar, Juvenal, Sallust, Livy, Tacitus and other Roman authors. In addition to that some Greek and mathematics were usually taught, as well as ancient philosophy and French.[51] Suspicious of the bachelors of theology who taught in the old diocesan schools, the *gens de bien* hired lay teachers, often masters of arts, whom they wanted to be *bon philosophes*, *grecs*, and *humanistes*, to teach all this to their sons.[52]

Although in general no tuition fees were demanded and no one was denied access to the *collège*, the cost of maintaining a son at school were often prohibitively high for simple workingmen and peasants. It was not only that books and other materials had to be paid for, and sometimes room and board if one lived too far away to go home every evening, but a son in school meant one hand less in the workshop or on the field. Consequently, the *collèges* were predominantly populated by the sons of the more prosperous families.[53] These fortunate fellows went there for a period of about ten years, between the ages of approximately six and sixteen, separated from the adult world, and subjected to a daily regime of strict order, regularity and hard work, in which the mastery of the ancients was the central purpose. Everyone of them who had gone through this experience bore its stamp for the rest of his life.[54] It is not exaggerated to say that the *collèges* effected a profound cultural revolution: thanks to these schools the renaissance, which had until then been a affair of a handful of *érudits*, was disseminated throughout the realm, influencing in particular the class of people that met all the mental and material conditions 'pour quelque jour parvenir grandement'.[55]

In the *collèges* a new type of man was nurtured, the *civis* of the *res publica*, whose values were taken directly from the ancients. All the books put in the boys' hand praised a specific lifestyle and specific virtues, grafted almost exclusively onto the ancients, especially the Romans. Their models were the virtuous patricians of the glorious Roman republic.[56] Neither the merchant, nor the *gentilhomme* could serve as a model to them.[57] The merchant's life of trade and commerce was demeaning, so they were taught, and the noble's life of conspicuous spending, hunting, duelling, and brawling was coarse, idle and empty-headed.[58] The word *nobilitas* was on everybody's lips, but this should not be interpreted as a wish to pass for a *gentilhomme*. For those kind of 'nobles' they felt only scorn. 'We recognize him from his pompous way of walking', wrote the principal of the *collège* of Amiens in 1584, 'we hear him bragging about the nobility and antiquity of his house and race; he knows nothing of the liberal arts and gives himself up, instead, to the tragic exercise of the hunt; his body's prowess is dedicated to the service of Bacchus and Venus; in the manner of monkeys, he copies the ways of princes'. Gambling, thievery and murder are his pastimes. He swears, blasphemes, and does violence to his people. And 'he shows contempt for the magistrates, *officiers*, bourgeois, and inhabitants of the town, whom such "noblemen" (..) speak of, contemptuously, as *roturiers* and *vilains*, although most of them live more nobly than they do'.[59] This sort of diatribe is typical of the circles associated with the *collèges*.

The idea of nobility that was taught in these schools was in many ways different. Their model was of Greek and Roman rather than feudal origins, the core ideal of which was citizenship rather than knighthood.[60] What exactly this entailed, cannot be explained in a few words. We will return to the subject in the following chapters. Some of its most marked features should be named here, however. The principal quality of a noble man, in the classicist meaning of the word, was his disinterested patriotism. This set him clearly apart from both the bourgeoisie and the feudal nobility. The merchant, engrossed in the acquisition of property, lacked disinterestedness. To be sure, the possession of property was an indispensable prerequisite to a noble life, but the process of acquiring it was ignoble. To be able to serve the commonwealth disinterestedly, one must have leisure, and not have to earn one's living every day. For the same reason (and others, of which later) land was considered the best kind of property. Especially when rented out to tenant-farmers, almost no work was necessary to be assured of a continuous and fairly stable flow of income over the years.

If all this set the *gens de bien*, in their own eyes, apart from the bourgeoisie, it also associated them in more than one way with the feudal nobility, whose ideas about *vivre noblement* were in some respects quite similar. Yet, at the same time there were crucial differences between the world view of these two groups. When observing these wealthy *roturiers* purchasing noble estates and ennobling offices, changing their names, and selling their interest in *marchandise*, one should not jump to the conclusion that they wished to become old-style *gentilshommes*. They pursued a different kind of *nobilitas*. Their heroes were the *viri illustres* of antiquity, not the great knights of the middle ages.

The *gentilhomme*, when assuming governmental tasks, served his personal overlord rather than his *patrie*. The *gens de bien* on the other hand learnt from the ancients that as *officiers* they would be serving the prince as head of the commonwealth; an entirely different political conception.[61] The *gentilshommes* scorned both the merchant and the *officier* for their lack of martial virtues. To him enthusiasm of letters was pedantic and effeminate. Fighting was the highest purpose of his life. The *gens de bien* loved nothing so much as books, and regarded fighting as a civic duty, which had to be resorted to only if no justice could be had by other, more peaceful means.[62] In view of all this it is no wonder that in the sixteenth-century *gens de bien* were widely regarded as a 'fourth estate', a 'body separate of the nobility' as well as of the third estate.[63]

The embrace by the *gens de bien* of the classical ideal of disinterested patriotism and everything it encompassed, sealed a trend that had existed for some time, but as a result of the influence of the *collèges* became much more powerful and irreversible: the *Aristokratisierung* of the bourgeoisie. Their prolonged immersion in the ancients in the *collèges* taught the merchants' sons that the way of life of their fathers was ignoble, but that nobility was within reach, because it was more a matter of life-style and disposition than genealogy. Acquiring the status of nobility and seeking a governmental office, which had for centuries been the most promising way to advancement in the world, now became something transcending mere self-interest in the restricted sense of the word, and obtained a more exalted, lofty stature as the good and noble life *par excellence*. Entirely derived from the ancients, this idea of nobility was explicitly and deliberately contrasted with the 'false' feudal idea of nobility.[64]

3.2. Noblesse et nobilitas

The alumni of the *collèges* were the people who manned the royal offices everywhere and at all levels in the realm. These were the *sénéchaux* and *baillis*, the *conseillers* and *présidents*, the *maîtres des requetes* and *intendants*.

These were the *gens de robe*, on their way to become the *noblesse de robe*. These were the men who posed a threat to the military nobility, the *noblesse d'épée*. And these were the men who pointed the way to a solution.

This is what happened. Around the turn of the century the civil wars were over. Declaring that France was worth a mass to him Henry IV had become a Catholic. Religious as well as political liberties were guaranteed to the Huguenots by the Edict of Nantes. With expedient moves like this the king managed to buy off virtually all internal opposition, whereafter he could begin to focus on restoring the wealth and the power of the realm. Like most of his predecessors and successors he believed that this required further centralization and hence a strengthening of royal authority. It followed logically that particularisms of all kinds had to be vigorously resisted, and potential centers of sedition had to be either liquidated, or reformed and regulated in such a way that they henceforth served royal policy.

It was in this context that the king's attention was drawn to the *collèges*, the number of which had increased steadily in the century past, quite unnoticed by the government which had been too busy with other things most of the time. Now they were just about everywhere. Each single town of some, and many of little or no importance had one. Moreover, these schools were completely independent of both the church and the state and without exception, affluent *roturiers* were the main beneficiary.[65] Not surprisingly such a state of affairs was widely regarded as objectionable and dangerous by the elites within the kingdom, including those *gens de bien* who had already secured high governmental office and noble status.

There were reasons enough to fear unrestricted learning. Both the church and crown had apprehensions about the heretical and freethinking ideas the pupils in the *collèges* derived from the classical books they read in unexpurgated editions.[66] Ordinary mortals had no need of all this knowledge; it was sufficient to teach them how to read, write and count, and to behave like a good Christian and subject.[67] All this learning was detrimental to the state, because the *enfants de la ville* who had completed *collège* tended to abandon the productive and useful occupation of their fathers in favor of an *office*.[68] Both statesmen and clerics presumably believed that 'the study of literature is an activity appropriate only to a small minority of man. (..) More farmers are needed than magistrates, more soldiers than priests, more merchants than philosophers, more artisans than men of letters, more hard-working bodies than dreamy and contemplative spirits. Scholarship and science should remain exceptional pursuits'.[69]

The nobility had its own reasons for concern, as we have seen. For a long time its interest in the *collèges* had remained very limited. Nobles did not usually sponsor them, or send their sons to such a school for their education.[70] Protracted study of literature enfeebled body and mind, and was to be avoided. As the century drew to its close, however, more and more nobles came to realize the importance the *collèges* had assumed. Here a class of thoroughly educated layman was bred, well-trained for governmental service, which was in the process of outbidding the nobility. What to do under these circumstances? Of course there were many nobles who reacted to this predicament with a great clamor of indignation, insisting that the *collèges* be shut down and everything returned to 'normal'. But, whether or not such views at any time expressed the feelings of the majority within the nobility, there evidently was no future in them. The only sensible solution for the nobility was to qualify itself. Around the turn of the century this was finally grasped, and more and more noble scions began to flock into the *collèges*.[71]

The policy eventually adopted reflected the interests and concerns of all three, the crown, the church, and the nobility. It involved shutting down most *collèges*, and turning the remaining few into elite institutions under clerical supervision, serving only the very rich and well-born.[72] Although it was not successful in all respects -in the eighteenth century there were still *collèges* everywhere in France-[73] this policy did by and large achieve its aims. In the course of the seventeenth century all the independent, secular, humanist *régens* were replaced by teachers belonging to a religious order, particularly Jesuits and Oratorians, under whose guidance most of the *collèges* slowly drifted into insignificance.[74] First-rate schools where one could get a thorough classical education became expensive and rare. Sending their sons to one of them was far beyond the means of a bourgeois, no matter how wealthy he may have seemed in the eyes of the populace. Hence, the *collèges* became the preserve of an exclusive *côterie*, consisting of the sons of the high robe and the most prominent families within the *noblesse d'épée*, many of whom were expected to take part, be it as *présidents*, as generals, or in some other prominent capacity, in future affairs of state. This was the nobility that really counted in the ancien régime.

It was a mixture of the robe and the sword. To be sure, the segregation between these two elites did not vanish just because and as soon as their scions began to go to the same schools. Ancient preconceptions are not that easily overcome. Yet, once the *collèges* had made them classmates for a number of years, giving them ample opportunity to associate with each other, the mental walls that had until than securely divided the *gentilshommes* and the *robins* were bound to come down sooner or later. Presumably, the boys' discovery of existing affinities ensured this -the shared condition of rentiership, the rejection of commerce as something demeaning, the adoration of the country life, the knowledge of being destined to govern the realm, and the exclusive education they jointly received, which set them, as one elite, apart from the population at large, and reinforced these preconceptions.

A second repercussion of these developments was that a classical education and a classicist outlook were increasingly looked upon as typically noble attributes. This primarily affected the nobles themselves, who gradually but unmistakingly began to put less emphasis on concepts derived from the medieval warrior ethos when speaking of themselves and the place in society they were entitled to, and instead of that more and more began to refer to classical -chiefly Roman- examples, notions, and doctrines. The recognition of a connection between nobility and classicism made the long-standing *robin* claim to such a status much more plausible and acceptable. They had been staunch classicists for a long time, always busy imitating the Roman *nobiles*, serving the *res publica*. If the *noblesse d'épée* derived its self-image from the ancients, surely the robe, which had done so for a long time was equally justified in calling itself a *noblesse*? This line of reasoning may not have been logically flawless, but it was convincing anyway.

This development should not be thought of as some ideological *volte face* on the side of the sword, involving a complete rejection of convictions formerly held, and a conversion to a new and utterly different faith. It was nothing of that kind. As has been set out, classicism was not regarded as something entirely at odds with the traditionally espoused warrior ethos. On the contrary, the nobles, given their essentialist frame of mind, tended to equate medieval and classical concepts whenever possible -such as the medieval knight and the Roman *eques*-, which enabled them to a large extent to adopt this ideological reorientation without acknowledging that such a reorientation was in fact implicated.[75] And in addition to that, some typically 'feudal' elements of the picture of the world traditionally endorsed by the nobility were retained, incorporated into the newly acquired classicist framework, and eventually subscribed to by the nobility with a *robin* background, the practice of duelling being the most obvious example. Henceforth, a classical education was an indispensable prerequisite for social advancement. It is a sign of the times that monsieur Jourdain, the hero in Molière's *Le Bourgeois Gentilhomme*, hired a philosopher. Had the play been written a century earlier this would have been incomprehensible. A century after its first publication on the other hand a *roturier* hiring a philosopher to help him behave like a nobleman was still as relevant a topic as it had ever been. Up till the revolution a solid grounding in the ancients remained the core of an aristocratic education,[76] and a *sine qua non* to social ascent.

This overriding cultural importance of the ancients to the self-conception and the world view of the nobility of the ancien régime has received scant attention from older historians of the age. But in view of the fact that the nobility tended to be regarded as an anachronistic leftover from the past by these authors, without much significance, this is hardly amazing. Only now, after a generation of unprecedented research and scholarly debate, we gradually begin to realize that this frame is severely distorted, and has to be discarded in favor of a new one, the outlines of which are still vague and sketchy. One thing is beyond dispute however: the 'appeal to antiquity'[77] is a key to a genuine understanding of the age. The question is what did antiquity mean to the elite of the ancien régime?

NOTES

1. Herodotus, *Histories*, II.167

2. Bitton 1969, p.1

3. Tacitus, *Germania*, XIV

4. Bloch 1968, p.436

5. Duby 1980

6. Keen 1984, p.2

7. See Huizinga 1955, ch.4-7, whose account of this period has become classic. It contains an extensive, though rather cynical analysis of chivalry.

8. Berman 1983, p.301; Ganshof 1976, pp.4-5

9. Berman 1983, p.302

10. Berman 1983, p.302; Preston and Wise 1970, p.67 The stirrup improved the horseman's stability, enabling him to use his sword more forcefully, and to deliver powerful thrusts with a lance without toppling from the saddle. According to Berman the stirrup and the horseshoe were imported from the east, where they were used by Eurasian tribes. Preston and Wise on the other hand claim that their origins can be found in the Mediterranean world.

11. Howard 1976, pp.2-3

12. Berman 1983, pp.301-302

13. Jansen 1981, p.106

14. Ganshof 1976, p.5

15. Ganshof 1976, p.19

16. Ganshof 1976, p.16

17. In the middle ages this union was never complete. There always remained vassals without landed property.

18. The prevalent form of property from the ninth century onwards was a conditional kind of property, a tenement called *beneficium, feodum* or fief. See Ganshof 1976, p.106 ff. Prior to that estates were mostly granted in full ownership: *allodum*.

19. Ganshof 1976, p.19.

20. Jansen 1981, p.106

21. Ossowska 1972, p.135

22. Ossowska 1972, p.135

23. Barber 1974, pp.71-155

24. It is sometimes argued that the cult of courtly love was a kind of romanticism: the idea that love was an authentic feeling that should be honored, even if it contradicted the demands of tradition and law. This can hardly be true. Until the middle of the eighteenth century feelings were regarded as experiences that should be controlled by the ratio or by virtue. If feelings determined a man's action they had got out of hand. Besides, the cult of courtly love was paired with an elaborate etiquette, which is completely at odds with the ideal of genuineness in the romantic sense. Rather than a cult of authentic feeling, it was a cult of inauthenticity, in which feeling and behavior were in a great measure imitative, ritualized, and standardized.

25. Painter 1977, pp.7-24

26. Jouanna 1976, p.657

27. Hexter 1976, pp.48-49

28. Schalk 1986, p.175

29. Howard 1976, ch.1, pp.1-19

30. Howard 1976, p.20 It should be noted, in this context, that during the first half of the sixteenth century the infantry to a large extent consisted of foreign -Swiss and German- mercenaries. Although the number of French foot-soldiers began to rise significantly from the 1530's onwards they seem to have been outnumbered by the foreigners until about 1550. See Bitton 1969, p.30

31. Bitton 1969, pp.30-31

32. Bitton 1969, p.43

33. Bitton 1969, pp.1-5

34. E.g. Le chevalier d'Arc, *La Noblesse Militaire ou le Patriote François*, Paris 1756

35. Roberts 1967, p.195

36. Bitton 1969, p.40

37. Proved for the first time in the Battle of Nieuwpoort between the Dutch and the Spanish on the second of July 1600

38. Hexter 1976, ch.4, pp.45-70; Bitton 1969, pp.46-47

39. Huppert 1977, p.18, p.74

40. See Hinze 1928, p.14, p.491n33

41. See Ford 1968, p.107; Salmon 1975, pp.37-47

42. Bitton 1969, p.44

43. Chartier et al. 1976, p.168, p.179

44. Quoted in Bitton 1969, p.47. See also Hexter 1976, p.58n1

45. Hexter 1976, pp.63-64

46. Goubert and Roche 1984, vol.II, p.214

47. Huppert 1984, p.xii, xiv

48. Huppert 1977, pp.59-63

49. Huppert 1977, pp.59-60

50. Huppert 1984, p.9, p.58. The author seems to have changed his mind on this issue. In Huppert 1977, pp.82-83, it is argued that 'there is no clear connection between the curriculum of the *collèges* and the skills required of royal magistrates in the *baillages* or even in the *parlements* (..) if the *collèges* and the law schools were indispensable *pour voguer* in the sixteenth century, it was not for the professional preparation they dispensed but rather for the general culture they had to offer and for the habits and manners they inculcated'.

51. Huppert 1977, pp.77-78

52. Huppert 1984, pp.51-52

53. Huppert 1977, pp.71-72

54. Huppert 1984, pp.75-77

55. Huppert 1977, pp.59-60

56. Huppert 1977, p.90

57. Nor the priest, whose life of celibacy, prayer, and otherworldliness was regarded as uncivic.

58. Huppert 1977, p.73; Huppert 1984, p.86

59. Quoted in Huppert 1977, pp.86-87

60. Huppert 1977, p.90

61. Hexter 1976, pp.69-70 Note that Hexter is talking about 'the sixteenth-century aristocrat'. That seems to be too broad, at least in the case of sixteenth-century France. At that time this way of thinking about the 'body politic' was still something typically *robin*. It became an 'all-aristocratic' creed only in the seventeenth century, after the nobility of the sword had decided to 'renounce its ignorance'.

62. Huppert 1977, pp.90-102

63. Huppert 1977, p.46

64. Huppert 1977, ch.4, pp.24-33

65. Huppert 1984, p.111

66. Huppert 1977, p.66; Huppert 1984, ch.7, pp.92-103 Zealous Catholics of course were also afraid of another heresy: Protestantism. See Huppert 1984, p.xi

67. Huppert 1984, p.117

68. Huppert 1984, p.116

69. Quoted in Huppert 1984, p.121, from a Jesuit memoir.

70. Huppert 1977, p.67

71. Chartier et al. 1976, p.170

72. Huppert 1984, ch.9, pp.116-129

73. Goubert and Roche 1984, vol.II, p.212

74. Huppert 1977, p.121

75. Huizinga 1955, p.71

76. Doyle 1990, p.49

77. Gay 1977, vol.I, title of book I

CHAPTER FOUR

THE MEANING OF ANTIQUITY

*As yet, everyone has found in the ancients
whatever he needed or wanted; most of all himself*

Schlegel[1]

1. Readings of antiquity

'But it is an easy thing, for men to be deceived, by the specious name of liberty; and for want of judgement to distinguish, mistake that for their private inheritance, and birth-right, which is the right of the public only. And when the same error is confirmed by the authority of men in reputation for their writings on this subject, it is no wonder if it produce sedition, and change of government. In these western parts of the world, we are made to receive our opinions concerning the institution, and rights of commonwealths, from Aristotle, Cicero, and other men, Greeks and Romans, that living under popular states, derived those rights, not from the principles of nature, but transcribed them into their books, out of the practice of their own common-wealths, which were popular (..). And because the Athenians were taught, to keep them from desire of changing their government, that they were freemen, and all that lived under monarchy were slaves; therefore Aristotle puts it down in his *Politics*, (*lib*.6 *cap*.ii) *In democracy*, liberty *is to be supposed: for it is commonly held, that no man is* free *in any other government*. And as Aristotle; so Cicero, and other writers have grounded their civil doctrine, on the opinions of the Romans, who were taught to hate monarchy (..). And by reading of these Greek, and Latin authors, men from their childhood have gotten a habit, under a false show of liberty, of favoring tumults, and of licentious controlling the actions of their sovereigns, and again of controlling those controllers; with the effusion of so much blood, as I think I may truly say, there was never any thing so dearly bought, as these western parts have bought the learning of the Greek and Latin tongues.'[2] (author's emphasis)

These lines by the political philosopher Hobbes, written in the 1640's in France, where the author had sought refuge when parliament and king came to open war in Britain, are highly interesting, because they are a testimony to both the extent and the drift of the influence of Roman and Greek antiquity on the political thought of the age. But a telling phrase alone does not prove anything yet. 'Roman and Greek antiquity' is so broad a notion that it could include almost anything. Hence, the first questions to be answered are: what exactly did the nobility of the ancien régime learn from their reading 'of the books of policy, and histories of the ancient Greeks, and Romans', that was so much abhorred by Hobbes? What did the nobility know of antiquity? What aspects of antiquity did it value and emphasize? What parts of antiquity did it find congenial and inspiring?

Most of these questions have already been given some consideration in the previous chapters. Concisely summing up our main conclusions here may be useful. We learned first of all that the French aristocracy of the ancien régime was classically minded through and through -at least the wealthier *échelons* within it. The curriculum of the schools to which the aristocracy sent its sons was dominated by the ancients. Its libraries were filled with the works of the ancients. The aristocracy adorned its *hôtels* and its gardens with classicist busts and statues, often representing Greek and Roman statesmen, philosophers, and generals. Its correspondence was packed with casual allusions to and quotations from ancient poets and historians. The minds of the French nobles were stocked with classical images and examples. In short, the culture of antiquity pervaded the lives of the members of the aristocracy, reinforcing its separateness from the common people, that entirely lacked such a culture, and providing it with a pervasive and distinctive code of values.

In addition to this we learned that the origins of the classicism of the French aristocracy go back to sixteenth-century *robin* circles, which devised a classical education for their offspring, as a 'means of arriving', i.e. a way to acquire an *office*, and eventually noble status. The old, 'feudal' aristocracy long remained contemptuous of education and learning, regarding it as pedantic and effeminate, and incompatible with the life of action led by a noble warrior, but around the turn of the century the *épée* began to 'renounce its ignorance', as it became aware of the fact that the *robins* were gradually replacing the 'old' nobles in governmental positions, because they were infinitely better educated. The seventeenth century subsequently saw a complex process of *rapprochement* between the two groups, to which the now shared classical education and classicist outlook contributed substantially, eventually resulting in a relatively unified top-layer within French society, which tended to view itself largely in terms derived from the ancients.

If the social and political thought of the French aristocracy of the seventeenth and eighteenth century was in fact heavily indebted to the ancients, as is maintained here, it should be determined exactly how much one knew, and what were judged to be true and valuable insights. For the use that is made of a body of knowledge depends upon two things. It depends in the first place on the extent of that knowledge, and in the second place on one's particular fields of interest. The Greeks and the Romans have had a tremendous influence on western civilization, especially since the renaissance, but that influence has never been unequivocal. Ancient literature has been read, interpreted, and explained in multifarious and conflicting ways, not only because an ever increasing stock of information became available, but also because every age stressed those aspects of the classical heritage that suited its tastes and preferences best. As a result of this our own perception and use of the ancients differs substantially from that of the French aristocracy of the ancien régime.

1.1. Knowledge of antiquity

To begin with, our knowledge of the Greeks and the Romans is much greater. Anyone who wants to know anything about these peoples, their way of life, and their thinking, has at his disposal the findings of a profession which has made considerable progress in the past two centuries. First of all, some important ancient manuscripts were rediscovered. In 1816 B.G. Niebuhr located Gaius' *Institutiones*, first published in 161 A.D., in the cathedral of Verona.[3] Fragments adding up to about a quarter or a third of Cicero's *De Re Publica*, of which only *Somnium Scipionis* -Scipio's dream- and a few quotations by other authors had been known earlier, were found in 1820.[4] A substantial part of Aristotle's *Constitution of Athens* was uncovered in 1891. And quite a few other new discoveries were made. Nevertheless, these discoveries were not the principle cause of the growth of our knowledge of antiquity. The book-finders and antiquarians of the renaissance had done a thorough job, and had left few manuscripts unearthed. Most progress has been made in the analysis and interpretation of well-known texts, not in finding more texts.

This is largely due to the simple fact that later scholars could stand on the shoulders of their predecessors. In addition to this, the advances in other branches of the arts and sciences, most notably in archaeology, contributed significantly to the growth of our knowledge of antiquity.[5] A wealth of inscriptions has been dug up, incised in clay tablets and chiseled in the stone remnants of walls and pillars. Loads of papyri, the normal writing-material until after 100 A.D., have been rediscovered, as well as statues, coins, utensils, etcetera, each and everyone a piece of additional evidence, corroborating or disproving the textual accounts we already possessed.

As a third explanation of the growth of knowledge of antiquity a new attitude to history is sometimes mentioned. In earlier times historians supposedly freely criticized and judged the past, which was regarded as a store-house of *exempla*, inciting us to be virtuous, and to eschew the vices. Livy's definition of history as 'a record of the infinite variety of human experience plainly set out for all to see; (..) (in which) you can find for yourself and your country both examples and warnings; fine things to take as models, base things, rotten through and through, to avoid',[6] is often quoted to substantiate this view. In the nineteenth century value-judgements and moralizing supposedly receded into the background, to be replaced by a new ideal of writing history: the disclosure of *wie es eigentlich gewesen*.[7] This is said to have resulted in a novel stress on objectivity, thoroughness, detachment, detail, and proof, which led to the aforementioned progress in the study of the ancients.[8]

But this is exaggerated, and chiefly inspired by an improper comparison between different kinds of writers, and different genres of books. One should carefully distinguish real scholars and *érudits* from *literati* and *philosophes* who used works of scholarship to further their own, often politically motivated, causes. The principles and the aims governing the work of seventeenth- and eighteenth-century scholars were much the same as those of their nineteenth- and twentieth-century successors. The ambition to show 'what had really happened' is considerably older than the previous century. Like their nineteenth- and twentieth-century heirs, many *érudits* of the ancien régime were more interested in getting to know the truth about the past than about moral rectitude, and searched their sources for the minutest pieces of evidence as scrupulously as their successors. The case of Edward Gibbon, probably the most celebrated among them, is illustrative. His huge *Decline and Fall of the Roman Empire*, which appeared in intervals between 1776 and 1788, is a monument of passionate but reasoned erudition, despite its bias against Christianity. Gibbon's engrossment in getting the facts right was so complete, that he scarcely got round to a moral judgement of the developments he was describing. Of course his investigations were to some extent structured and directed by his preconceptions and value-judgements, but that does not warrant the conclusion that he had a frivolous approach of the truth, and was essentially interested in teaching his readers a moral lesson.

Conversely, though many nineteenth and twentieth-century historians have proclaimed that it is the task of their profession only to determine 'what really happened', and not to judge it, most of them have been unable to live up to this ideal, if indeed they ever strove to, in their own publications. Theodor Mommsen, the author of an acclaimed *Roman History* (1854-6), which covered the rise and fall of the Roman republic, and superseded all the earlier books on that subject, is a fine example of this failure. This scholar was the virtual embodiment of objectivity, thoroughness, detachment, detail and proof. Yet, inspired by the German nationalist aspirations of his time, he unabashedly moralized about Cicero -pictured as weak and unprincipled-, Caesar -pictured as a genius and the savior of the *patria*-, and many other *dramatis personae* of the history of the Roman republic.[9] And Mommsen was not exceptional in this respect.[10]

For all that, the idea that in the nineteenth century a new attitude to history gradually developed, that encouraged and furthered the study of antiquity, is not entirely chimerical. Its quintessence, however, is not a novel stress on objectivity, thoroughness, detachment, detail and proof, but a shift in epistemological perspective, away from classicist essentialism. Irrespective of the question whether this new perspective is in any sense superior to its predecessor, the beliefs central to it -the singularity, incomparability, incommensurability, and underived worthiness of every age- altered the way historians and scholars of adjacent disciplines looked at the past, at least to some degree, and in doing so definitely furthered classical scholarship. Aspects which had always seemed insignificant and without interest, now began to draw attention and were analyzed in unprecedented detail, as a result of which the knowledge of antiquity steeply increased.

It is not easy to explain this in the abstract, but an illustration might prove helpful. It pertains to archaeology, a field of research closely related to classical studies, in which a similar change of epistemological perspective occurred in the same period. For, contrary to what is sometimes asserted, archaeology is not an invention of the nineteenth century. It had existed for centuries. If anything, archaeology is a child of the renaissance. What changed, however, was its aim. It had long remained intimately related to artistic pursuits. Not coincidently, the interest in and demand for ancient works of art arose in the fifteenth and sixteenth century, simultaneously with the rediscovery on a grand scale of ancient literature. The Medici pope Leo X was the first to appoint an overseer of the antiquities of Rome -Raphael-, charged among other things with the excavation of ancient works of art.[11] As a consequence of the growing classicism of the aristocracy the interest in and demand for these pieces of art steadily expanded in the following centuries, turning archaeology into a prospering line of industry, in which many people participated. Since the excavations were guided by the idea of classical art as a standard of taste and beauty, the excavators were mainly interested in well-preserved works of art and other artistic objects, and tended to neglect everything not falling within these boundaries. In a more philosophical language: the archaeology of those days was tuned to the ideas of eternal value, immortal beauty, unchanging merit, and supra-historical standing, all of which are unequivocally of an essentialist nature. In such an epistemological cosmos their is evidently no room for incommensurability and all that, because the value of everything depends entirely on its affinity with the one, Platonic ideal, and can therefore be compared with anything else. It follows by implication that everything only remotely or not at all related to this ideal is of little or no value, and should not be given too much attention. Hence the limited concern for the ordinary, the plain, and the insignificant.

The replacement of the essentialist by a new, modern perspective, that occurred in the first decades of the nineteenth century, profoundly altered the aim and subject-matter of archaeology. Henceforth, not the timeless mattered but the temporary, not the universal but the unique, not the seriate but the singular. The question was posed 'wie es eigenlich gewesen' in a past epoch, irrespective of the 'transcendental' meaning of that epoch. In answering this question many things, including ordinary, everyday items, which had seemed wholly insignificant before, acquired a new status and began to be studied minutely, because they possibly conveyed important information on this question. Once this point of view prevailed the earlier neglect of the unspectacular seemed thoughtless and irresponsible, and the new approach much more objective and scientific. Though strictly spoken this is untrue, that does not alter the fact that the rise of this new perspective provided a substantial incentive to archaeologal research, and thus effectively contributed to the subsequent widening and deepening of our knowledge in this field. More or less the same goes *mutatis mutandis* for classical studies.

If in terms of sheer *quantity* the available knowledge of Greece and Rome has grown drastically over the past two centuries, the *distribution* of this knowledge on the other hand has fallen off just as drastically, ever since the beginning of the nineteenth century, but especially from the eighteen-eighties onwards.[12] For the greater part, antiquity has become the domain of the scholarly specialist. As we have seen, this was utterly different in the ancien régime. After the nobility of the sword had started to 'renounce its ignorance' and send its sons to *collèges* and universities, whose curricula consisted of little else than the study of classical languages and literature, an intimate knowledge and easy familiarity with the subject quickly established itself as the mark *par excellence* of good breeding, distinguishing the top-layer within seventeenth and eighteenth-century French society from the ordinary mortals. To these people, who dominated their society in every respect, a good education was more or less synonymous to being well-read in the classical authors. This meant much more than just having gone through them, as can be gathered from the fact that many members of this elite were sufficiently proficient in the classics to effortlessly quote and recognize quotes from ancient authors. They cherished the classics as teachers both of style and wisdom. They constantly compared themselves to the heroes of antiquity, who were role models to them, eminently worthy of imitation. Whether one examines the curricula of the elite's *collèges*, the contents of its members' libraries, their letters, the fashionable and learned journals, one always encounters persons, places, writers or events from antiquity.

Surprisingly little has been written about this. A few books have appeared on the influence of antiquity on the enlightenment *philosophes*,[13] a few on its influence in the revolution,[14] but to the knowledge of the present author no extensive study has as yet been written addressing this subject. Of course, if the aristocracy was of little consequence, no more than a reactionary force fighting in the rear-guard of history, and ideas are not important anyway, belonging to the superstructure of social development, there would be no pressing need for such a study. Tracing the origins and the evolution of the social-economic forces in the vanguard of history - the bourgeoisie and the proletariat, and their respective 'modes of production'- is, from that point of view, both more relevant and more rewarding. In view of the long-lasting predominance of this belief in the historical and political sciences, it is no wonder that the aristocracy in general and its ideas in particular have been neglected.

1.2. Römertum

What cannot escape notice when analyzing the classicism of the ancien régime's aristocracy is its one-sidedness. The same picture emerges wherever one looks: the schools' curricula, the private libraries, the quotes and references in books, journals and letters. Antiquity to the aristocracy meant first and foremost Roman antiquity. The ancient Greeks definitely came in second place, and compared to the Romans played only a minor role in the nobility's mental world. There is abundant evidence for this. As one distinguished student of the Greek and Roman influence on western civilization put it, 'people often admired Greek literature from a distance, like an Alp, but they were at home in Latin'.[15] A thorough and comprehensive knowledge of Latin was common coin within the elite, a similar familiarity with the Greek highly exceptional even among the intellectual 'leaders' of the age.

It is not that the Greek historians, philosophers, playwrights and oratorians were completely unknown. They were not. Many of their works were generally available, and the library of many a nobleman contained at least a few; significantly, however, mostly in French or Latin translations. Hardly anyone read the Greeks in the original. By itself this obviously does not prove much; on the contrary, the existence of translations shows that the ancient Greek authors were appreciated. Nevertheless, the fact that virtually no one was sufficiently in command of the language to be able to read the Greeks in the original, whereas fluency in Latin and an intimate, firsthand knowledge of the Roman authors on the other hand could be expected of every *gentilhomme* of substance, makes clear that much more weight was attached to the latter. Consider for instance the cases of two such noblemen, both of whom belonged to the most erudite, the most esteemed, and certainly the most influential men of their times, Michel de Montaigne (1533-1592) and Charles-Louis de Secondat, baron de Montesquieu (1689-1755).[†]

[†] Interestingly, Montaigne and Montesquieu in many respects led remarkably 'parallel lives'. To name only the most conspicuous biographical similarities: both were noblemen from the Gascogne, both were *officiers* in the parlement of Bordeaux, and both retired in their prime in order

Montaigne's own *Essays* bear eloquent testimony to the nature and extent of his knowledge of the ancients on virtually every page. In one of them, called 'On educating children', he offers us his recollections of his own earliest education -which by the way was hardly less extraordinary than the one received by J.S. Mill almost three centuries later. 'Latin was my mother-tongue', writes Montaigne.[16] 'The expedient found by my father was to place me, while still at the breast and before my tongue was untied, in the care of a German (..); he was totally ignorant of our language but very well versed in Latin. (..) he had me continuously on his hands. (..) He had two others with him (..). They never addressed me in any other language but Latin. As for the rest of the household, it was an inviolable rule that neither he nor my mother nor a manservant nor a housemaid ever spoke in my presence anything except such words of Latin as they learned in order to chatter a bit with me. (..) I was six years old before I knew French any more than I know the *patois* of Périgord or Arabic.'[17] Montaigne *père* did not deem it necessary to appoint another tutor to teach the young man some Greek as well. That, he thought, he could do himself. Given the fact that he knew only a little Latin and it is very unlikely that he new more Greek, this says enough about the value attached to an extensive knowledge of the latter language.[18] The result was predictable: in one place Montaige says that Greek is a language 'which I scarcely understand at all',[19] in another he states that he does not like to read the Greeks, 'since my judgement cannot do its job properly on the basis of a puerile and apprenticed understanding', [20] in yet another that 'I can see none of the beauty of that language'.[21] Montaigne does not say much about his subsequent schooling at the *collège de Guyenne* in Bordeaux -according to the author at that time 'the best in France'[22]- and nothing at all about the courses he seems to have taken at the universities of Bordeaux and Toulouse, but we know that in these institutions too Latin was omnipresent and Greek secondary at best.

In the essay 'On books' Montaigne gives an account of his favorite books.[23] He begins with expressing his preference of the ancients. In poetry he ranked Virgil, Catullus, Lucretius, and Horace above all others. He admired Virgil's *Georgica* in particular; he regarded it as the best piece of poetry ever written. But Lucan and Terence were also poets Montaigne highly

---

to lead a life mainly devoted to study and writing. However, there are also some significant dissimilarities, in particular with regard to their respective noble status. Montaigne's nobility was rather recent. His great-grandfather, a wealthy large-scale merchant, had bought the castle Montaigne in the fifteenth century. Montesquieu's credentials on the other hand were rather more secure. The nobility of his family was of much longer duration, going back more than two centuries. And, though not of great eminence, it belonged to the *épée* at least as much as to the *robe*.

esteemed. Of the other authors he mentions Plutarch stands out, whom he considers 'his man in all respects'. He read the *Parallel Lives* and the *Moral Essays* in the celebrated Amyot translations, published respectively in 1559 and 1572, which remained the standard translations in France throughout the ancien régime.[24] Seneca he was also fond of. Cicero he finds conceited and his style tedious and verbose, but the works in moral philosophy, the oratory, and the *Letters to Atticus* are nevertheless alluded to as important to him. Diogenes Laertius, whom he read in both a Latin and a French translation,[25] and Caesar are the last ancient authors he says to study 'for pleasure and profit'.[26] The striking absence of the Greeks is readily apparent. Montaigne's intellectual horizon with regard to the ancients seems to have been almost exclusively Latin. Though the author he admired most -Plutarch- was a Greek, he was a very 'Romanized' Greek, both in the choice of his subject and in its treatment. And besides, he could be read in French. The conclusion that Montaigne's antiquity was by and large Roman is confirmed if one takes a look at the *Essays* as a whole.[27] The book is virtually covered with Latin citations; they appear on almost every page. Greek citations, on the contrary, are scarce, and it has been shown that most of them are taken from doxographic books like Diogenes Laertius' *Lives of the Philosophers*, or from anthologies. Montaigne knew little or no Greek tragedians, historians or philosophers at first hand. In Roman literature on the other hand he was exceptionally well-read.

What about Montesquieu?[28] This nobleman's earliest education was less extraordinary than Montaigne's. At the age of eleven he was sent to the Oratorian *collège de Juilly* near Meaux, which was considered to be among the foremost in the country. Even the *grands* sent their sons to Juilly. Here Montesquieu stayed for five years. Central to the curriculum of the *collège* was the study of Latin and of Roman literature.[29] The study of Greek, though always cultivated at Juilly, was secondary. Among other things the pupils were required to read Terence, Sallust, Virgil, Horace, Livy, Tacitus, and Caesar.[30] We have the manuscript of a notebook Montesquieu wrote in this period, called *Historia Romana*, which consists of 78 pages of questions and answers in Latin on Roman history *ab urbe condita* until the principate. Upon his return from Juilly in 1705 until 1708 Montesquieu seems to have studied law at the university of Bordeaux, where, like everywhere else, Roman law stood first, although the study of French law had recently been introduced.[31]

We have little direct evidence on his scholarly pursuits from this point onwards, but there is enough indirect evidence to suggest that classical studies were a major part of them, especially Roman studies. To begin with, Montesquieu's library at La Brède, which has survived unscathed, contains a wealth of Roman literature.[32] A look at Montesquieu's own literary development is perhaps even more revealing. A large part of what he wrote prior to the *Spirit of the Laws* pertained directly to Rome and the Romans. Around 1709 he wrote an hagiographic essay entitled *Discourse on Cicero*. In 1716 he gave a lecture, called *Dissertation on the Politics of the Romans concerning Religion*, at the *Académie de Bordeaux*, of which he had become a member that same year. In 1724 he submitted a *Discourse on Sylla and Eucratis* to the illustrious *Club de l'Entresol* of which he had likewise become a member. In 1734 finally Montesquieu's *Considerations on the Causes of the Grandeur of the Romans and their Decadence* were published. But the *Spirit of the Laws* itself too is full of allusions to, discussions of, and references to Rome and the Romans, as even a quick browse through its contents will reveal. It all adds up to a picture of a man with a deep and lifelong interest in the problems of antiquity, who studied the ancients, particularly the Romans, throughout his adult life, and who in due course acquired a vast knowledge of their writings. Montesquieu's own assertions are telling. In chapter XIV of the *Considerations* he exclaims that 'I can let nothing pass which serves to make understand the genius of the Roman people' a sentiment reiterated in the opening sentence of chapter XI.13 of the *Spirit*: 'One can never quit the Romans'. That says it all.

What exactly drew both Montaigne and Montesquieu towards the study of the Romans? What made them spend so much time on this subject? What made them believe in its supreme importance? A nineteenth- or twentieth-century student of the Romans would probably speak of 'the Roman legacy' and 'our debt to Rome' to justify his pursuits, or say that he studied antiquity for its own sake, but not so Montaigne and Montesquieu. Neither of them was an antiquarian, or -with regard to Rome- a genealogist, exhuming historical roots. They are not primarily interested in the Roman origins of French or, for that matter, western civilization.

They looked upon Rome not as a foundation stone but as a looking-glass. Roman history to them is not the history of an ancient people, whose institutions and ideas heavily influenced western civilization, but the prime example of a history of civilization as such. When Montesquieu writes: 'I am strengthened in my maxims when I find the Romans on my side',[33] he asserts that the Roman experience reflects universal laws governing human life and society. When Montaigne writes that he cherishes Terence, it is because 'I find him wonderful at vividly depicting the movements of the soul and the condition of our customs; at every hour our own action bring me back to him',[34] when he writes that the ancient historians are 'his right hand', it is because in their books 'man in general, whom I seek to know, appears (..) more alive and more entire than anywhere else'.[35] To Montesquieu and Montaigne the history of ancient Rome was a metaphor. They studied it to know themselves, to understand their own time, and to make sense of the history of their own country.

2. Field of interest

Classicism shaped the outlook of the aristocracy. But that 'classical antiquity' was not classical antiquity 'as a whole', or even 'as we see it today' -which is not 'as a whole' either. To the aristocracy of the ancien régime classical antiquity's first and foremost meaning was Roman antiquity. This needs to be stressed, since our own view of the ancients is utterly different. It is important to be aware of that disparity in order not to misapprehend the classicism of the ancien régime's aristocracy.

2.1. Griechentum

To us, as far as it still is a subject of consideration to the non-specialist, antiquity is almost synonymous to Greek antiquity, more particularly to Plato and Aristotle, fifth-century Athens, Homer and, to a lesser extent, the three great philosophic schools of the Hellenistic world, the stoics, the epicureans, and the skeptics. The Romans are standardly depicted as in most if not all respects inferior to and dependent upon the Greeks. The judgement passed on the Romans by Bertrand Russell in his *History of Western Philosophy* is typical. 'The Greeks were immeasurably their superiors in many ways: in manufacture and in the technique of agriculture; in the kinds of knowledge that are necessary for a good official; in conversation and the art of enjoying life, in art and literature and philosophy. The only things in which the Romans were superior were military tactics and social cohesion. (..) After the Punic Wars, young Romans conceived an admiration for the Greeks. They learnt the Greek language, they copied Greek architecture, they employed Greek sculptors. The Roman gods were identified with the gods of Greece. The Trojan origins of the Romans was invented to make a connection with the Homeric myths. Latin poets adopted Greek metres, Latin philosophers took over Greek theories. To the end, Rome was culturally parasitic on Greece. The Romans invented no art forms, constructed no original system of philosophy, and made no scientific discoveries. They made good roads, systematic legal codes, and efficient armies; for the rest they looked to Greece.'[36]

Evidently, a 'transvaluation of values' has occurred with regard to classical antiquity. Men used to speak of the ancients and think of the Romans, we speak of the ancients and think of the Greeks. Naturally, one is tempted to ask what caused this transvaluation, when and where it began and how the new view of antiquity spread. But this is essentially a story that belongs to the modern age, not to the ancien régime. Throughout the eighteenth century the intellectual and moral orientation of the educated remained predominantly Roman.

To be sure, from approximately the 1750's on, some scholars and *literati* began to take a deeper interest in Greek antiquity. This turn to Greece assumed greatest significance in Germany, where the works of Winckelmann (1717-1768) on the history of ancient art influenced much more than the prevalent idea of beauty.[37] In his *Thoughts on the Imitation of Greek Works in Painting and Sculpture* (1755) but particularly in his *History of the Art of Antiquity* (1764) he expounded the theory that the great artistic achievements of the Greeks were associated with their 'free' society.[38] This theory stirred the fascination of the German *literati* -Lessing, Goethe, Schiller, Herder, Hölderin, Friedrich and August Wilhelm von Schlegel, Wilhelm von Humboldt, and others- who now began to see ancient Greece as the fountain of beauty and truth. Through their works the new 'philhellenism' was transmitted to the reading public in Germany and later also abroad.[†] The growing sense of relevance of the Greeks eventually changed the public's whole view of antiquity.

Previously rather dimly perceived as a culture only peripherally connected to European civilization Greece came to be conceived as one of its principal sources and pillars. Little by little Rome receded into the background. When that happened, however, the eighteenth century had already passed well into the nineteenth.[39] We will return to Winckelmann and the 'philhellenists' in the last chapter. In the meantime it seems safe to say that before the turn of the century classicism remained chiefly Roman in origin and inspiration. Significantly, even the political thought, the oratory, and the symbolism of the radical French revolutionaries, who were fanatical classicists, was still mainly Roman.[40]

As we have seen Greece was not entirely a blank. Many Greek authors were known and read, if only in translation. Nevertheless, there is no denying that previous to the nineteenth century the elite remained relatively indifferent to the Greeks. How to explain this? It is too facile an idea that this indifference was the result of ignorance. Knowledge generally is the effect of a concern with a subject rather than its cause. Obviously, such concern presupposes an awareness of the importance of the subject, but not -and that

---

[†] The turn to Greece was not wholly German-made. In England, the Society of Dilettanti, a club of art-loving gentlemen founded in 1732, in 1751 sent a painter and an architect, Nicholas Revett and James Stuart, to Athens to make drawings of the architectural and artistic remains of the city. Their sketches were published in 1762 as *The Antiquities of Athens, Measured and Delineated.* (Three subsequent volumes appeared in 1789, 1794, and 1830.) Then the Dilettanti sent an similar expedition to what had once been Greek Asia which resulted in a *Antiquities of Ionia* in two volumes, published in 1769. These and other books did much to introduce the fashion that spread throughout Europe in the early nineteenth century. See Highet 1985, p.307; Turner 1981, pp.37-38

is the point- much knowledge of that subject. This provides us with a clue to our problem. If we want to know what attracted the German 'philhellenists' and, a few decades later, the nineteenth-century social and intellectual elite to Greece, what made them desire to know more about it, we have to ask what they were concerned with. If these concerns differed from the concerns of the previous era and were closely linked up with the Greek experience, whereas the concerns of the ancien régime's elite were linked up more with the Romans, this would not only explain the shift but also provide us with a clearer idea of the exact nature of seventeenth- and eighteenth-century classicism.

2.2. The lure of democracy

To the extent that knowledge of classical antiquity has not become the domain of the scholarly specialist, and is still sought by laymen, this is usually done in order to throw some light, historically or philosophically, on specific features of modern society, or themes of contemporary social thought, like democracy for example. This subject is of great concern to us, and makes us feel the need to study antiquity, where its origins are to be found. Naturally, in view of this concern, our attention is predominantly focused on the Attic *polis* of the sixth, fifth and fourth century B.C. By studying it, we hope to learn something about the achievements and shortcomings of our own political system, behavior, and thought.[41] The fact that the Athenians of this period established, lived in, squandered, and rebuilt a democracy, and reflected on this experience for the first time in history, not only gives their affairs an immediate urgency to us, but has also lead many of us to think that in Athens, particularly during the fifty years between the end of the Persian and the beginning of the Peloponnesian war, antiquity had reached its zenith, its *Sternstunde*, its finest hour. In a very real sense, classical antiquity to most of us *is* Athens between, say, 600 and 300 B.C.[42]

Although non-specialist interest in other episodes and aspects of ancient Greek history -particularly in Homeric poetry and Hellenistic philosophy- is by no means non-existent, it pales before the interest in the life and letters of Athens. Glancing over the virtually infinite number of books and articles on ancient Greece that have appeared in the past two centuries it is immediately apparent that those about Athens in the so-called 'classical age' constitute the most notable slice. This cannot be explained simply by the fact that most of our sources for this period concentrate on Athens. Not that that is untrue. In fact, the sources concentrate overwhelmingly on Athens.[43] The striking thing is that we tend to concentrate on this period, and see it as the climax of antiquity. Books and articles on the period 'from Solon to Socrates'[44] or rather 'to Aristotle' outnumber by far those on the preceding and succeeding period. But even more significantly, the last mentioned periods are often looked upon respectively as a prelude and an aftermath of this 'classical age'.

This 'Athenaecentrism' is a conspicuously post-revolutionary phenomenon. With the exception of the German 'philhellenists', Athens by and large failed to capture the imagination of ancien régime's elite. Although it was not entirely ignored, it was mentioned only infrequently, usually in a highly critical or even hostile fashion. To the extent that ancient Greece was a concern to the French aristocracy Sparta was in favor more than Athens, though against the Lacedaemonians too there were strong reservations. It was generally agreed that Sparta's attractive features were outweighed by its unattractive features. It was thought to have had a free, strong and stable polity, lacking the political unrest and party strife characteristic of Athens, but its interference with private property and its excessive *austérité* made it an unlikely candidate for emulation. In the second half of the eighteenth century some enthusiasm for Sparta did emerge, but not within aristocratic circles. The main writers associated with it in France were Rousseau, Helvétius, and particularly Mably, who was the best classicist and the most celebrated political theorist of the three.[45] But their influence, as political theorists at least,[46] was limited more or less to that class of petty *officiers* who manned the Constituent Assembly in the nineties.[47] They were much too egalitarian to suit the taste of most *gentilshommes* of the ancien régime. Moreover, even in the writings -and the minds- of these authors and their followers Sparta did not replace Rome, but was merely upgraded and added to the Quirites as a source of inspiration.

Hence, the question why a change from the previous emphasis on Rome to that on Greece occurred, what was behind this shift in interest, is more than a quaint footnote in the history of ideas. Given the fact that this reorientation was more the cause than the effect of an increase in the knowledge of ancient Greece, it seems legitimate to conclude that much of what attracted the educated classes of the nineteenth and the twentieth century in Greece, must have appeared to be of minor importance, irrelevant, or even repellant to the elites of the seventeenth and eighteenth century. If we can find out what all of a sudden made ancient Greece seem so attractive and ancient Rome so uninteresting, this could provide us with some important clues as to some fundamental differences between the culture of the ancien régime and that of the emerging modern society. What contributed most conspicuously to the change of focus from Rome to Greece was doubtlessly the resurgence of the democratic ideal. But on a deeper level the rise of romanticism must be designated as the main culprit.[48] Even though it aimed to save some essential features of the classicist ideal for modernity, it effectively destroyed the cultural footing of the old order: *Römertum*. We will go into this in the final chapter of this book. But first, we must acquire a better understanding of the meaning of *Römertum* -the classicism of the ancien régime.

NOTES

1. Friedrich Schlegel, *Fragmente*, in: *Werke in Einem Band* 1982, p.44, 'Jeder hat noch in den Alten gefunden, was er brauchte oder wünschte; vorzüglich sich selbst.'

2. Hobbes, *Leviathan*, XXI

3. Highet 1985, p.690n4

4. Reynolds 1983

5. Highet 1985, p.468

6. Livy, praefatio

7. Highet 1985, p.473 incl.n7. The phrase 'wie es eigentlich gewesen' has become something of an adage of the modern historical profession. It is derived from the preface to the first edition of Leopold von Ranke's *Geschichte der Romanischen und Germanischen Völker von 1494 bis 1514* (1824), where the author argued that 'man hat die Historie das Amt, die Vergangenheit zu richten, die Mitwelt zum Nutzen zukünftiger Jahre zu belehren, beigemessen: so hoher Ämter unterwindet sich gegenwärtiger Versuch nicht: er will bloß zeigen wie es eigentlich gewesen'.

8. Highet 1985, ch.21, pp.466-500

9. Highet 1985, pp.475-476

10. Thomas Macaulay was notorious for his perpetual judging. Nor was his equally famous French contemporary, Fustel-de Coulanges, whose influential *La Cité Antique* (1864) is sometimes described as the first detailed analysis and scholarly treatment of the *polis*, beyond *partis pris*.

11. Highet 1985, p.16

12. Highet 1985, p.466

13. Gay 1977, vol.I; Mat-Hasquin 1981; Chevalier 1987. Of course virtually every book on a specific *philosophe* goes into that thinker's 'formative years' and the literature that influenced him, but usually these chapters have little bearing on the plot, so to speak.

14. Mossé 1989

15. Highet 1985, p.348

16. Hensel 1928, p.67

17. Montaigne, *Essais*, I.26

18. Montaigne, *Essais*, I.26, lists as one of the consequences that only Latin should be spoken to him or in his presence that 'mon père et ma mère y apprirent assez de latin pour l'entendre, et en acquirent à suffisance pour s'en servir à la nécessité'.

19. Montaigne, *Essais*, I.26

20. Montaigne, *Essais*, II.10

21. Montaigne, *Essais*, II.10

22. Montaigne, *Essais*, I.26

23. Montaigne, *Essais*, II.10

24. Friedrich 1991, p.71 As a matter of fact, even the contemporary Pleiade-edition of the *Vitae* is still based on that translation.

25. Hensel 1928, p.70

26. The few other ancient authors Montaigne names in this essay, are not discussed -the elder Plinius-, or compared unfavorably to those already mentioned -Martial to Catullus, Sallust to Caesar-, or treated with some disdain -Plato's dialogues are said to be 'traînants' and 'étoufflant par trop sa matière'.

27. See Hensel 1928, pp.67-94; Friedrich 1991, pp.44-82; Highet, 1985, pp.185-193

28. See Shackleton 1961; Chaimowicz 1985; Levin 1973

29. Hamel 1867

30. Hamel 1867, p.231

31. Shackleton 1961, p.8

32. Desgraves (ed.) 1954

33. The first sentence of book VI.15.

34. Montaigne, *Essais*, II.10

35. Montaigne, *Essais*, II.10

36. Russell 1979, XXIX, pp.283-284

37. Rehm 1952

38. Rawson 1991, p.309; Winckelmann 1764, IV.1

39. The displacement of Rome by Greece was a highly complex process, the commencement and the completion of which are easily pinned down, but the description of which is hard. It had a different pace in different countries, and was sometimes temporarily reversed. In Germany the reaction to philhellenism set in already in the first decade of the nineteenth century. The emergence on the stage a few decades later of the towering figure of Theodor Mommsen assured that Rome retained its position in Germany for years. See Rehm 1952, p.21, pp.277-278 See on the development in nineteenth-century Britain, Livingstone 1932; F.M. Turner 1981

40. Highet 1985, p.390ff; Parker 1937; Mossé 1989; Rawson 1991, p.263

41. Farrar 1989, ch.I, pp.1-14

42. Cf. Zimmern 1969; Ehrenberg 1964; Tarkiainen 1966; Knauss 1964; Finley 1973; Ehrenberg 1975; Davies 1978; Raaflaub 1985

43. Davies 1978, p.18

44. The title of Ehrenberg 1975

45. Rawson 1991, ch.15 and 16

46. Taking a broader stance Rousseau was of course the most well-known of the three. But it should be remembered that in the eighteenth-century public eye Rousseau was the author of *Julie, ou la Nouvelle Heloïse* (1761), *Emile* (1762), and the *Confessions* (1781) rather than of the two *Discours* (1750 and 1754) and the *Contrat Social* (1762). If the number of reprints is a measure of one's success as an author, Rousseau's success as a political theorist was fluctuating indeed. Immediately after the first appearance of the *Contrat Social* thirteen French editions followed, and many translations. Between 1763 and the Revolution there was but one single reissue. Then a second hausse began. Between 1789 and 1799 no fewer than thirty-two French editions appeared. See Palmer 1959/64, vol.I, pp.119-120

47. Cobban 1973, p.182

48. Palmer 1959/64, vol.I, pp.14-15

CHAPTER FIVE

ROMAN TRADITIONS

> *The best and most just man is happiest, and he is
> that man who is kingliest and is king of himself;
> while the worst and most unjust man is the most
> wretched and he, in his turn, happens to be the
> one who, being most tyrannical, is most tyrant of
> himself and of the city*
>
> *Plato*[1]

1. Of law and letters

The notion of the ancients is not equivocal. It means different things at
different times. Men used to speak of the ancients and mean the Romans,
today we speak of the ancients and mean the Greeks. A similar ambiguity
recurs in speaking of the Romans. *Römertum* means different things to
different men. Indeed, the meaning of ancient Rome is particularly ambivalent. For, as its students since the renaissance have remarked, it seems to have
had a split political and moral identity. On the one hand, ancient Rome
possessed a republican identity, embodied in the works of literature and
history that have come down to us. On the other hand, it possessed an
imperial identity, embodied mainly in the *Corpus Iuris Civilis*, the Justinian
codification of Roman law. Moreover, these two political and moral identities
are not only different, they are in many ways each other's opposite. As a
consequence, the vindication of one of these identities usually implies a
rejection of the other.

1.1. Modern imperialism

If today this antithesis plays no role *in politicis* anymore, it is because we are
all, unwittingly, 'imperialists' now. In fact, these principles seem to be so
self-evident today, that it has become hard for us even to understand the
principles of the Roman republic, let alone to see them as providing a viable
alternative to ours. They have become relics of the past, more or less
forgotten; there is no need to fight them, either in speech or in print. Hence,
the first two centuries A.D. are at present commonly considered by the
historians to make up Rome's 'Golden Age'.[2] Especially the second century
is often singled out as the happiest period in Roman history. It witnessed the
reign of the five 'good emperors' -Nerva, Trajan, Hadrian, Antoninus Pius,

and Marcus Aurelius- who succeeded in preserving internal peace and external security for most of the century.[3] This was the period in which *pax Romana* ruled the world.

By the first third of the second century the Roman empire had attained its widest extension. The legitimacy of the *princeps'* rule was secure. Republican opposition against the empire, which had been quite intense in the second half of the first century as a result of the misrule of Nero and Domitian, had withered away.[4] The problem of imperial succession, which intermittently plagued the empire from Augustus' rule onwards until its final demise, was met, for the time being, with prudence and some luck: lacking legitimate sons of their own the successive emperors each adopted a male successor of ascertained merit. (Things went wrong only when Marcus Aurelius, who had a son, preferred him to several other competent candidates, and thereby saddled the empire with another Nero.)[5] A growing bureaucracy administered the affairs of state fairly efficiently. The army had turned, likewise for the time being, from a source of turmoil into a pillar of order and security for both the citizen and the state. The conscription of citizens was by and large abandoned. Under the empire the legions consisted mostly of professional soldiers, whose main task had become the defense of its frontiers.[6] Hence, the prospect or reality of warfare hardly interfered with the population's daily life anymore.

The enduring peace and security generated a climate of confidence that made possible quite a tremendous economic development. Although there was little technical improvement of any consequence, agriculture, industry and trade flourished like never before. Commercial relations both within the frontiers of the empire and with countries outside were carried to an unprecedented high.[7] As a result, prices fell across the board, turning past luxuries only the happy few could afford into products that were within the reach of the many. In effect, the prosperity enjoyed by the population of the empire was not only greater than in any previous -or, for that matter, later-period in its history, but it was also more widely distributed; the common people shared in it to some extent. This was reflected in the average level of expenditure, as well as in the average level of education. At no other time in Roman history the ability to read and write was more widespread.[8] A concomitant development was the further growth, in size and number, of cities. The second century marks the culmination of urbanization in antiquity.[9] Not until the nineteenth century did town life again acquire a like importance. In its wake, construction thrived. The amphitheaters, bridges, temples and other public buildings from this period exhibit a stupendous technical proficiency.[10] Furthermore, an excellent system of roads throughout the empire neared its completion towards the end of the second century, likewise unparalleled until the nineteenth century, fostering business and even some tourism.[11] Finally, this was also the period in which Roman juris-prudence reached its highest level ever.[12] The largest part of Roman law as we know it, is from these centuries.[13] Presumably, law played a central role in this society. It must have pervaded the life of the Romans.

In sum, these facts seem to provide a convincing underpinning of the idea that the second century A.D. was Rome's Golden Age. It brought things most of us hold in high esteem, like peace, general prosperity, the rule of law, and widespread liberty in the 'negative' sense[14] of being left free 'to culti-vate one's garden'.[15] The republican institutions seem to stand in stark contrast to these: warfare, poverty, and the total(itarian) commitment of the individual to the state seem to be their main principle, or at least their effect; a thoroughly reprehensible condition for man.

1.2. Ancient republicanism

In the ancien régime things were different. Indeed, it is possible to epitomize the whole political discussion in that era in terms of the antithesis between empire and republic. Strange though it may seem now, it was central to the debate. The experience of the ancient Romans was of the highest authority and exemplary value. If it could be shown that one had them on one's side, the battle was virtually won. In chapter two we introduced the two parties to the debate: the party defending the conventional aristocratic view, the *thèse nobiliaire*, and the party which supported strong kingship, the defenders of the *thèse royale*. This latter faction, determined to show that absolute monarchy was the best form of state, had to defend that the Roman empire was superior to the republic. Accordingly, it tried to substantiate that the ancients themselves had proved that absolute monarchy was the best form of state. In addition to this, it tried to annex Roman law to the nature of the French government.

Those who defended the aristocratic cause did exactly the opposite. They aimed to prove that the empire was a tyranny, and the best form of state was that of the Roman republic, viz. a mixed government, in which there could be only a limited prerogative for the king. In the eighteenth century this point of view was eloquently expressed by Montesquieu,[16] in his *Considerations*: 'Augustus (that is the name flattery gave to Octavius) established order, that is to say a durable servitude; since, when sovereignty is usurped in a free state, one calls *rule* everything that can found the unlimited authority of a single man, and one names *trouble, dissension, bad government* everything that can maintain the honorable liberty of the subjects'.[17] (author's emphasis) And Roman law, the defenders of the aristocratic cause argued, had nothing to do with the nature of the government of France.

This judgement was widely shared by the seventeenth- and eighteenth-century noblemen. Throughout the ancien régime the idea prevailed within this class that from the beginning the Roman empire was a reprehensible political system, a *civitas servitus*. This judgement stemmed *linea recta* from ancient Roman literature; it was based on a reading of Cicero, Sallust, Livy, Tacitus, Caesar and a handful of others; a reading that obviously must have differed considerably from that of the royalists. Hence, the subject of this chapter: the nature and meaning of Roman law and *belles lettres* in the political and moral debate of the ancien régime.

1.3. Roman law
One of Rome's most enduring achievements was its creation, development, and ultimate codification under the emperor Justinian of a corpus of law, which after its rediscovery around the end of the eleventh century was gradually adopted throughout continental Europe as a primary source of law, and still lives on in the national legal codes of today. In the political debate in the ancien régime Roman law played a great role. As has been set out, most future sovereign court officers and royal magistrates studied law at one of France's universities, where for a long time Roman law was virtually the sole subject studied. Admittedly, canonical law was part of the curriculum too, but many of the maxims of the latter reflected the influence of the former. Even after *le droit français* had been introduced by order of Louis XIV in 1679, Roman law remained the main subject at the universities' law schools.[18]

The authority of Roman law was constantly invoked by the royalist authors to legitimate the claims of absolutism. *Quod principi placuit leges habet vigorem*, they quoted from the Digests: whatever pleases the prince has the force of law. Moreover, *princeps legibus solutus est*: the prince is free from the operation of the laws, the law binds all except himself, he is above the law.[19] That is not to say that the royalist authors believed that the king could do no wrong because he determined what was wrong. Only a small minority among them held a view that came close to such a position, most notably Hobbes. But he, significantly, was despised with equal fervor by both the royalists and their opponents. Views such as Hobbes' point forward to the positivist political thought of the nineteenth and twentieth century, developed by Bentham, John Austin, Kelsen and the like, culminating in the ominous inference that 'a wrong-doing state would be a contradiction in itself',[20] simply because the state decides what is right and hence, by implication, also what is wrong.

These crafty deductions have little in common with the mainstream royalist political thought of the ancien régime. Virtually all pre-revolutionary royalist authors distinguished, in a classicist fashion, between the *pouvoir absolu* of a monarch and the *pouvoir arbitraire* of a tyrant, the former advancing *le bien commun*, the latter oppressing the population to further his own private goals. They insisted that the royal power had to be of the first kind, absolute but not tyrannical. There could be no countervailing powers, only subordinate powers. To give weight to this position the royalists regularly invoked the authority of Roman law.

It is not that the political meaning of the *Corpus Iuris Civilis* was completely straightforward. Most of it had no political significance at all. The bulk of it consists of administrative law, ecclesiastical law, criminal law, and above all civil law in the narrower sense of the word. It is largely devoted to questions of the safeguarding, preservation, and transmission of property rights. Matters of constitutional law are by and large passed over in silence. And this goes for our other Roman legal sources as well.[21] Roman law was first and foremost a source of *ius privatum*. Acceptance of the authority of Roman law thus did not necessarily bring with it an absolutist *parti pris* in politics. Moreover, it could be and sometimes was used politically by some of the most radical opponents of absolutism.[22] The tenor of the constitutional precepts of Roman law apparently left at least some scope for anti-absolutist interpretations.

One of the precepts mentioned above, for instance, was the subject of a recurring debate: *quod principi placuit legis habet vigorem*. In its entirety, it reads: *quod principi placuit legis habet vigorem, utpote cum lege regia, quae de imperio eius lata est, populus ei et ad eum suum imperium et potestatem transferat* -whatever pleases the prince has the force of law, since the people have by royal law transferred to and upon him all their own power and sovereignty. The issue was whether the transference spoken of here was a mere delegation or a willing away for good. In the first case, the people were at liberty if necessary to revoke the transference and retake their *imperium et potestas*. Arguments to this effect were sometimes expressed.[23]

Another example of the use the authority of Roman law by anti-absolutist writers was the application to the sphere of constitutional law of a private law argument justifying violence in case of self-defence -*vim vi repellere licet*, one can repel force with force- in order to legitimize political resistance to a tyrannical king.[24] Notwithstanding these qualifications, however, there is no question that, all in all, Roman law has to be associated with the king's party in the politics of the ancien régime. There is no better proof of this than the fact that its authority was constantly invoked by royalists throughout the ancien régime, whereas its authority was savagely attacked by the theorists of the aristocratic party. This means that both sides must have regarded Roman law as essentially absolutist in tenor.

The discussion therefore centered on the question of the applicability of this law to the government of France, rather than on its contents. The core of the argument was whether the French institutions were founded by the Franks who had entered Gaul as conquerors, or were a heritage of the Romans, the

French kings taking the place and succeeding to the rights of the Roman emperors. In the first case, which was the position held by the aristocratic party, the direct applicability of Roman law had to be denied.[25] In the second case, the status of the French king was equivalent to that of the Roman emperor. The royalists had a fixed formula for it: *rex Franciae in regno suo est imperator regni sui*. In French: *le roy de France est empéreur en son royaume*.[26] Developed in the thirteenth-century to articulate royal independence vis-à-vis the pope and the German emperor, this doctrine was used more and more for domestic purposes: to emphasize the king's prerogative vis-à-vis the nobility.

The aristocratic counterattack was launched in the sixteenth century, when one of the nobility's greatest theorists ever, François Hotman, published a book entitled *Antitribonian*. Written in 1567, but probably first published only in 1603,[27] it is a closely reasoned rejection of the idea of Roman law as an immediately valid authority in the state of France.[28] Hotman's attack is directed both against its relevance and its alleged perfection.[29] The *Corpus Iuris Civilis* is irrelevant, because 'the forms of these two commonwealths are not in any way alike',[30] and 'laws should be accommodated to the form and condition of the commonwealth, not the commonwealth to the laws'.[31] This goes for the realm of public law as well as that of private law. In public law, for example, the Roman system was based on a division of citizens into patricians and plebeians, whereas French law departs from a threefold division into nobles, *roturiers*, and serfs.[32] In private law too, many French institutions are not only different from the Roman, but do not even have a counterpart, Hotman asserted.[33]

Moreover, the *Corpus Iuris Civilis* is a treacherous guide to Roman law. It is the product of an age that for Hotman was the nadir of classical virtue. The men who compiled it were provincials who were juridically incompetent and did not understand the Roman spirit. The laws of the republic, when Rome was at the peak of its virtue, were slighted. The commentaries of the illustrious two Catos, of Quintus Mucius Scaevola, and of Servius Sulpicius Rufus, who lived in the illustrious days of the republic, do not appear in it. The edicts of the later emperors on the other hand are recorded at length and in great detail. 'I leave it to anyone of sound and healthy judgement', Hotman remarked,' to consider how much equity is to be found in these rescripts of infamous tyrants, who more rightly deserve the name of abominable and devilish monsters than that of Roman emperors.'[34] To learn about the best Roman institutions one should study the ancient historians rather than Roman law.[35] Hotman's attack set the tone. His views became staple fare in the aristocratic tradition.

1.4. Roman belles lettres

The moral and political tenets of Roman literature on the other hand seem to have made it a natural ally to the aristocratic party, since it was constantly used to substantiate the political claims of the nobility.[†] This partiality is not as clear-cut as one would wish it to be, however. The thing is that the ancient Romans were also invoked by most of the royalist authors of the ancien régime, to support their own political ideas. Given the tremendous authority of the ancients that is hardly surprising. But it brings on the question to what extent it is really useful and accurate to associate Roman literature with the aristocratic party.

And yet, even a casual glance at what we possess of Roman literature must bring the reader to the conclusion that most of it is politically anti-absolutist and republican in tone and sentiment, and is hence unlikely to be drawn upon in support of royalist claims. Without exception, the authors from the days before the principate who wrote about Roman politics -including Caesar- extolled the republic and attributed the rise of the Romans to the excellence of their institutions.[36] If they felt 'alienated' from their society, it was not because they believed a monarchy to be a superior form of state, but because they held that the *vetus res publica* had become corrupted though and through. This was a theme taken up time and again. It is forcefully expressed by Sallust in his *Bellum Catilinae*, when he exclaims that the commonwealth was great when the forefathers bequested it to posteriority, but by gradual changes it has ceased to be the noblest and the best, and has become the worst and most vicious.[37]

The principate brought no radical break with this tradition of nostalgia. Augustus wanted to be and was hailed primarily as the restorer and protector of the ancient constitution, and outwardly his government conformed to republican forms. All the republican magistracies and assemblies continued to function, although their real political power was diminished. More than

---

[†] The notion of Roman *belles lettres* is used in a fairly loose fashion here. They include all genres of literary work, except the legal. For our purpose, however, the most important are the works of history, the biographies, and the moral treatises, because these are our main source of information on Roman political and ethical thought. Moreover, it would be wrong to categorically exclude all Greek literature, since it always continued to play a role, even though a relatively minor one, as compared to Roman literature. Most importantly, however, in some cases what we now consider to be Greek literature, because it is written in Greek by a Greek, was regarded more or less as a part of the Roman heritage in the ancien régime. That goes in particular for Polybius' *Histories*, Dionysius of Halicarnassus' *Roman Antiquities*, Plutarch's *Parallel Lives* and *Moral Essays*, Appian's *Roman History*, and Dio Cassius' *Roman History*. Although written in Greek these works are largely devoted to the Romans and their history. In addition to that, they were usually read either in a Latin or in a French translation. We have to keep this in mind when we speak of Roman literature, and its influence in the ancien régime.

anything else perhaps, the use of the term *princeps* to signify Augustus' constitutional position bears witness to this seeming reverence of the republican tradition. It was a concept used in the republican political vocabulary to denote the *princeps senatus*, the first citizen, superior to all other citizens, not in rights but in *auctoritas*, i.e. commanding general respect and obedience by virtue of his great achievements in the service of the *patria*, necessarily linked in the mind of the Romans to great moral virtue.[38] Another indication of the fact that the Romans continued to think of their political system in terms of the vocabulary inherited from the republic is that the Roman state continued to style itself *Senatus Populusque Romanus*. Although this constitutional doctrine increasingly turned into a mere façade, a formal shell, the idea of a *res publica restituta* continued to be upheld for a surprisingly long time, and was dropped only towards the end of the third century A.D., when the title *dominus et deus* was officially adopted by Aurelian,[39] in belated recognition of the fact that the emperor was not a first citizen, but a master of subjects.

Since the official constitutional doctrine of the principate was built upon the idea of a restored republic, the writers of the age could glorify the republican past without being automatically disloyal to the emperor. As a result, much of the writing retained a definitely republican flavor, without being clearly or at all oppositional. The works of Virgil, Livy, Horace, Dionysius of Halicarnassus, Suetonius, and the younger Pliny are cases in question. On the other hand, the official doctrine also prevented the bulk of the opposition that did exist from becoming really 'revolutionary'. The only writer to outrightly reject the principate as a tyranny seems to have been the poet Lucan in his *Pharsalia*.[40] Opposition largely took the form of a condemnation of specific emperors -Caligula, Nero, and others- who allegedly perverted the principate, rather than of a condemnation of the principate itself. Even a writer like Tacitus, who viewed the official doctrine as a sham, intended to cover up the monarchical structure of the government, did not advocate revolutionary action directed against the 'system', because he had grave misgivings about the possibility of a return to the republican order. In his view, the loss of the pristine virtues of the forefathers had made such a return illusory.

There were also some writers who, on the basis of the textual evidence, can neither be classified as republicans nor as royalists, the most important of them being Plutarch. Although there are some indications that the Spartan mixed government established by Lycurgus was his 'all-time favorite', it plays only a marginal role in Plutarch's oeuvre. He apparently believed that there was no place for a mixed constitution in his own time.[41] In contrast to Tacitus, however, this belief did not deject Plutarch or make him cynical. He did not regard a monarchy as an inherently objectionable form of government.

To Plutarch all depends on the question whether the king rules in the interest of the people or not, which is determined by his moral and intellectual qualities, rather than by constitutional design. Consequently, he does not censure the Roman emperorship as such, but can be very critical of specific emperors who did not live up to his ideal of kingship.

Obviously, the politically equivocal nature of most of these writings, the almost complete lack of clear-cut renunciations of the imperial status quo, gave the royalist authors of the ancien régime at least some latitude, but they can scarcely have been really content with the argumentation of the Roman writers in defense of their support of the principate, i.e that it really was a restored republic, or that people had become too corrupt for a republic. What they needed was a positive justification of a monarchy as preferable on principle, and not merely more practical under the circumstances. But there were hardly any self-confessed royalists among the Roman writers. One of the few coming close to such a position is Seneca, particularly in his treatise *De Clementia*, addressed to the then still youthful emperor Nero, and intended to guide him toward the ideal of a merciful king.[42] Dio Cassius is another author who seems to prefer a monarchy to a republic, because the second is allegedly unstable.[43] Finally, Ammianus Marcellinus, the 'last' of the great Roman historians, might also be called a royalist. But he essentially belongs to a different historical period, that of the dominate. In his *Rerum Gestarum* the absolute power of the emperor is taken for granted. Ammianus clearly did not envisage any alternative to the imperial system. There is no effort to show the superiority of a monarchy and no argument as to the inferiority of the other constitutions -except a tyranny. Hence, his political stance is not self-conscious enough to label him a royalist theorist.

Summing up, we cannot but conclude that the royalist authors of the ancien régime had little to fall back upon, when they wanted to make use of Roman literature to support the king's political cause. And, to make matters even worse for them, the opposite seems to be true with regard to the aristocratic cause. In fact, it is no exaggeration to say that the whole of Roman literature exhibits a definite bias in favor of the aristocracy. Writing about a republican government the Roman authors generally side with the 'few' against the masses. Even those among them with a Greek background, like Plutarch, of whom more democratic sympathies might be expected, prove to be no exception to this rule. They consistently distrust the common people and think of them as shortsighted and rather emotional, and therefore incapable of governing the republic by themselves. The people need the political leadership of an aristocratic minority. This partiality of the Roman authors comes to the fore no less succinctly in their writings on princely government. Although the political primacy of the emperor is hardly disputed, they generally held that he should consult the senate on his policies and reserve all the major magistracies to the *nobilitas*. If an emperor passed over the aristocracy and turned to the low-born or even to freedmen as counselors, this was regarded as a sure sign that he had become a tyrant. In short, the fact that the aristocracy of the ancien régime saw Roman literature as a historical vindication of its natural right to govern seems anything but far-fetched.

2. The royalist reading of Roman letters

A confirmation of this conclusion comes from unexpected quarters. One of the most lucid of all royalist political philosophers in Europe, Thomas Hobbes, warned in his *Leviathan* against Roman *belles lettres* in a language that cannot be misconstrued.[44] 'And as to rebellion in particular against monarchy; one of the most frequent causes of it', he argued, 'is the reading of the books of policy, and histories of the ancient Greeks, and Romans; from which young men, and all others that are unprovided of the antidote of solid reason, receiving a strong, and delightful impression, of the great exploits of war, achieved by the conductors of their armies, receive withal a pleasing idea, of all they have done besides; and imagine their great prosperity, not to have proceeded from the emulation of particular men, but from the virtue of their popular form of government: not considering the frequent seditions, and civil wars, produced by the imperfection of their policy. From the reading, I say, of such books, men have undertaken to kill their kings, because the Greek and Latin writers, in their books, and discourses of policy, make it lawful, and laudable, for any man so to do; provided before he do it, he call him tyrant. For they say not *regicide*, that is, killing of a king, but *tyrannicide*, that is, killing of a tyrant is lawful. From the same books, they that live under a monarch conceive an opinion, that the subjects in a popular commonwealth enjoy liberty; but that in a monarchy they are all slaves.'[45] However, Hobbes' warning as to the seditious effects of the ancient books of policy and history was profoundly deviant and hence not taken seriously. Classical education had become sacrosanct by the end of the sixteenth century, as witnessed by the fact that in 1598 the educational system of the *collèges* was formally approved and endorsed by a royal statute.

Perhaps nothing is more illustrative of the sacrosanctity of Roman literature than the fact that they formed the principle part even of the education of the successive *dauphins*. One would have expected something else, in view of its subversiveness. Apparently, the suppression of Roman literature that Hobbes seems to argue for, was out of the question. All the royalist writers could do was to try to remove its sting, an undertaking which required quite a bit of creativity.[†] To prove this, let us take a look at how they proceeded. A sample of three major absolutist theorists from different periods of time should suffice to inform us on the issue.

2.1. Guillaume Budé

The fame of Budé, a leading French humanist, rests primarily on the *Annotationes in Quator et Viginti Pandectarum Libros* (1508), which constitute the first systematic attempt at a philological study of the original significance of the *Digests*, abandoning the medieval interpretation of Roman law in feudal terms.[46] In the last month of 1518 and the first month of 1519 Budé composed a book addressed to Francis I that was meant to instruct him in the rights and duties of a prince.[47] These are presented in the form of an inventory of *exempla* of celebrated *dicta* and *actiones* of and on ancient princes and generals, drawn to a large extent from Plutarch, Pliny the Elder, Aristotle, Suetonius, Lucan, Livy, Homer, Appian, Juvenal, Quintilian and other pagans.[48]

Perusing the *Education of a Prince* (1547) one could easily get the impression that virtually every state in antiquity was a monarchy. We hardly

---

[†] Certainly, criticism of the curriculum gradually mounted in royalist circles. In 1766 a series of articles on the issue by an anonymous writer was published in the physiocrat periodical *Ephémér-ides du Citoyen*. Speaking of a school where the *grands* sent their sons, he writes, 'I find there a large number of pupils engaged in receiving what is called an education. Eight or nine years must be spent in these public institutions. Then I examine the way in which this precious part of a young man's life is usually spent. For every day I find eight or nine hours sleep, which is very necessary, and about four hours for meals and recreation, which are also indispensable. Of the remaining twelve hours, I see more than six are spent in putting Latin into French or French into Latin. (..) Such an education is excellent for future grammarians or Latin teachers, but is it suitable to the duties of a great lord? It seems obvious that the children of the great nobility have only a very limited need for these things, but a very urgent need for a number of others. (...) By their birth these people are destined to be the eye, the hand, and the voice of sovereign authority in the administration of the state. How could they carry out these important functions without being thoroughly familiar with the principles of natural law and the law of nation, without having studied the interior constitution of the monarchy, its origins and variations, without knowing about relations with other states and their good or bad influences on public tranquility?' Cited in Forster (ed.) 1969, pp.306-309 In other words, classical education was attacked by some royalists, but not because of its seditious nature that turned young men of birth into rebels against the monarchy. It was attacked because one began to have doubts about its *utility* for the monarchy. Just like two centuries before, when one had begun to grasp that a nobility without an education was of little use to the monarchy, apprehension was now growing that a nobility with a classical education was of little use either. See Gay 1977, vol.II, ch.X.1, pp.497-516; In spite of the censure however the old system of classical education was by and large retained, and only abolished after the Revolution. Up till then, if one wanted to know whether a person had received a good education one asked, 'does he know his ancient authors well?' See Hayek 1979, pp.195-196; Sicard 1970

hear anything about tyrannies, and the other forms of state the ancients used to discern are almost completely ignored. Only a few times Budé explicitly refers to states that are not a monarchy: Athens and Carthage are referred to as a *seigneurie*. But significantly they are consistently alluded to in a disparaging context. These *seigneuries* maltreat their 'men of great spirit and courage'. For instance, the great general and historian of the Peloponnesian war, Thucydides, was exiled by the Athenians, just like Themistocles, the 'very ingenious and very eloquent war chief' who defeated the Persians under Xerxes in the battle of Salamis.[49] The latter retired to the court of the Persian king where he was hospitably received and made a very rich man.[50]

If these comments on *seigneuries* are no more than short asides, that goes for Budé's discussion of tyranny as well. It is mentioned three times only, twice in connection with Dionysius *père* and *fils*, who are called kings of Sicily 'by force and not by right and by the goodwill of their subjects'.[51] Neither one of them is portrayed as 'an animal that lives on human flesh', however.[52] On the contrary, Dionysius *père* had obvious virtues. Among other things,[53] the following is recounted of him. 'Once he heard that there was a citizen of Syracuse, a very rich man, who had hidden in the ground a large treasure-chest. He ordered that citizen to come to him and commanded him to bring him his treasure-chest, which he did, except that he retained a part with which he bought a piece of property where he went to stay, and abandoned the country. When Dionysius the tyrant heard of this, he demanded to have a talk with him, and when he had come, gave him back all his money while saying: "I rend it to you because you have started to use it, but take heed as of now that in the future you will not leave unused a thing that is invented for the use of men".'[54]

And Dionysius *fils* may have been a 'bad spirit full of felony',[55] but his being chased away from Sicily shortly after the death of his father was caused, Budé seems to suggest, by the fickleness of the people. 'My father made himself king at a time when the Syracusians were tired of living in a democracy, that is to say a popular state, and demanded as of then one or more leaders (..). But at the time when I succeeded him the Syracusians were tired of tyranny', Dionysius the younger is said to have declared.[56] All in all, this is a remarkable portrayal, since Budé must have been aware of the criticism levelled at these tyrants, by for instance Aristotle in the *Politics*,[57] pseudo-Aristotle in the *Economics*,[58] Plato in his seventh letter, and Cicero in the *Tusculan Disputations*.[59] However, as has already been indicated, the problem of tyranny is treated as a minor point by Budé.

By far the largest part of the *Education of a Prince* is devoted to an account of the great deeds and wise sayings, and to a lesser extent the shortcomings, of ancient kings and generals. Significantly, Julius Caesar is praised to the skies. 'Julius Caesar, the first of the caesars and the one who transformed the government of Rome into a monarchy, was a man of the greatest heart and the highest spirit of which there is a record in history, and who most approximated the courage and the virtue and the fortune of Alexander.'[60] Budé is quite prepared to praise great Roman generals from the days of the republic as well, like Fabius Maximus,[61] the two Scipio's,[62] Marius,[63] and particularly Pompey.[64] Yet, he concentrated on the personal qualities of these men, and largely disregarded the constitutional setting. Sobriety, clemency, courage, prudence, magnanimity, liberality, eloquence, dignity and the like are lauded in a ruler, obsequiousness, intemperance, ire, fear of death, vainglory, pusillanimity, effeminacy and the like are censured. In short, Budé furnishes his royal reader with a thoroughly classicist catalogue of virtues. Even the sections which are based on the Bible, in which king Salomon has a leading part, are pervaded with a classicist rather than a Christian morality.[65]

The few times the senate and the people of Rome are mentioned, it is unfailingly done to convey their ignorance and lack of judgement. The account of Fabius Maximus' defeat of Hannibal, which is clearly based on one of Plutarch's biographies, is exemplary in this respect. 'When Hannibal had already gained several victories over the Romans in Italy, Fabius, who was called Maximus, that is to say the very great, was sent against him. When he had arrived at the encampment, Hannibal, who had always had to deal with hasty captains who aspired to nothing but combat, was surprised that Fabius stayed always up in the mountains without showing himself to him, and nonetheless kept his enemies on a tight reign, so that they could neither inflict any harm on the country, nor supply themselves easily. Therefore, Hannibal wanted to incite Fabius to give battle to him, and provoked him with disdain and all other methods he knew, causing as much annoyance as he was capable of, so that the army of Fabius wanted nothing but to fight.'

In Rome the senate and the people began to speak of him as 'a weak and conceited captain'. His friends advised him to give in and 'give battle, to satisfy everyone', but 'Fabius remained master of himself and his army', and 'responded with a singular constancy, that a captain who, for fear of what people say, refrains from doing what is useful and advantageous, and harmful to the enemy, must be regarded as more fainthearted and petty, than he who does not dare to give battle until he knows that it will be to his benefit'. In the end 'Hannibal and his army had worn themselves out and money and supplies fell away, and Hannibal confessed that he had found his master. When one heard in Rome of the prudence of Fabius, which had put an end to Hannibal's streak of fortune, and that his band (of soldiers) diminished day after day, everybody held him in high esteem'.[66] The message is clear. A king should be a father to his people,[67] putting their safety and prosperity first. The people on the other hand should not interfere with his government, and be willing to obey him. Otherwise the realm will be put in danger.[68]

2.2. Jean Bodin

If Budé evaded the issue of the form of state, and reduced the political thought of the ancients to a set of ethical precepts, something over half a century later Jean Bodin went into the offensive, and scrutinized the ancient sources for evidence as to the superiority of a monarchy. The results are presented in his *Six Books on the Republic* (1576), a great work of over 1,000 pages, that is a true monument of the classicist spirit.[69] The reader encounters the ancients on virtually every page. There is no question that Bodin regarded them as the measure of all things politic. Both his classification of forms of state and his thoughts on the nature of the various forms of state are heavily dependent on the ancients. He revered them deeply. Yet, he retained his independence, and did not let them dominate him.

This comes to the fore quite clearly in his treatment of mixed government, the form of state championed by the aristocratic party. He admits that many of the ancient authors took the view that a 'melange of three republics' was the best of all forms of state.[70] However, a mixed state cannot exist; a state can merely appear to be one. There are but three kinds of state: monarchy, aristocracy, and democracy.[71] 'Each one of the three may be laudable or vicious', that is to say all three have a good as well as a corrupted form.[72] 'To combine the incompatible, viz. the monarchy with a popular state and a *seigneurie*, is an impossible thing, and cannot even be imagined. If, as has been set out, sovereignty is an indivisible matter, (..) how can it be assigned to a prince, the *seigneurs*, and the people at the same time?'[73]

In contrast to Hobbes, whose deductive mind led him to depend essentially on an impossibility theorem to prove that a 'melange' could not exist, Bodin predominantly relied on historical evidence, derived from the ancients themselves. 'Experience is the master of all things, and a touchstone, that provides the resolution to all the disputes one can have.'[74] He respected the ancients too much to simply discard them, as Hobbes did seventy-five years later. 'If reason had not forced me to hold the contrary, perhaps the authority of such grand personages would have convinced me. We must demonstrate, therefore, with good reasons, that it is an error, including reasons and examples they themselves have given.'[75]

The examples from ancient history Bodin discusses are Sparta and the Roman republic.[76] Polybius and others, he writes, 'asserted that the state of the Lacedaemonians was composed of three parts, since there were two kings, and also a senate of twenty-eight which represented the aristocracy, and five ephors, who symbolize the popular state'.[77] Furthermore, 'they have given as an example the state of the Romans, which according to them was a mixture of a royal, a popular, and an aristocratic state. And it is clear, says

Polybius, that the royal power is vested in the consuls, the aristocracy in the senate, and the democracy in the assemblies of the people. Dionysius of Halicarnassus, Cicero, (..) and others have followed him in this. But it has no justification'.[78] In reality Sparta was an aristocracy, as is shown by Plutarch, who has recounted the true history of the state of the Lacedaemonians, 'which before him had not been understood at all, either by Plato, or by Aristotle, or by Polybius, or by Xenophon'.[79] And Livy has demonstrated that Rome was a democracy ever since the kings had been chased away, except in the two years when the ten commissioners ruled to correct the customary law, and changed the state into an aristocracy, 'or, more accurately, into an oligarchy', i.e. the corrupted form of the rule of the few.[80]

Book VI chapter IV of the *Six Books* is entitled: 'On the comparison between the three legitimate republics, that is the popular, the aristocratic, and the royal state, and that royal command is best'. [81] In its opening sentence Bodin concludes that all aspects of the state have been amply dealt with in the foregoing chapters, and that all that rests is to know the advantages and disadvantages of each form of state, and to determine which one is the best. This is the chapter in which one can find Bodin's systematic defense of the superiority of a monarchy vis-à-vis an aristocracy and a democracy.[82] To an overwhelming degree the argument depends on *exempla* drawn from the ancients. As to democracies 'does one want any better judgement or testimony than that of Xenophon? "I cannot", said he, "approve of the state of the Athenians, because they have espoused a form of state in which the worst are always on top, an the men of honor and virtue are kicked around". If Xenophon, who was one of the greatest captains of his age (..) made such a judgement about his own republic, which was the most democratic, and among the democratic the most esteemed and well-ordered -or *pour mieux dire*, as Plutarch said, the least vicious- how would he have judged the other democracies and ochlocracies?'[83]

The Roman republic banned Rutilius, Metellus, Coriolanus, the two Scipio brothers, and Cicero, Ephesos banned the virtuous Hermodorus, in Athens one chased away Aristides the just, let Themistocles die in exile, jailed Militiades, and executed Socrates.[84] And although Phocion, 'the most complete and virtuous man of his age, was elected captain and leader forty-eight times and never received any blame, a demagogue nevertheless stood up before the people and, without regard to any consideration of due process for him or his companions, asked whether it would please them that one brought to death Phocion and his companions. All rose -not a single one remained seated- and, raising their hand condemned them'.[85] When Phocion asked why his companions had to die too, the people replied: because they are your friends.[86] 'The popular state is counter to *gens de bien*', it rejects the wise and virtuous minority it needs the most.[87]

Furthermore, if we take counsel in Plato, we find that he called a democracy a market where everything could be bought. And Aristotle agrees with him.[88] In a popular state 'every office is sold to the highest bidder, and the magistrates resell *en detail* what they have bought *en gros*. Thus, in Rome Marius did not eschew to come up with a load of money to buy the votes of the people. And Pompey did the same'.[89] Also, 'those who are so full of admiration for the popular state of the Romans, should not lose sight of the seditions and civil wars that always troubled that people. (..) "We have witnessed", said Cicero, "often in the middle of an assembly of the people, that stones were thrown from all sides, and swords drawn, not that often, but nevertheless too often"'.[90] The republic hardly saw a decade without civil war or a sedition, whereas Augustus established a peace that lasted for a long time, even after his death.[91]

If one analyzed all the democracies that ever existed, one would find that they were almost always at war either with each other or internally, or that they were only apparently governed by the people, and in reality ruled by a few citizens or the 'wisest among them who took the place of the prince and the monarch'.[92] 'During the time when the republic of Athens was fine and flourishing, it was governed by the senate of aeropagites. And when their power was diminished, Pericles -says Thucydides- was its true monarch, although it was in appearance a popular state.'[93] 'In the same fashion, we can say that the popular state of the Romans was really governed by the senate, and the authority of the senate was based on men like Menenius Agrippa, Camillus, Papirius Cursor, Fabius Maximus, Scipio, Cato, Scaurus, Pompey.'[94] A popular state cannot survive without wise pilots, but once these have gained hold of its 'rudder', they always make themselves master of the state and use the people to mask their control.[95]

An aristocracy is not much better than a democracy, according to Bodin. Those who believe that an aristocracy is the best form of state, because a assembly of *seigneurs* has more judgement and wisdom than one man alone, are mistaken. They forget that counsel and command are two different things. 'The advise given by several good minds may be better than one, (..) but to decide, to conclude, to command, one is always better than several.(..) Add to this that ambition is so natural between equally powerful *seigneurs*, that some of them would rather see the republic perish, than admit someone to be wiser than they. Others, who do recognize it, are too ashamed to change their opinion, fearing even the smallest loss of reputation.'[96] The difficulty of reaching an authoritative decision Bodin clearly considered to be the gravest shortcoming of an aristocracy. At best, it would lead to indecisiveness, but more likely to disputes among the few who rule, as a result of which sooner or later 'the most unruly and ambitious go over to the people and ruin the aristocracy'.[97] It is impossible for a state, which is like a body, to have more than one head, 'just like the emperor Tiberius said to the senate: otherwise it is not a body, but a hideous monster with several heads'.[98]

Even in democracies and aristocracies the advantages of a single ruler are recognized. Many of them appoint one in precarious situations. Even the Romans did so. 'Trepidi patres, said Livy, ad summum auxilium decurrunt, dictatorem dici placet': when they are overcome by fear the fathers resort to the ultimate expedient, and decide to name a dictator.[99] 'In extreme situations the Lacedaemonians also appointed a magistrate with powers comparable to a dictator, which they called a harmost. (..) That is why Tacitus has said that great and fair exploits require that the commanding power be in the hands of one personage.'[100] Thousand other examples could be put forward that prove unequivocally the necessity of having one commander, not only in war, when the danger is greatest, but also in peacetime. 'For just like an army is badly lead and most of the time defeated, if it has several generals; the same fate awaits a republic which has more than one seigneur, whether as a consequence of dividedness, of diversity of opinion, of the diminution of power that results when it is given to many, of the difficulty of agreeing and deciding, of the fact that the subjects do not know whom to obey, of the leaking of things that should remain secret, or of all these things together.'[101]

All the people of antiquity that were guided by nature have had no other form of state than a monarchy. 'Even all the ancient peoples of Greece and Italy, before they became depraved and corrupted by ambition, had nothing but kings and monarchs.'[102] One marvels at the fact that the Roman republic and the Spartan aristocracy have lasted four hundred years or so, but forgets that many large and mighty monarchies have lasted one thousand or twelve hundred years without a change of constitution.[103] 'If we are looking for authorities, we will find that the greatest personages that have ever lived, have held that the monarchy was the best form of state, viz. Homer, Herodotus, Plato, Aristotle, Xenophon, Plutarch, Philo, Apollonius, Saint Hieronymus, Cyprian, Maximus Tyrius, and many others.'[104] A very interesting list of authorities indeed, especially in view of the names not mentioned.

2.3. Jacques-Bénigne Bossuet

Bishop Bossuet (1627-1704), who was tutor to the *dauphin* from 1670 to 1680, and one of the most notable defenders of absolute monarchy in the whole of French political thought, believed that Roman *belles lettres* were an important source of the political knowledge a prince needed to have in order to govern wisely.[105] In 1681 he published a *Discourse on Universal History*, dedicated to the *dauphin*, whose edification and instruction was the immediate and explicit purpose of the book.[106] It centers on the progress of the Catholic religion, but is full of references to the Romans and closes with a lengthy discussion of their rise and fall. That 'great empire', Bossuet reminded his royal pupil, 'which has engulfed all of the world's empires and has given rise to the greatest kingdoms of our world -the empire whose laws we still respect and which we consequently should know better than any other. You are aware, of course, that I am speaking of the Roman empire. You have studied the entire course of its long and memorable history. (...) The world has never seen a prouder and bolder, but also a more steadfast and tradition-bound, as well as a more astute, industrious, and patient people than that of Rome'.[107] Significantly, Bossuet is speaking of 'the Roman empire' in a broad sense here, encompassing the time from its alleged founding in 754 B.C. to 800 A.D., when Charlemagne 'was elected emperor by the Romans and founded the new empire'.[108] The bishop was fully prepared to discuss the republic too.

Bossuet's starting-point is the conviction that monarchy is the most natural form of government.[109] 'The whole world began with monarchies; and almost the whole world has preserved itself in that state, as being the most natural', he argued.[110] 'Rome began in this way, and finally came back to it, as if to her natural condition.'[111] 'If it is the most natural, it is consequently the most durable, and from this the strongest as well. It is also the most opposed to division, which is the essential evil in states, and the most certain cause of their ruin.'[112] Not surprisingly then, Augustus appears in the *Discourse* not as the harbinger of a protracted servitude, as Montesquieu had called him, but as a peacemaker.[113] The people of Rome were 'weary and exhausted by that long period of civil war and in need of tranquility (..)'.[114] Augustus, who 'exercised absolute power',[115] gave it to them. The civil war had been engendered by the republic itself, 'which carried within it the seeds of its destruction, namely, the constant jealousy directed by the people against the senate or, rather, by the plebeians against the patricians',[116] Behind this lay an excessive love of liberty. 'It was a fundamental tenet of the republic to regard liberty as an integral part of being a Roman. A people nurtured in that spirit (...) was unwilling to accept any laws but its own. (...) Enjoying the most essential rights of royalty, the people somehow assumed the attitude of a king. It was willing enough to be advised, but refused to be forced, by the senate. Any seemingly overbearing action, anything outstanding, in a word, anything that offended or seemed to offend the equality which a free society demands, became suspect to this touchy people. (...) Rome thus saw that the love of liberty, on which its state had been founded, created division among the estates composing it. (...) Smoldering or openly displayed at various times, but always alive in the Roman consciousness, these feelings eventually caused the great change occurring at the time of Caesar and then those changes that followed'.[117] For a considerable time internal dissention was kept within bounds by the senate, by constantly provoking new occasions for war against other nations, which united the two estates in the defense of their country, but when there was no longer anything to fear from the outside, especially after the fall of Carthage, the love of liberty was carried to an excessive degree of sensitivity, and the subsequent internal divisions wrecked the republic.[118] The survival of the republic had depended on continuous warfare, as a consequence of which it had been naturally inclined to encroach upon other nations.

The republic was a warrior-state, which 'had brought political and military science to the highest point of perfection'[119] and thus subjugated the world. This was cruel and unjust. 'Strength is given to us to preserve what belongs to us and not to usurp what belongs to others.'[120] It emanates from the desire to dominate, which is justly condemned by the Gospel. Under the emperors though, Rome lost its spirit of conquest, and was 'more interested in self-preservation than expansion'.[121] If the republic brought war, the monarchy brought peace. Moreover, if the republic brought inequitable conquests, the monarchy brought good government of the conquered nations.[122] Most importantly, the laws of Rome were introduced everywhere.[123] Roman citizenship was gradually extended. The public offices, even the highest, were gradually given to the conquered people as well. In the end, 'all the subjects of the empire felt themselves to be Romans'.[124] All nations were molded into a single one, as a result of which 'the world enjoyed a profound tranquility', [125] in which agriculture, commerce, navigation, and the arts and sciences flourished.[126] The empire had its weaknesses too, the bishop admitted, especially the all-powerful army, which could make and unmake emperors at it saw fit,[127] but that was nothing as compared to the upheavals in the republic.

This is the gist of Bossuet's version of Roman history. By cleverly emphasizing some aspects and toning down others he managed to sketch a picture that throws a rather favorable light on the empire and depreciates the republic, without disregarding any of the sources. There is no trace of cunning or deceit in this; it merely reflects the values and aims of the royalist 'party'. *Summum bonum* is the 'general tranquility' that enables everyone to live in peace and prosperity. An equitable system of law and an absolute ruler are necessary to achieve this. Without them party strife will tear the country apart. In the light of this view, it is easily comprehensible that Bossuet had little faith in the Roman republic.[†]

[†] On the other hand, Bossuet's writings also bear witness to the fact that many sides of the republic unquestionably held a great attraction for him. Apparently without perceiving the contradiction with his general political outlook, he for instance praises the love of poverty and *patria* of the Roman people in the early republic, and criticizes the increasing love of luxury and

Against this background the use the bishop makes of Polybius is very suggestive. As is well-known the latter is the author of the most influential exposition and eulogy of the theory of mixed government in antiquity.[128] Not a word is said about this theory. Indeed, Polybius' authority is brought forward to prove that the republic was not viable. 'Rome was bound to go back under the power of one individual. And this came about so naturally that Polybius, who lived in the most flourishing age of the republic, foresaw, simply by observing the configuration of circumstances, that the Roman state would revert to a monarchy in the long run.'[129] This is an interesting interpretation of the theory of the cycle of political constitutions, the *politeión anakuklósis*, expounded by Polybius in book VI of his *Histories*. Bossuet gives the impression that Polybius agreed that a monarchy was the most natural form of state, to which other forms would sooner or later return. But there is no textual evidence to support that idea.

Polybius argues that 'every kind of state is liable to decay'.[130] A mixed government, however, which unites in it all the good and distinctive features of the best governments'-i.e. kingship, aristocracy, and democracy-, has a much greater stability than any of those governments in themselves. For they are 'formed on one principle' and therefore 'soon perverted into the corrupt form which is proper to it and naturally follows on it', whereas in a mixed government 'the force of each (is) being neutralized by that of the others', so that the constitution will 'remain for a long time in a state of equilibrium like a well-trimmed boat'.[131] Hence, 'it is impossible to find a better political system than this'.[132] Rome, Polybius repeatedly asserts, has such a mixed government.[133]

Obviously, all of this runs counter to the most fundamental doctrines of absolutism, and Bossuet cannot possibly have subscribed either to the idea of the longevity of a mixed government, or to the praise bestowed on it by Polybius. What the bishop refers to when he appeals to the *Histories* to support his view that the Roman republic would revert to a monarchy, is Polybius' admittance that 'this state, more than any other has been formed and has grown naturally, and will undergo a natural decline and change to its contrary'.[134] 'Naturally' here means: according to the theory of the cycle of political constitutions.[135] Nothing lasts forever, is Polybius' message.[136]

A monarchy degenerates into a tyranny. That is subsequently overthrown

---

pursuit of self-interest at a later, 'corrupted', time. And he compares virtuous and unified Rome in its early days, still a poor and agricultural country with an admirable militia composed only of citizens, with a declining Carthage, riven by factions, where the citizens cared only about their wealth and the army consisted of foreign mercenary troops 'which are often as dangerous to those who pay them as to those against whom they are employed'.

and replaced by an aristocracy, which in its turn degenerates into an oligar-chy. That is overthrown too, and replaced by a democracy, which eventually degenerates into mob-rule -an ochlocracy-. Finally, that is replaced by a monarchy, and the cycle starts all over again.[137] Bossuet turns this into the message that the republic could last only a relatively short time, as it would necessarily end in mob-rule which is naturally followed by a return to monarchy. Implicitly, the Polybian cycle of constitutions is changed from an inevitability into a fearful possibility, that won't be triggered as long as the king doesn't become a tyrant. Ancient history teaches the causes and pattern of revolutions in a monarchy, and therewith the prudence required of a king.

However, it was not principally as a theorist of constitutional change (and stability) or as the predictor of the republic's demise that Polybius was esteemed by royalists like Bossuet. They valued him mainly as one of the most accurate military historians of Rome, from whom it could be learned that 'the most warlike nations yielded to the Romans', not because of their greater physical strength or courage, but above all because of their incompara-ble military discipline, which was 'the cornerstone of their empire'.[138] Bossuet believed that the French could still learn something from that. 'It was one of the finest features of the Roman militia that spurious valor was not recognized. The spurious maxims about honor which have been the downfall of so many among us were not even known in a nation so eager for glory.'[139] Evidently, the 'spurious maxims about honor' that are condemned here are an allusion to the medieval warrior-ethos of individual prowess still popular within the nobility. As we will see further on, Polybius' fame within the aristocracy was founded on entirely different grounds.

2.4. Awkward assumptions

Summing up, it is clear that royalist authors did not slight or ignore Roman *belles lettres*, but that they tried hard to take the sting out of them by playing down the anti-monarchical aspects in the ancient authors, and stressing the flaws and drawbacks of the republic. In fact, their acceptance of the authority of ancient Roman literature is unmistakably selective. They by and large ignored or explicitly denounced the latent or manifest republicanism that is present in many if not most of the Roman authors. Ancient sentiment on this point was clearly opposite to what the royalists endorsed. Particularly the idea of a mixed government as the best form of government was unacceptable to them, and much time and effort was put into disproving the viability or possibility of that form of government.

At the same time, however, the royalists were initially not prepared to reject the principles of Roman political thought, and develop a new, 'modern' political science. Most conspicuously, the classical typology of forms of government figured prominently in their own political writings. But most importantly, they wholeheartedly embraced the system of ethics that was fundamental to Roman political thought. This seems to be the key to an understanding of the reasons behind the royalist endorsement of Roman literature. Men like Budé, Bodin, and Bossuet believed that the ethical precepts given by the Romans -their catalogue of virtues and vices- constituted indispensable practical knowledge for every gentleman involved in governing the country, above all the prince himself. It is this aspect of Roman literature they were really concerned with and thought of as valuable irrespective of time and place.

It is clear then that their eclecticism put the royalists in an intellectually awkward position. The political and moral thought of the Romans is a closely-knit structure, in which all elements are somehow linked to each other, so that it is virtually impossible to embrace some elements and reject others without getting into nasty contradictions. Caught in this predicament the royalists gradually began to abandon the classical moral and political 'paradigm', and to start searching for an entirely different way of legitimizing the monarchy, based on notions like the free circulation of goods and the utility to society of self-interested behavior, which evolved out of the concepts central to that other 'paradigm' of Roman law. This is a very interesting story, since it essentially deals with one of the foremost intellectual roots of what is sometimes called 'modernity'. Yet, it is often overlooked that this new moral and political discourse, though originating in the eighteenth century, became widely influential only after the revolution, and is therefore only of minor consequence to the developments in the ancien régime. Even in the second half of the eighteenth century the ancient Roman historians, orators, philosophers, and poets were still far and wide regarded as the masters of political and moral thought, even though their mastery was increasingly questioned. Hence, a true comprehension of the political and moral thought of the ancien régime presupposes a thorough knowledge of the Roman view of ethics and politics as laid down in their *belles lettres*. It is high time we took a closer look at it.

NOTES

1. Plato, *Politeia*, 580b-c

2. This is Gibbon's expression, but the view is shared by many others. See e.g. Homo 1941. who speaks of this period as 'l'apogée'; Cf. Grant 1974, whose book bears the title *The Climax of Rome*.

3. Cary 1957, ch.XXXVII-XXXIX, pp.628-701

4. Adam 1970, pp.68-72. Even a traditionalist like Tacitus probably believed that a return to the republic would be impossible: in his eyes men had become 'ready for slavery'. Tacitus, *Annales*, III.65 See on the issue of Tacitus and republicanism: Wirszubski 1950, pp.160-167; Syme 1958; Chaimowicz 1985, ch.III, pp.42-61. They all agree that Tacitus was no republican. But the evidence that he wasn't is circumstantial. Tacitus nowhere rejects republicanism as an ideal. His position seems to be rather that republicanism has become unattainable, because the Romans, particularly the aristocracy, have become morally degenerated. Clark 1956, p.111, is probably right when he writes that Tacitus' 'heart was on the side of the republican past, his head on the side of the imperial present'.

5. Cary 1957, p.703

6. Keppie 1984, ch.VII, pp.172-198

7. Cary 1957, pp.666-672

8. Cary 1957, pp.690-691

9. Cary 1957, pp.672-674

10. Cary 1957, pp.674-685

11. Cary 1957, p.690

12. Kunkel 1982, ch.7.3.1

13. Feenstra 1992, p.400

14. Berlin 1979, ch.III, pp.118-172

15. The expression is Voltaire's. See *Candide*, last sentence.

16. Gay 1977, vol.II, p.325

17. Montesquieu, *Considérations sur les Causes de la Grandeur des Romains et de leur Décadence*, ch.XIII

18. Curzon 1920; Coing 1979, p.35

19. *Digests*, I.4.1 and I.3.31 respectively. See Huchthausen (ed.) 1991, pp.220-221

20. Kelsen 1945, ch.VI, p.305

21. Schulz 1963, p.46, p.81, pp.138-193. The lack of treatises on imperial constitutional law is understandable, because in the empire such law belonged to the *arcana imperii*. Moreover, the decay of politics in the civic sense, in combination with the engrossment of the population in private pursuits, obviously didn't boost the demand for such treatises. It is more difficult to

explain the absence of a substantial body of republican literature of constitutional law. One would expect a keen interest in constitutional codes, but nothing of that kind apparently existed. Even in the Law of the Twelve Tables, according to tradition dating from 450 B.C., and praised by Livy, III.34.6 as the *fons omnis publici privatique iuris* -the fountain of all public and private law- only rules of civil law are laid down. See Kunkel 1982, 2.2

22. See Skinner 1979, Vol.II, pp.123-134, who describes the birth of these political arguments in the renaissance; Ullmann 1975, pp.214ff

23. And angrily refuted by the royalists. See for instance, Filmer 1991, pp.64-65, 'certainly the law there intends no more than to note *the particular fact* of the people of Rome, and not *a general right* of all other people'.

24. Skinner 1979, vol.II, pp.124-125

25. These are Montesquieu's words. See *L'Esprit des Lois*, VI.24

26. Albertini 1951, p.34; Franklin 1973, p.6; Shennan 1968, pp.280-282

27. Franklin 1966, p.36n2

28. The title of the book refers to Tribonianus, the chief member of the commission of jurisconsults that was appointed by Justinian to compile the *Corpus Iuris*.

29. Franklin 1966, pp.46-58

30. Hotman, quoted in Franklin 1966, p.49

31. Hotman, quoted in Franklin 1966, p.46

32. Hotman, quoted in Franklin 1966, p.47

33. Hotman, quoted in Franklin 1966, p.51

34. Hotman, quoted in Franklin 1966, p.53

35. Hotman, quoted in Franklin 1966, pp.55-56

36. This is not to say that Caesar was a convinced republican. In fact, according to one widely held view he intended to overthrow the republic and establish a monarchy. See e.g. Suetonius, *Vitae*. However, this is no more than an guess. Neither in the *Commentarii de Bello Gallico* nor in the *Commentarii de Bello Civili* one can find scorn for the constitution and an explicit or implicit endorsement of the aim to change the form of state.

37. Sallust, *Bell.Cat.*, V.9

38. This definition of *auctoritas* is slightly too individualistic. A distinguished lineage was a definite asset in this respect.

39. Ruling from 270 to 275

40. Kopp 1969, pp.63-131

41. Aalders 1968, pp.124-126; Aalders 1982, ch.IV-V, pp.28-44

42. Kopp 1969, pp.9-10; Adam 1970, pp.20-63

43. See Dio Cassius, *Roman History*, LII The key passage is the dialogue between Maecenas and Agrippa

44. Hobbes, *Leviathan*, ch.XXIX

45. Hobbes, *Leviathan*, ch.XXIX

46. But also on *De Asse et Partibus Eius* (1514), in which the question of the Roman measures of weight and money was for the first time systematically addressed. See Bolgar 1977, pp.309ff, p.376

47. See Bontemps et al. 1965, pp.1-11 It did not have a title, and wasn't published until 1547, when it appeared in three editions at the same time.

48. G. Budé, *L'Institution du Prince*, Paris 1547, reprinted in Bontemps et al. 1965, pp.77-139

49. Budé, *Institution*, on Thucydides: 18r.-18v.

50. Budé, *Institution*, on Themistocles: 38v.-40v, on Carthage: 41r.-42r.

51. Budé, *Institution*, 45v.-46r., 110r.-112v. They are usually referred to as tyrants of Syracuse. Tyranny is mentioned the third time in connection with Sulla's dictatorship, which Budé erroneously believes to have lasted twenty-six years. See 82r.-86v.

52. One of Cato's dicta about kings. See Plutarch, *Cato Maior*, c.8

53. Budé, *Institution*, 45v.-46r.

54. Budé, *Institution*, 111v.-112v

55. Budé, *Institution*, 110v.

56. Budé, *Institution*, 111r.-111v

57. Aristotle, *Politica*, 1311b40ff, where it is said of the younger Dionysius that he was never sober, and therefore held in contempt by the citizens; and 1313b16ff. where it is said that the elder Dionysius taxed his subjects so heavily that in five years the value of everything possessed was paid in.

58. Pseudo-Aristotle, *Oeconomica*, 1349a14-1350a5 and 1353b20-1353b27, where the reader is told, among other things, that on one 'occasion, being in want of money, he asked the citizens to give him contributions; but they declared that they had nothing to give, Accordingly he brought out his own household goods and offered them for sale, as though compelled to do so by poverty. When the Syracusans bought them, he kept a record of what each had bought, and when they had paid the price, he ordered each of them to bring back the articles which he had bought'.

59. Cicero, *Tusculanae Disputationes*, V,57ff.

60. Budé, *Institution*, 60r

61. Budé, *Institution*, 68r.-70r.

62. Budé, *Institution*, on Scipio the elder, 72r.-72v., on Scipio the younger, 78r.-79v.

63. Budé, *Institution*, 80v.-82r.

64. Budé, *Institution*, 86v.-98v.

65. Budé, *Institution*, 26v.-35v., 114v.-117v.

66. Budé, *Institution*, 68r.-69r

67. Budé, *Institution,* 10v.

68. Budé, *Institution,* see 108v.

69. The 2nd edition of 1583 has been used.

70. Bodin, *Republique,* II.I, p.254

71. Bodin, *Republique,* II.I, p.252 This does not imply that Bodin, like Hobbes, believes that tyranny is merely the name of monarchy 'disliked'. In fact, he differentiates between three kinds of monarchy. See pp.272-273: 'Or toute Monarchie est seigneurale, ou Royale, ou Tyrannique: ce qui ne fait point diversité de Republiques, mais cela provient de la diversité de gouverner la Monarchie. Car il est bien difference de l'estat, & du gouvernement: qui est une reigle de police qui n'a point touchee de personne (..). Donc la Monarchie Royale, ou legitime, est celle où les subjects obeissent aux loix du Monarque, & le Monarque aux loix de nature, demeurant la liberté naturelle & proprieté des biens aux subjects. La Monarchie Seigneurale est celle où le Prince est faict seigneur des biens & des personnes par le droit des armes, & de bonne guerre, gouvernant ses subjects comme le pere de famille ses esclaves. La Monarchie Tyrannique est où le Monarque mesprisant les loix de nature, abuse des personnes libres comme d'esclaves, & des biens des subjects comme des siens. La mesme difference se trouve en l'estat Aristocratique & populaire (..) le mot de Tyrannie se prend aussi pour l'estat turbulent d'un peuple forcené, comme Ciceron a tresbien dit.'

72. Bodin, *Republique,* VI.4, p.937 The corrupted form of a monarchy is a 'monarchie tyrannique'. A 'monarchie seigneurale' is not a corrupted form. It is a good monarchy as well, though of a different kind, that can be found mainly in Asia. 'Si nous voulons mesler & confondre l'estat seigneural avec l'estat tyrannique, il faudra confesser, qu'il n'i a point de difference entre le droit ennemi en faict de guerre, & le voleur: entre le juste Prince & le brigand: entre la guerre justement denoncee & la force injuste & violente, que les anciens Rommains appeloyent volerie & brigandage.' See p.278 The corrupted form of an aristocracy is an oligarchy. See e.g p.260 The corrupted form of a democracy is called both ochlocracy and 'la tyrannie de tout un peuple'. He believes it to be the most dangerous of tyrannies. 'Toutesfois elle n'est point encores si mauvaise que d'Anarchie, où il n'y a forme de Republique, ny personne qui commande, ou qui obeisse.' See pp.937-939 Could it be that Bodin was the first to use the concept of anarchy in this sense? The notion of *anarchia* was familiar to the ancients, but they associated it with the corrupted form of democracy. See e.g. Plato, *Politeia,* 558c4

73. Bodin, *Republique,* p.254

74. Bodin, *Republique,* p.969 'L'experience est la maistresse en toutes choses, & comme la pierre de touche, qui fait la resolution de toutes les disputes qu'on peut faire.' His 'empiricist' emphasis on experience was not coupled with a nominalist historicism, however. Bodin was a convinced essentialist. See p.252 'Il est certain, que pour avoir les vrayes definitions & resolutions en toutes choses, il ne faut pas s'arrester aux accidents qui font innumerables, mais bien aux differences essentielles & formelles: autrement on pourroit tomber en un Labyrinthe infini, qui ne reçoit point de science.'

75. Bodin, *Republique,* p.253

76. In addition to these two, he also discusses some cases of alleged modern 'estats composés': Venice, the German empire, and France. Venice and the German empire are aristocracies, Bodin argues. And to say of France that it is 'aussi composé des trois Republiques, & que le Parlement de Paris tenoit une forme d'Aristocratie, les trois estats tenoyent la Democratie, & le Roy representoit l'estat Royal: qui est une opinion non seulement absurde, mais aussi capitale. Car

c'est crime de leze maiesté de faire les subjects compagnons du Prince souverain'. See Bodin, *Republique*, pp.260-263

77. Bodin, *Republique*, p.255

78. Bodin, *Republique*, II.I., pp.257-258

79. Bodin, *Republique*, p.257

80. Bodin, *Republique*, p.260 Bodin refers to the famous episode in early Roman history (453-451 B.C), when all normal offices of government were abolished and a board of ten -the *decemviri*-was appointed, to reduce Roman law to a written code. See e.g. Livy, III.33-55

81. Bodin, *Republique*, pp.937-972

82. Bodin argues that there is no need to include the three 'vicious' forms in the comparison, since the best form of state is found by comparing the three 'good' forms. See *Republique*, p.937

83. Bodin, *Republique*, p.939

84. Bodin, *Republique*, p.944

85. Bodin, *Republique*, p.944

86. Bodin, *Republique*, p.944

87. Bodin, *Republique*, p.942

88. Bodin, *Republique*, p.940

89. Bodin, *Republique*, p.944

90. Bodin, *Republique*, p.945

91. Bodin, *Republique*, p.969

92. Bodin, *Republique*, p.945

93. Bodin, *Republique*, p.945

94. Bodin, *Republique*, p.946

95. Bodin, *Republique*, pp.946-947

96. Bodin, *Republique*, p.966

97. Bodin, *Republique*, p.954

98. Bodin, *Republique*, p.966

99. Bodin, *Republique*, p.963

100. Bodin, *Republique*, p.964

101. Bodin, *Republique*, p.965

102. Bodin, *Republique*, p.968

103. Bodin, *Republique*, pp.968-969

104. Bodin, *Republique*, p.969

105. Floquet 1864; Goyet 1965; Keohane 1980, ch.8, pp.241-261; Rébelliau 1905

106. Bossuet, *Discours sur l'Histoire Universelle*, introduction. The English edition by Ranum has been used. Citations are from this edition. As Ranum sets out in his editor's introduction, Bossuet also had some less immediate purposes with the book: to expound the principles of Gallicanism, to warn Louis XIV that the kingdom ran the risk of divine punishment because of his sexual license, and to defend the historicity of the Bible.

107. Bossuet, *Discours*, ch.6, pp.339-340

108. Bossues, *Discours*, p.25, p.109, p.370

109. In the second great treatise he had set out to write for the benefit of the *dauphin*, the *Politique Tirée des Propres Paroles de l'Escriture Sainte*. After Bossuet had written the first six books of this treatise in the seventies of the seventeenth century, he set it aside and did not take it up again until 1700, when he wrote the final four books. The *editio princeps* dates from 1709. Citations are from the English edition by Riley, that appeared in 1990.

110. Bossuet, *Politique*, p.47

111. Bossuet, *Politique*, p.46

112. Bossuet, *Politique*, p.47

113. Bossuet, *Discours*, pp.69-70

114. Bossuet, *Discours*, p.368

115. Bossuet, *Discours*, p.368 Bossuet actually speaks of 'the house of the Caesars' exercising absolute power.

116. Bossuet, *Discours*, p.360

117. Bossuet, *Discours*, pp.360-361

118. Bossuet, *Discours*, p.370

119. Bossuet, *Discours*, p.370

120. Bossuet, *Discours*, p.356

121. Bossuet, *Discours*, p.368

122. Bossuet, *Discours*, p.357 Admittedly, Bossuet does not draw a sharp line between republic and empire as to the way the conquered nations were governed by the Romans, but it is clear that his commentary on the way the Romans governed conquered countries centered on the empire.

123. Bossuet, *Discours*, p.360

124. Bossuet, *Discours*, p.359

125. Bossuet, *Discours*, p.359

126. Bossuet, *Discours*, pp.358-359

127. Bossuet, *Discours*, p.371

128. Aalders 1968, especially ch.XII, pp.85-106

129. Bossuet, *Discours*, p.371

130. Polybius, *Histories*, VI.57.2

131. Polybius, *Histories*, VI.10

132. Polybius, *Histories*, VI.18.1 See also VI.10.14 and VI.3.7

133. Polybius, *Histories*, VI.10.13-14; VI.11.11

134. Polybius, *Histories*, VI.9.12-14

135. Polybius, *Histories*, VI.4.11-13

136. See especially Polybius, *Histories*, VI.5.4-6 'When owing to floods, failure of crops or other such causes there occurs such a destruction of the human race as tradition tells us has more than once happened, and as we must believe will often happen again, all arts and crafts perishing at the same time.'

137. Needless to say, this is a simplification of Polybius' cycle theory, particularly with regard to his views on monarchy. He distinguishes between (a) primitive despotism, where the man who excels in bodily strength and courage rules over the rest, (b) kingship, which follows it and is based on excellency of judgement and reasoning powers, and (c) tyranny, which is the degenerated form of kingship, characterized by pleasure-seeking, voluptuousness, love of luxury, and other vices of 'over-civilization'. See VI.5-7

138. Bossuet, *Discours*, pp.344-346 In addition to discipline Bossuet names 'the greater skill in the use of weaponry, in the deployment of troops, and in using the vicissitudes of the engagement', i.e. technical, strategic and tactical superiority. Perhaps the most influential military handbook of the age was a commentary on Polybius; Lipsius' *De Militia Romana Libri Quinque; Commentarius ad Polybium*, published in 1594, which inspired the widely copied military reforms of Maurice of Orange, who had been Lipsius' pupil at the University of Leyden. See Hahlweg 1941; Oestreich 1969; Momigliano 1977, pp.92-93

139. Bossuet, *Discours*, p.346

PART III

THE APPEAL FROM THE ANCIENTS

CHAPTER SIX

THE MAN OF HONOR

*Strenuously, we have to find our way back to this
(rhetorical-humanist) tradition*

Gadamer[1]

The greater the difficulty, the greater the splendor

Cicero[2]

1. A common concern

Is it possible to say that the ancient Romans shared a common conception of politics and morality, to speak of *the* Roman tradition in politics and morality? Perusing modern historical work on the Romans one would hardly believe it. Modern *academia* has become very sophisticated in the discovery of distinction and development, and conceives of this way of looking at things as the scientific approach *par excellence*. Hence, a considerable part of academic production now consists in making finer and finer distinctions, not only between historical periods, but also between authors, between the 'early' and the 'mature' work of each author, between the *capita* of each book, and so on. And yet, sometimes a historian still dares to argue that notwithstanding all the differences between the various authors, a common perspective can be traced in Roman literature. 'The ideal of the nobility of the republic', it is asserted in a well-known book on the subject, 'became the standard of the governing class of the empire. (..) Molded into a tradition of quite extraordinary longevity and vitality, it formed to the end of the Roman empire in the west the most potent influence on all educated Romans. It became, in a word, *the* Roman tradition'.[3]

This is not to say, of course, that Roman political and moral thought was a static whole, in which the meaning of the central conceptions changed not at all as time went on. The recognition of change is the reason why one speaks of a tradition in the first place. The point of using that notion is to acknowledge development without lapsing into an extreme nominalism that discerns only differences, and is blind to the permanence and continuity of moral and political ideas. The present author has no quarrel with those who see endless variety in Roman literature. But as long as we focus on the ancients in this way, it will remain impossible to grasp what the mind of the ancien régime saw in them. Departing from an essentialist ontology this mind looked for permanence and continuity everywhere, and discarded the differences as much as possible. The mind of the ancien régime was tradition-bound. To understand it, we have to follow in its footsteps.

1.1. Rulership

How could that tiny settlement on the banks of the Tiber, twenty miles upstream from the shores of the Mediterranean sea and surrounded by many similar settlements, grow into an empire of unprecedented dimensions and power, stretching out over three continents and uniting a vast number of peoples under one banner? How did the Romans manage to impose their will first upon their near neighbors -the Etruscans, the Latins, the Aequi, the Samnites, the Sabines and others- and subsequently upon Epirus, Illyricum, Greece and Macedonia, Carthage, Pontus, Gaul, Numidia, Syria, Spain and so on? What qualities helped the Romans to achieve supremacy over so many other nations? And why did the Roman state change into an abject tyranny just when it had crushed most of its enemies?

These perplexing questions, which are basically concerned with the issue of *rulership*, were undoubtedly the principal reason behind the keen interest of the ruling class of the ancien régime in the ways and means of the ancient Romans. To posterity the Romans were the archetypical rulers, and thus anyone interested in the factors that uphold and destroy rulership quite naturally sought advise with them first. Obviously, this applied to the French aristocracy of the seventeenth and eighteenth century. It is no wonder therefore that these noblemen turned to the ancient Romans for counsel and example.

They did not have to perform a hermeneutical *tour de force* in order to get some answers, since the Roman authors were themselves absorbed by these questions. Polybius (c.200-118 B.C), who wrote his *Histories* at a time when all was still quite well, was mainly concerned with Rome's rise to power. As he says at the beginning of book VI, he aims to show his readers 'how it was and by virtue of what particular (..) institutions that (..) nearly the whole world was overcome and fell under the dominion of Rome, a thing the like of which had never happened before'.[4] About a century later, Sallust (c.86-35 B.C.) already strikes a different note. His *Bellum Catilinae* begins with 'a brief account of the institutions of our forefathers in peace and war, how they governed the commonwealth, how great it was when they bequeathed it to us, and how by gradual changes it has ceased to be the noblest and the best, and has become the worst and most vicious'.[5] And in Livy the causes of Rome's decay and the collapse of the ancient constitution have become a central concern. 'I invite the reader's attention', Livy writes in the celebrated preface preceding book I of the *Ab Urbe Condita*, 'to the (..)

serious consideration of the kind of lives our ancestors lived, of who were the men, and what the means both in politics and war by which Rome's power was first acquired and subsequently expanded; I would then have him trace the process of our moral decline, to watch, first, the sinking of the foundations of morality as the old teaching was allowed to lapse, then the rapidly increasing disintegration, then the final collapse of the whole edifice, and the dark dawning of our modern day when we can neither endure our vices nor face the remedies needed to cure them'.[6]

The core of the answer Polybius, Sallust, Livy, and their fellow-writers gave to the question of Roman imperial rulership, is that it was the consequence of the Roman 'spirit', reflected in the *res publica* as well as in the individual. The notion of rulership -on various levels, with different shades of meaning- was central to the Roman mind. Rulership and related concepts like domination, authority, command, control, leadership, pre-eminence, were fundamental to the Roman view of the world, society, and man. To their mind verticality was self-evident, something that goes without saying. Horizontality, parity, equality, notions so close to the heart of the Greeks of the fifth and the fourth century B.C., were quite foreign to the Romans. The instincts of the latter were much more aristocratic than those of the former. (It is hardly surprising then that the French nobility of the ancien régime turned to the Romans, whereas we tend to focus on the Greeks when considering antiquity.)

When the starting-point of a political and moral philosophy is a cluster of basic notions connected with the idea of horizontality, the idea of verticality with all of its connotations is bound to appear as antithesis, denial, negation. If horizontality is thought of as the underlying property of the good, the just, and the right, the opposites of these are sure to be associated with verticality. Interestingly, this is not true the other way round. When a cluster of basic notions connected with the idea of verticality is the starting-point, like for instance rulership and domination, not the idea of horizontality and its ramifications will appear as antithesis, but notions like servitude and slavery. Departing from horizontality both rulership and servitude tend to be seen as bad; when verticality is the standard, only servitude is considered bad. Rulership on the other hand is seen as good. On such a view horizontality i.e. equality must be considered unstable or even impossible, since horizontal associations go against the very essence and the natural ambitions of man conceived of as a ruler. Relevant inequalities will automatically establish the pre-eminence of the superior associate. The question is merely: what are relevant inequalities, what makes a man superior, what is it that makes him a ruler?

1.2. Virtus
The answer lies in the interesting concept of *virtus*, that has gradually fallen

into disuse in the modern era. It is commonly translated as 'virtue', but it is also -though less often- rendered as 'excellence' or 'good quality'. This concept was fundamental to the moral and political thought of the Romans. Rulership, independence, mastery, control: it depended on *virtus*, and could be preserved and extended only if one possessed *virtus*, if one was virtuous. So what did it mean to be virtuous?

Etymologically, *virtus* delineated the quality thought to be particular or proper to a man -*vir*-, just like *iuventus* for example delineated the quality peculiar or proper to a young man -*iuvenis*. Hence, the most elemental meaning of *virtus* is 'manliness'.[7] In the course of time, the overtones of the concept multiplied and one began to speak of *virtus* in the plural. It was even extended to qualities thought proper to women and other 'non-males'. Chastity -*pudicitia*- and gracefulness -*venustas*- for instance came to be considered as female *virtutes*.[8] To the extent that this occurred the link with the original meaning of *virtus* as manliness was cut of course. But such a severance remained rather exceptional. In common usage *virtus* continued to be linked with the notion of manliness, even after the concept had proliferated into *virtutes*. The most elaborate catalogue of Roman virtues, Cicero's *De Officiis*, a book which played a key role in classicist moral and political thought, must be perceived as an elaboration on the original virtue of manliness, as the product of the application of this virtue to different aspects of a man's life as a ruler.

The ancient Roman authors were very much preoccupied with the idea of *virtus*. Their description of both men and peoples was couched in terms of *virtus*, their judgement as to a man's or a people's worth was based on their estimation of the *virtus* of those concerned. Even a superficial encounter with ancient literature makes this apparent. Likewise, it is relatively easy to get at least some idea of what *kind* of qualities the Romans designated as virtues. The first thing that strikes the mind when reading them is that they admired and called virtues qualities like courage, discipline, and fidelity. It is much harder to understand the *nature* of the Roman virtues. What were they: abilities, inclinations, talents, character-traits, dispositions, capacities, or maybe something else? It is hardly possible to really understand the classicism prevalent in seventeenth- and eighteenth-century France, if this question is passed over in silence.

2. The nature of virtue

What probably makes it so hard to understand the nature of the Roman virtues is that our entire moral language has changed. It is not only that we often regard other forms of behavior as morally good, but rather that after the revolution the whole concept of virtue seems to have gradually vanished from our moral language. In a recent book on the classical virtues a British philosopher has argued that they were 'dispositions of character that enabled men to live good and happy lives'.[9] That is correct, but not very illuminating, since nothing is said about the nature of these dispositions.[10] *Virtus* was not inborn, but had to be chosen, had to be pursued, had to be achieved, and had to be preserved. The Romans emphasized the effort that was needed to acquire qualities -physical as well as spiritual-, whereas the moderns tend to see such qualities principally as endowments, as inborn capacities, as 'gifts of nature'. To the ancients a physical or psychological quality was predominantly a product, to the moderns it is predominantly a resource.

It is true that the latter are still capable of admiring some of the physical and psychological qualities the Romans praised and esteemed, like for instance strength and courage. But their admiration of these qualities has no moral overtones. To be strong and courageous is not a sign of moral goodness to the moderns. Strength and courage are by and large regarded as 'accidents of fortune'. To have either or both of these qualities is therefore sheer luck, and can only be praised in the way one praises a breeding bull, a racing horse, or a beauty queen. Conversely, not to have these qualities can hardly be judged a moral shortcoming. Lack of strength and courage are still commonly seen as forms of weakness, but not as moral weakness. It is just plain bad luck if one does not possess enough of these resources.

Clearly, it makes sense to speak of morality only to the extent that something is the result of choice, of volition, of agency, and not of circumstances, of compulsion, of determinants, whether it is an action, an occurrence, or a quality. If one 'cannot help it', moral categories do not apply. *Force majeure* was a valid moral excuse to the Romans no less then to us. Opinions begin to diverge, however, when one asks what constitutes *force majeure*. The moderns tend to see both physical and psychological qualities, like strength and courage, as 'given', as belonging to a person's 'make-up'. They are not (primarily) the result of a choice. One does not *choose* to be strong and not feeble, courageous and not cowardly, one *is* strong and not feeble, courageous and not cowardly. The Romans on the other hand stress the volitional aspect of both physical and psychological qualities. 'First of all', writes Cicero, 'we must decide who and what we wish to be, and what kind of life we want.'[11] Each has to choose the path of life -*via vivendi*- that he will take. This choice is above all a moral choice: it is the choice between the life of vice and the life of virtue.

2.1. The battlefield of the mind

Xenophon's story about the young Heracles, narrated in his *Memorabilia*, that was well-known to the Romans, is probably the most celebrated parable dealing with this choice.[12] It tells of the youthful Heracles who sits pondering which road to take: the path of virtue or the path of vice. Two women appear, one voluptuous and the other modest. The first bids him to follow her and promises him to lead him along the most pleasant and easiest road. 'You shall taste all the sweets of life, and hardships you shall never know.'[13] When the woman has named a few of these 'sweets of life' she has in store for him, Heracles asks for her name. 'My friends call me happiness', she says, 'but among those that hate me I am nicknamed vice'.[14] Then the second woman, who represents virtue, addresses Heracles, and says that if he takes the road that leads to her he will perform great and noble deeds. 'But I will not deceive you', she immediately adds, 'for of all things truly good and fair, the gods give nothing to man without toil and effort.'[15] It is a hard and long road she offers him.[16]

This parable is quite informative as to the nature of *virtus*. To begin with, it makes clear that *virtus* is not an inborn endowment. If there are virtuous and vicious men it is not because they are so by nature, but because they decided on the right or the wrong path of life. Of course, one might pose the question why some choose the path of virtue and others the path of vice. Isn't that caused by the fact that the first have sufficient moral fiber to begin with, and the second a want of it? This remark misses the point. Xenophon's parable not only tells us that (every) man has to choose, but also that (every) man is capable of choosing the path of virtue. Moreover, this choice between the path of virtue and the path of vice should not be thought of as a once-in-a-lifetime once-and-for-all decision. It is rather the moral aspect of every decision a man has to take. Every time he has to choose he is confronted with the two different paths, the morally right one and the morally wrong one. Hence, this Roman way of thinking in terms of virtue and vice constitutes a radical moralization of life. Everything one does becomes a question of ethics.

Note: everything one does, not everything one thinks or feels. *Virtus* is emphatically not a pure state of mind, a spirit that is free from vicious thoughts or feelings. *Virtus* implies a rejection of vice, and hence presupposes a choice between them. Vice 'exists' within the breast of even the most virtuous man; otherwise, we could not speak of a choice between virtue and vice. A pure mind/heart does not have to decide which path to follow. It cannot be vicious and therefore cannot be virtuous either. The moral language of virtues simply doesn't apply to such cases. Or rather: 'a pure mind/heart' is a concept that belongs to a different moral language. For the Romans what counts is the deed, not what lies behind it.[17] It is not that the spirit does not count at all, but only in the deed it is revealed whether a man is virtuous. The mere fact that his thoughts or feelings are virtuous or vicious is in itself of no account.

In the second place, the metaphor used -the hard and long path of virtue versus the easy and pleasant path of vice- is highly significant. The adjectives tell us unequivocally that the choice between virtue and vice is anything but 'equitable'. The odds are heavily against the path of virtue. So why bother at all? Why not take the pleasant and easy path, if the other one is so troublesome and demanding? Is it worth it? To a Roman these questions would have made little sense. For what we are talking about, he would say, is the choice between rulership and slavery, between mastery and submission, and to his mind it was clear which of the alternatives is preferable.

However, the knowledge that we are morally obliged to choose the path of virtue does not by itself make this an easy choice. The path of vice is very tempting; after all, it is easy and pleasant, whereas the other one is long and hard. Consequently, the choice of virtue must be thought of as something that is the result of a mental struggle that has been won. It is a heroic victory over a mighty enemy within our own breast, a victory that has to be gained time and again, because the enemy cannot be eliminated for good. One must always be *en garde*. To sit back and relax, to enjoy the fruits of one's labor, to slacken in one's efforts quickly reduces a man's resistance and leads him on to the path of vice. No one can afford to take his virtue for granted. Behind these ideas lies an interesting model of the human mind. In this model the mind is thought of as a battlefield on which a recurrent struggle takes place between two opposite, antagonistic forces: virtue and vice.

2.2. Ratio et imitatio

History never repeats itself, the moderns tend to believe; it is essentially a line, not a circle.[18] The ancients took the opposite view. They saw history as a process of eternal recurrence. There is, they believed, nothing essentially new under the sun. Particular events are reflections, illustrations of underlying causes that have the same force everywhere. Hence, the killing of Caesar was considered an instance of the universal rule that tyrants are sooner or later violently removed. Not even the Gods or frequently invoked *fortuna* stood outside the causal chain. They explain occurrences that cannot be explained otherwise, but they never effect a deviation from the general pattern. For instance, *fortuna* can play a role in a military victory of a consul or the downfall of an emperor. It can be a (partial) cause of an occurrence, but these occurrences are in themselves always recognizable as a variant of some pre-existent, known pattern. *Fortuna* operates within this pattern. It cannot bring about something entirely new and unclassifiable. It does not add anything. There is no creation *ex nihilo*. The world is a closed system, so to speak.

If *inventio* is nothing, it follows that *imitatio* is everything. To understand the present and foretell the future, which allows us to take charge of events, one must study the past, the life of earlier generations. History sets forth the causes and consequences of everything, and shows us where the paths of virtue and vice lead. It provides us with crucial information, viz. *exempla*, 'fine things to take as models, base things, rotten through and through, to avoid'. In this view, the self is not a creative force, but it is neither a dwindling focus of causal determinants; it is a center of choice. The Roman self does not invent new options, but it selects from given options that are identical for everyone. *Imitatio* does not imply passive obedience of the self to 'history'. The past can teach us what options there are to choose from, it does not impose a choice upon us.

Imitatio is reserved to man, as opposed to animals. It is tied up with the study of the past, which presupposes an extrication from one's immediate surroundings. An animal cannot do that. It 'adapts itself only in responding to the senses, and only to something that is present at hand, scarcely aware of past or future'.[19] *Imitatio* is made possible by the fact that man possesses reason -*ratio*-, which 'enables him to perceive consequences, to comprehend the causes of things, their precursors and their antecedents, so to speak; to compare similarities and to link and combine future with present events; and by seeing with ease the whole course of life to prepare whatever is necessary for living it'.[20]

Imitatio, made possible by the *ratio*, enables man to choose. Animals cannot choose; they respond mechanically to immediate stimuli. Therefore they can neither be virtuous nor vicious. Man can be virtuous or vicious because he possesses reason, because he is capable of choice. However, it does not follow that man could rationally choose the path of vice over that of virtue. When reason commands he is aware of the choice, but will always choose the path of virtue, because that path is better for him, and reason always choses what is better. It is only when reason lies dormant that vice will result. This is not the result of a choice, since choice presupposes *imitatio*, which is possible only by using the *ratio*. Without *ratio* no *imitatio*, without *imitatio* no choice, without choice only impulse, and impulse in man equals vice, since, unlike an animal, he could do better. The virtues are all the result of the use of reason, that is: the control, the restraining of the impulses by means of reason. Vice results when reason lies -partially or wholly-dormant, which sets the impulses free.

'The soul is divided into two parts, one of which is gifted with reason, while the other is destitute of it. When then we are directed to be masters of ourselves, the meaning of the direction is that reason should be a curb upon recklessness. As a rule, all men's minds contain naturally an element of weakness, despondency, servility, a kind of nervelessness and flaccidity. Had human nature nothing else, no creature would be more hideous than man: but reason, the mistress and queen of the world, stands close at hand and striving by her own strength and pressing onward she becomes completed virtue.'[21]

Consider the four cardinal virtues Cicero distinguished in *De Officiis*.

Practical wisdom -*prudentia*- demands that 'we should not take things that have not been ascertained for things that have, and rashly assent to them', but take time and care when pondering over any matter.[22] Justice -*iustitia*- is tantamount to refraining from injustice, which stems from fear, avarice, neglect, laziness, the craving for influence or positions of command, honor and glory, and other urges.[23] Justice is viable only when these urges are submitted to reason. Courage -*fortitudo, magnitudo animi*- requires that we 'empty ourselves of every agitation of the spirit',[24] in order to 'remain unperturbed in difficult times, and (..) not be thrown (..) off one's feet, but rather hold fast to reason'.[25] Appropriateness -*decorum*- means first of all: conforming to one's role and position, keeping up appearances, but also: not giving offence, respecting the feelings of others. *Decorum* means behaving like a man, not like a beast, but also conforming to one's particular station; it alludes to something we call good manners. 'Let our standing, our walking, our sitting and our reclining, our countenances, our eyes and the movements of our hands all maintain (..) seemliness'.[26] This includes among other things a pleasing mode of speech, ease and charm in conversation, modesty and dignity in dress, a restraint in expressing emotion, tact and timing, and observance of established customs. To achieve this the desires must be rendered obedient to reason. 'If impulses overstep their bounds, if, leaping away, so to speak, whether attracted by something or repelled, they are not adequately restrained by reason, then indeed they transgress due measure and limit'.[27]

Clearly, the Roman idea of *virtus* hinges on the control, the regulation, the moderation of the appetites, the impulses by reason. The virtues are the corollary of what might be called self-discipline, self-control, self-restraint, or self-conquest, at least if these are not understood as disciplining, controlling, restraining, or conquering of the self, since that would be anachronistic. What is involved is not the disciplining of the 'self', but of the 'passions' -to use a slightly obsolete but time-honored expression- by reason. Since the desires cannot be extinguished for good and are always ready to take over command, the choice of the path of virtue has to be reaffirmed constantly. Reason can never take a rest; it can never refrain from its efforts to submit the desires. This is not a mere theoretical effort. Submitting the desires means *acting* in disregard of these desires. It is emphatically not an endeavor to exorcise them from one's mind. Self-discipline is a practice, a *habitus*, a *hexis*: it has to be practiced continuously; and in practicing it we *are* virtuous.

2.3. Health and strength

The Roman authors perpetually associated self-discipline with bodily health and strength, which considerably illuminates the nature of this practice. Health and its opposite, sickness or disease, as well as strength and its opposite, weakness, are not only regarded as metaphors of virtue and vice, but also as direct repercussions, as well as presuppositions of virtue and vice. Staying healthy and curing a disease entail a certain way of life, that is opposite to a life devoted to 'pleasure' and 'self-indulgence'. It is a life of abstention from too much food, too much drink, too much play, too much sleep. One should not eat before one is hungry, and should eat only to assuage one's hunger. A cold breakfast and a frugal dinner are much to be preferred over a lavish banquet.[28] One should not drink before one is thirsty, and only to quench the thirst. On active service the elder Cato, the embodiment of *virtus*, 'drank nothing but water, except that occasionally when he was parched with thirst he would ask for vinegar, or when his strength was exhausted add a little wine'.[29] Drinking parties are to be shunned. One should not play unless one has 'given time enough to weighty and serious matters'.[30] One should not sleep unless one is tired from toil and hardship. Let not 'the tedium of having nothing to do make you long for sleep'.[31] Self-indulgence makes a man fat. So fatness demonstrates a lack of virtue. This is what Caesar referred to when he said: 'I'm not much afraid of these fat, long-haired people. It's the other type I'm more frightened of, the pale, thin ones'.[32] In addition to being a (possible) *sign* of vice, an unhealthy state of the body also *makes* it virtually impossible to be virtuous. A healthy body is both an indication and a precondition of virtue. When the body is not healthy it paradoxically takes the lead, which is explained by the fact that the Romans linked many impulses to the body. Only when the body is healthy it can be submitted to reason, it can be made the instrument of reason.

The metaphor of strength and weakness entails the same way of life, which is hardly surprising since one cannot be strong unless one is healthy, but it adds an element. To become and stay strong it is not sufficient to abstain from unhealthy practices. One has to be prepared to train long, hard and without floundering as well.[33] Bodily weakness betrays an unwillingness to work, and hence a lack of virtue. Moreover, it makes virtue almost unattainable. 'We must exercise the body, training it so that when it has to attend to business or endure hard work it is able to obey counsel and reason.'[34] If we don't exercise the body it will desert us when we most need its assistance: in times of uncertainty and danger for instance, when virtue is really indispensable. 'Look at the training of the legions, the double, the attack, the battle-cry, what an amount of toil it means! Hence comes the *animus* in battle that makes them ready to face wounds. Bring up a force of untrained soldiers of equal *animus*: they will seem like women.'[35]

Self-discipline is a practice. Like any practice it can to a large extent be learned only by practicing it. Actual experience, the Romans believed, was the best teacher. The art of war is learned mainly on the battlefield, they argued, the law mainly in the courts, and politics mainly in the *comitiae* and the senate. When preparation was deemed necessary it usually took the form of an apprenticeship. 'Theoretical' training also had its place, but only to the extent that it assisted man in taking the right decisions in practical life. The study of (Roman) history in particular was considered important, because the deeds of virtuous men from the past were seen as a major source of practical guidance on the path of virtue. One way or the other, the *imitatio* of *exempla* was central to the Roman approach.

3. Honor

To act in a virtuous way is to act honorably -*honestus*. Honor is not identical to virtue. It is the crown, the prize of virtue.[36] The Romans wavered in deciding whether honor was or was not supposed to make man act virtuously. It was sometimes rejected as an incentive of virtuous behavior. One should only desire to be virtuous. Then honor will follow like a shadow.[37] *Honos praemium virtutis*.[38] But more often the reader encounters the idea that nature has made men 'enthusiastic seekers after honor',[39] and that it is from this spring that virtue is born.[†] In any case, the Roman *nobilitas* -and the classicist French aristocracy that followed in its footsteps- believed that honor, since it was closely linked to virtue, was something quite different from the desires, and that there should be no trade-off between them. Honor must

---

[†] In their more pessimist mood authors like Cicero and Seneca reject the dependence of honor on popular approval. In the *Tusculanae Disputationes*, II.64 for instance Cicero argues that 'there is no audience for virtue of higher authority than the approval of *conscientia*'. Honor can 'find joy in itself'. It does not stand in need of glorification and publicity. Similar utterances can be found in Seneca, *Epistulae ad Lucilium*. However, it is evident that both in Cicero and Seneca this view was born of frustration of being politically sidetracked. In happier days both authors had expressed a different opinion. Turned philosopher they began to subscribe to the Platonic critique of appearance, which detaches being from seeming, and therefore virtue from honor or seemliness. But in their heart they remained partisans of the politicians, historians, rhetoricians, poets, and tragedians, to whom form and substance, outside and inside, honor and virtue still were a unity. Significantly, even in the *passus* just quoted Cicero felt compelled to add that applause need not be avoided, 'for all things done well tend to be set in the light of day'. In any event, even in their most pessimist moods both Cicero and Seneca are still well within the bounds of the 'honor ethic', although the 'public' is depersonalized and internalized. Of course, in this process they move from 'shame' to 'guilt', but the reasons for feeling ashamed or guilty are no different than before. The line between 'shame' and guilt' moralities has probably never been very rigid. As Williams 1993, ch.4, has recently set out, one even finds the internalized other in Homer. In the *reasons* for feeling ashamed or guilty one finds more fundamental differences between moralities. For instance, cowardice would clearly be a reason for a Roman to feel ashamed or guilty, whereas a romantic would feel ashamed or guilty for very different reasons, such as inauthenticity or unoriginality. See about the spuriousness of the distinction between shame-cultures and guilt-cultures also Cairns 1993, pp.14-47

always be put in first place: it has the quality of a 'categorical imperative'.[40]

Just like the notion of virtue the notion of honor seems to have almost vanished from the landscape of contemporary moral discourse in the western world. That is no coincidence. After all, honor without virtue is an empty shell that is harmful to man. To the *gentilhomme* of the ancien régime on the other hand nothing mattered more than his *honneur*.[41] Though there was some disagreement as to its exact meaning, the notion of *honneur* -and the related concept of *honnête homme*: the honorable man- was central to the moral discourse of this era.[42] To assert that tax-exemption was the core of nobility and that the honorific rights attached to that status were only secondary, and to ridicule controversies of etiquette like the famous 'affaire du bonnet'[†], about which feelings often ran high, and which called forth great quantities of literature, betrays an utterly modern outlook: to play up a matter of honor is today conceived of as slightly ludicrous.[43] It overlooks the fact that in the ancien régime such things were anything but sinecures.

3.1. The desire for recognition

The honorable man is someone who is respectable, admirable, commendable, praiseworthy, laudable, above reproach. The honorable man is the virtuous man, because his virtue makes him respectable, admirable and so on. Yet, to have a knowledge of his own virtue is not sufficient to make a man honorable. Others should know it too: he must be actually well-regarded and esteemed for it. So an honorable man is a man of good or eminent reputation. His honor depends on the respect shown to him, the admiration for him by others.

Honor is intimately related to pride, in the sense of high self-respect. Self-respect presupposed respect by others. The proud man was the honored man. Behind this lay the idea that man's identity consists of his 'public' face(s). He understands himself entirely in terms of his social roles. Significantly, the Roman notion of *persona* means mask, role, actor playing a role, or social/legal position.[44] In the classical/classicist view, man has a primary need for 'extraspection'. Because his identity depends on his 'public' face(s), it is of the utmost importance what others expect of him and what they think of his performance. Both the Roman and the French noblemen were very much concerned with the impression they made on others. *Decorum* must always be observed, 'for what is seemly is honorable, and what is

---

[†] This affaire centered on the question whether a president of the *parlement* of Paris should remove his *mortier* -his cap- when asking a peer's opinion and whether the latter could remain covered in answering. With an utter lack of empathy Ford 1968, pp.177-178, calls the affaire a 'mock drama'. For a full account see Grellet-Dumazeau 1913.

honorable is seemly'.[45]

Who were these 'others'? Who were the *arbitri honorum*? Whose impressions counted? Of course a nobleman should keep up appearances under all circumstances, but only other man of honor could ultimately judge the honorableness of a gentleman's behavior. The *multi* had no full conception of honor. Therefore, their opinion was of secondary importance. Most significant was what the *boni* thought.[46] Respect and admiration was sought primarily of those who were respectable and admirable themselves. It was a greater source of pride to be praised by the few who were most highly esteemed than by the many who were of little account.[47]

To be dishonored was essentially to lose the respect of others. It was the punishment for not behaving honorably. A man then loses his 'face'. To be dishonored is to be put to shame. Shame is the opposite of pride. It results when a man makes a bad impression. But only an honorable man can be dishonored. The man without honor is beyond shame. He does not care what others may think of him. To the classical/classicist mind shamelessness was a sign of utter depravation. This is what Plutarch referred to when he wrote of Cato the elder that he liked to see young men blush.[48]

Honor demanded that a man insist on being treated with due respect: with *pietas*. Not to be treated in such a way was an insult. It was dishonorable not to treat others with due respect -to insult them-, but it was still more dishonorable to allow others to treat oneself without due respect. That would turn the insult into a humiliation, which was about the most horrendous thing that could happen to a man of honor. To prevent humiliation 'satisfaction' had to be obtained. Sometimes an apology sufficed, but often damages had to be paid, or some sort of revenge was taken, in which case bloodshed was not shunned. The highly interesting phenomenon of the duel, which was introduced in France around the beginning of the sixteenth century and rapidly became an extremely popular method within the nobility to settle matters of honor, is such a way to obtain 'satisfaction'.[49]

Because humiliation is an unbearable prospect the honorable man will go to any length to prevent it. Even death is better than humiliation. Honor is worth risking one's life for. It is even worth the certainty of death, indeed suicide if necessary. The man who accepts a loss of face to save his life -or, worse, his goods- cannot be a man of honor. On the contrary, he is utterly despicable: cowardly if he fears for his life and avaricious if he fears for his goods.[50] To modern man the idea that one's honor is worth more than one's life seems rather peculiar. Most of us even have grave doubts whether honor is worth more than our goods. After all, of what value is it to me if my honor is saved, but I am no longer alive to notice and enjoy it? Foolish pride! To the Roman *nobilis* and the French *gentilhomme* such a view was ignoble, typical of the low-born and ill-bred. To overcome the fear of death was the most honorable thing imaginable.

To a nobleman it was of supreme importance to be remembered well, to be honored by and a source of honor to his descendants, which is explained by the fact that not the individual consciousness but the *gens*, the lineage was central to his conception of personhood. (Note that a *gentilhomme* was a *homo gentilis*, a man who belonged to a *gens*.) Dishonor is not a mere individual humiliation, but a humiliation of the whole *gens*, ancestors as well as contemporaries and descendants. Every nobleman is expected to keep up and increase the honor of the lineage. Honor is a heritage that must be well preserved and handed on to later generations. Hence, the honorable deeds of the ancestors are expected to be a stimulus to the living, who in their turn should set an example to their offspring. The honorable man will forever remain a source of pride to his descendants: his honor makes him 'immortal'. The man who was prepared to look death straight into the eyes, if honor so demanded, could rest assured of his remembrance.

If the nobleman was obliged to defend his own honor in order to uphold the honor of his *gens*, it was also the other way round. He must defend the honor of the members of his *gens* to uphold his own honor. It was very dishonorable not to do so. A man could not stand by and assert that what happened to other members of the *gens* was of no concern to him. It was very much his concern. On the other hand, if a member had dishonored the *gens* the others could and should punish that person -by disinheritance, ostracism, or even homicide if the shame brought on the family was great enough- in order to restore the honor of the *gens*.

The notion of honor was emphatically inegalitarian. The honorable man is not merely a man who succeeds in avoiding dishonor; he is a man who distinguishes himself, who stands out, who commands respect. 'One judges men's actions here not as good but as fine, not as just but as great; not as reasonable but as extraordinary', writes Montesquieu.[51] The man of honor does not pursue equal honor, he wants to surpass the others in honor. At this point the notion of honor touches on and becomes equivalent of the notion of glory -*gloria, la gloire*.[52] Glory is the superlative degree of honor.

3.2. The duty towards oneself

The most complete honor -and glory- were due to those who had performed the greatest services to others -*gratiae*-; not in the way the servant serves, who follows the orders of his master, but as a patron and benefactor. Such a man commanded not only admiration and respect but also gratitude. Hence, honor implied more than a 'negative' moral code consisting of prohibitions. The code of honor demanded a certain behavior: *noblesse oblige*. Honor entailed the duty to serve and protect others: family, friends, and dependents particularly. But the greatest honor was to serve one's country in a military or civil office. Significantly, the Roman concept of *officium* reflects all three of these aspects: it refers to duty, service, and public office.

To the moderns the concept of duty is complementary to the concept of right. My right implies your duty to refrain from everything that interferes with this right or to help me 'effectuate' my right. In classical/classicist thought duty is more than the outflow of another person's right. To a large extent the duties of a gentleman were the consequence of his honor. He could easily forsake his duty and act dishonorably even if he did not infringe on someone else's rights. When a gentleman spoke of his duty he was concerned mainly with what he owed to his own honor, not with what he owed to others as of right.

This duty could be very exacting. Honor sometimes demanded the sacrifice of one's life, especially when a man's *patria* was involved. 'What good man would hesitate to face death on her behalf, if it would do her a service?'[53] Hence, *in extremis* honor required the rejection of the most powerful impulse known to man and beast: the desire of self-preservation. More generally, honor demanded that a man sacrifice his immediate impulses, desires, and passions. Only if he succeeded in keeping these in check he could and would serve and protect society. Perhaps the most telling example of this concerns the defense of the realm, generally considered a particularly noble *officium*. When wounded in battle and 'the flames of pain are kindled, most men are frightened beyond measure',[54] and tempted to turn their back on the enemy in order to save their life. Because this is only natural it constitutes a great problem for society, for if many soldiers were to give in to these impulses the defense of the realm would collapse.

Honor and dishonor are the carrot and the stick held out by society to incite a soldier to overcome his fear. The same 'logic' applied to all other impulses, whether painful or pleasurable. For instance, 'men whom money does not move are (..) most greatly admired. If that quality is observed in someone, they regard him as tested by fire',[55] the reason being that such men would not refuse or try to avoid taking a public office when more money could be made elsewhere, and once in office they could not be bribed or put under pressure by threats to confiscate their property. One could therefore rest assured that they would not put their private interest before the common good.

3.3. The bond between virtue and honor

Virtus is self-control, mental rulership. Honor is the crown of *virtus*. Honored is he who has performed great deeds. Such deeds can be performed only if one is able to reject and transcend one's immediate impulses; they are in fact defined by such a rejection and transcendence. Plainly, that is often in one's own longer-term interest. A man has to forego present consumption and save if he wants to enjoy a good standard of living when he has become too old and feeble to earn a living. But the sacrifice his honor demands of him implies not merely that of letting the long run prevail over the short run. It also implies a renunciation of one's own interest for the benefit of others. Writes Cicero, 'a brave and great spirit is in general seen in two things. One lies in the disdain for things external, in the conviction that a man should admire, should choose, should pursue nothing except what is honorable and seemly, and should yield to no man, nor to agitation of the spirit, nor to fortune. The second thing is that you should, in the spirit I have described, do deeds which are great, certainly, but above all beneficial'.[56] 'A spirit which is ready to face danger, but is driven by selfish desire rather than the common benefit should be called not courage, but audacity.'[57] Put more bluntly, 'if greatness of spirit were detached from sociability (*communitas*), and from the bonding between humans, it would become a kind of brutal savagery'.[58] Hence, ultimately *virtus* is not mental rulership *per se*, but self-control with a social purpose. Honor is supposed to warrant this.

It is little wonder then that the possibility of a rift between virtue and honor was one of the most important issues in classical/classicist political theory. To begin with, the occurrence of anti-social, selfish virtue was widely recognized. It was even argued that 'the more outstanding an individual is in greatness of spirit, the more he desires complete pre-eminence, or rather to be the sole ruler'.[59] Such were the men who established tyrannies. However, this problem could be solved within the 'logic' of the classical/classicist moral framework. For though a tyrant may be quite virtuous, he is not generally honored. Therefore, he must rule by force and severity: he must be feared. But men hate the man they fear, and wish to see him dead. As long as an inkling of virtue is left in some of his subjects a tyrant cannot feel safe and will sooner or later be assassinated.[60] It is only when virtue has been completely extinguished that all is lost: then men are ready for slavery.[61]

Another rift between virtue and honor occurred when the concern for reputation produced deceit instead of virtue. This too was not conceived of as a remote possibility, but as a clear and present danger. For it was much less laborious and dangerous to pretend to be virtuous -to boast- than to really be it, and therefore very tempting: one acquired the prize of honor without the performance it was supposed to reward. To boast of great deeds performed in war and politics was much easier than to actually perform them. Yet, there were some drawbacks. First, deceit could succeed only as long as the falsehood was not detected. One's real behavior had to be covered up. However, such secrecy was almost impossible to attain in the most honorable station in life: public office. In effect, deceit was only feasible in the relative invisibility of the private sphere of the household. But whatever one pretended to have done there could only be a much more limited source of pride. So, this problem too could be solved within the 'logic' of the classical/classicist moral framework. Any man who unjustly boasted to have acted honorably was bound to be put to shame by others, who had observed his actual behavior. Hence, to prevent dishonor it was better to stick closely to the facts.

3.4. The problem of the private sphere

But there is more to the theme than this. Classical/classicist thought was deeply concerned with what might be called 'the problem of the private sphere'. Because it was believed that virtue hinged on its being honored, the private sphere of the household, where behavior was much less visible than in the public sphere, constituted a moral problem. The temptations of vice were likely to become too strong with insufficient social control, it was believed, and because virtue required constant practice it was impossible to settle for a double standard of keeping up appearances in public and secretly surrender to vice in private. Sooner or later vice would spill over into the public sphere and contaminate it. Someone who mistreated his family could be expected to mistreat his people when called to public office.

The Romans drew the obvious conclusion: private morals must be supervised.[62] In 443 B.C. they established the office of *censor*, which was regarded as the most honorable of all offices.[63] 'Its powers were very extensive and they included the right to inquire into the lives and manners of the citizens.'[64] As Dionysius of Halicarnassus remarks: 'The Athenians gained repute because they punished as harmful to the state the indolent and idle who followed no useful pursuits, and the Lacedaemonians because they permitted their oldest men to beat with their canes such of the citizens as were disorderly in any public place whatever; but for what took place in the homes they took no thought or precaution, holding that each man's house-door marked the boundary within which he was free to live as he pleased. But the Romans, throwing open every house and extending the authority of the censors even to the bed-chamber, made that office the overseer and guardian of everything that took place in the homes; for they believed that a master should not be cruel in the punishments meted out to his slaves, nor a father unduly harsh or lenient in the training of his children, nor a husband unjust in his partnership with his lawfully-wedded wife, nor children disobedient toward their aged parents, nor should brothers strive for more then their equal share; and they thought there should be no banquets and revels lasting all night long, no wantonness and corrupting of youthful comrades, no neglect of the ancestral honors of sacrifice and funerals, nor any other things done contrary to propriety and the advantage of state'.[65]

(Interestingly, Greek indifference, as described by Dionysius, seems to have been anything but complete. It is true that they did not know the office of *censor*, but there is sufficient evidence that at least to some extent private morality was regarded as 'publicly' relevant. Both Aeschines and his enemy

Demosthenes for instance argued that a man who is wicked in private relations could not be trusted with public office.[66] And Aristotle asserted in the *Politics* that 'since men also cause revolutions through their private lives, some magistracy must be set up to inspect those whose mode of living is unsuited to the constitution'.[67] Hence, it is safe to assume that in Greece too the freedom to live as one pleased, to which Dionysius refers, was usually limited.)

The idea of privacy -a sphere of action that should be free from 'public' interference,[68] in which man could rightfully 'occupy his days or hours in a way which is most compatible with his inclinations or whims'[69]- was foreign to the ancient mind precisely because the ancients regarded such liberty as dangerous. The idea of privacy is linked to the 'emancipation' of the inclinations and whims mentioned, Hence, it obviously made the distinction between virtue and vice redundant. But this is all part of the rise of modernity. The men of the ancien régime still endorsed the ancient view. The private life of a man had not yet acquired the distinctive sanctity it was to obtain in the modern age. The writers of the seventeenth and eighteenth century would have been shocked by J.S.Mill's contention that 'the only part of the conduct of any one, for which he is amenable to society, is that which concerns others. In the part which merely concerns himself, his independence is, of right, absolute'.[70] That is to say, in the part which merely concerns himself he was at liberty to do whatever he wanted. That, a classicist would have argued, amounted to a license for licentiousness. He was not concerned with the question how the violation of man's private life could be prevented, but with the question how private life and the demands of virtue could be combined.

It is no accident that the most radical champions of virtue, from Plato to Rousseau, proposed to extend the public sphere to the point of completely eliminating private life.[71] The particular must merge into the universal, the individual into the collective. Obviously, neither private property nor leisure fit into such a conception, since both 'distance' the individual from the collective. However, such political reductionism never gained the upper hand in the classical/classicist tradition. Even the radicals had grave doubts about the possibility of rooting out private life. In general, the necessity of a duality of private and public was accepted, although it is hard to find detailed justifications of private life. The predominant stance in classical/classicist thought seems to be that the private was somehow basic to life and therefore indispensable, but that as little as possible should be left to it. It was a matter of dispute what belonged to the private, but all agreed that hypertrophy of this sphere beyond the bare minimum was sure to effect corruption and hence the demise of the public sphere, i.e. the state. The private sphere was suspect. One could not do without it, but it could easily degenerate into a cover for everything that could not stand up to examination.

As a consequence, it was felt that one had a right to comment on each other's private life. What the moderns disapprovingly call gossip and see as a breach of individual liberty, was considered legitimate censure -reprehensio- by the ancients.[72] Those who challenged public opinion in their private life faced scorn and dishonor. Also, no one was exempt from justifying his private life before the bar of public opinion. To avoid criticism a prudent man asked advise and sought approval before taking a decision on a private matter.[73] In effect private life was not very private at all. Man was to a large degree a public man.

Cicero's remarks in *De Officiis* are revealing. He is at pains to make clear that his withdrawal from public life was not voluntary. Because one man -Caesar- had come to dominate everything, the senate had been suppressed and the lawcourts destroyed, there was nothing worthy of him that he could do in the senate-house or in the forum. When the republic was still run by the men to whom it had entrusted itself, he had devoted all his concern and all his thoughts to it. Even now he had not surrendered to grief or pleasure. He had not become idle, but had used his leisure honorably: by writing about philosophy he served his fellow Romans as best as he could.[74]

Summing up the purport of this paragraph, we have seen that the classical/classicist notions of virtue and honor were but two sides of the same coin. No honor, no virtue. Hence, the overriding importance of, and the great sensitivity as to matters of honor. The fact that actions pertaining to one's honor, such as a harakiri, a vendetta, or an *affaire du bonnet*, are incomprehensible, ridiculous, or merely uncivilized to many of us, is a token of our estrangement from the ancient idea of virtue. It is true that some of us believe that the answer to many of our own social problems lies in a revaluation of that idea. But are they aware that such a return to traditional morality entails a restoration of a code of honor?

In view of the inseparability of honor and virtue it is obvious that the possibility of virtue no longer being honored was the most serious moral problem of the classical/classicist age. If that happened the moral framework inevitably broke down. If man loses his admiration of *virtus* or his readiness to honor it, the incentive to practice it is gone, and men will give in to their immediate desires, one argued. Vice will quickly become rampant in society and mental rulership a thing of the past. And because the ancients aligned such mental rulership to political rulership and its loss to political servitude, the question what caused such moral 'corruption' and how to prevent it was also one of the major issues in their political thought. Four factors were considered decisive by the ancients: the role of leadership, the type of society, the structure of politics, and *humanitas*. We must turn to these now. In discussing these factors the nature of the link between mental rulership and slavery and their political counterparts will become clear as well.

4. The role of leadership

It is possible to read Roman literature as a series of reflections on the theme of rulership or leadership: mental, social or political, and imperial rulership, which were conceived of as analogous phenomena. Throughout their history rulership remained the Romans' ideal *par excellence*.[75] It was valued so highly because it was associated with order, stability, harmony, strength, independence, and maturity, whereas its opposite -servitude or slavery- was associated with chaos, weakness, unsteadiness, discord, dependence and immaturity. The well-being of an entity, be it an individual or the *res publica*, depended on its being well-ordered.

The Romans believed that order was the effect of a submission of the impulsive to the rational, the lower to the higher, the lesser to the better, the base to the noble. It was established by the noble and had to be consciously maintained by it, for the base had a propensity to rise in rebellion. If such a rebellion were to succeed, order would break down and chaos would ensue. Hence, order depended basically on the vigor and the determination of the leadership. Subversive elements of various kinds, dangerous to order were believed never to be far off. And their elimination was impossible: they were in the nature of things. In the interest of the entity as a whole these 'agitators' had to be kept under control.

4.1. The pervasiveness of rulership

On one level Roman literature is about mental rulership, self-control, self-discipline, sobriety, moderation of the appetites, mastery of impulses. *Virtus* always implies such excellences. They are indeed key aspects of the notion of *virtus*. True, the belief that it is important to restrain the immediate desires is not foreign to modern moral language. But in that case self-restraint has a merely instrumental and therefore conditional value. To the ancients on the other hand self-restraint was an unconditional value that must be held onto under all circumstances. The alternative was mental slavery. A man who could not resist his desires was their subject, their slave, ordered around by them, obeying their commands. Such a man had lost control. His soul was not well-ordered, not in harmony with itself.

The opposite, the negation, of mental rulership is mental submission, and not obedience, although submission implies a kind of obedience. The Romans believed that there was a different kind of obedience which should be applauded. Not surprisingly, these were respectively the obedience to vice and to virtue. Obeying the temptations of vice was easy. It meant letting go, giving in. Obeying the commands of virtue on the other hand was always difficult. It meant rejection and overcoming one's 'animal' inclinations, it took self-discipline. Hence, this kind of obedience was really part of what mental rulership signified. Without it mental rulership was impossible. He who wants to rule himself must first learn to obey himself.

The same 'logic' of rulership and submission operates between different persons and between different nations. The ancients held that there was a close analogy between the command of others and the command of oneself.[76] The structure of society at large was considered more or less identical to the structure of the subject, both in health and corruption. Phrased alternatively, the individual was taken as a society within.[77]

But it is not only that they are of a similar nature, there is also a causal relationship between the different levels of rulership. Only the man capable of ruling himself was considered capable of ruling others and ruling them well. 'The sovereign must first gain command of himself, must regulate his own soul and establish his own character (èthos).'[78] If he fails to do so and is swayed by his passions, he disregards and possibly destroys the well-being of those under his command. A general who is fearful, audacious, or irate jeopardizes the victory of his army and endangers the lives of his soldiers. A king or a consul who is avaricious and lustful is likely to expropriate the citizens and rape their spouses. Also, others may take charge of the situation and use him for their own purposes. If he is a coward he may be threatened, if he is avaricious he may be bribed, if he is vain his judgement may be clouded by flatterers, and so on. So lack of mental rulership is associated with deficient social rulership, which in its turn is linked to social disorder and decline.

It was believed to be in the interest of everyone that the best, the most virtuous, should take the lead, in both the private and the public realm. Roman literature breathes of hierarchy and guardianship, not equality and democracy. Most if not all social relations were relations of inequality: a husband was superior to his wife, a father to his children, the senior to the junior, a *patronus* to his *clientes*, a *magistratus* to a *privatus*, and the *boni* or *optimi* to the *multi*. Even in friendship -*amicitia*- and sexual relations the Romans seem to have believed that there must necessarily be a superior and an inferior.[79]

The verticality of human relations was taken for granted. Hierarchy, that is rulership and obedience, was the unquestioned presupposition. Moral and political issues were consistently approached as problems of insufficient and inadequate rulership and obedience. The notion of hierarchy itself was never challenged. Only hierarchy ensured order, and therefore only hierarchy stood between man and chaos. Obviously, the modern conceptions of morality and politics differ fundamentally from this ancient conception. In fact, to the moderns relations of rulership and obedience are of a morally and politically questionable status, and acceptable only if they can ultimately be reduced to a horizontal relation. Because the individual is a *Ziel an sich*, and hence equal in value/worth to all others, there is a strong presumption in favor of equality in all spheres of life. The classical/classicist mind has no *rapport* with such beliefs. It expected hierarchy everywhere. Horizontality, if possible at all, must be unstable and ephemeral. Verticality is natural and will therefore prevail. As a consequence, classical/classicist moral and political thought was not much concerned with the problem of rulership *as such*. Verticality was not seen as standing in need of justification. It was mainly concerned with the problem of assuring good and avoiding bad rulership.

4.2. Auctoritas

Good rulership was paternalistic rulership. The superior is supposed to take heed of the inferior, but he is not to let the inferior rule over him. What counts is the well-being of the whole (of all), which can be secured only if the inferior is kept in its place. To achieve that the superior has to give the inferior what is due to it. He is not to use the inferior as a mere means to his own ends. The superior is responsible for the good of the inferior, for it is part and parcel of the whole and needs guidance.

A general for instance should never ignore the mood of his men and ruthlessly impose his will upon them. That would precipitate mutiny. But neither should he make a bid for popularity by letting them have their way: an army that commands its commander cannot be successful in battle. A general must assure that his men willingly and gladly submit to his commands. The key-word here is respect. If he commands the respect of his men, if they look up to him, he will generally be obeyed. This idea is fundamental to the classical/classicist conception of ethics and politics. Of course, it is Roman in origin. There seems to be no Greek equivalent. The verticality of human relations was justified by the *auctoritas* of the superior.[80] *Auctoritas* is not the legal right to command; that was called *imperium* and *potestas*.[81] It referred to a moral authority based on superior *virtus*, establishing confidence and trust -*fides*[82]- in the capacity to lead, and a willingness to obey, in recognition of the fact that the other knows better. *Auctoritas* had to be gained and confirmed time and again; it could always be lost. Respect could not be taken for granted: it had to be commanded. To achieve that one had to give proof of outstanding virtue.[83]

The greater one's *auctoritas* the higher one could rise in rank. And the higher one's rank, the greater one's *auctoritas*. So rank was intimately linked to the degree of moral authority. Since this in its turn was linked to *virtus*, and that, it will be remembered, to *honor*, it is manifest that the latter were matters of degree also. The highest ranks were the most honorable ranks, but also the ranks of which most was expected in terms of virtue. A low position in the hierarchy brought only limited honor, but it shielded from censure at the same time. Hence, in contrast to the moderns who tend to regard behavioral norms as universal, the ancients advocated differentiation. The more exalted one's rank, the greater one's obligations and responsibilities, and the stricter the rules of conduct. What is dishonorable for a man of high rank need not be dishonorable for someone of a lower rank.[84]

Since order and the general well-being were believed to depend on a submission of the lower to and by the higher, a breakdown of order was conceived of as a consequence of failing leadership, of lacking *auctoritas* and *eo ipso* a want of virtue of the leader or leaders. This is an ever recurring theme in the literature. The base is naturally fickle, but can usually be kept on the right track when skillfully directed by the noble.[85] Victory or defeat in battle, obedience or insurrection of the *multi*, the rise and decline of the state: ultimately everything depends on the *auctoritas* and the *virtus* of the *boni*. These are the linchpins of the system.

The senators, writes Cicero in *De Legibus*, 'shall be a model for the rest of the citizens. If we secure this we shall have secured everything. For just as the whole state is habitually corrupted by the evil desires and the vices of its prominent men, so is it improved and reformed by *continentia* on their part. (..) For it is not so mischievous that men of high position do evil -though that is bad enough in itself- as it is that these men have so many *imitatores*. For, if you will turn your thoughts back to our early history, you will see that the character of our most prominent men has been reproduced in the whole state; whatever change took place in the lives of prominent men has also taken place in the whole people. (..) A transformation takes place in a nation's character when the habits and mode of living of its *nobilitas* are changed. For that reason men of the upper class who do wrong are especially dangerous to the state, because they do not only indulge in vicious practices themselves, but also infect the whole commonwealth with their vices; and not only because they are corrupt, but also because they corrupt others, and do more harm by their bad *exemplum* than by their sin.'[86]

4.3. Disciplina

The counterpart of *auctoritas* was *disciplina*.[87] If the first was expected of the leaders, the second was required of the led. *Disciplina* might be defined as submission to the authority of a superior. If *auctoritas* guaranteed order, it did so by establishing *disciplina*. The latter was considered the corollary of the first. *Disciplina* implied obedience to the command of a superior, but it was emphatically not like the obedience a slave owed to his master. A slave has no choice. He is subjected and forced to obey. His principal motives are 'selfish': fear of punishment, food, money, and the hope for manumission. He stands outside the logic of virtue and honor. *Disciplina* on the other hand is a building-stone of this logic. It is a kind of obedience that is the opposite of slavish: it is honorable. Although breaking *disciplina* was punished -often severely[†]- fear of punishment was not conceived of as the stimulus upholding it.[88]

This is brought out very clearly by the story of the mutiny of the Roman army at the German frontier in the year 14 A.D., recounted in Tacitus' *Annals*. Germanicus, the commander, succeeds in restoring *disciplina* mainly by convincing the soldiers that their behavior is disgraceful, whereupon they kill the instigators of the mutiny themselves.[89] Afterwards, 'there was still a savage feeling among the troops and a desire to make up for their lunacy by attacking the enemy. Honorable wounds, they felt, on their guilty breasts, were the only means of appeasing the ghosts of their fellow-soldiers'.[90] When the Germans attacked, 'Germanicus rode up to the twenty-first brigade and shouted that now was the time to wipe out their mutiny; by one rapid stroke their disgrace could be turned into glory'.[91]

Disciplina implies obedience but it is not slavish. The obedience of a slave is a different matter altogether. The obedience inherent in *disciplina* is that of a free man. Both the *servus* and the *liber* must obey their superiors, but that does not mean that their positions are somehow comparable. Verticality was everything, but it was not always the same thing. This consideration was central to Roman and classicist thought, and serves particularly well to highlight the distance that separates the ancients from the moderns, who are inclined to equate obedience and unfreedom or servitude.

The two different species of obedience were linked to two different species of rulership, *principatus* and *dominatio*, only the first of which was compatible with *libertas*.[92] The second characterized the relationship between a *dominus* and a *servus*. The *princeps* directed his inferiors essentially by his *auctoritas*, the *dominus* by force and violence. The first was obeyed out of respect, the second out of fear. The first served the interests of his inferiors, he is a *pater*, a *custos*, whereas the second served only his own interests, using his inferiors as mere instruments.

[†] Compare the famous story of the consul Manlius Torquatus who had his son beheaded for not obeying his command not to fight, even though the young man, named Titus Manlius, had been challenged by an enemy and killed him in battle. When he victoriously returned to the camp and told his father what had occurred, the latter replied: 'Titus Manlius, you have respected neither consular *imperium* nor your father's *maiestas*, you have left your position to fight the enemy in defiance of my order, and, as far as was in your power, have subverted *disciplina militaris*, on which the fortune of Rome has rested up to this day. (..) I belief that you yourself, if you have a drop of my blood in you, would agree that the military discipline which you undermined by your error must be restored by your punishment. Go, lictor, bind him to the stake'. Livy, XIII.7

Dominatio as such did not have a pejorative connotation. Significantly, *dominium* was the term used by Roman law for the -absolute- rights of ownership over private property. What was thought of as odious was the treatment of free men as if they were slaves, as if they were a piece of private property. At the same time, one could expect to be treated as a free man only if one showed proper deference for one's superiors, appropriate *disciplina*. *Licentia* made men fit for slavery; in such circumstances order could be maintained by a *dominus* only. Hence, in the Roman conception discipline and freedom are two sides of the same coin; and the twin concepts of *licentia* and *servitus* are their opposite. *Disciplina* sets man free, *licentia* enslaves him.

The ancient concept of liberty was closely tied to the notion of virtue. *Libertas* was important because it went hand in hand with *virtus*. In the modern moral languages no trace of that connection has remained. Today liberty is valued for its role in utility-maximization or self-realization. As a consequence, the content and the boundaries of modern liberty differ substantially from that of its ancient counterpart. The fact that we share with the Romans a concern for liberty must not be taken for a sign that we are concerned with the same thing.

For the ancients in the end everything boiled down to the question of *virtus*, an approach which has lost much of its appeal to the moderns. Having set out its meaning and having sketched the main pillars of the conceptual edifice built around *virtus*, it is time to take a closer look at how exactly it could be propagated and preserved, and what caused its loss.

NOTES

1. Gadamer 1990, p.29, 'Wir müssen uns den Rückweg in diese (rhetorisch-humanistische) Tradition mühsam bahnen.'

2. Cicero, *De Off.*, I.64, 'Quo difficilius, hoc praeclarius.'

3. Earl 1970, p.7

4. Polybius, *Hist.*, VI.2.3-4 In the later books of this work, especially XXXI.25, Polybius describes a decline in moral standards, especially after the war with Perseus that ended, victoriously of course, in 168 B.C.

5. Sallust, *Bel.Cat.*, V.9

6. Livy, praefatio

7. Cic., *Tusc.Disp.*, II.43. See also Earl 1970, p.20; Mitchell 1991, pp.14-15

8. On chastity, see e.g. Livy, I.57ff about Lucretia; on gracefulness see Cicero, *De Off.*, I.130

9. Casey 1991, p.v

10. See Cicero, *De Fin.*, V.36, V.38

11. Cicero, *De Off.*, I.117

12. See Xenophon, *Mem.*, II.1.21-34. Cicero refers to it in *De Off.*, I.118

13. Xenophon, *Mem.*, II.1.23-24

14. Xenophon, *Mem.*, II.1.26

15. Xenophon, *Mem.*, II.1.27-28

16. The metaphor of the easy road of vice and the hard road of virtue can already be found in Hesiod, *Works and Days*, 287-298. It is quoted, somewhat freely, in Plato, *Politeia*, 364d: Vice in abundance is easy to choose/ the road is smooth and it lies very near/ while the gods have set sweat before virtue/ and it is a long road, rough and steep.

17. It is true that the Roman authors sometimes seem to argue that the motive behind the deed and not the deed itself determines its moral value. See e.g. Cicero, *De Off.*, I.44 where true liberality is distinguished from sham liberality, in that the latter does nor stem from goodwill but from ostentation. However, as *De Off.*, II.55-56 makes clear, true and false liberality are different deeds. There are deeds that serve others or the community as a whole, and there are deeds that ultimately serve only the giver himself. Only the first kind of deeds are really liberal.

18. The roots of this conception of history are older than romanticism. It is tied up primarily with the notion of creation *ex nihilo*, which is Christian in origin. What the romantics did was to link the notion of creation to the self instead of to God. See Arendt 1990, pp.27ff

19. Cicero, *De Off.*, I.11

20. Cicero, *De Off.*, I.11

21. Cicero, *Tusc. Disp.*, II.47

22. Cicero, *De Off.*, I.18

23. Cicero, *De Off.*, I.23-28

24. Cicero, *De Off.*, I.69

25. Cicero, *De Off.*, I.80

26. Cicero, *De Off.*, I.128

27. Cicero, *De Off.*, I.102

28. E.g. Plutarch, *Cato Maior*, c.4.

29. Plutarch, *Cato Maior*, c.1

30. Cicero, *De Off.*, I.103

31. Xenophon, *Mem.*, II.1.30

32. Plutarch, *Caesar*, c.62

33. Cicero, *Tusc. Disp.*, II.55

34. Cicero, *De Off.*, I.79; cf. Seneca, *Ep. ad Luc.*, VIII.5

35. Cicero, *Tusc. Disp.*, II.37

36. Cf. Aristotle, *Eth. Nic.*, IV.3

37. Cicero, *Tusc. Disp.*, I.109; Cf. Cicero, *De Leg.*, I.44-45

38. Cicero, *Brut.*, 281

39. Cicero, *Tusc. Disp.*, II.58-59

40. Cicero, *Tusc. Disp.*, II.30; II.46

41. Relevant are Billacois 1986; Kiernan 1988, esp.ch.9; Neuschel 1989; Chaussinand-Nogaret (ed.) 1991; Best 1982, ch.1, pp.3-26; on honor in antiquity see Fisher 1992; Cairns 1993; Jaeger, vol.I, ch.I entitled 'Nobility and Arete', pp.3-14; Adkins 1975

42. Höfer and Reichardt 1986, pp.7-73

43. Ford 1968 surprisingly makes this mistake. See pp.27-29 and 177-178

44. Oksenberg-Rorty 1976, pp.309-311; the *locus classicus* is of course Cicero, *De Off.*, I.107

45. Cicero, *De Off.*, I.93

46. Cf. Cicero, *Tusc. Disp.*, I.110; III.3; Cicero, *Pro Sest.*, 96-98, where the true men of honor, the *optimates*, who want but what is best for all, are contrasted with the *populares*, who wish everything they do and say to be agreeable to the masses.

47. Cicero, *Tusc. Disp.*, III.3; V.103-104

48. Plutarch, *Cato Maior*, c.9

49. Baldick 1970, esp. ch.IV, pp.49-62; Cuénin 1982

50. Cf. Sallust, *Bel.Iug.*, 67.3

51. Montesquieu, *Esprit*, I.4.2

52. Knoche 1983, pp.420-445

53. Cicero, *De Off.*, I.57

54. Cicero, *De Off.*, II.37

55. Cicero, *De Off.*, II.38

56. Cicero, *De Off.*, I.66

57. Cicero, *De Off.*, I.63

58. Cicero, *De Off.*, I.61

59. Cicero, *De Off.*, I.64

60. Seneca, *De Ira*, II.xi.3: 'He must fear many whom many fear'; *Ep. ad Luc.*, XIV.10

61. Cicero, *De Off.*, II.23-25; Tacitus, *Ann.*, passim

62. Veyne 1992, pp.161-181

63. Meyer 1948, p.156

64. Plutarch, *Cato Maior*, c.16

65. Dionysius of Halicarnassus, *Rom. Ant.*, 20.13.2-3 Quoted in Nicolet 1988, p.78 Cf. Pericles' assertion, in Thucydides, *Pelop. War*, II.37, that 'we are free and tolerant in our private lives'.

66. Moore jr. 1984, p.154

67. Aristotle, *Pol.*, 1308b20ff

68. Cf. Lukes 1973, ch.9, pp.59-66

69. Constant, *De la Liberté des Anciens et des Modernes*, p.311

70. J.S.Mill, *On Liberty*, ch.I, p.73

71. See Plato, *Laws*, 5.739b-e; Rousseau, *Contrat Social*, I.IX

72. Cicero, *Tusc. Disp.*, III.50; Cf. Veyne 1992, p.172

73. Veyne 1992, p.173

74. Cicero, *Tusc. Disp.*, II.50; *De Off.*, II.2 and III.2 In the same vein, for instance Sallust, *Bell.Cat.*, III and IV, and *Bell.Iug.*, III

75. Cf. Heinze 1960, pp.9-27. Esp. p.26 'Die Römer alter Zeit sind (..) Machtmenschen, der einzelne wie das Volk als Ganzes, und die Macht, nach der sie verlangten, ist anerkanntes Höherstehen, Herrsch- und Befehlsgewalt.'

76. Cf. Foucault 1984, III.2

77. Jaeger vol.II, p.207, pp.347-357, about 'the close relation of the state and the soul' in Plato's *Politeia*

78. Plutarch, *To an Uneducated Ruler*, 780b in: *Moralia* Vol.X

79. Cicero, *Lael.*, c.13: 'Friendships (..) are formed when an exemplar of shining goodness makes itself manifest, and when some congenial spirit feels the desire to fasten to this model.' This clearly suggest a vertical relationship. Even more explicit is c.19: 'A particular important point between one friend and another is this. The superior must place himself on an equality with the inferior.' Cf. Foucault 1984; P.Veyne, 1992, pp.204-205

80. Heinze 1960, pp.43-58; Meyer 1948, pp.244-246; Lütcke, 1968 part I, 'Der Auctoritas-Begriff vor Augustin', pp.13-63

81. Meyer 1948, 109ff

82. Heinze 1960, pp.59-81

83. See on authority Friedrich 1972; Arendt 1977, 'What is Authority?', pp.91-141 Both authors repeat Mommsen's felicitous expression in *Römisches Staatsrecht*, that *auctoritas* is more than advise, but less than command. It is advise which cannot be safely disregarded.

84. Cf. Sallust, *Bell.Cat.*, LI.12-14

85. Cf. Sallust, *Bell.Iug.*, LXVI.2

86. Cicero, *De Leg.*, III.30-32

87. Meyer 1948, p.246

88. Cf. Sallust, *Bell.Iug.*, C.5; Xenophon, *Oeconomicus*, XIII.9 'Men can be made more obedient by word of mouth merely, by being shown that it is good for them to obey. But in dealing with slaves the training thought suitable for wild animals is also a very effective way of teaching obedience.' In Cicero, *De Off.*, II.87 Cicero mentions that, as a young man, he translated the *Oeconomicus*.

89. Tacitus, *Ann.*, I.16-I.48

90. Tacitus, *Ann.*, I.49

91. Tacitus, *Ann.*, I.51

92. The *locus classicus* is Pliny the younger, *Panegyricus*, 45.3 See Klein (ed.) 1969 passim, but esp. the contributions of Wolfgang Kunkel, pp.68-93, and Lothar Wickert, pp.94-135; Hans Kloesel 1983, pp.120-172; Chaimowicz 1985, ch.3 entitled 'Der Gegensatz Monarchie-Despotismus'.

CHAPTER SEVEN

THE SOCIETY OF UNEQUALS

Treat your inferiors as you would be treated by your betters

Seneca[1]

1. The society of the ancestors

The spirit of Roman literature is in a sense oppressively pessimistic. Most Roman authors lamented the moral and political condition of their own days and were firmly convinced that in the past things had been much better. The forefathers -*maiores*-, who had raised Rome from obscurity to greatness, had been paragons of *virtus*. But everything had changed for the worse. Vice had spread like a deadly plague, plunging the *res publica* in a destructive civil war that threw everything into confusion and prepared the way for tyranny.

1.1. The mos maiorum

This diagnosis of the historical development of Rome as a process of decline naturally prompted a strong nostalgia and a tendency to turn to the *maiores* for wisdom and guidance.[2] These were revered. Writes Cicero, 'beyond question our ancestors have adopted better regulations and laws than others in directing the policy of government. What shall I say of the art of war? In this sphere our countrymen have proved their superiority by valor as well as in an even greater degree by discipline. (..) When we come to natural achievements, apart from book-learning they are above comparison with the Greeks or any other people. Where has such *gravitas*, where such *constantia*, *magnitudo animi*, *probitas*, *fides*, where has such surpassing *virtus* in every field been found in any of mankind to justify comparison with our *maiores*?'[3]

It followed, obviously, that the corruption of standards, the degeneration of morals, was the result of deviating from the ways of the *maiores*. 'Before our own time the customs of our ancestors produced excellent men, and eminent men preserved our ancient customs and the institutions of their forefathers. But though the *res publica*, when it came to us, was like a beautiful painting, whose colors, however, were already fading with age, our own time not only has neglected to freshen it by renewing the original colors, but has not even taken the trouble to preserve its configuration and, so to speak, its general outlines. For what is now left of the 'ancient customs' on which (the poet Ennius) said 'the commonwealth of Rome' was 'founded firm'? They have been, as we see, so completely buried in oblivion that they are not only no longer practiced, but are already unknown.'[4] The message is clear: only if one sticks to the *antiqui mores* and *maiorem instituta* corruption can be prevented.

As has been set out, such a 'conservatism', which looks upon the past as exemplary to the present, is equally characteristic of the views of the nobility of the ancien régime. Significantly, its roots in antiquity are predominantly Roman. Greek thinking about morals and politics is more 'nomothetical'; Plato and Aristotle in particular seem to lack historical nostalgia. No appeal is made by them to a virtuous *patrios politeia*.[5] That the post-revolutionary social theorists -except the reactionaries- turned to the Greeks instead of the Romans probably had something to do with this. The Romans' habitual invocation of the *mos maiorum* cannot have appealed to men who had just turned their back on what had formerly existed.

Since the ancient customs of the *res publica* were their criterion of good and bad, it was inevitable that the study of its early history excited a great deal of interest and was taken up with some zeal by the Roman writers, just like, much later, the aristocratic historians of the ancien régime were to focus on the early history of France. When exactly the 'good old days' changed into the 'bad new days' is not entirely clear, but the second century B.C. is referred to as a turning-point by some of the foremost Roman writers. Sallust for instance refers to the final destruction of Carthage in 146 B.C.[6] Polybius refers to the wreckage of the Macedonian monarchy in 168 B.C.[7] And Livy to the Galatian campaign in 189 B.C.[8] In any case, the general approach was that of contrasting the new i.e. vicious with the old i.e. virtuous.

More significant than the question when things went wrong is the question why they went wrong. Since the classical/classicist mind appraised the ultimate springs of human action in moral terms, it perceived the onset of corruption as succumbing to the temptations of vice, as failing moral fiber. But why exactly the temptations of vice gradually overwhelmed the Romans is something difficult to derive from the literature. On the one hand, since they conceived of morality as the ultimate spring of human action, everything is in the end explained by virtue or vice, which logically implies that virtue and vice themselves cannot be explained by anything still more profound. And yet, the Romans were well aware of the force of circumstance. There are many *passus* analyzing and rebuking tempting circumstances, and calling for their suppression. Prosperity occasions insolence,[9] solitude grows idleness,[10] leisure and luxury demoralizes the warlike spirit of soldiers,[11] protracted peace enervates,[12] and so on. The moral decline of Rome is related to some 'material' development, such as the lack of enemies after the destruction of Carthage, and the import of luxury from the Middle East, which are said to have undermined the virtue of the Romans.

The contradiction is manifest, but that does not seem to have vexed the Romans. They focused more on analogy than on causality. A certain type of society went together with virtue, another with vice. And if they were little outspoken on the relation between *Unterbau* and *Überbau*, they were very articulate on the substance of both. The society that best exemplified *virtus* was ancient Rome; the state as it had been in the glorious days of the *maiores*.

1.2. The rural bias

What were its main features? An appropriate place to start looking for an answer to this question is *De Agri Cultura*,[13] the earliest extant Latin prose work we possess, and the sole surviving text of Cato the Elder (234-149 B.C), the embodiment of Roman virtue. This 'role-model' asserts right at the beginning of that treatise that 'when (the ancestors) were trying to praise a good man they called him a good farmer and a good tiller of the soil, and the one who received this compliment was considered to have received the highest praise. (..) It is from among the farmers that the bravest men and the sturdiest soldiers come, and the gain they make is the most blameless of all, the most secure, and the least provocative of envy, and the men engaged in this pursuit are least given to disaffection'.[14] Panegyrics like this, celebrating the virtues of the farmer and healthy, rustic life on the farm can be reproduced *ad nauseam*.[15]

It would be quite off the mark, however, to conclude that Roman literature exhibits a proto-romantic idealization of the peasant world.[16] In fact, its general spirit and outlook are overwhelmingly aristocratic, and deeply contemptuous of the common people, the *vulgus*, including the peasantry.[17] The praise of farmers one finds scattered through Roman literature signifies something else. The farmer stands for life in the country -*rus*-, as opposed to life in the city -*urbs*.

The Roman bias in favor of rural life comes to the fore quite blatantly in the composition of the two most important republican assemblies, the *comitia centuriata* and the *comitia tributa*. In both assemblies voting took place on the basis of originally territorial *tribus*, i.e districts or constituencies. From 241 B.C. on there were thirty-five of such tribes, four *tribus urbanae* and thirty-one *tribus rusticae*. (Within each tribe individual suffrage was the rule, a simple majority being decisive, and no minimum quorum being required.) In both *comitiae* every tribe had one single vote. This by itself conferred a huge numerical advantage on the rural tribes. But what made the inequality really glaring was the fact that the four urban tribes were each much larger than the rural tribes, and contained most of the 'second-rate' citizens, so to speak, i.e. the *proletarii*, the freedmen, and many of the allies.[18] How to make sense of this bias?

'The city creates luxury, from which avarice inevitably springs, while from avarice audacity breaks forth, the source of all crimes and misdeeds. On the other hand, this country life (..) teaches thrift, carefulness, and justice', Cicero proclaimed in his *Pro Roscio*.[19] And Varro, in his treatise on agriculture, argued that 'it was not without reason that those great men, our ancestors, put the Romans who lived in the country ahead of those who lived in the city. For as in the country those who live in the villa are lazier than those who are engaged in carrying out the work on the land, so they thought that those who settled in town were more indolent than those who dwelt in the country.'[20] Evidently, the Romans believed that country life was productive of virtue, and city life brought forth vice. To the modern reader it presumably is not immediately obvious why this must be the case. The key to this enigma lies in the specifically urban means of livelihood: trade for profit. That was considered dishonorable and demeaning. As to agriculture, on the other hand, 'there is no kind of gainful employment that is better, more fruitful, more pleasant and more worthy of a free man'.[21]

Four distinct but related reasons for this evaluation can be traced in the literature, all centering on the idea that the rural mode of subsistence evokes virtue, whereas the urban mode of subsistence produces vice. It was argued first of all that the *goal* served by farming was morally superior to that served by trade, since it was concerned with the production of necessities, upon which survival depended. Trade on the other hand thrives by supplying goods that are not only superfluous, but positively damaging to the moral health of society, viz. luxury-goods.

Secondly, it was argued that the *activity* of farming requires various virtues, such as *labor* -willingness to endure toil-, *patientia*, *industria*, *frugalitas*, and *parsimonia*. Farming hardens a man's body and mind. The means by which traders earned their bread on the other hand, smelled of vice. Traders do not really produce anything, but merely replace goods from one place to another. And when goods are in scarce supply, they increase their prices. Hence, they make a profit out of the misery of others. The virtue of entrepreneurs is a theme conspicuously absent from Roman literature.

Thirdly, farming is not a full-time occupation. Between sowing-time and harvest-time the farmer must abide his time, waiting for his crop to ripen and mature, for the weather to change, for the spring to set in. This leaves him with enough spare time 'to attend to his friends and the city'.[†22]

[†] The Greek word for spare time, which could be devoted to friends and the city is *scholè*. Its opposite is *ascholia*, which refers to work. Interestingly, the Roman notion of spare time -*otium*- does not have the same connotation. For the time devoted to friends and the city were subsumed under its opposite: *negotium*. *Otium* belongs to the private sphere. It is the time neither devoted

Finally, the *social constraints* upon the farmer and the trader are different in two important ways. Primo: farming produces *rootedness*, trade volatility. The farmer has a stake in the land, which makes him much less mobile than the trader. Also, his means of livelihood are much more secure than those of the trader, who can make huge profits one day and go broke the next. As a consequence, the farmer is a lot more predictable and trustworthy than the trader. In contrast to the latter, he can be relied upon to take a keen interest in and to take part in the preservation of the realm.

Secundo: the farmer depends on no one for his livelihood; he is *independent*. He can therefore speak for or against anyone, as he wishes. He can afford to be proud. The trader in contrast is dependent upon the favorable opinion of others. Trade therefore demands, or at least goads into deception. 'Those who buy (..) and sell again immediately, should (..) be thought of as demeaning themselves. For they would make no profit unless they told sufficient lies, and nothing is more dishonorable than *vanitas* -misrepresentation-.'[23] Moreover, traders are likely to be sycophants; they cannot speak their minds freely, but have to fawn upon their customers and swallow their pride.[†]

When speaking of an independent farmer the Romans had in mind a man with a secure property title in his own piece of land, i.e. a freeholder. Tenant farmers and farm workers -also country dwellers- are looked upon as inferior, because they possess no landed property, and are therefore considered much less independent. As a consequence, this section of the rural population stands largely outside of the logic of virtue and honor. It simply cannot afford it.

---

to work, nor to public office. Both Sallust, e.g. *Bel.Cat.*, IV.1; *Bel.Iug.*, III.3, and Cicero, *De Off.*, II.2-4, III.1, repeatedly feel the need to ensure their readers that their *otium* was well used, and that they should not be suspected of indifference -*socordia*-, moral corruption -*desidia*-, and laziness -*inertia*.

[†] The ancients were certain that trade must involve deceit. Cf. Paul Veyne, 1990, pp.52-53, 'In order to make money, the merchant falsifies the value of things. He sells space, an incorporeal entity that does not belong to him. Time, too, belongs to no one, and that is why it is dishonest to lend money at interest. Commerce is no less dishonest. Furthermore, the merchant, thanks to his position as an intermediary, inflates the prices of goods as he passes them on. This is his profit. People are convinced that he is responsible for the dearness from which he gains. We know that matters are less simple, for the marginalists have taught us that scarcity and the market are the only sources of the value of goods. (..) But the naive mind does not see matters like that. (..) For the naive mind thinks that value arises from below. It believes in labor-value. It would agree that if one were to manufacture knick-knacks lacking in any utility whatsoever, but 'with lots of work in them', then these would possess a lot of value. Labor-value alone is the basis of the *iustum pretium*. The merchant, however, is said to falsify the just price, for he inflates it without incorporating any additional labor in the object concerned.'

1.3. Poverty of two kinds
This dividing line is not to be taken for the dividing line between rich and poor. The man of independent means, as the Romans conceived of him, is not necessarily rich, nor is the rich man necessarily of independent means. A trader may be extremely wealthy, but that does not make him a man of honor. As long as he remains a merchant his position is too insecure to warrant his independence. True, 'if (..) men trade on a large and expansive scale, importing many things from all over, and distributing them to many people without misrepresentation, that is not entirely to be criticized', but it is only 'when such men are satiated, or rather satisfied, with what they have gained, and just as they have often left the high seas for the harbor, now leave the harbor itself for land in the country, it seems that we have every right to praise their occupation'.[24] (Imagine the son of a wealthy merchant from Paris or Bordeaux in, say, 1700 A.D. reading this passage at the *collège*.) A freeholder on the other hand may be quite poor, but as long as his land allows him to provide for himself and his family, he is a man of independent means, and virtue and honor are within his reach.

In fact, there is an important streak in Roman literature glorifying an austere and simple life-style. A well-known *exemplum* of such a life-style is the episode of Cincinnatus being called from his farm to lead the country. Livy's account sets it squarely down. 'Now I would solicit the particular attention of those numerous people who imagine that money is everything in the world, and that honorable rank and *virtus* are inseparable from wealth: let them observe that Cincinnatus, the one man in whom Rome reposed all her hope of survival, was at the moment working a little three-acre farm (..). A mission from the city found him at work on his land -digging a ditch, maybe, or ploughing. Greetings were exchanged, and he was asked (..) to put on his toga and hear the senate's instructions. This naturally surprised him, and asking if all was well he told his wife Racilia to run to their cottage and fetch his toga. The toga was brought, and wiping the grimy sweat from his hands and face he put it on; at once the envoys from the city saluted him, with congratulations, as *dictator* (..).'[25] Roman literature abounds in such stories. One could easily get the impression that poverty and virtue were inseparable to the Roman mind. That, however, is not the case. For one finds with the same authors the view that poverty is vile and dishonorable, and that riches and honor go together.[26] Does that mean that they were inconsistent? Should we conclude that in praising poverty, they were 'doing little more than providing a nostalgic reminder that past rustic virtue was the foundation of present glory and grandeur', which had little to do with their actual life and thought?[27]

That seems unlikely. Such a conclusion disregards the pervasiveness of the idea of virtue in the Roman conception of the good life. As in everything else, the Romans distinguished between a virtuous and a vicious species of both the poor and the rich. The poverty of the virtuous is essentially self-willed. It is the poverty of a man who refuses to serve the goddess of *pecunia*, because he has set his aims much higher. Like Cato Maior such a man observes the ancestral custom of working his own land, is content with a cold breakfast, a frugal dinner, the simplest clothing, and a humble cottage to live in, and such a man thinks it more admirable to renounce luxuries than to acquire them.[28] This is the poverty of a land-owner who could devote his life to accumulation, but thinks of that as despicable. His land is meant to assure his independence, not to maximize his income. (However, this does not imply that for the Romans farming was a matter of strict subsistence, that excluded the sale of farm products. Selling what one had produced oneself was not regarded as trade.[29]) The vicious poor on the other hand are those whose poverty is not self-willed. This poverty is not a renouncement of, an abstention from luxury, but the squalor of being reduced to begging, stealing, lying, and cheating for a living, which to the Roman mind was closely linked to the lack of landed property, and therefore considered a predominantly urban predicament. It is only this kind of poverty that is regarded as vile and dishonorable by the Romans.

The Roman view of manual labor is a reflection of this understanding of poverty. Contrary to what is sometimes maintained an undifferentiated contempt for such labor is hard to find in Roman literature.[30] *Exempla*, like the one's above about Cincinnatus and Cato, stressing the merit of working the land with one's own hands, are so common that such a conclusion seems unwarranted. Contempt for manual labor was clearly limited to a specific type, viz. that of handicraftsmen and non-agricultural workmen.

In Xenophon's *On Estate Management*, translated by the young Cicero,[31] the craftsman -*banausos*- is compared in the most unfavorable terms with the farmer -*georgos*. The crafts 'spoil the bodies of the workmen and the foremen, forcing them to sit still and live indoors, and in some cases to spend the day at the fire. The softening of the body involves a serious weakening of the mind. Moreover, these crafts leave no spare time for attention to one's friends and the *polis*, so that those who follow them are reputedly bad at dealing with friends and bad defenders of the country'.[32] By comparison, farming 'seemed to be easiest to learn and most pleasant to work at, to give the body the greatest measure of strength and beauty, and leave the mind the greatest amount of spare time for attending to the interests of one's friends and the *polis*. Moreover, since the crops grow and the cattle on a farm graze outside the walls, farming seemed (..) to help in some measure to make the workers valiant. And so this way of making a living appeared to be held in the highest esteem by our states, because it seems to turn out the best citizens and most loyal to the community'.[33] The essential distinction, for the

Romans, was not between intellectual and manual occupations, but between activities aspiring to *honestas*, and those aiming at mere *utilitas*.[34]

1.4. Wealth of two kinds

As has been set out, the distinction between the virtuous and the vicious poor was parallelled by a similar distinction with regard to the wealthy. Both the way wealth was acquired and the way it was spent were considered morally relevant. As to the former: it was evidently in bad taste to discuss such matters.[35] One simply had money.[36] The little that was said about it leaves no doubt that acquisition was honorable, if and only if it concerned landed property. Indeed, of such property one could scarcely possess enough, provided it was 'pursued by means that are free from dishonorableness'.[37] Not much is said as to which means are meant, but unquestionably the most honorable was land acquired by warfare; everything in the logic of virtue lead up to that conclusion. Marriage and inheritance were also honorable means to that end, of course. But land purchased with profits made in trade smelled of the vicious activity that made the purchase possible, and was therefore much less esteemed; that too followed from the logic of virtue.

Nouveaux riches were suspect.[38] Plutarch tells us that, when Sulla boasted of his achievements in the Libyan campaign of 107-105 B.C., one member of the aristocracy said to him: 'There is certainly something wrong about you, who have become so rich when your father left you nothing at all'.[39] The Romans found it hard to believe that one could become wealthy quickly, that is in an honorable way. And this belief was not groundless, for it was very difficult indeed for a family to augment its wealth substantially, unless it already was wealthy.[40] Unlike the moderns the ancients did not have a liking for the self-made man. It was assumed that anyone somersaulting into great wealth must have used all means available to achieve this end: falseness, servility, avarice, ruthlessness. Obviously, such a man was without honor, without virtue. Ancient riches was the most respectable riches.

If Roman literature is rather short-winded on the question of acquiring wealth, the opposite is true of how to make use of it. This topic is discussed at much greater length. Evidently, honor was considered to be more 'at home' in, more befitting to this domain. Acquiring wealth was uncomfortably close to seeking wealth, which was of course dishonorable. It is as if wealth was morally acceptable only if it was acquired by chance, as a side effect of an honorable pursuit, if it fell into one's lap, so to speak. Hence, even warfare was dishonorable, if it was waged with the goal of obtaining booty.[41]

And yet, wealth -that is to say landed property- was not to be despised. Although a life of respectable -'genteel'- poverty was possible, the highest, most glorious stations in life were open only to those of great opulence. The honorable man of moderate wealth -the small landowner- had to be satisfied with a relatively subordinate position. Like the great landowner he was *a man of independent means*. Like him he did not depend on others for a living. So like him he could speak his mind freely, and detachedly ponder over all aspects of an issue, without having to take into consideration the popularity of his decision. Like him his rootedness in the soil ensured that he would take an active interest in the well-being of the country. And like him he had sufficient spare time to engage in public affairs. But the small landowner, as opposed to the great landowner, lacked the funds necessary to occupy one of the foremost positions in society. Only those who were rich in land -the *locupletes*- satisfied all preconditions for the highest positions of leadership. In addition to the independence, the rootedness, and the spare time, which they shared with the small landowners, they had the money required to provide for the necessary education and the expenses that went with each *officium*.

Hence, the Roman view of how to make proper use of wealth was closely tied to their conception of leadership of the *res publica*. Wealth must be used in the service of the state. The latter is the *ultima ratio* of the former, the former the *sine qua non* of the latter. Cutting the bond between them was catastrophic. Wealth turned to private use -*luxuria*- was one of the most dangerous forms of moral corruption, and government by the poor and the needy was equal to asking for bribery and plunder. This being the situation two questions arise. How to ensure that the wealthy -the great landowners- dominate society and have the main say in the government of the *res publica*? And how to ensure that they use their wealth correctly, viz. for public purposes? The first question leads us on to the structure of Roman politics. We must turn to that now. The answer the Romans gave to the second question, which deals with what is perhaps the most important issue in classical/classicist political theory, the *humanitas* of the elite, will be discussed thereafter.

2. The structure of politics

The Romans did not conceive of themselves as a *Volk*, a race, or a nation, but as a *civitas*. Being Roman meant having all the rights and duties of a *civis Romanus*, which were acquired simply by enrolment in the *census*, the list of citizens. As is generally known, the Romans granted citizenship to aliens, not excluding recent enemies, far more liberally than any other ancient people. It is not entirely clear how to explain this uncommon hospitality. However, what matters here are merely the criteria for admission to citizenship. Both advocates and adversaries of liberal admission used arguments that were exclusively political and moral in nature. Discussions about the cultural match of aspirant citizens, that carry such weight in modernity, are not to be found in Roman literature, which is hardly surprising, of course, for the variable 'culture' is of romantic origin.[†]

In the last analysis, Roman citizenship signified that the person and property of its possessor was protected by the *civitas* -'all for one'. In return, the *civis* was expected to maintain and support the *civitas* with his services, goods, and counsel -'one for all'. *Ius* and *officium* were to be in balance, for if the burden was too heavy the bond would break. The *officia* were fourfold: they involved military service, payment of taxes, political deliberation, and the exercise of political command. The citizen was, by his nature, a soldier, a taxpayer, a voter, and an office-holder. By his nature, because if the citizen refused to take up his *officia*, the *civitas* would fall apart, his *iures* would dissolve, and his citizenship would be in shambles.[42]

The ancients were well-aware that free-riding was an acute and permanent temptation for every citizen; an *officium* is after all a duty, a burden. To have only rights and no duties is a naturally appealing vision to man. His animal spirits draw him towards it. But giving in to this vision entails the demise of the *civitas*. Therefore, the animal spirits have to be resisted and overcome. And that is accomplished by *virtus*. Without *virtus* no *officium*, without virtue no duty. Hence, it is to the domain of *officium* rather than to the domain of *ius*, that the ideal of *virtus* appertains. The discharge of

---

[†] That the discussion was held in political and moral terms is shown for instance by Tacitus, *Annales*, XI. 23-24. In the year 48 A.D. the emperor Claudius proposed to enlarge the senate with the chiefs of those tribes of northern and central Gaul with long-standing treaties with Rome. The proposal aroused much discussion. 'Italy is not so decayed, said some, that she cannot provide her own capital with a senate. In former times even peoples akin to us were content with a Roman senate of native Romans only; and the government of those days is a glorious memory. To this day, people cite the ancient Roman character for their models of courage and renown. (..) Do we have to import foreign hordes, like gangs of prisoners, and leave no careers for our own surviving aristocracy, or for impoverished senators from Latium? Every post will be absorbed by the rich men whose grandfathers and great-grandfathers commanded hostile tribes, assailed our armies in battle, besieged the divine Julius Caesar at Alesia.' Etcetera. The emperor defended his proposal, predictably, with an appeal to the *maiores*, with the following arguments. 'The experience of my own ancestors, notably of my family's Sabine founder Clausus who was simultaneously made a Roman citizen and a patrician, encourage me to adopt the same national policy, by bringing excellence to Rome from whatever source. For I do not forget that the Julii came from Alba Longa, the Coruncanii from Camerium, the Porcii from Tusculum'. The enfranchisement not merely of individuals but of whole peoples 'reinvigorated the exhausted empire. This helped to stabilize peace within the frontiers and successful relations with foreign powers. Is it regretted that the Cornelii Balbi immigrated from Spain, and other equally distinguished men from southern Gaul? Their descendants are with us; and they love Rome as much as we do. What proved fatal to Sparta and Athens, for all their military strength, was the segregation of conquered subjects as aliens. Our founder Romulus, on the other hand, had the wisdom -more than once- to transform whole enemy peoples into Roman citizens within the course of one day'.

duty was burden, but is was also a sign of virtue, and therefore an honorable burden.[43] In other words, honor was the rightful reward for the discharge of duty, which signified virtue. The three terms form an equation, which has a stable solution only when each one is given its due weight.[†]

2.1. Unequal citizenship

In principle, every citizen had the four duties mentioned above. Everyone could be soldier, taxpayer, voter, and magistrate. There was no division of society in functional orders, like the medieval distinction between *bellatores*, *laboratores*, and *oratores*. However, it would be erroneous to conclude that citizenship as conceived by the Romans was an egalitarian concept. It was in fact thoroughly hierarchical, much more so than its Greek counterpart. To grasp this we have to consider the features of Roman citizenship in greater detail.[44]

As mentioned above, the *census* was its backbone. The Romans attributed the design of the *census* to Servius Tullius, the sixth king of early Rome. If so, it was long-lived, for in the last century of the republic it was still in force, albeit with some modifications. The *census*, made up in principle every five years by two *censores*, categorized all citizens, on the basis of various qualifications. For the Romans not all men were equal.

Apart from the fact that many residents -most notably slaves- did not even appear on the civic roll, not every citizen was a full citizen -*civis optimo iure*. There were many -freedmen, allies, women- who had some, but not all the rights and duties of full citizens. The wives and daughters of citizens were not allowed to vote or stand for office, but came under the protection of Roman law. Freedmen could vote, but were barred from service in the army as well as from political office. And many allies were given citizenship without the right to vote -*civitas sine suffragio*-, but with combat duty.

The full citizens were also categorized. Until about 200 B.C. they were

---

[†] The picture drawn here of the nature of *ius* and *officium* and the relationship between them is beautifully symmetrical and intuitively appealing, but it may be to some extent a construction rather than a reconstruction of Roman thought. Most importantly, it is clear that the Romans used the concept of *ius* not only in opposition to the concept of *officium*. For instance, they referred to voting and political office not merely as duties, but also as rights: respectively as *ius suffragio* and *ius honorum*. Part of the answer to this puzzle is obviously that the meaning of neither *ius* nor *officium* is completely captured by translating these concepts as a (subjective) right and a duty. As has already been set out the Roman notion of *officium* has a connotation of honor and virtue, and therefore of privilege and entitlement. Clearly, that implies that it is in some respects close to our concept of a (subjective) right. Similarly, the concept of *ius* entails an element of what we would call duty, which comes to the fore in the fact that its primary meaning is (objective) law, or rule, rather than (subjective) right. Contrary to a (subjective) right one does not possess a law, but obeys it.

divided into five hierarchical *classes*, basically according to the amount of property each owned,[45] although the censors were free to deviate from this rule, if a man's merit or demerit gave them reason to do so. Each class was divided into a set number of *centuriae*. The first class consisted of eighty such *centuriae*, the second, third, and fourth of twenty, and the fifth of thirty. Finally, there were five special *centuriae*. Two attached to the first *centuria*, composed of carpenters, two attached to the fifth, composed of buglers and trumpeters, and one *infra classem*, composed of the propertyless, who were classified by a head count, on account of which they were designated as *capite censi* or *proletarii*: they who possess only offspring -*proles*.[46] At the top of the hierarchy, above the five classes, the wealthiest citizens were enrolled in eighteen *centuriae* of *equites*, bringing the number of *centuriae* to a total of 193. Towards the end of the third century B.C. or possibly in the early part of the second the number of *centuriae* assigned to the various classes was modified. Many elements of this change are obscure, but it is clear that henceforth, the first class consisted of seventy *centuriae*. Since the number of equestrian and proletarian *centuriae* remained the same, as well as the total number of classes and *centuriae*, ten *centuriae* must have been added to one or more of the other classes.

The purpose of this rather intricate looking system was threefold. It served as the basis of the distribution of military, fiscal, and electoral *officia* over the citizens. Each *centuria* was expected to furnish the same number of soldiers and the same amount of tax, and possessed one vote in the *comitia centuriata*. Because the *centuriae* were extremely unequal in size -the number of poor far exceeded the number of rich[47]- the rich contributed substantially more in blood and money than the poor. But at the same time, it gave the rich a disproportionate influence *in politicis*. Under the 'original' system the equestrian and first class *centuriae* together had a majority of votes in the *comitia centuriata*, viz. 98 out of 193. After the reform the equestrian and first class *centuriae* together had only 88 out of 193 votes, as a consequence of which the preponderance of the rich was somewhat reduced, but it would be far of the mark to conclude that something approaching democratic equality had been established.[48]

De facto and *de iure*, Roman citizenship was and remained an elite affair. Even the *census*, the footing of civic life, was inegalitarian in principle as well as in fact. And the other features of the system only reinforced the verticality. In perusing the ancients authors, nothing comes to the fore more clearly than this, and there is no question that the Romans thought everything was very admirably arranged that way. They had no taste whatsoever for democratic equality. It is highly significant in this respect that even in the first century B.C., when *discordia* had gripped the elite and had divided it into two antagonist factions, known as *populares* and *optimates*, even the former never proposed democratic reforms, although it 'wanted (its) actions and (its) words to be pleasing to the people at large'.[49]

The Romans had little faith in democracy. Generally, under such a government 'liberty prevails everywhere, to such an extent that not only are homes one and all without a master, but the vice of anarchy extends even to the domestic animals, until finally the father fears the son, the son flouts his father, all sense of shame disappears, and all is so absolutely free that there is no distinction between citizen and alien; the schoolmaster fears and flatters his pupils, and pupils despise their masters; youths take on the gravity of age, and old men stoop to the games of youth, for fear they may be disliked by their juniors and seem to them too serious. Under such conditions even the slaves come to behave with unseemly freedom, wives have the same rights as their husbands, and in the abundance of liberty even the dogs, the horses, and the asses are so free in their running about that men must make way for them in the streets. (..) The final result of this boundless license is that the minds of the citizens become so squeamish and sensitive that, if the authority of government is exercised in the smallest degree, they become angry and cannot bear it. On this account they begin to neglect the laws as well, and so finally they are utterly without a master of any kind'.[50] The resulting chaos engenders tyranny.[51]

This description leaves no doubt as to what was considered the shortcoming of a democracy: it lacked hierarchy, without which no order was believed possible. It brought about a confusion of ranks, as a result of which no one knew his place any longer. The Greek infatuation with popular government was regarded with scorn. In his *Pro Flacco*, Cicero contrasted the Romans with the Greeks. 'All the states of the Greeks are managed by irresponsible seated assemblies. And so, not to discuss this later Greece, which has long been troubled and vexed by its own devices, that older Greece, which once was so notable for its resources, its power, its glory, fell because of this defect alone -the undue freedom and irresponsibility of its assemblies. Untried men, without any experience in any affairs and ignorant, took their places in the assembly and then they undertook useless wars, then they put factious men in charge of the state, and they drove most deserving citizens out of the country.'[52]

Citizenship Roman style was a deeply aristocratic concept. The social ties that held Roman society together were those of authority, rather than of fraternity. It was a 'communitarianism' of the 'right' rather than of the 'left', which is part of the explanation why the ancien régime's elite was drawn towards it (and also why most present-day 'communitarians' turn to Greece instead of Rome).

2.2. The nobilitas

Most pronounced was the aristocratic character of Roman citizenship in the rules concerning the eligibility for public office -civil, military, and religious. At first Roman society was divided into two orders, the *patricii* and the *plebei*. Tradition has it that the distinction was political and went back to Romulus. He allegedly selected a hundred heads of *gentes* to form a consultative body, the *senatus*. These, Livy maintained, were called *patres*, and their descendants *patricii*.[53] Under the monarchy and in the early republic these patrician families had a monopoly on public office, the *ius honorum*. Whatever its true historical origin, the order of patricians acquired all the features of a nobility of birth, reserving the rank of patrician to children of patrician parentage.

However, in the fourth century B.C. the plebeians won the right to all major public offices, as a result of which the distinction between patricians and plebeians lost its political decisiveness. Yet, this so-called equalization of the orders did not constitute an introduction of the principle of horizontality in Roman society. For, following the admittance of plebeians to public office a new nobility emerged, composed partly of plebeians and partly of patricians, the *nobilitas*. This coterie became the nucleus of the Roman ruling class, with a more or less hereditary claim on the highest offices of state and on membership of the senate, even though *nobilitas* never became a legal rank.[54]

Nobilitas is derived from the verb *noscere*, to know, to recognize. So the root meaning of nobility is something like 'the man who is known by others'. Obviously, the basic antinomy of *nobilitas* is 'the unrenowned'. Because of his 'humble and obscure background' the common man is not as well known as a noble scion. For from early youth 'the eyes of all are cast on (the latter). They examine whatever he does, the very way in which he lives; he is as it were, bathed in so brilliant a light that no single word or deed of his can be hidden'.[55] In short, they know him for what he is.

As the etymology of the concept makes clear, nobility and fame were primarily associated with the doing of great, i.e. extraordinary things, rather than good things.[56] The nobleman was admired and feared by the common man because he is capable of doing things they are not, rather than loved or hated because he promotes their well-being or fails to do so. A noble act need not necessarily be associated with the good, the just, and the reasonable. This primitive notion of the noble is still central to the deliberations of the Homeric warrior-kings. Justice -*dikaiosunè*- and reasonableness -*sophrosunè*-, are at best minor elements of Homeric *aretè*. However, by the time of Plato and Aristotle this dangerous moral ambiguity of the noble was successfully domesticated, by linking the doing of great deeds to the service of the community.[†57] Naturally, the celebration of egotistic noble fearlessness and ruthlessness remained an undercurrent, but it could resurface in all its force only when romanticism turned the self into the focal-point of existence.[58] To the romantics we also owe the 'insight' that the noble might indeed justify the evil, the unjust, and the unreasonable.[59] In the ancien régime the concept of nobility was still securely tied to the idea of serving the well-being of the whole.[60]

It is not entirely clear who was considered *nobilis*. Perhaps plain criteria did not exist. In any case, the sources fail to give them. Probably the lower fringes of nobility were contested, as they were in the ancien régime. It is certain that all descendants of consuls were called noble.[61] But the descendants of other high magistrates as well as families of patrician stock were probably also included.[62]

2.3. Novitas

Before Augustus turned the *nobilitas* into a closed caste, it was possible for rich and talented men to ennoble themselves and their family -and acquire a place in the senate- by securing one of the high magistracies. Such men were called 'new men' -*homines novi*.[‡] Presumably, it was not too difficult to do. According to Cicero 'innumerable men' had achieved it.[63] However, it was almost impossible for a *homo novus* to reach the highest rung of the ladder: the consulate. 'The nobility used to pass on the consulship from one to another of their own number, and any *homo novus*, however distinguished and however remarkable his achievements, was regarded as unworthy of the office, as if he were polluted.'[64] It has been calculated that between 366 B.C. and 63 B.C. only fifteen *homines novi* were elected to the consulate, the last one of course being Cicero.[65] Indeed, five out of six consuls were not merely

---

[†] By the time of Plato and Aristotle, justice had long been accepted as an important virtue, but if it wasn't for their work, 'popularized' by Cicero, the western tradition would perhaps not have accorded such a central moral place to justice. On this view, Plato's and Aristotle's foremost merit would be that they 'humanized' the warrior-ethic. Note, by the way, that Aristotle and particularly Cicero are more aristocratic that Plato, since only the latter tries to explain all the virtues in terms of justice.

[‡] It seems clear that this is the definition of *homo novus*. See e.g. Sallust, *Bel.Iug.*, LXIII.6-7. It follows that if the *nobilitas* was restricted to the descendants of consuls, a *homo novus* must have been a man first in line of his family to hold consular office. But Gelzer 1962/64, vol.I, pp.39-50, who vindicates such a narrow definition of *nobilitas*, maintains that *homines novi* were all who were first in line to hold an office of state, in which case a much larger number of men were included. On the other hand, Brunt 1982, p.5, who defends the broad definition of *nobilitas* going back to Mommsen, argues that 'as a general rule, the first consul of every plebeian house was a *novus*'. This would imply a much smaller *nobilitas*, and also cut the link between *nobilitas* and *novitas*.

of noble, but of consular descent.[66]

It seems that even the *nobilitas* was highly stratified. A huge gulf separated those who could boast of a long line of consular ancestors, had been consul themselves, had led major military campaigns, and had governed important provinces, from those of more unassuming descent, whose nobility was still of a tender age, and who had held only lesser magistracies. The former, often referred to as *nobilissimi* and *principes*, dominated the discussions in the senate, whereas the latter were so rarely called upon to speak in the senate that they were colloquially known as *pedarii* -they who vote with their feet.[67]

A *homo novus* who became a consul was conceived of as an anomaly, not only by the *nobilitas*. There is no doubt that the population at large too had a preference for noblemen as magistrates. The Roman people never considered itself fit to rule. The classical Roman world view, still predominant in the eighteenth century, accords to everything and everyone a fixed place in a hierarchy. Upward, or for that matter downward, movement was possible, but by the nature of things had to remain exceptional, if the hierarchy was to stay intact.[68]

The social distance between the *nobilitas* and the rest of the population is pointedly illustrated by the fact that, although the three most celebrated *homines novi* of the republic -Cato the elder, Gaius Marius, and Cicero- all came from equestrian families, that social background apparently did not count for much. Marius, we are told by Plutarch, 'was born of parents altogether obscure and indigent, who supported themselves by daily labor'.[69] Cicero's mother was 'well-born and lived a fair life', but of his father so little was known that 'some would have him the son of a fuller, and educated in the trade, others carry back the origin of his family to Tullius Attius, an illustrious king of the Volscians'.[70] And Cato's ancestors were 'almost entirely unknown', even though in the ensuing sentence Plutarch mentions that Cato's great-grandfather served with valor in the cavalry, which implies that he must have been an *equis*.[71]

2.4. The parvenu's protest

Throughout their career all three faced slights and spiteful allusion to their lineage by the *nobilitas*. And all three reacted in a way typical of the *parvenu*, viz. by proclaiming the primacy of *virtus*, contrasting their own 'true' nobility with the merely formal nobility of the *nobiles*. The *locus classicus* of this *topos* of the upstart, is Marius' address to the people in Sallust's *Bellum Iugurthinum*, which deserves to be quoted at length.

'Compare me now, Quirites, a new man with those haughty nobles. What they know from hearsay and reading, I have seen with my own eyes or done with my own hands. What they have learned from books I have learned by service in the field; think now for yourselves whether words or deeds are worth more. They scorn my *novitas*, I their worthlessness. (..) For my part, I believe that (..) the bravest is the best born. But if they rightly look down on me, let them also look down on their own *maiores*, whose nobility began, like mine, in *virtus*. (..) Even when they speak to you or address the senate, their theme is commonly a eulogy of their ancestors; by recounting the exploits of their forefathers they imagine themselves more glorious. The very reverse is true. The more glorious was the life of their ancestors, the more shameful is their own baseness. (..) The glory of the ancestors is, as it were, a light shining upon posterity, suffering neither their virtues nor their faults to be hidden. Of such glory I acknowledge my poverty, Quirites, but -and that is far more glorious- I have done deeds of which I have a right to speak. Now see how unfair those men are. What they demand for themselves because of others' *virtus* they do not allow me as the result of my own, no doubt because I have no family portraits -*imagines*- and because mine is a new nobility. And yet surely to be its creator is better than to have inherited and disgraced it. Their ancestors have left them all that they could: riches, *imagines*, their own illustrious memory. But *virtus* they have not left them, nor could they have done so; that alone is neither bestowed nor received as a gift. They say that I am common and of rude manners, because I cannot give an elegant dinner and because I pay no actor or cook higher wages than I do my overseer. This I gladly admit, Quirites, for I learned from my father and other righteous men that elegance is proper to women but toil to men, that all the virtuous ought to have more fame than riches, and that arms and not furniture confer honor. Well then, let them continue to do what pleases them and what they hold dear, let them make love and drink, let them pass their old age where they have spent their youth, in banquets, slaves to their belly and the most shameful parts of their body. Sweat, dust and all such things let them leave to us, to whom they are sweeter than feasts.'[72]

Whether Marius' accusation of noble incompetence was true or not is not the issue here. What his speech proves, irrespective of its veracity, is how little the *nobilitas* was prepared to accept an outsider as one of theirs, and how insecure Marius' himself believed his position really was. The Roman people held that leadership in war and in peace was the responsibility and the privilege of the *nobilitas*. A commoner claiming high public office seemed not to know his place in the great chain of being, and thus to upset the natural order. Hence, the terms of Marius' defense: it is not he but they who upset it.

Summing up, it appears that to the Roman mind the seemingly egalitarian concept of citizenship did not stand in the way of a division of society in two ranks or classes, on the one hand those who are alternately called the best -*optimi*-, the good -*boni*-, the few -*pauci*-, the rich -*locupletes*-, and so forth, and on the other hand the many -*multi*-, the unreliable -*improbi*-, the poor -*egentes*-.[73] What all these designations convey is that the Romans conceived of the world as made up of leaders and led. It is significant that *Senatus Populusque Romanum* was the proper name of the *res publica*. In the notion of *nobilitas* all of these ideas come together. The *nobiles* are the good, the few, the rich, the famous, the polite, the honorable. They are the best, they man the senate. In a sense, they inhabit a different material and spiritual world than the many, who are poor and stand -partially or wholly- outside the logic of honor and shame. In a sense, the Romans argued, all this made the *nobiles* more completely, more fully human, because less like the animals, than the common people. Their mode of being showed man at his best.

3. The socialization of the noble

As we saw, wealth -landed property- was the most important criterion of classification. For those without substantial landed property the gate to public office, to fame and glory, to immortality, was hermetically closed. From a modern point of view this seems highly unequitable. After all, merit doesn't follow wealth? And yet, even parvenus like Marius and Cicero never questioned the legitimacy of that criterion. They opposed their own virtue to the longer lineage of the *nobilitas*, not to its greater wealth. Apparently, they agreed that wealth was a *sine qua non* of virtue and the right to hold public office.

The ancients believed that they had good reasons to think so. To begin with, the poor were likely to misuse the power given to them. They could easily be bribed, and would probably plunder the treasury and the population. Not necessarily to enrich themselves: if a poor ruler were to refrain from such misuse, he would be unable to cover his expenses. For in Rome the magistrates were unsalaried. They had to live off their own means. To work for money was considered incompatible with the holding of an *officium*. For even if it left enough spare time, it implied dependence. Since the poor did not have a secure and independent source of income they had to earn their daily bread. In effect, they lacked independence, time, and money.

3.1. The few and the many

But the argument is more profound than that. What the above signifies is that the poor are necessarily too much concerned with the economic,[74] with their own interest, with *utilitas*, to be able to ascend to the political, to the interest in others, to the sphere of *honor*. They are too much imbued in the material to be able to rise to the spiritual. Because their base is so narrow, they cannot reach very high. On top of this, the poor tend to be ruled by impulse rather than reason, by short-term gratification of the senses, rather than long-term considerations of what is best. As a consequence, they are likely to neglect even *utilitas*, and succumb to pleasure -*voluptas*.

Here we have the distinction between the pleasurable, the useful and the honorable, that played such a prominent part in classical/classicist thought. The moral world of the common man lies between the poles of pleasure and utility. When he is good he will prefer the useful to the merely pleasurable. The noble man on the other hand should transcend both the pleasurable and the useful, and strive for the honorable. This cannot be expected of the common man; he is too poor for that. His 'honor' lies entirely in his being useful, whereas the true honor of the nobleman lies in something that goes beyond the useful, and is in the classical sense of the word not useful. That is to say: it is not immediately linked to the economic, to the material, to narrow self-interest. As always Cicero sums it up beautifully. 'Mankind falls into two classes, one unlearned and rustic, which always prefers *utilitas* to *honor*, and the other educated and urbane,[75] which places *dignitas* above all else. Consequently, the latter class of people give the first place to *laus*, *honor*, *gloria*, *fides*, *iustitia*, and all other virtues, while the former class puts the profits and emoluments of gain first. And also *voluptas*, which is the greatest enemy of the virtues and adulterates the true essence of the good by deceptive imitations, and which is most eagerly pursued by the worst, who place it above not only honorable things but also necessary things.'[76]

The destiny, the purpose of life of the commoner and the noble, the poor and the rich, are utterly different. Therefore they should also have a different upbringing, acquire a different kind of knowledge. The schooling and training of the first should be directed at *utilitas*. They should learn a trade, become craftsmen. Tellingly, the Romans regarded carpentry, medicine, and architecture as respectable trades, because of their great usefulness to the state. 'The crafts that are least worthy of approval', on the other hand were 'those that minister to *voluptas*: fishmongers, butchers, cooks, poulterers, fishermen, (..) perfumers, dancers, and the whole variety show.'[77]

The *nobilitas* too should be educated. The Romans did not consider wealth a sufficient condition for rulership. On the contrary, wealth that was not accompanied by the knowledge and the intent to use it in the right way, was particularly dangerous. But this elite education had to focus on something quite distinct, viz. on the creation of fine magistrates, great leaders of the state in war and peace. Its aim was emphatically uneconomic, use-less. Politics was its subject-matter, the capacity to excel in public office, of doing great deeds in the service of the state, its goal, *virtus* its standard and *honor* its device.

3.2. Prudentia

The kind of knowledge that had to be acquired by the *nobilitas* was unlike the knowledge of the craftsmen, which might be called technical or instrumental knowledge. But it was also unlike the knowledge of the philosopher, *sapientia*, for whom understanding of the whole scheme of things human and divine is the ultimate goal. The knowledge that the state's leaders had to possess was neither technical, nor theoretical. It was called practical knowledge: *prudentia*.

The meaning of this concept has been lost to modern thought. To be sure, we still speak of prudence sometimes, but in a more superficial sense. 'It might not be just, but under the circumstances it is the most prudent thing to do'; that is how we speak of prudence. Hence, it has the connotation of hard-hearted *Realpolitik* and unauthentic affability. To call a judgement or an act prudential is to recognize that it is smart and serviceable, but also morally not entirely right.

Related notions are judgement, tact, *Urteilskraft*, good taste, and common sense. The fact that prudence and its virtual synonyms seem more and more to disappear from our vocabulary indicates that the modern mind is ill at ease with these notions. They are not only a negation of what seems subjective, and therefore limiting one's freedom to do one's own thing, but are also rather undefinable. Therefore modern man would rather deny that they point out a kind of knowledge and keep silent about them.[†]

The Romans on the other hand regarded *prudentia* as supremely important. Cicero called it *ars vivendi*,[78] and 'the knowledge of things to be sought for and things to be avoided', i.e. virtues and vices.[79] Action, not reflection, is the aim of practical knowledge. Practical knowledge is knowledge how to act. For the prudent man, study is a means, not an end. He should not spend too much time on it and confine himself to the essentials of a subject-matter. Furthermore, his study should be action-oriented: it should

---

[†] The story of how the notion of knowledge became narrower, is part of the larger account of the rise of modernity. The culprit is the epistemological tradition that is usually said to have begun with Francis Bacon, to have been refined by Descartes, Locke and Hume, and to have been perfected by the logical positivists of this century. It has two variants: modern rationalism and empiricism. It has denounced both theoretical knowledge -*sophia* or *sapientia*- and practical knowledge -*phronèsis* or *prudentia*-; the first as unverifiable metaphysical speculation, and the second as a matter of valuation instead of fact. Both kinds of knowledge were hence reduced to the status of the merely subjective, the remaining field of objectivity being technical or instrumental knowledge. Because this kind of knowledge has expanded enormously over the last centuries, the empiricist/rationalist view has become predominant, and has convinced many that the subject-matters traditionally seen as theoretical or practical knowledge -such as metaphysics, law, history, and political science- should be approached as technical or instrumental knowledge as well, if they are to count as knowledge at all. The appeal of empiricism/rationalism to the modern mind can be understood only if one also sees its multifarious links with extra-scientific features of modernity. Its historical rootedness in *technè* -the knowledge of the common man- is particularly significant.

be concerned with finding solutions rather than causes. Looking for causes is important only to the extent that it helps to find solutions. There is no need to go any further. In this sense, the gentleman is always an amateur, a dilettante; the *savant*, or for that matter any professional, never a gentleman. Knowing too much about a subject is a sign of boorishness and pedantry. It proves that one does not lead a life of action. But practical knowledge is more than the antonym of theoretical knowledge. It is more than merely knowledge how to act. The action it is supposed to make possible and enhance is not just any action, but action towards the good, the virtuous. Practical knowledge is knowledge of *virtus*. Thus it is moral knowledge. In contrast with instrumental knowledge, which is also action-oriented, practical knowledge is concerned with the ends of life, with the good life.

The good life for whom? As has been set out, there was a permanent danger lurking in the background that noble feelings of superiority and disdain vis-à-vis the common man would cause the noblemen to revert, as Nietzsche said, to 'die Unschuld des Raubtier-Gewissens': the innocence of the predator's conscience.[80] Cicero was well aware of and more than a little worried about this danger. He repeatedly belabors the point that leadership requires that one is committed to the pursuit of the common good; otherwise, nobility becomes depraved and is misdirected to evil ends.[81] The 'Herrenmoral' should be checked and balanced by the 'Sklavenmoral', the competitive virtues by cooperative or social virtues. There are two of such cooperative or social virtues: '*iustitia*, the most splendid of the virtues, on account of which men are called *bonus*; and *beneficentia*, which is connected with it, and may also be called kindness -*benignitas*- or generosity *liberalitas*'.[82] It is due to these that the fellowship of men with one another -*societas*-and the communal life -*communitas*- are held together.[83]

The just man is the good man; but, as will be remembered, *vir bonus* was also the nobleman. Apparently, Cicero was reminding the *nobilitas* of something. There is no doubt that one man in particular was in his mind: Gaius Iulius Caesar, the outstanding aristocrat who had usurped all power, whose excellence was connected with his viciousness. Let that be a warning, Cicero seems to argue. For 'it is a hateful fact that loftiness and *magnitudo animi* all too easily give birth to an excessive desire for preeminence'.[84] The conclusion is that 'if the loftiness of spirit that reveals itself amid danger and toil is empty of justice, if it fights not for the common good -*pro salute communi*- but for its own advantages, it is a vice. It is not merely unvirtuous; it of a barbarous nature and revolting to *humanitas*.'[85] Hence, the supreme importance of the 'quieter' virtues: their prime purpose is the domestication, the 'socialization' of the strong and the mighty.[†]

3.3. Iustitia

Without justice the state would fall apart. 'For just as in the music of harps
and flutes or in the voice of singers a certain harmony of the different tones
must be preserved, the interruption or violation of which is intolerable to
trained ears, and as this perfect agreement and harmony is produced by the
proportionate blending of unlike tones, so also is the *civitas* made harmonious
by agreement among dissimilar elements, brought about by a fair and
reasonable blending together of the highest and the lowest orders and those
in between, just as if they were musical tones. What the musicians call
harmonia in song is *concordia* in the *civitas*, the strongest and best bond of
permanent union in any *res publica*; and such a pact can never be brought
about without *iustitia*.'[86]

The opposite of *concordia* is *discordia*, which means social conflict,
social strife. *Concordia* therefore connotes a situation of social accord and
tranquility, of peace within the *civitas*. It was considered of supreme
importance, for without it victory in warfare was impossible. Indeed, the
enemy was likely to take advantage of the situation to attack either the *res
publica* or its allies. Internal peace was conceived of as the *sine qua non* of
collective survival. And justice was its linchpin.[‡] Furthermore, *discordia* also

---

[†] A celebrated exposition of this *topos* of primal power, based on sheer force, which is
subsequently 'humanized' and put in the service of justice, can be found in Polybius, *Histories*,
VI.5 'What then are the beginnings I speak of and what is the first origin of political societies?
When owing to floods, famines, failure of crops or other such causes there occurs such a
destruction of the human race as tradition tells us has more than once happened, and as we must
believe will often happen again, all arts and crafts perishing at the same time, then in the course
of time, when springing from the survivors as from seeds men have again increased in numbers
and just like other animals form herds -it being a matter of course that they too should herd
together with those of their kind owing to their natural weakness- it is a necessary consequence
that the man who excels in bodily strength and in courage will lead and rule over the rest. We
observe and should regard as the most genuine work of nature this very phenomenon in the case
of the other animals which act purely by instinct and among whom the strongest are always
indisputably the masters -I speak of bulls, boars, cocks, and the like. It is probable then that at
the beginning men lived like this, herding together like animals and following the lead of the
strongest and bravest, the ruler's strength being here the sole limit to his power and the name we
should give his rule being monarchy. But when in time feelings of sociability and companionship
begin to grow in such gatherings of men, then kingship has struck root; and the notions of
goodness, justice, and their opposites begin to arise in men.'

[‡] To the Romans peace -*pax*- always meant first and foremost internal peace. External peace was
considered a mixed blessing. Following Polybius, *Histories*, VI.18.2, who declared that an
external enemy assured *concordia*, many Roman authors saw warfare as the means *par excellence*
to avert social discontent. Especially Livy abounds in references to this point. But see also

ushered in the overthrow of the constitution, for it was a sign that some or all classes of citizens were dissatisfied with the status quo. *Concordia* on the other hand assured stability *-firmitas*. Hence, the importance of *iustitia*, which was considered indispensable in bringing about social accord.

Iustitia is defined as granting to every man what is his own: *suum quique*.[87] In *De Officiis* Cicero explains that this implies 'first, that one should harm no one; and secondly, that one serve the common interest'.[88] What comprises 'harm', depends on a person's legal status. It was impossible to be unjust towards slaves. They were subject to the legal *dominium* of another person, and technically as much his property as his house, over which the master had absolute power. Consistently, Roman law allowed the slave-owner to punish, sell or kill his slaves at will. Abusing a slave was in effect equal to inflicting harm on his master. And a master abusing his own slave was harming himself; not in the last place because the abuse demonstrated a lack of *continentia* on the side of the master.[89]

Justice becomes relevant only when a person is *persona sui iuris*, possessing rights of his own. That is to say, anyone who was not a slave; all free persons. The Romans spoke of *servitus* on an individual and on a collective level. It made as much sense to them as it makes to us to say that a people was being enslaved or held in slavery. As *servitus* was the opposite of *libertas*, the twofold meaning of the first concept shows that the latter was also used in two ways: to denote the freedom of the *civis* as well as the freedom of the *civitas*.[90] *Iustitia* upholds liberty in both senses.

The citizen is harmed when his freedom in respect of public or private

---

Plutarch, *Cato Maior*, c.26-27. Cato, sent out on a diplomatic mission to Carthage, found out that the second Punic war had by no means crushed or impoverished the city. On the contrary, 'he found it teeming with a new generation of fighting men, overflowing with wealth, amply stocked with weapons and military supplies of every kind, and full of confidence at this revival of its strength. He drew the conclusion that (..) unless they found means to crush a city which had always borne them an undying hatred and had now recovered its power to an incredible extent, they would find themselves as gravely threatened as before.' Upon his return to Rome, whenever in the senate 'his opinion was called for on any subject, he invariably concluded with the words: "And furthermore it is my opinion that Carthage must be destroyed!"'. Everybody knows this *dictum* of course, but the continuation of the story is perhaps less well known: 'on the other hand Publius Scipio Nasica made a point of adding the phrase, "And in my view Carthage must be spared!"' Let it not be thought that it was weakness or benevolence that made him say so. 'Scipio had already observed, no doubt, that the Roman people was by this time indulging in many excesses, and that the insolence occasioned by its prosperity prompted it to cast aside the control of the senate and force the whole state to follow in whichever direction the impulses of the masses might lead. *He was therefore in favor of keeping the fear of Carthage hanging over the people as a check upon their arrogance* (emphasis added), and he evidently also believed that although Carthage was not strong enough to threaten the Romans, she was not so weak that they could afford to despise her.' Here we have the doctrine that external war promotes internal peace.

law is violated. The most important freedom in respect of public law was the *ius sufragii*, the right to take part in the political deliberations and vote. 'To be deprived of the suffrage (..) would be tyrannical.'[91] The most important freedom in respect of private law is the freedom of the citizens 'to hold on to what is theirs'.[92] The law protects the citizens and their private property against ill-treatment -*iniuria*- and theft -*furtum*.[93] Without it the *res publica* cannot survive. Cicero insisted that the protection of private property is no less essential than the protection of the citizen himself. It is necessary even among bandits. 'For if anyone steals or snatches something from one of his fellows in banditry, he leaves no place for himself within the gang of bandits.'[94] Stealing is coequal to 'a violation of the law of human fellowship'.[95]

As to the legal protection of the citizens against ill-treatment, the sources are somewhat vague in their pronouncement of what was considered ill-treatment. Physical ill-treatment such as causing mutilation or a fracture was of course punishable. In addition to that at some time or another some insults, whether 'real' -like the spitting in someone's face-, verbal or written, seem to have come under the law as well, drawing honor into the sphere of the law. This is confirmed by a passage in *De Re Publica*, quoted by St.Augustine, in which Cicero says that 'our Twelve Tables, though they provided the death penalty for only a few crimes, did provide it for any person who sang or composed a song which contained slander or insult to anyone else. This was an excellent rule, for our mode of life ought to be liable to judgement by the magistrates and the courts of law, but not by clever poets; nor ought we to be subject to disgrace unless we have an opportunity to answer and defend ourselves in a court of law'.[96]

On the other hand, there is sufficient evidence to suggest that the legal prohibition of slander and libel of private persons -*laesae maiestatis* was an entirely different matter- were far from being considered crucial. Roman literature and law hardly mention them in a legal setting, even though it is obvious that the ancients were great slanderers. Cicero for one was quite fond of making cruel jokes at the expense of his legal opponents and enemies. This aroused a good deal of ill-feeling against him, we are told, but legal repercussions are never even hinted at.[97] And neither, for that matter, were 'extra-legal' repercussions. Montaigne, for one, was highly amazed that, contrary to the custom in his own days 'of exactly weighing and measuring words and making that a question of honor, (..) it was not like that in ancient times among the Greeks and the Romans. It often seemed strange and new to me to watch them giving each other the lie and insulting each other without it starting a brawl. Their laws of duty took some other road than ours. (..) Words were avenged by words alone, without further consequence'; that is to say, without a demand for satisfaction in the form of a duel.[98] Tellingly, the idea of conceiving of invective as a legal matter never seems to enter Montaigne's mind. In that at least the ancien régime was at one with the ancients: honor was one thing, the law another.[†]

[†] Montaigne certainly was not the only one wondering about the ancients' apparent indifference to invective. To the mind of the ancien régime reputation was so important that it was generally considered a part of one's private property. See e.g. Adam Smith, *Lectures on Jurisprudence*, rep.of 1762-63, I.10ff. 'The first and chief design of all civil governments is (..) to preserve justice among the members of the state and prevent all encroachments on the individuals in it, from others of the same society. (..) Justice is violated whenever one is deprived of what he had a right to and could justly demand from others, or rather when we do him any injury or hurt without a cause. (..) First, he may be injured as a man; secondly, as a member of a family; and thirdly, as a citizen or member of the state.(..) A man merely as a man may be injured in three respects, either first, in his person; or secondly, in his *reputation*; or thirdly, in his estate.' (emphasis added) In his discussion of reputation Smith distinguishes between *iura perfecta* and *iura imperfecta* In I.14ff. he asserts that 'perfect rights are those which we have a title to demand and if refused to compel an other to perform. What they call imperfect rights are those which correspond to those duties which ought to be performed to us by others but which we have no title to compel them to perform; they having it entirely in their power to perform them or not. (..) But when we use the word right in this way it is not in a proper but a metaphorical sense. (..) The former are the rights which we are to consider, the latter not belonging properly to jurisprudence, but rather to a system of morals as they do not fall under the jurisdiction of the laws'. A man is injured in his perfect right 'when one endeavors to bring his character below what is the common standard among men. If one calls another a fool, a knave, or a rogue he injures him in his reputation, as he does not then give him that share of good fame which is common to almost all men, perhaps 99 of 100'. Imperfect rights see to one's reputation as far as it transcends the standard level. 'If one calls another an honest good natured man, tho perhaps he deserved a much higher character' one merely violates his moral right, behaving improperly rather than against the law. Hence, the honor due to a gentleman, as opposed to the respect due to all men, is not a question of law, but of *decorum*. In II.135ff. Smith elaborates on the *iura perfecta*. They are divided into real affronts, 'which are done by some action in presence of others, that tends to make one meanly thought', verbal affronts, and written affronts i.e. libels. As to real affronts 'the law has been apt to consider these rather in the sense they were taken by the old law (i.e. Roman law, A.K.) than in that which is suitable to the customs of modern times, That is, rather as assault or battery than as an affront; and accordingly has given but a very small satisfaction for them. And to this in a great measure may be ascribed the great frequency of duelling.' This is a highly informative passage. It tells us that (1) in speaking of *iura perfecta* Smith neither meant positive law nor unchanging natural law, but a law suitable to modern times, that (2) duelling is the effect of a non-conformity of positive law to this suitable law, and that (3) the positive law of his own days did not, by and large, recognize and enforce man's *iura perfecta*. Smith admits that 'the smallness of the punishment had not indeed the effect of introducing duels into Rome, but the different circumstances of the nations easily accounts for that', according to him. Much the same goes for verbal affronts, like giving the lie. 'It is entirely from *this new notion of honor* (emphasis added) that the injury of such affronts arose. This owed its first origins to the judicial combat which was established by law, but has several other concomitant causes which have kept it up till this day, after the judicial combat has been 300 or 400 years in disuse. Before that time these injuries were considered merely by the hurt they did the person, and the punishment is accordingly very small, and so inadequate to the injury that no

Justice demands that one should harm nobody else, but it demands something else as well. 'There are some who (..) claim to be attending to their own business, and appear to do no one any injustice. But though they are free from one type of injustice, they run into another: such men abandon the *vita societatis*, because they contribute to it nothing of their devotion, nothing of their effort, nothing of their means.'[99] The argument seems to be that one cannot expect the *civitas* to protect its *cives* against harm, if these in their turn refuse to contribute to its protection. Private rights can be maintained only when the public *officia* are not dodged. What your country can do for you depends on what you do for your country.

Man is led by his vices to commit injustice. Cicero explicitly mentions fear -*metus*-, *avaritia*, and the desire for power -*opes*-, and he alludes to *luxuria* and *ambitio*, as reasons why harm is inflicted,[100] and he reports as causes of the second type of injustice the wish not to incur enemies, toil, or expense, as well as *neglegentia*, laziness -*pigritia*-, *inertia*, and the pursuit of some private business.[101]

One category of unjust men is singled out by Cicero: those who mind their own business. He seems to be particularly worried about them. This category consists not of entrepreneurs, but of philosophers, chiefly epicurean and Platonist. Both schools advise their followers to stay aloof from public life, the first in the name of happiness, the second in the name of truth. 'Disdaining the very things for which most men vigorously strive and even fight one another to death, they count them as nothing.'[102] These men should know better; they embody reason, the highest faculty of man. And they are the teachers of mankind; their instruction ought to strengthen the ties of community, not to severe them. Otherwise, 'learning (..) would seem solitary and barren'.[103]

Now let us go back to the concept of *prudentia*. Practical knowledge is knowledge how to act virtuously. It is moral knowledge, concerned with the

---

one will think it worth his while to sue for it. We see that formerly those actions and words which we think the greatest affronts were little thought of. Plato in his dialogues commonly introduces Socrates giving the lie to those whom he converses with, which is taken as no more than ordinary conversation.' As to written injuries or libels, finally, Smith maintains that, being more malicious and deliberate, these are generally more severely punishable by law. But much depends on the form of government. In aristocratic governments they are punished with more severity than in monarchical governments, 'for a libel which would not affect the king, as being too much above such scandal, would greatly irritate a lesser lord'. But it is in democracies that libels are least taken notice of. Of course Rome serves as an example. 'In old Rome, in the monarchical and aristocratical governments, the publishers of libels were punished with death. (..) But in the time of the democratical government of Rome this punishment, which was a very unreasonable one, was taken away, and great freedom in this respect indulged to the people. But when the monarchical form of government was again restored, the old punishment returned.'

realization of the ends of life, with the good life. In its turn, the good life is primarily defined as the common good, *salus populi*.[104] Hence, serving the community as a leader of men is the destiny and the duty of the prudent, i.e. the noble man; therein he can show his virtue. But this conception of the good life is clearly a different, more restrictive, view of the good life. It is the good life of the nobleman as opposed to that of the commoner.

Apparently, there are two distinct conceptions of the good life, one in which the *boni* and the *multi* share, but also another which is the privilege of the first. The virtue that is associated with the good life in general, and is therefore the virtue relevant and pertaining to all men, outstanding and ordinary, is *iustitia*. It is the precondition of *libertas* and *concordia*, and thus a warrant against tyranny -*servitus*- and civil war -*discordia*-.

It is fraught with meaning that the ancient historians portrayed the introduction of the Twelve Tables -according to the Romans the fountain of their laws- as the result of popular agitation against the unlimited power of the consuls. Livy has it that 'on several successive days (the tribune Gaius Terentillus Arsa) made inflammatory speeches to the mob, inveighing bitterly against the arrogance of the patricians as a whole and more particularly against the excessive powers of the consuls, which he denounced as intolerable in a free *civitas*. Consul, he declared, might be a less hateful word than king, but in actual fact consular government was even more oppressive than monarchy, in that the country had taken two *domini* in place of one, both of them with unlimited, infinite power, who without any sort of check upon themselves used the whole terror of the law with all the penalties it sanctioned for the crushing of the common people. "Therefore", he said, "it is my intention to propose a measure which will put a stop to this irresponsibility. Five commissioners must be appointed to codify the laws which limit and define the *imperium* of the consuls; that done, the consuls will be bound to use against the people only the power granted to them by popular assent, instead of giving the force of law, as they do at present, to their own arbitrary passions"'.[105]

If it is true that there is a deep relation between justice and ordinary life, it is perhaps not surprising that today, in the age of the common man, all the other virtues seem to have eclipsed into insignificance beside the virtue of justice. To the classical/classicist mind such an immersion in one of the virtues, albeit an important one, would have been the height of imprudence: lack of practical knowledge.

To the ancients justice was not even the only cooperative or social virtue. As has already been set out, they discerned a second social virtue, viz. *beneficentia*, which is also called *benignitas* or *liberalitas*. This virtue is connected with justice, in that it is also supposed to hold together the community and fellowship of men. It comprises both kindness expressed in

personal services and in giving money.[106] Judging from the number of
capita in *De Officiis* devoted to this subject, Cicero considered it of the
greatest consequence.

3.4. Beneficentia

If justice is a virtue for all men, *beneficentia* is within the reach of outstanding men only. For it depends on one's capabilities, financial and otherwise,
and these are naturally distributed very unequally. It is every citizen's duty
not to harm anyone, and to serve the common interest. These are expected of
both the few and the many. But the few have an *officium* in addition to these:
the duty of *beneficentia*. 'Nothing is more suited to human nature.'[107]

The political significance of *beneficentia* stems from the typically
aristocratic preoccupation with the question how to make the many submit to
the command or power of the few, how to bring about the obeyance of the
masses to the elite. But at the same time, like justice, it purges the overriding
power of the strong of its primitive egotism, and turns its strength to a good,
social use.

Cicero distinguishes various reasons of submittance, the worst being fear
and the best love.[108] Fear is the mode of the tyrant, but it is a poor basis of
power, for men hate the man they fear, and will sooner or later dispose of
him. Hence, 'those who wish to be feared cannot but themselves be afraid of
the very men who fear them.'[109] When one of the flatterers of Dionysius the
elder, the tyrant of Syracuse, named Damocles, 'dilated in conversation upon
his troops, his resources, the splendors of his despotism, the magnitude of his
treasures, the stateliness of his palaces, and said that no one had ever been
happier', the tyrant replied, '"Would you then (..) like to have a taste of it
yourself and make trial of my good fortune?" On his admitting his desire to
do so Dionysius had him seated on a couch of gold covered with beautiful
woven tapestries embroidered with magnificent designs, and had several
sideboards set out with richly chased gold and silver plate. Next a table was
brought and chosen boys of rare beauty were ordered to take their places and
wait upon him with eyes fixed attentively upon his motions. There were
perfumes, garlands; incense was burnt; the tables were loaded with the
choicest banquet; Damocles thought himself a lucky man. In the midst of all
this display Dionysius had a gleaming sword, attached to a horse-hair, let
down from the ceiling in such a way that it hung over the neck of this happy
man. And so he had no eye either for those beautiful attendants, or the richly
wrought plate, nor did he reach out his hand to the table; presently the
garlands slipped from their place of their own accord; at length he besought

the tyrant to let him go, as by now he was sure he had no wish to be happy'.[†110]

It is better to be loved by the masses.[‡] This love -*amor*- is a kind of friendship -*amicitia*- or concord.[111] It comprises admiration -*admiratio*-, trust -*fides*-, and good will -*benevolentia*.[112] Not surprisingly, Cicero singles out justice as a particularly important virtue to secure the friendship of the crowd. It is the virtue the common man most of all takes an interest in. But other virtues can make the relationship even better. From this *beneficentia* derives its meaning. It is supposed to inspire and express gratitude -*gratia*-, sealing the bonds of friendship.[113]

Beneficentia is shown in two ways, 'either by personal services, or by giving money. The latter is easier, especially for a wealthy man; the former, however, is both more brilliantly illustrious, and more worthy of a brave and notable man. For both involve a liberal willingness to gratify others; but the one draws upon the money-chest, the other upon one's virtue'.[114] Financial generosity has clear drawbacks. It drains the very source of kindness, it tends to corrupt the receiver, and it brings robbery in its wake. 'For when men, because of their giving, begin to be in need themselves, they are forced to lay hands on others' goods.'[115] Nevertheless, 'sometimes one should give money; that type of kindness should not be entirely rejected'.[116]

'In general there are two kinds of men who give amply, the one extravagant -*prodigus*- and the other *liberalis*. The extravagant, with their banquets, their gladiatorial performances, their spectacular provisions of

---

[†] The *exemplum* of Dionysius the elder was staple fare in the ancien régime. Every educated person must have been acquainted with it. The sword hanging over Damocles' head has even become proverbial. But the other stories that were told about the tyrant are no less amusing and instructive. Cicero, *Tusc.Disp.*, V.58-59, tells us among other things, that 'he went so far as to have his daughters taught the use of the razor that he might not put his neck at the mercy of the barber; accordingly the young princesses, reduced to the mean employment of drudges, shaved their father's hair and beard like mere hairdressers; and all the same, when they were older, he took the iron utensil out of the hands of these girls and arranged for them to single his hair and beard with red-hot walnut shells'. Furthermore, 'having surrounded the chamber in which he slept with a wide trench and fitted a gangway over the trench by means of a small wooden bridge, we are told that he drew in this bridge himself as often as he closed the door of the chamber'. The point is that the tyrant can trust no one of some standing -not even his own family. He has to surround himself with creatures who are entirely dependent upon him: slaves or others of low descent, and foreigners. Hence, the view was established that a monarch associating with such people was a token of impending tyranny.

[‡] There is yet another option. Submittance may be effected by 'lavish distributions' or 'financial reward', that is to say the masses' loyalty can be bought. But 'things are in a bad way when what ought to be achieved through virtue is attempted by means of money'. Cf. Cicero, *De Off.*, II.21-22

games and wild animals in combat, pour out their money on things for which they will be remembered briefly, if at all. The liberal, however, out of their resources, ransom captives from bandits, or assume their friends' debts, or help them to finance their daughters' marriage, or give them assistance in acquiring and enlarging their property.'[117]

This is not a limitative enumeration of the targets of extravagant and liberal spending. What Cicero wants to point out is that true liberality is concerned with real needs, whereas extravagance gratifies only the pleasures of the moment. Hence, 'the former is the mark of a serious and great man, the latter of those who flatter the people, as it were, using pleasures to tickle the fickle fancies of the masses'.[118] Thus, liberality must be considered a virtue, but prodigality is a vice.[119] In fact, 'to be able to act with liberality (..) is without a doubt the greatest fruit that money can bear'.[120] One certainly 'must attend to one's personal wealth, for it is despicable to let that slip away, but in such a way that there is no suspicion of *illiberalitas* or *avaritia*.'[121] It is fitting, therefore, to be bountiful in giving to others what is due to them, and avoid harshness in exacting what is due from them. 'Being fair, affable, often yielding much of what is rightfully one's own, certainly shunning ligitation as far as possible, and perhaps even a little further than that.'[122] In addition to all this, hospitality must be praised, for it is also a kind of liberality.[123]

In theory at least *liberalitas* pertained exclusively to the private sphere. Indeed, what was considered generosity there, constituted a form of corruption in the public sphere. Buying votes, raising an army with one's own resources, and the distribution of corn at a low price or free of charge, at the expense of the treasury, were all seen as detrimental to the state.[124] The generosity that is expressed by personal services on the other hand need not be limited to the private sphere. Help and assistance may 'be bestowed both on the nation as a whole and on individual citizens'.[125] Though undoubtedly the nature of these services was manifold, legal counsel and defense and the administration of public affairs counted as the foremost *beneficia*, regarding respectively individuals and the body politic. If well done, these were the most excellent ways of serving one's fellow citizens and the *res publica* as a whole, because these were the pillars which most supported *iustitia*.[126]

NOTES

1. Seneca, *Ep.ad Luc.*, XLVII.11: 'Sic cum inferiore vivas, quemadmodum tecum superiorem velis vivere'. Cf. *Scriptores Historiae Augustae*, Vita Alexandri Severi, 51: 'quod tibi fieri non vis, alteri ne feceris', known as the Golden Rule.

2. Cf. Roloff, 'Maiores bei Cicero', in: Oppermann 1983, pp.274-322

3. Cicero, *Tusc.Disp.*, I.2; Cf. Cicero, *De Rep.*, I.34; I.70

4. Cicero, *De Rep.*, V.1 This fragment was known through Augustine, who quoted it in *De Civitate Dei*, II.21

5. This is not to say that Greek historic nostalgia did not exist at all. In the works of the fourth-century orators Isocrates and Demosthenes for instance it can be found in abundance. But compare Thucydides, *Pelop. War*, I.1: 'After looking back into (the past) as far as I can, all the evidence leads me to conclude that these periods were not great periods either in warfare or in anything else'.

6. Sallust, *Bell.Cat.*, X

7. Polybius, *Hist.*, XXXI.25

8. Livy, XXXIX.6

9. Plutarch, *Cato Maior*, c.27

10. Cicero, *De Off.*, II.3

11. Sallust, *Bell.Cat.*, XI

12. Tacitus, *Agricola*, 11

13. Also known as *De Re Rustica*.

14. Cato, *De Agri Cult.*, I.1

15. E.g. Cicero, *Pro Roscio*, 50; Cicero, *De Senec.*, 51-60; Horace, *Epod.*, II 'Happy the man who, far away from business cares, like the pristine race of mortals, works his ancestral acres with his steers'; Virgil, *Georg.*, II.458-68; Xenophon, *Oecon.*, V-VI

16. The idealization of the peasant dates from the second half of the eighteenth century. As is to be expected Rousseau was the trendsetter. It is still very much alive today. The Rousseau of the twentieth century -Heidegger- also put his trust in peasants. Allan Megill in his *Prophets of Extremity*, p.135, recounts that Heidegger, after receiving his second call as an *Ordinarius* to the prestigious university of Berlin, withdrew from the city and returned to his hut in the *Schwarzwald*. 'I listened to what the mountains and the forests and the farms said. I came to my old friend, a 75-year-old-peasant. He had read about the call to Berlin in the newspaper. What would he say? Slowly he fixed the sure gaze of his eyes on mine, and keeping his mouth tightly shut, he placed his true and considerate hand on my shoulder -ever so slightly, he shook his head. That meant -absolutely no!'

17. MacMullen 1974, pp.28-32; e.g. Horace, *Odes*, III.1 'I hate the uninitiated crowd and keep them far away'.

18. In the last two centuries of the republic the *comitia tributa* was the chief legislative body. In addition to that, it elected the *magistratus minores*. The legislative power of the *comitia centuriata* was by and large limited to declarations of war. Further, it elected the *magistratus maiores*, i.e. the consuls, the praetors, and the censors. See Nicolet 1988, p.84, p.224 ff.; Sherwin-White 1987; Loewenstein 1973, pp.106-113

19. Cicero *Pro Roscio*, 75

20. Varro, *Rer. Rust.*, II, praef.1; III.1.4 'And not only is the tilling of the fields more ancient -it is more noble. It is therefore not without reason that our ancestors tried to entice their citizens back from the city to the country.' A reference to the Gracchii?

21. Cicero, *De Off.*, I.150-151

22. Xenophon, *Oecon.*, see infra.

23. Cicero, *De Off.*, I.150

24. Cicero, *De Off.*, I.151

25. Livy, III.26

26. In the introductory chapters of Sallust, *Bell. Cat.*, XII and XXXVII, for instance, poverty is most emphatically lauded, and the onset of wealth is pointed out as the main cause of the moral decline of the nation, but at the same time Sallust takes the side of the rich and prominent, and speaks most depreciatingly of the poor masses.

27. Wood 1991, p.118; see for a comparable judgement MacMullen 1974, p.116n91

28. Plutarch, *Cato Maior*, c.4

29. Giardina, 'The merchant', in: Giardina (ed.) 1993, p.260

30. See for such a view Wood 1991, p.118; MacMullen 1974, p.114

31. Cicero, *De Off.*, II.87

32. Xenophon, *Oecon.*, IV.2-3

33. Xenophon, *Oecon.*. VI.9-10

34. Morel, 'The craftsman', in: Andrea Giardina (ed.) 1993, p.214

35. Cicero, *De Off.*, II.87

36. MacMullen 1974, p.117

37. Cicero, *De Off.*, II.87; cf. I.92

38. See esp. Juvenalis, *Sat.*; Petronius *Sat.*

39. Plutarch, *Sulla*, c.1

40. MacMullen 1974, pp.88-102

41. In *De Off.*, I.34-40 Cicero distinguished two kinds of just wars. On the on hand those fought for survival, and on the other hand those fought for honor and glory. The first kind involves existence the second rulership. Presumably, this scheme excludes wars for profit. See however, II.85 which seems hard to reconcile with this view.

42. Nicolet, 'The citizen; the political man', in: Giardina (ed.) 1993, pp.16-25

43. Cicero, *De Off.*, II.4, 'honoribus inservire coepi'

44. Most enlightening on this topic is Nicolet 1988

45. Originally, only landed property was taken into account, but probably from the end of the fourth century B.C. on other kinds of property were also included in the calculation.

46. Livy, I.43

47. In Cicero's days there were apparently more citizens in the proletarian *centuriae* than in all other *centuriae* taken together.

48. The ancient texts are not particularly lucid about the reform. And the text of the most articulate *passus* -Cicero, *De Rep.*, II.39-40- is uncertain, because it rests on a medieval correction of the manuscript. A long tradition of scholarship, going back to the sixteenth century, has it that the reform brought the total number of *centuriae* to 373, extrapolating the seventy *centuriae* of the first class to the other classes (18+(5x70)+5=373). This goes counter to the aforementioned *passus* of Cicero, however, and it is not attested by any text. See Nicolet 1988, pp.221-222

49. Cic., *Pro Sestio*, 95; See Meyer, 'Vom Griechischen und Römischen Staatsgedanken', in: Klein 1966, p.80

50. Cicero, *De Rep.*, I.67 Cicero here paraphrases Plato, *Politeia*, 562c-563e. Of course, the readers of the ancien régime had no knowledge of this exact *passus*, as this work was rediscovered only in the nineteenth century, but it is representative of the way the Romans thought about democracy. Under certain circumstances, it might work for some time, but chances were that it quickly degenerated into a form of mob-rule.

51. Cicero, *De Rep.*, I.68

52. Cicero, *Pro Flacco*, 7.15-16

53. Livy, I.9

54. The *nobilitas* possessed one legal privilege, the *ius imaginum*. See Polybius, *Hist.*, VI.53-55 Due to its avoidance of intermarriage with plebeians, the ancient patriciate had shrunk considerably by the end of the republic. Of the seventy *gentes* of the early republic only fifteen or so are represented in the late-republican senate. Augustus turned the *nobilitas* into a closed caste. Consequently, after the second century A.D. the *nobilitas* had disappeared from the annals of history. See Gelzer, 1962/64, vol.I, pp.147-150

55. Cicero, *De Off.*, II.44

56. Cf. Montesquieu, *Esprit*, IV.2 'On n'y juge les actions des hommes comme bonne, mais comme belle; comme juste, mais comme grandes; comme raisonnables, mais comme extraordinaire'.

57. Adkins 1975

58. Significantly, Homer's writings were highly esteemed by the romantics, whereas earlier generations had judged them uncouth and barbaric. See Highet 1985, ch.19

59. Praz 1970

60. Cicero, *De Off.*, II.29-38, clearly recognizes the force of sheer admiration as a ground for accepting rulership.

61. The classic accounts of the Roman *nobilitas* are still Mommsen, *Römisches Staatsrecht*, (1871/88) and Gelzer. 'Die Nobilität der Römischen Republik' (1912) and 'Die Nobilität der Kaiserzeit' (1915), both included in Gelzer 1962/64, vol.I, pp.17-135 and 136-153 resp. The first treatise is translated with some revisions as *The Roman Nobility*, Oxford 1969. *Contra* Mommsen, Gelzer defends the view that *nobilitas* was confined to those whose ancestors included a consul or a military tribune with consular powers.

62. Brunt 1982, who defends Mommsen's view against Gelzer's revisionism.

63. Cicero, *Pro Plancio*, 60

64. Sallust, *Bel.Iug.*, LXIII.6-7

65. Gelzer 1962/64, vol.I, pp.59-60

66. Brunt 1982, p.15

67. Gelzer, 1962/64, vol.I, pp.50-57; Beard and Crawford 1985, p.48

68. Plato's *Politeia* is of course the paradigmatic statement of this world view. Cf. Lovejoy 1964

69. Plutarch, *Gaius Marius*, c.3; Sallust, *Bell.Iug.*, LXIII Marius 'had in abundance every qualification (for the consulship), except an ancient lineage'.

70. Plutarch, *Cicero*, c.1

71. Plutarch, *Cato Maior*, c.1 'Now it being the custom among Romans to call those who, having no repute by birth, made themselves eminent by their own exertions, new men or upstarts, they called even Cato himself so, and so he confessed himself to be as to any public distinction or employment, but yet asserted that in the exploits and virtues of his ancestors he was very ancient.'

72. Sallust, *Bell.Iug.*, LXXXV

73. See Hellegouarc'h 1972; The jurists of the classical period of Roman law distinguished between *honestiores* and *humiliores*. See Garnsey 1970, pp.221-233

74. Here, and in the following the notion of economics is used in its ancient rather than its modern sense.

75. Cicero uses the words *humanus* and *politus* here. The present author translates 'educated' and 'urbane', in order to stress the contrast with the unlearned -*indoctus*- and rustic -*agrestus*- referred to in the same sentence. This is not as free a translation as it might appear at first sight. See infra.

76. Cicero, *De Part.Orat.*, 90

77. Cicero, *De Off.*, I.150-151 Carpentry is mentioned in Cicero, *De Rep.*, II.39

78. Cicero, *De Fin.*, V.16

79. Cicero, *De Off.*, I.153

80. Nietzsche, *Zur Genealogie der Moral*, Erste Abhandlung, 11

81. Cicero, *De Off.*, I.26; I.62-64; I.157

82. Cicero, *De Off.*, I.20

83. Cicero, *De Off.*, I.20

84. Cicero, *De Off.*, I.64

85. Cicero, *De Off.*, I.63

86. Cicero, *De Rep.*, II.69 Because it is quoted by St.Augustine in *De Civ.Dei*, II.21 this passage was known in the ancien régime.

87. Cicero, *De Off.*, I.15; *De Leg.*, I.19; *De Fin.*, V.65-67; *Digests*, I.I.X.1; St.Augustine, *De Civ.Dei*, XIX.21

88. Cicero, *De Off.*, I.31

89. At *De Off.*, I.41 Cicero argues that we should be just even to slaves, which seems to contradict the general use of the concept of *iustitia*. Probably, Cicero stretches the meaning of the word at this point. What he means is perhaps that one should treat his slaves with *clementia*, and employ *severitas* when one cannot otherwise control them. Cf.II.24 One's honor demands it. On Roman slavery, see: Veyne 1992, pp.51-70; Finley 1980; Vogt 1974

90. See Wirzubski 1950, p.3; Cicero, *De Rep.*, II.43

91. Cicero, *De Rep.*, II.39

92. Cicero, *De Off.*, II.73; Cf.II.78 'It is the proper function of a citizenship and a city to ensure for everyone a free and unworried guardianship of his possessions.' On the basis of utterances such as these, it has been argued, most recently by Wood 1988, p.132, that 'Cicero (..) is the first important social and political thinker to affirm unequivocally that the basic purpose of the state is the protection of private property. Thereby he is the first, with some qualification, to offer a non-ethical conception of the chief end of the state. Unlike Plato and Aristotle, he does not conceive of the state fundamentally in moral terms, that is, as a means of shaping human souls, of creating men of virtue'. Hence, Cicero appears as a proto-Lockean apologist of private property. This conclusion seems one-sided, to say the least, and evidently inspired by Marxist preconceptions of the course and the purpose of history.

93. This is a slight simplification. On the various kinds of *delicta privata*, see Kaser 1986, pp.226-235. On *crimina*, see Mommsen 1899

94. Cicero, *De Off.*, II.40

95. Cicero, *De Off.*, I.21 *Iustitia* is what makes the difference between conquest and theft on a grand scale, between states and large robber bands. Cf.St.Augustine, *De Civ.Dei*, IV.4, who probably derives the whole of his argument from Cicero, *De Rep.*, III.23ff, which is lost. Interestingly, the crook in Sylvester Stallone's 1993 movie 'Cliffhanger' obliquely refers to St.Augustine: 'Kill a few and you're a murderer, kill a million and you're a conqueror'.

96. Cicero, *De Rep.*, IV.12; St.Augustine, *De Civ.Dei*, II.9 Horace was apparently worried about the possibility that his writing might get him into trouble. See *Sat.*, II.1, where it is said that 'the courts take cognizance of and pass judgement upon any person writing ill of another'. The *Codex* also addresses the question of insult -*convicium*- in various places. See Mommsen 1899, pp.784-808 E.g.IX.35.5 *Veritas convicii non excusat iniuriam*, an insult is not remitted if it is true.

97. Plutarch, *Cicero*, c.27 and passim

98. Montaigne, *Essais*, II.18

99. Cicero, *De Off.*, I.29

100. Cicero, *De Off.*, I.24-26

101. Cicero, *De Off.*, I.28

102. Cicero, *De Off.*, I.28 Cicero is referring to Plato's teachings here, but his comment applies to the epicureans with equal force.

103. Cicero, *De Off.*, I.157

104. Cicero, *De Leg.*, III.8

105. Livy, III.9 Cf. Cicero, *De Off.*, II.42 'This, therefore, is manifest: the men who are usually chosen to rule are those who have a great reputation among the masses for justice.'

106. Cicero, *De Off.*, II.52

107. Cicero, *De Off.*, I.42

108. Cicero, *De Off.*, II.23ff As usual, Cicero's use of concepts is not wholly consistent. For the sake of clarity, his syntax is somewhat streamlined by the present author.

109. Cicero, *De Off.*, II.24

110. Cicero, *Tusc.Disp.*, V.61-62; Cf. Cicero, *Leal.*, 52-53

111. See Hellegouarc'h 1972, p.42: 'L'*amicitia* peut (..) être envisagée à deux points de vue extrêmement différents: d'abord comme un bienfait, assuré par la parfaite rectitude morale des *amici*, et qui se présente pour ceux qui sa pratiquent comme une sorte d'idéal, qu'il est souhaitable de rechercher le plus possible sans pouvoir jamais esperér l'atteindre totalement; en second lieu comme un instrument de l'action politique que les grands leaders ont à leur disposition et dont ils se servant au mieux de leurs intérêts, en se tenant le plus possible éloignés des considérations de caractère moral ou sentimental.' Cf. Cicero, *Lael.*, 18-19 'Friendship cannot exist except among the *boni*'. Cicero is speaking of *amicitia* in the full sense here, which is attainable only to those who are virtuous. At *Lael.*, 22 it is contrasted with the vulgar and mediocre kind of friendship. Cf. *De Off.*, III.45

112. Cicero, *De Off.*, I.31ff

113. Cf. e.g Adam Smith. *Theory of Moral Sentiments*, II.ii 'Of justice and beneficence', which depends heavily on Cicero

114. Cicero, *De Off.*, II.52

115. Cicero, *De Off.*, II.52-54

116. Cicero, *De Off.*, II.54

117. Cicero, *De Off.*, II.55-56

118. Cicero, *De Off.*, II.56-63

119. Cf. *De Off.*, II.57-60; Cicero admits of some exceptions. 'I do realize that even in the good old days it had become a tradition in our city to demand splendor from the best men in their aedileships.' In this and similar situations 'there is a case for lavish distribution'. However, it remains 'of its nature contrary to virtue; but due to circumstances, it may be necessary'.

120. Cicero, *De Off.*, II.64

121. Cicero, *De Off.*, II,64

122. Cicero, *De Off.*, II.64

123. Cicero, *De Off.*, II.64

124. Veyne 1990; Cicero, *De Off.*, II.60 points in a different direction, but that seems to be a rather isolated remark.

125. Cicero, *De Off.*, II.65

126. Cicero, *De Off.*, II.65-73

CHAPTER EIGHT

THE POLITICS OF NOBILITAS

> *All those who have preserved, aided, or enlarged*
> *their fatherland are certain of a special place in*
> *heaven*
>
> *Cicero*[1]

1. Humanitas

Nothing is more suited to human nature than *beneficentia*, Cicero declares, but that does not mean that it is a duty for all men. Most are not in the position to be beneficent. For *beneficentia* is the preserve of those who possess money and leisure. Money must be available in great quantity, to enable liberal spending;, and without leisure one does not have time to be of service in law and politics. Hence, *beneficentia* presupposed a secure source of -consider-able- income, which did not take up much of one's time.

1.1. Land and leadership

Not unreasonably, it was assumed that agriculture, the ownership and exploitation of arable land, meets these needs most completely. The laborer, the craftsman, and the professional all lack both time and money. The trader might be rich sometimes, but his wealth is not secure; each day could bring bankruptcy and leave the trader destitute. The ownership of landed property on the other hand guaranteed a continuous flow of income and left sufficient spare-time, particularly to those who possessed enough to employ overseers and rent out a part of their property to tenant-farmers. Such *rentiers* were more or less exempted from the necessity to work for a living, from the need to provide for their self-preservation every day. The question how to spend one's time and money was an important issue only to this elite. To the common man it hardly pertained: he spent his time working and sleeping, and his money on food and shelter. He had little choice. The constraints of scarcity did not give him any leeway, but pointed out with great clarity and severity the direction he must take. For the common man the answer to the question 'What to do?' was easy and obvious.

For the great landowner things were different. He was destined to dominate society, but he could do so in two ways; either in his own interest, or for the common good -like a tyrant or like a monarch. The first way was conceived of as in a sense more natural. Humankind was originally governed despotically. But the second way was the better, civilized way. The great landowner still dominated society, but he now dominated it by putting himself at its service. This masterful link between domination and service, between overriding strength and assistance, was forged mainly by the idea of *beneficentia* as a virtue particularly becoming to the noble man of honor. If *iustitia* assuaged the potentially destructive and murderous puissance of the great, *beneficentia* converted them into powerful protective shields of the common people.

The great landowners lead a life that differs substantially from ordinary life. Their leisure and their money enables them to transcend the sphere of production and reproduction, to which most people are condemned, and serve society at large. If ordinary life is largely concerned with self-interest, with the merely useful, the life of the great is largely devoted to the general interest, to the honorable. This is the good life for the few. *In concreto*, it meant a life devoted to serving others in positions of authority, especially in law and politics.

The preparation for such a life was necessarily different from the preparation one needed for ordinary life. The common man must learn a trade, like bakery, painting, or medicine. As has been set out, this involves a specific type of knowledge, viz. technical, or instrumental knowledge. Law and politics on the other hand are of a distinct epistemological nature: as is evident from their Roman names, they were considered to be forms of *prudentia*: *iurisprudentia* and *prudentia civilis* respectively.

It will be remembered that *prudentia* was believed to be a higher form of knowledge than instrumental knowledge, because it is directed at the aims of life. '*Prudentia* is the knowledge of what is good, what is bad and what is neither good nor bad. Its parts are memory, intelligence, and foresight. Memory is the faculty by which the mind recalls what has happened. Intelligence is the faculty by which it ascertains what is. Foresight is the faculty by which it is seen that something is going to occur before it occurs.'[2] No free man can do completely without. Without *prudentia* freedom is unthinkable. But if the leaders of society were to be without *prudentia*, that would be truly disastrous. For them *prudentia* is the single most important type of knowledge. Consequently, the education of the great should essentially aim at the improvement and mastery of *prudentia* and leave the more profane type of knowledge to the common man (and the more exalted type -*sapientia*- to the philosopher or the priest).

The ancients gave much thought to the education of the few, considerably more so than to the education of the many. But they had good reasons for this. First of all, practical knowledge is a lot harder to acquire than instrumental knowledge. For it is the knowledge of the most perplexing of all objects: man himself. Secondly, the well-being of the community depends on the quality of its leaders. If they fall short and make mistakes, the consequences are likely to be grave. And finally, the nobleman remains a dangerous animal whose *Raubtiergewissen* cannot be extinguished for good. Each and every generation must be tamed by a proper education.

This was an education that was baptized a humanist education by the scholars of the renaissance, because Ciceronian *humanitas* was its aim and justification. The so-called *artes liberales*, denoting all the studies that befit the liberal i.e. beneficent man, were central to its curriculum. Explicitly and self-consciously elitist it was indeed imperative that the many did not get such an education, for the exclusive concentration on the honorable by the few was conceivable only if the many took care of the merely useful.

1.2. The liberal arts

These liberal arts, which were also called *humanae* or *bonae* by the Romans, and in the ancien régime were referred to as the *studia humanitatis*, were intended to infuse the noble pupil with practical knowledge, in order to prepare him for his future role as a leader of the state. It was to some extent a matter of debate, of course, what subjects contributed to the nurturing of *prudentia* and should therefore be included in the curriculum. But rhetoric, moral and political philosophy, and the study of law and history were on everyone's list.

That it is necessary for the future statesman to have an intimate knowledge of the law, particularly constitutional law, is obvious. He must know everything of the rights and duties of the various organs of state. In addition, he should be conversant in civil law, as well as in international law, if he is to be prepared for his coming office. The guiding principle behind all this was the idea of *die Hoheit des Rechts*. The political man was conceived of as a guardian of the law, not as a policy-maker, who could use the law as his instrument. Change was the problem, not the solution. Good politics was inspired and guided by the past.

Sensibly therefore the study of history was considered of the utmost importance. Through the study of the past one becomes familiar with the traditions and principles of one's own nation, with the *mos maiorum*, the bolstering of which was considered the *ultima ratio* of politics. Moreover, history provides the student with a treasury of moral *exempla*, both good and bad, of the virtuous and vicious deeds of the men of old. And finally, it provides indispensable information about the *conditio humana* in general. It discloses to the student the world at large and the ways of men, and is thus an important addendum to one's own actual experience. 'To be ignorant of what occurred before you were born is to remain always a child.'[3]

But the study of law and history alone is not sufficient. The statesman should also be schooled in moral and political philosophy. The parts of philosophy dealing with the mysteries of nature and the subtleties of logic can safely be left to the philosopher, but the part that is concerned with human nature -man's psychological make-up- and the fundamental mechanisms relating to the establishment and governance of political communities, give an understanding no statesman can afford to neglect.[4]

The Romans never had any doubt that the purpose of all this knowledge was mastery *in politicis*. Therefore, *doctrina* must not turn into something that is pursued for its own sake. It should support the demands of public life, not interfere with them.[5] The study of the liberal arts does not seek to create scholars or sages, but men with good sense and good judgement, who are able to take the right decisions. Hence, the curriculum must concentrate on the outlines of the various subjects, and be content to take from them what is of practical use to the statesman.

This being the criterion, it is not surprising that the Romans gave a high place to the art of *eloquentia* in the education of the few. Indeed, they regarded this as so essential to the statesman that they often referred to such a man simply as *orator*. Rhetoric was a field badly spoken of by the philosophers for being concerned with appearances rather than reality, with style rather than substance. But practical necessity must have been more forceful than theoretical protest, because in spite of this the study of rhetoric was the capping-stone of the humanist education, reflecting the fact that wisdom unspoken or badly articulated is socially and politically impotent. It needs the help of artful and persuasive speech to have real effect. Otherwise, it remains introverted and quarantined. 'It is better to speak at length, provided one does so wisely, than to think, however penetratingly, without eloquence. For speculation turns in on itself, but eloquence embraces those to whom we are joined in *communitas*.'[6]

Indeed, *ratio* and *oratio* are but two sides of the same coin. Each one is helpless and truncated without the other. Reason needs the assistance of speech to assert its superiority. Reason is manifested in speech. Speech is reason in action. The command of reason depends on speech. 'What other power could have been strong enough either to gather scattered humanity into one place, or to lead it out of its brutish existence in the wilderness up to our present condition of civilization as men and citizens, or, after the establishment of *civitates*, to give shape to laws, tribunals, and civic rights?', Cicero asks his readers -rhetorically.[7] That is to say, without *ratio et oratio* man would have lived like the animals: entirely dependent upon his senses for his knowledge and his brute force for the creation of social order. From this point of view, the art of persuasion is eminently human and humanistic.

But there is yet another reason why *eloquentia* was regarded by the ancients as indispensable to the statesman, which probably carried at least as much weight in practice. As has been set out, verticality and analogy were fundamental principles in the Roman view of man and society. Within the breast of each man reason and the passions vied for pre-eminence, the good man being governed by reason. By analogy, society should be governed by its most rational element, the best and the brightest. The common man, being volatile, unpredictable, and impetuous, must be restrained and controlled by the former. Since it was the statesman's function not only to discover the best course of action, but also to secure its acceptance and implementation by the people, he should not merely be highly rational, but also capable of molding the spirit of the latter, inspiring them to virtuous endeavors, and deflecting them from pernicious courses. But because the rationality of the many is not as well developed as his, the statesman must also appeal to their passions, and to the *auctoritas* or lack of it of the main actors, to win them over. The orator's appeal to their reason -*logos*- must be assisted by an appeal to their emotions -*pathos*- and their faith in persons -*ethos*.

1.3. Ethos and pathos

It is this unabashed use of these two strategies of 'irrational' persuasion which perhaps accounts most of all for the bad reputation of rhetoric in philosophical circles, both ancient and modern. Interestingly, however, what seems repugnant to them differs. What most offended Plato *cum suis* was that *ethos* and *pathos* polluted the pure rationality of discourse; what most offends the modern philosophers is that they are an expression of an haughty attitude vis-à-vis the people, who apparently are not taken seriously. From a Platonic perspective *ethos* and *pathos* are too egalitarian, from a modern philosophical perspective they are not sufficiently so. But of course in this respect the statesman, both ancient and modern, though prepared to listen respectfully to what the philosopher has to say, shrugs his shoulders, for he knows that *ethos* and *pathos* are indispensable to him.[8]

Ethos refers to what is called 'image' today. The persuasiveness of an orator partly depends on what his audience thinks of him. 'Attributes helpful to the orator are a mild tone, a countenance expressive of modesty, gentle language, and the faculty of seeming to be dealing reluctantly and under compulsion with something you are really anxious to prove. It is very helpful to display the tokens of *facilitas*, *liberalitas*, gentleness, *pietas*, and a disposition that is pleasing and not grasping or covetous, and all the qualities belonging to men who are upright, unassuming and not given to haste, stubbornness, strife, or harshness, (and) are powerful in winning *benevolentia*.'[9] Without a good *ethos* it is virtually impossible to be convincing. 'Accordingly the very opposites of these qualities must be ascribed to our opponents.'[10] Of course, the best way to achieve a good 'image' is it to be what one wishes to seem. For 'everything false drops swiftly like blossom; and pretence can never endure'.[11]

Pathos is the appeal to the feelings of the audience, most commonly, says Cicero, those of love, hate, wrath, envy, compassion, hope, joy, fear, and vexation.[12] To make effective use of this instrument of persuasion the statesman has to be an astute psychologist. Therefore, the nature, the objects and the causes of the human emotions must be a major subject in the liberal arts curriculum.

Take envy -*invidia*-, for instance. Since it is the fiercest and most widespread of all emotions, its repression and stimulation are particularly powerful tools of persuasion. A thorough knowledge of the psychology of envy is therefore imperative. 'Now people are especially envious of their equals, or of those once beneath them, when they feel themselves left behind and fret at the others' upward flight. But envy of their betters also is often furious, and all the more so if these conduct themselves insufferably, and overstep their rightful claims on the strength of pre-eminent rank or prosperity. If these advantages are to be made fuel for envy, it should before all be pointed out that they were not the fruit of *virtus*, next that they even came by vice and wrong-doing, finally that the man's *honor* and *gravitas*, though credible and impressive enough, are still exceeded by his arrogance and disdain. To quench envy, on the other hand, it is proper to emphasize the points that those advantages were the fruit of great exertion and great risks, and were not turned to his own profit but to that of other people. And that, as for any renown he himself may seem to have won, though no unfair recompense for his risk, he nevertheless finds no pleasure therein, but casts it aside and disclaims it altogether. And we must by all means make sure (..) that the belief in (his) prosperity shall be weakened, and that what was supposed to be outstanding prosperity shall be seen to be thoroughly blended with *labor* and sorrow.'[13] This is what Cicero has to say about *invidia* in *De Oratore*, his most celebrated treatise on eloquence. But much more is to be learned about it, and about all the other emotions. The student must give them a lot of thought, so that the statesman can handle them well. The study of literature -*les belles lettres*- was considered the most important theoretical source and guiding-light in this field as well.

To sum up, the study of the liberal arts is meant as a course in practical knowledge, the type of knowledge needed by the leaders of state. *Eloquentia* tops it off. It is the most practical of all forms of practical knowledge, since it provides the bridge that connects theory and practice, learning and life. But even *eloquentia* is turned into book-learning by the pedants of this world, and presented as a system of fixed rules that should be learned by heart. That approach mistakes the beginning for the end. For the best teacher in these matters is actual experience: *usus*. The consummate *orator* is made in practice. Schooling in the precepts of the art of rhetoric is only the first step.[14]

The obvious follow-up was legal advocacy, in Cicero's opinion at least.

As a lawyer in a court of law one could exert *beneficentia*, and at the same time practice and enhance one's oratorical skill. Thus, the bar was a perfect preparation and stepping-stone for magisterial office. It is true, however, that in ancient times the bar never became a required step in the *cursus honorum*, the career of office, which significantly began with the military tribuneship.[15] This reflects the fact that most Romans 'consider that military affairs are of greater significance than civic', an opinion Cicero disputes.[16] 'Many achievements of civic life have proved greater and more famous than those of war.'[17] It bespeaks of Cicero's great influence on the classicism of the ancien régime, that in those days the bar did become an alternative stepping-stone to high magisterial office.

1.4. Clementia

Humanitas is not only *prudentia*. It has a broader meaning.[18] *Humanitas* also alludes to virtues like *clementia* -mercy- and *mansuetudo* -gentleness-,[19] and to the virtues of *decorum* and *urbanitas*.[20]

Clementia and the like pertain principally to relations with inferiors. It is a moral obligation for the superior to treat his inferiors with mercy and gentleness. *Clementia* is very much an aristocratic virtue, germane to hierarchical societies with great inequalities of power. Mercy is asked from men who are the arbiter of life and death, whose power over others is virtually unrestricted. It is significant that Seneca wrote a treatise on mercy for the young Nero. The power of the emperors was indeed unlimited. Temperance could therefore only come from within the young man's breast. 'Of all men none is better graced by *clementia* than a king or a prince', writes Seneca, 'for great power confers grace and glory only when it is salutary. It is surely a baneful power, that is strong only in harming'.[21] 'It is mercy that makes the distinction between a king and a tyrant as great as it is.'[22] This is not to say that *clementia* was a specifically imperial virtue. It applied to all men of august rank, and even to the Roman people as a whole, in its relation to vanquished enemies.[23] But it does seem to have gained weight parallel to the centralization of power. Or is it a coincidence that of all people it is Julius Caesar whose name is forever associated with *clementia*?[24]

In a passage of great beauty Sallust contrasts the *clementia Caesaris* with the austerity of his contemporary Cato the younger in an apparent attempt to explain the success of the Roman people in conquering the world as a result of the presence of both kinds of virtue in the leaders of state. 'The former became famous for his *mansuetudo* and his *misericordia*, the latter obtained prestige by *severitas*.'[25] Caesar's *clementia* is associated with his *beneficentia* and *munificentia* -great generosity-, with his inclination to give, help, and forgive. Cato's *severitas* on the other hand is associated with *integritas*, and his incorruptibility. 'One was a refuge for the unfortunate, the other a scourge for the wicked. The *facilitas* of the one was applauded, the *constantia* of the other. Finally, Caesar had schooled himself to work hard and sleep little, to devote himself to the welfare of his friends and neglect his own, to refuse nothing which was worth the giving. He longed for great power, an army, a new war to give scope to his *virtus*. Cato, on the contrary, cultivated *modestia*, *decorum*, and above all *severitas*. He did not vie with the greedy in greed nor with the factious in factiousness, but with the virtuous in virtue, with the self-restrained in moderation, and with the blameless in *abstinentia*.'[26]

The man of perfect *virtus* would have to combine the virtues of both Caesar and Cato. He would have to possess *clementia* as well as *severitas*. Too much forgiveness and compassion induce laxity and corruption. Too much austerity on the other hand goes counter to *humanitas*. Plutarch's comment on the elder Cato's belief that it was his duty to sell slaves who had become too old to work, rather than feed useless mouths, is interesting in this respect. 'In my judgement, it marks an over-rigid temper for a man to take the work out of his servants as out of brute beasts, turning them off and selling them in their old age, and thinking there ought to be no further commerce between man and man than whilst there arises some profit by it. We see that kindness or humanity has a larger field than bare justice to exercise itself in; law and justice we cannot, in the nature of things, employ on others than men; but we may extend our goodness and charity even to irrational creatures and such acts flow from a gentle nature, as water from an abundant spring. It is doubtless the part of a kind-natured man to keep even wornout horses and dogs, and not only take care of them when they are foals and whelps, but also when they are grown old. (..) If it were for nothing else, but by way of study and practice in humanity, a man ought to prehabituate himself in these things to be of a kind and sweet disposition.'[27] Hence, it is not that Cato was unjust in selling his old and useless slaves; he had every right to do so. But by his failure to abstain from using his right, he showed that he lacked *clementia* and therefore (a part of) *humanitas*.

1.5. Decorum
The third and last aspect of *humanitas* concerns what the Romans called *decorum* and *urbanitas*. The last term is helpful, if only because it has a definite opposite, viz. *rusticitas*, which instantly gives an idea of the meaning of these notions. For *rusticitas* is of course the derogatory qualification pertaining to country-dwellers, implying a lack of refinement and polish, ignorance and boorishness, a dirty appearance and uncouth behavior, gullibility and shyness, a provincial pronunciation, and so on.[28] *Urbanitas* hence consists in elegance and politeness, culture and savoir-faire, seemliness

in appearance and speech, tact and propriety, etcetera.

As has already been pointed out this feeling of superiority of the city-dweller vis-à-vis the country-dweller does not imply a general disapproval of country life. Classic and classicist thought abounds with panegyrics of bucolic *virtus*. Moreover, the city is conventionally censured as a cesspool of vice. But, irrespective of how this may look at first sight, the Romans were far from ambiguous or contradictory about the issue of town versus country. A gentleman lives off the land, but in the city, at least most of the time. Commonly, he will withdraw to his estate only in the summertime, when the city is too hot and dusty, and politics are at a low anyway.

Romantics tend to regard *urbanitas* and *decorum* as a superficial concern with appearance and demeanor, passing over the things that are really essential in judging a man. From such a point of view, these virtues can be interpreted only as a form of snobbery.[29] But there seems to be more to it than just snobbery, although that undoubtedly is part of the motivation. The significance of *urbanitas* and *decorum* derive from our duty to 'exercise a respectfulness towards men, both towards the best of them and also towards the rest. To neglect what others think about oneself is the mark not only of *arrogantia*, but also of utter laxity'.[30] It complements justice. For 'the part of justice is not to harm a man, that of a sense of shame not to outrage him. Here is seen most clearly the essence of *decorum*'.[31]

What is at stake is ultimately a sense of respect for the feelings of others. The *homo urbanus* eschews everything displeasing and inappropriate, so that others will approve of him and regard him well. Obviously, self-interest will readily support the demands of delicacy in this case, particularly when the man in question has political ambitions. After all, one does not make too many friends by being rude and impertinent.

The logic of pride and shame guides the process of adaption to circumstances. Seemliness is honorable, unseemliness is shameful. The man who knows what is appropriate possesses judgement, which is of course a species of practical knowledge. His good manners, his politeness, are a matter of style, but they point to something beyond, viz. both to insight into human nature and to respect for one's fellows. Consequently, if a man carefully guards *decorum* this may be taken as a sign that he would be a trustworthy guardian of the general interest and an able leader of the state. *Decorum* is therefore much more than merely a matter of manners.

The most extensive description of what *decorum* entailed is given in Cicero's *De Officiis*, toward the end of the first book. As that author tells us there are two sides to *decorum*. It is concerned with a general duty applying equally to all men, and with a specific duty depending on the particular situation of each man. The general duty is to look and act like a reasonable being, in recognition of our common superiority over the brute beasts. If reason commands and impulse obeys, only then we are truly human. Composure and moderation in expression, appearance, and behavior gives proof of such control within the soul and is therefore seemly. Anger, fear, and excessive pleasure on the other hand are all unseemly, for the faces, the voices, the gestures, and the postures aroused by these passions bear witness to their lack of self-control. Hence, the general side of *decorum*; it is simple and straightforward.

That is not the case with the determination of what is proper and fitting for a man in relation to his background and circumstances. For what is acceptable and even honorable in one station or situation, may be outrageous and inexcusable in another. General rules cannot be given with regard to this second side of *decorum*. Everything depends on the place, the time, and one's position. That is not to say, however, that nothing at all can be said about it. Cicero gives a number of interesting examples of the different standards demanded from youths and older men, from male and female, from magistrates, private citizens, and foreigners, and so on. For instance, the male must venture to behave with dignity, whereas gracefulness is expected of the female.[32] Also, our way of speaking, among other things, must be attuned to the situation. 'Oratory should be employed for speeches in law courts, to public assemblies, or in the senate, while conversation should be found in social groups, in philosophical discussions, and among gatherings of friends, and may it also attend dinners!'[33] And even while having a conversation one must never loose sight of propriety. Every participant should be given a turn. The subjects discussed should be tuned to the interests of the company. If the subject is serious, it must be treated with gravity, if lighthearted, with wit. 'And just as there was a reason for beginning (a discussion), so let a limit be set for its conclusion.'[34] Furthermore, 'one's standing ought to be enhanced by one's house, but not won entirely because of it; the master should not be made honorable by the house, but the house by the master. (..) A notable man ought to be concerned that his house is spacious; for he will have to receive many guests there and admit to it a multitude of men of all sorts. On the other hand, a grand dwelling can, if there is emptiness there, often bring disgrace upon its master, and very much so if once upon a time, with a different master, it had usually been thronging with people.'[35]

Is it necessary to say more? The general idea behind all these instances is clear. *Decorum* and *urbanitas* are the finishing touch, so to speak, of *humanitas*. They round off the classical/classicist idea of nobility. Modesty and dignity of dress and deportment, ease and charm in conversation, an elegant mode of speech, a restraint in deed and word that avoids excitement and dispiritedness, a sense of tact and timing, a broad cultural and intellectual sophistication that is never pedantic and pretentious, urbane wit and gentility, and the like, are all the marks of the gentleman. And although *decorum* and *urbanitas* may not be the most crucial of the noble virtues, they are nevertheless characteristic attributes of the true *homo humanus*.

2. Mixed government

These deliberations on human nature, society and politics seem to point unequivocally in the direction of an aristocratic form of government. If we had not possessed ancient writings dealing specifically with forms of state, it would probably have been most prudent to assume that an aristocratic government was the prevailing governmental ideal in antiquity. But instead of such an espousal our sources reveal a widely-held preference for a 'mixed' form of government, a *regimen mixtum*.

One cannot help but wonder what would have come of the influence of the ancients on later western history if not this notion but that of an aristocratic government had topped off their social and political thought. Since that is not the case, however, we need not dwell on this issue. The ideal of a *regimen mixtum* apparently exerted a greater attraction on the ancient writers. As a consequence, the concept of a mixed government became a crucial notion in the political thought of later times. To depict its influence is one of the main aims of the fourth part of this study. But before we can begin studying its *Wirkungsgeschichte*, the meaning of the concept must be articulated, as well as its relation to the general tenets of Roman thought.

2.1. The origins of the doctrine

The notion of a mixed government presupposes that there are or can be 'pure' or 'simple' governments, which can be blended. At quite an early stage the ancients had developed the idea that there were essentially only three types of government: rule by one, rule by a few, and rule by the many. Herodotus already distinguished between them.[36] But there is no indication in his *Histories* that he was aware of the possibility, not to mention the desirability, of a mixture. The earliest of our sources to speak of that is Thucydides, who argues in his *Peloponnesian War* that during the first period after the removal of the oligarchy in 411 B.C. 'the Athenians appear to have had a better government than ever before, at least in my time. There was a reasonable and moderate blending of the few and the many, and it was this, in the first place, that made it possible for the city to recover from the bad state into which her affairs had fallen'.[37] Hence, both the ancient typology of governments and the ideal of the mixed government go back to the fifth century B.C.[38]

In the following century these doctrines were further developed. The typology of governments reached its final shape in Aristotle's *Politics*. 'Sovereignty necessarily resides either in one man, or in a few, or in the many. Whenever the one, the few, or the many rule with a view to the common good, these governments must be correct; but if they look to the private advantage, be it of the one or the few or the mass, they are deviations.(..) The usual names for right governments are as follows: monarchy aiming at the common interest: kingship; rule of more than one man but only a few: aristocracy (..); political control exercised by the mass of the populace in the common interest: *politeia* (..) The corresponding deviations are: from kingship, tyranny; from aristocracy, oligarchy; from *politeia*, democracy.'[39] Although later terminology with regard to the rule of the many was still to shift somewhat, this typology became the backbone of all subsequent theories of government in antiquity and later, until the modern age.

Aristotle's treatment of the concept of the mixed government on the other hand was less definitive. He distinguishes between various mixed governments. Some are a blending of two 'pure' governments, others a blending of three; some are very stable, others less so. Aristotle is most concerned with the analysis of oligarchies and democracies, not because these are his favorite governments, but because they predominated empirically.[40] He asserts that a *politeia* is a mixture of oligarchy and democracy.[41] But he does not seem to believe that all good governments are mixtures of bad ones. In sum, one must conclude that analytically as well as normatively Aristotle's discussion of the mixed government ultimately leaves the matter somewhat at a loose end.

2.2. Polybius

The classic theorist of the ancient theory of government is Polybius. In his version of the theory all the different strands come together and are combined into an elegant and consistent whole. Moreover, he is one of the two ancient authors we possess to explicitly apply the theory to Rome. The other one is of course Cicero, but as has been set out the contents of the treatise in which he deals most extensively with the theory of government -*De Re Publica*- were virtually unknown in the ancien régime, since the text as we have it was rediscovered only in the nineteenth century. Polybius presents his views in book VI of his *Histories*, which is introduced by the author as a theoretical *Exkurs* on the nature of the Roman government. Unfortunately, it has not come down to us unscathed, but enough has been preserved to give a good grasp of the general idea. Let us therefore take a closer look at it.

'Most of those whose object it has been to instruct us methodically concerning such matters', writes Polybius, 'distinguish three kinds of governments, which they call kingship, aristocracy, and democracy.'[42] But this is wrong. For 'it is by no means every monarchy which we can call straight off a *basileia* -kingship-, but only that which is voluntarily accepted by the subjects and where they are governed rather by an appeal to their reason than by fear and force. Nor again can we style every oligarchy an aristocracy, but only that where the government is in the hands of a selected body of the justest and the wisest men. Similarly that is no true democracy in which the whole crowd of citizens is free to do whatever they wish or purpose, but when, in a community where it is traditional and customary to reverence the gods, to honor our parents, to respect our elders, and to obey the laws, the will of the greater number prevails, that is to be called a democracy. We should therefore assert that there are six kinds of governments, the three above mentioned which are in everyone's mouth and the three which are naturally allied to them, I mean monarchy, oligarchy, and *ochlocracy* -mob-rule.'[43] Although at some points the terminology is at variance with Aristotle's, it is obvious that we have a very similar typology of governments here.

The next step in Polybius' argument is an elaboration of the idea that all of these governments are instable and destined to go through an eternal cycle of political revolutions, a *politeion anakuklosis*.[44] The first government 'to come into being is monarchy, its growth being natural and unaided; and next arises kingship, derived from monarchy by the aid of art and by the correction of defects'.[45] This original monarchy is a despotism or hegemony of the strongest. 'When owing to floods, famines, failure of crops or other such causes there occurs such a destruction of the human race as tradition tells us has more than once happened, and as we must believe will often happen again, all arts and crafts perishing at the same time, then in the course of time, when springing from the survivors as from seeds men have again increased in numbers and just like other animals form herds -it being a matter of course that they too should herd together with those of their kind owing to their natural weakness- it is a necessary consequence that the man who excels in bodily strength and in courage will lead and rule over the rest.'[46]

By insensible degrees this original monarchy then turns into a true kingship, as the notions of what is noble and just gradually arise. This is due to the faculty of reason, that distinguishes man from the animals, and invokes in him some idea of nobility and justice and their opposites. Now when the leading man consistently behaves in this way and apportions rewards and penalties in accordance with these ideas, the people 'yield obedience to him no longer because they fear his force, but rather because their judgement approves of him; and they join in maintaining his rule even if he is quite enfeebled by age, defending him with one consent and battling against those who conspire to overthrow his rule'.[47]

But sooner or later kingship changes into its vicious allied form, tyranny, which in its turn is replaced by an aristocracy. 'Aristocracy by its very nature degenerates into oligarchy; and when the commons inflamed by anger take vengeance on this government for its unjust rule, democracy comes into being; and in due course the license and lawlessness of this form of government produces mob-rule.'[48] Under this 'government' the people 'massacre, banish, and plunder, until they degenerate again into perfect savages and find once more a master and monarch'.[49]

2.3. The cycle of constitutions

The underlying causes of revolutionary change are always the same, Polybius tells his readers. It is invariably brought about by the immoderateness of those in power who have inherited a good government from their ancestors, and accordingly rule though no merit of their own. They take the government for granted and abandon themselves to the pursuit of their self-interest and their pleasures. Instead of protecting the people and serving the common interest, which is the ratio of all leadership, they misuse their power at the cost of the people. The hatred and indignation this evokes will eventually lead to the overthrow of the government.

Hence, the first true kings are busy all their lives 'fortifying and enclosing fine strongholds with walls and acquiring lands, in the one case for the sake of the security of their subjects and in the other to provide them with abundance in the necessities of life. And while pursuing these aims, they (are) exempt from all vituperation or jealousy, as neither in their dress nor in their food and drink (do) they make any great distinction, but (live) very much like anyone else, not keeping apart from the people. But (those who receive) their office by hereditary succession and (find) their safety now provided for, and more than sufficient provision of food, they (give) way to their appetites owing to this superabundance, and (come) to think that the rulers must be distinguished from their subjects by a peculiar dress, that there should be a peculiar luxury and variety in the dressing and serving of their food, and that they should meet with no denial in their amorous pursuits, however lawless.'[50] In this way kingship is changed into a tyranny.

However, tyrannical behavior gives rise to intense resentment, as a consequence of which conspiracies begin to be formed. 'These conspiracies (are) not the work of the worst men, but of the noblest, most high-spirited and most courageous, because such men are least able to endure the insolence of princes.'[51] Eventually, the monarchy is abolished and an aristocracy established. 'For the commons, as if bound to pay at once their debt of gratitude to the abolishers of monarchy, (..) make them their leaders and entrust their destinies to them.'[52]

Now the process of degeneration begins anew. 'At first these chiefs gladly (assume) this charge and (regard) nothing as of greater importance than the common interest (..). But here again when children (inherit) this position of authority from their fathers, having no experience of misfortune (..) and having been brought up from the cradle amid the evidences of the power and high position of their fathers, they (abandon) themselves, some to greed of gain and unscrupulous money-making, others to indulgence in wine and convivial excess which accompanies it, and others again to the violation of women and the rape of boys. And thus converting the aristocracy into an oligarchy (arouse) in the people feelings similar to those of which (was) just (spoken), and in consequence (meet) with the same disastrous end as the tyrant.'[53]

When the people have either killed or banished the oligarchs, they turn the state into a democracy, assuming responsibility for the conduct of affairs themselves. 'Then as long as some of those survive who experienced the evils of oligarchical dominion, they are well pleased with the present form of government, and set a high value on equality and freedom of speech. But when a new generation arises and the democracy falls into the hands of the grandchildren of its founders, they have become so accustomed to freedom and equality that they no longer value them, and begin to aim at pre-eminence; and it is chiefly those of ample fortune who fall into this error. So when they begin to lust for power and cannot attain it through themselves or their own good qualities, they ruin their estates, tempting and corrupting the people in every possible way. And hence when by their foolish thirst for reputation they have created among the masses an appetite for gifts and the habit of receiving them, democracy in its turn is abolished and changes into a rule of force and violence. For the people, having grown accustomed to feed at the expense of others and to depend for their livelihood on the property of others (..) (will begin to) massacre, banish, and plunder' and thus destroy civil society.[54] Only the primitive form of despotic rule can now bring relief; with which we have come full circle in Polybius' cycle of political revolutions.

At this point the question arises, of course, whether there is a possibility to bring this cycle to a standstill. Polybius is quite positive that in the last resort no such possibility exists. 'That all existing things are subject to decay and change is a truth that scarcely needs proof', are the words with which he begins his conclusion of the *Exkurs* on the Roman government.[55] Thus, Rome's 'change for the worse (..) is sure to follow some day'.[56] However, it is feasible to stop the cycle for a substantial period of time. The man who has led the way here, according to Polybius, is Lycurgus, the illustrious law-giver who devised the Spartan government that survived longer than any other in the Greek world. He achieved this by 'not (making) his government simple and uniform, but (uniting) in it all the good and distinctive features of the best governments, so that none of the principles should grow unduly and be perverted into its allied evil, but that, the force of each being neutralized by that of the others, neither of them should prevail and outbalance another, but that the government should remain for long in a state of equilibrium like a well-trimmed boat'.[57] In other words, the secret of the political stability of Sparta lies in the fact that Lycurgus blended kingship, aristocracy, and democracy into a mixed government.

It is the same secret that explains the unprecedented success of the Romans, our author argues. 'The three kinds of government (..) all shared in the control of the Roman state. And such fairness and propriety in all respects was shown in the use of these three elements for drawing up the government and in its subsequent administration that it was impossible even for a native to pronounce with certainty whether the whole system was aristocratic, democratic, or monarchical. This was indeed only natural; for if one fixed one's eyes on the power of the consuls, the government seemed completely monarchical and royal; if on that of the senate it seemed again to be aristocratic; and when one looked at the power of the masses, it seemed clearly to be a democracy.'[58] In reality, 'none of the three is absolute, but the purpose of the one can be counterworked and thwarted by the others, none of them will excessively outgrow the others or treat them with contempt. All in fact remains in the status quo, on the one hand because any aggressive impulse is sure to be checked, and because from the outset each estate stands in dread of being interfered with by the others'.[59]

Polybius proceeds to recapitulate at some length the distribution of governmental powers among the consuls, the senate, and the people, as well as the means which enable each of these parts of the state, if they so wished, to counteract and co-operate with the others.[60] We will go into that subject shortly, but for the moment we are merely concerned with the general scheme of balancing political elements, not with the features of the balance.

2.4. Cicero

The last ancient writer to make a material contribution to the theory of mixed government was, predictably, Cicero. He is also the only author we possess who wrote about the theory of government in Latin.[61] Coming from Arcadia, Polybius wrote in Greek. And we have no direct or indirect knowledge of any writer from the imperial age to have carried on the tradition of reflection on mixed government, or any other government for that matter.[62] One can find a few scattered remarks in Dionysius of Halicarnassus, Cassius Dio, Plutarch, Tacitus, and some minor authors, but none of it is very substantial. Perhaps Tacitus captures the spirit of the thought of his age most accurately when he says, in his usual concise style, that a country is always either a democracy, or an oligarchy, or an autocracy. 'A mixture of the three is easier to applaud than to achieve, and besides, even when achieved, it cannot last long.'[63]

Hence, once again we end up with Cicero. His account of the mixed government in *De Re Publica* is very similar to Polybius'.[64] Although, as has already been said, the historical influence of the doctrine as it was set out in *De Re Publica* has been limited, since only a few passages of this treatise were known before 1820, it is worthwhile to summarize his views on this topic.

The government of a state must be granted either to one man, or two certain selected citizens, or to the whole body of citizens. In the first case we speak of a *regnum*, in the second of a *civitas optimatium*, in the third of a *civitas popularis*.[65] All of them have intrinsic shortcomings. 'In kingships the subjects have too small a share in the administration of justice and in deliberation. In aristocracies the masses can hardly have their share of liberty, since they are entirely excluded from deliberation for the common weal and from power. And when all the power is in the people's hands, even though they exercise it with justice and moderation, still the fairness -*equabilitas*- that results itself is inequitable, since it allows no distinctions in rank -*gradus dignitatis*.[66] In addition to these shortcomings, before every one of these three 'pure' forms of state 'lies a slippery and precipitous path leading to a certain depraved form that is a close neighbor to it'. A kingship easily degenerates into a *dominatus*, an aristocracy into the rule of the rich, and a democracy into 'the fury and license of the mob'.[67] Therefore, a fourth form of state is the most commendable, that form which is a well-regulated mixture of the three undegenerated 'pure' forms.[68]

Due to its *aequabilitas* such a mixed government has a greater stability.[69] That is to say, only this government gives to every element of the state what is due to it. 'The magistrates have enough *potestas*, the councils of the eminent citizens enough *auctoritas*, and the people enough *libertas*. As a consequence, no one has a reason to conspire against the government and it is safe from revolution.[70] Hence, the mixed government is an application of the general principle of justice to the state. *Suum quique*: to each his own. The government the *maiores* have handed down to us, writes Cicero, is precisely this mixed government.[71] If we are prepared to hold on to it, the Roman state will be preserved forever.

A first conclusion to be drawn from this overview of the ancient theory of mixed government is that its principal goal was the perpetuation of the status quo. Social and political stability was unmistakingly the purpose of the design. Yet, this must not be understood to mean that one simply sought peace and social tranquility. Polybius argued, as we saw, that both Sparta and Rome had a mixed government, but only the first of these was framed for the maintenance of the status quo in this sense. The Roman government on the other hand was tuned to the purpose of conquest and empire. Indeed, the ratio of Polybius' whole *Exkurs* is explicitly to give 'a knowledge how it was and by virtue of what peculiar political institutions that in less than fifty-three years nearly the whole world was overcome and fell under the single dominion of Rome'.[72]

An understanding of stability as *concordia*, i.e. harmony between the orders of society, would remove this difficulty. It is obvious that this is a better interpretation than the former, but a closer look reveals that it will not do either. For *concordia* is not the ultimate aim of a mixed government, although it is perhaps the most important means to reach this aim. The ultimate aim is: the preservation of the ancient constitution, the fundamental principles devised by the men of old on which the whole state is based. The idea, shared by Aristotle, Polybius, and Cicero, is that if everyone is happy with the status quo, no one will have an incentive to overthrow the constitution. If a mixed government establishes general concord, the latter is worthwhile only because it conserves the ancient constitution.

This ancient constitution consists of the *mos maiorum*, the ancient laws and customs to which a state owes its greatness. The form of state is an element of the ancient constitution of a state, but the constitution contains far more. A mixed government, surpassing all other forms of state in stability, is the best guarantee of the ancient constitution. Consequently, the ancient constitutions which include such a government are the constitutions with the greatest longevity.

This is not to say that all ancient constitutions which contain and are shielded by a mixed government are identical. Two states can have the same government, but nevertheless have a very unlike constitution in other respects. This explains the Polybian paradox, mentioned above, that both Sparta and Rome had a mixed government, but the first was tuned to peace, and the latter to war. Their respective ancient constitutions differ in other respects. 'As far as regards the maintenance of concord among the citizens, the security of the Lacedaemonian territory and the preservation of the freedom of Sparta, the legislation of Lycurgus and the foresight he exhibited were so admirable that one is forced to regard his institutions as of divine rather than human origin. (..) But as regards the annexation of neighboring territories, supremacy in Greece, and generally speaking an ambitious policy, he seems to me to have made absolutely no provision for such contingencies, either in particular enactments or in the general constitution of the state.'[73] 'It must be admitted that from this point of view the Lacedaemonian constitution is defective, while that of Rome is superior and better framed to the attainment of power, as is indeed evident from the actual course of events.'[74]

This provides us with at least a partial answer to the puzzle that was the starting-point of this paragraph. As has already been set out, the *mos maiorum* were central to the social and political thought of the Romans. The fact that a mixed government was part of these ancestral laws and customs, makes clear why the ancients predominantly vindicated such a form of government, instead of an aristocratic form of government, which on the face of it would have been more consistent, in view of the general tenets of their thought.

2.5. Aristocratic government

But more is to be said about the relation between the notion of mixed government and these general tenets than this. For if one looks closely enough at the way the writers of antiquity present this political blending of monarchy, aristocracy, and democracy, one must conclude that this is not a combination in which the different components are roughly of equal weight and influence. There is no parity of power. One element conclusively overshadows the other two. It should come as no surprise that this is the aristocratic element. The doctrine of mixed government has a bias towards aristocracy.

The aristocratic element stands as a tempering force between the democratic element on the one hand and the monarchical element on the other. It is largely due to this force that the two latter elements cannot wax immoderate. Thus, it prevents the corruption of the state into a tyranny or a mob-rule. It is necessary that the state has a monarchical element, if only because senates do not wage war. But there is always the danger that the generals turn on the people they are supposed to protect. Therefore, their powers must be carefully bound and circumscribed. As to the mass of the people, the ancient authors are at one that it is unavoidable that these have a say in the government of the state in order to give them an emotional outlet and an interest in its maintenance and thus to forestall revolution, but that given the people's fickleness and tempestuousness their say should under all circumstances be limited. In both cases, the principal restraining force is the aristocratic element within the state. It is true that this element in its turn is checked and balanced by the other two, but these checks are much less formidable than the restraints it places on the latter. In the last resort, a mixed government turns out to be a government in which the voice of the *boni* resounds with the greatest force.

Plutarch's remarks in his *Life of Lycurgus* capture this aristocratic bias of the tradition beautifully. 'Among the many changes and alterations which Lycurgus made, the first and of the greatest importance was the establishment of the senate, which having a power equal to the king's in matters of great consequence, and as Plato expresses it, allaying and qualifying the fiery genius of the royal office, gave steadiness and safety to the commonwealth. For the state, which before had no firm basis to stand upon, but leaned one while towards an absolute monarchy, when the kings had the upper hand, and another while to a pure democracy, when the people had the better, found in this establishment of the senate the central weight, like ballast in a ship, which always kept things in a just equilibrium; the (senate) always adhering to the kings so far as to resist democracy, and on the other hand supporting the people against the establishment of absolute monarchy.'[75] There is no doubt that Plutarch expresses a conviction that was generally held by the writers of antiquity, and not a personal idiosyncracy.[76] The aristocratic element within the state is the central element, on which the stability of the state ultimately depends. Hence, the virtue of this element guarantees the survival and flourishing of the state, and its corruption is the main cause of the state's decline. Even a mixed government will eventually be ruined if vice has infested the principal citizens of the state.[77]

The predominance of the aristocratic element in the Roman republic comes to the fore quite forcefully in the constitutional relations between on the one hand the senate and the consuls, and on the other the senate and the popular assemblies, the senate representing the aristocratic element, the consuls or the magistracy as a whole the monarchical element,[78] and the popular assemblies the democratic element.[79]

One of the most important sources on the relation between the senate and the magistrates is Cicero's *De Legibus*, which in contrast to *De Re Publica* was also available to the readers of the ancien régime. Most if not all of what he has to say in this book can also be found elsewhere, but here everything is summarized in a few pages, whereas in Livy for instance one has to piece the information together from the thousands of pages his work counts, and one does not have to be cynical to believe that conciseness was rewarded with greater influence. The constitutional laws listed in *De Legibus* are appropriate to a mixed government as described in *De Re Publica*.[80] As a matter of fact, 'they are practically the same as those of our own *civitas*', although some new rulings have been added. After all, 'the wisest and most balanced system has been devised by our own *maiores*'.[81] And the few innovations proposed are all meant to restore the ancient constitution, i.e to return to the true principles of a mixed government.[82]

The law dictates that 'there shall be two magistrates with royal powers': the consuls. They represent the monarchical element in the government. This means first and foremost that they hold the supreme military power -*militiae summum ius*. In the field there is no appeal from their orders. However, they are not free to do as they like. The safety of the people shall be their highest law -*salus populi suprema lex*-, a phrase destined to become one of the most important in the political thought of the ancien régime.[83] In general, the power of the consuls is far from absolute. Indeed, Cicero presents them as wholly subordinate to the senate, which is called the leader of public policy and the conductor of government.[84] This is a view one finds repeated in many of Cicero's writings, most equivocally perhaps in a famous passage of the *Pro Sestio*, where he asserts that in the constitution of the state, most wisely established by the *maiores*, 'the senate was set up as the guardian, the president, the defender of the *res publica*. They (i.e. the ancestors, A.K.) willed that the magistrates should be guided by the *auctoritas* of this order, and should act as if they were the *ministri* of this great counsel'.[85]

As far as the assemblies of the people are concerned, Cicero's constitutional law acknowledges them as the ultimate source of power within the state. *Res publica res populi est.*[86] They give law, elect the magistrates, and have important judicial responsibilities. And they indirectly determine the composition of the senate, since the latter is to consist exclusively of former magistrates.[87] Clearly, the people are to have a formidable range of constitutional powers. But, contrary to appearances, Cicero was not vindicating a doctrine of popular sovereignty. To begin with, due to the principle of gradual advancement to higher office -the *cursus honorum*-, electibility for all magistracies, except the lowest, was restricted to members of the senate.[88] It is these magistrates who preside over the popular assemblies, who can adjourn meetings, who instruct the people in regard to the matter in hand, who allow them to be instructed by other magistrates and private citizens, who can veto a bad measure, and who take the people's votes.[89] And it is to them that the ballots are to be shown, 'so that the people may enjoy liberty also in this very privilege of honorably winning the favor of the *boni*'.[90]

Cicero's ideas on this last issue -the ballot- can easily stand as a metaphor of his views on the constitutional relation between the people and the aristocracy. The first must have a say on the most important affairs of state, otherwise they would not be free.[91] But the *libertas* of the people must go hand in hand with the *auctoritas* of the senate, to ensure an equilibrium within the state.[92] 'Everyone knows that laws which provide for a secret ballot (..) (deprive) the *optimates* of their *auctoritas*.' The people must not be provided with a hiding-place, where they can 'conceal a mischievous vote by means of the ballot, and keep the *boni* in ignorance of their real opinion'.[93]

Summing up, it is clear that the doctrine of a mixed government as conceived by the ancients had a thoroughly aristocratic bias. The monarchical and the democratic element within the state play the second fiddle. They are subordinate to the aristocratic element, primarily in the sense that they are morally obliged to seek guidance and advise -*consilium*- from the latter, which consists of the most outstanding citizens.

It is true that from a legal point of view the *senatusconsulta* were 'merely' advisory. In case of disobedience the senate had no legal recourse. But the word 'merely' is an anachronism here, because it implies a qualification that is typical of modernity, viz. that legal rulings are somehow 'stronger' and more binding than rulings which lack this status. It should be remembered, however, that to the Roman mind things were different. An advise given by the senate possessed great *auctoritas* and did not need legal codification to deserve meticulous obedience, whereas a 'mere' legal ruling by the magistracy or the people meant little without the moral support of this august body. Thus, attempts by the magistrates or the people to act without the advise and consent of the senate were in a real sense breaches of the constitution. Such attempts violated the *dignitas* inherent in the aristocracy.

This was an idea which was to have a great future indeed.

2.6. Corruption

The *nobilitas* is the prop that keeps the ship of state afloat. The character of the most prominent men is reproduced in the *res publica*. As long as they are virtuous the state will flourish and be great. But as soon as they come under the sway of vice, the state will flounder and decay. For these men are imitated by the rest.[94] Thus they infect the whole *res publica* with their vices. The *nobilitas* must be free from dishonor and be a moral model for the rest of the citizens.[95] If one can secure that, one will have secured everything. On this view, the nobility bears a heavy responsibility. The rise and fall of nations depends essentially on its performance *in politicis* and *in societate*. The nobleman who refuses to play his pre-ordained role well, or accepts his exclusion from this role by the powers that be, forsakes his responsibility and is not worthy of his name. One way or the other, the decline of state is due to his ignoble behavior.

Perhaps most ignoble is the disuse or the misuse of power by the nobility. Its guardianship of the public interest implies that it must renounce its immediate private interest, a sacrifice that is much less expected of the common people. A failure to do so can be of two different kinds; it can be either an abandonment of the public interest to pursue one's private interest, or it can be the pursuance of one's private interest through the means that are at one's disposal for the sake of the public interest.

An example of the first kind of corruption would be a nobleman who refuses to stand for public office, because he aspires to acquire a fortune in trade. Such behavior demonstrates that one holds riches in higher esteem than the service of one's fellow men and country, which in its turn indicates that one is immoderately attached to material splendor and the things that money can buy: *luxuria* and *avaritia*. But other motives may also cause an abandonment of the public trust, laziness -*desidia*- for instance, and sensuality -*libido*-, or fear -*metus*. Whatever the reason, the moral argument is always the same. By giving in to these impulses one betrays the idea of nobility, which consists precisely in their transcendence. Behavior that is ruled by such impulses is low, mean, common, typical of the *vulgus*. What is at stake here is the abandonment of one or more of the duties of citizenship: paying taxes, serving in the army, going to the ballot, and standing for public office. If such an abandonment is widespread, the *res publica* perishes. It will either be overrun by a foreign enemy, or turn into a *regnum*. For instance, if the citizenry become content to pay mercenaries to fight for them instead of forming their own militia, they are sure to lose everything in the long run. For mercenaries have not half the fighting spirit of citizen-soldiers who defend their own country and children, and they are disloyal on top of that.[96]

Interestingly, there is in the ancient authors not a hint that the fall of the Roman republic was caused by a lack of civic spirit in any of the four possible senses. But that of course did not withhold later writers to criticize their own society on the basis of this logic.

The second kind of corruption is somewhat more ambiguous, morally. It is in a sense the opposite of the first kind. If that involved the abandonment of the public trust, this consists in making oneself its *dominus*. Such behavior reveals an immoderate desire for personal pre-eminence and power, without regard for the public interest. At this point authority becomes 'authoritarian'. The moral ambiguity of this kind of corruption stems from the fact that important elements of *virtus* must be present in a man if he is to succeed in or even begin with the implementation of such tyrannical designs. Cicero considered Julius Caesar the foremost example of such a man. He hated him with all his heart for overthrowing the *vetus res publica*; but almost in spite of himself he had to admit that he also admired Caesar for his many virtues. As a threat to the ancient constitution this second kind of corruption was probably considered more dangerous than the first, by Cicero anyway. As all aspiring tyrants do, these overambitious men seek the favor of the multitude, whose help they need to subvert the authority of the *optimates* and make themselves master over the state. They are called *populares*: friends of the people, because they wish everything they do and say to be agreeable to the masses.[97]

There have been popular leaders for a long time, but in the past these had always respected the limits set by the constitution. The real trouble started with the Gracchus-brothers, who went far beyond their predecessors in their efforts to cripple the authority of the *nobilitas*, most notably through a program of land redistribution from the rich to the poor.[98] Gaius, the youngest of the two, added insult to injury. 'Whereas in the past all popular leaders, whenever they rose to speak, had turned their faces to the right towards the senate-house and the part of the Forum which is known as the *comitium*, he now created a precedent by turning, whenever he addressed the people, to the left towards the Forum proper, and he made a regular habit of this procedure. Thus, by a slight change of posture and deviation from the normal practice, he raised an issue of immense importance and in a sense transferred the whole character of Roman politics from an aristocratic to a democratic basis; for what his action really implied was that the orators should address themselves to the people and not to the senate.'[99] No wonder that Cicero did not like the Gracchii. He and his fellow-*optimates* were convinced that they, and those who acted in their spirit, were in reality only after the crown.[100]

A nobleman cannot morally allow this to happen. To just stand there and watch passively how one is being excluded from one's rightful place in the constitution, would be truly ignoble. Hence, the nobleman is obliged to resist those who aim to change the state into a 'pure' monarchy or a 'pure' democracy. *A theory of resistance and tyrannicide is implicit in the classical idea of nobility.* Indeed, the killing of a tyrant is 'the fairest of all splendid deeds'.[101] 'For there can be no fellowship between us and tyrants (..) whom it is honorable to kill. (..) For just as the limbs are amputated, if they begin to lose their blood and their life, as it were, and are harming the other parts of the body, similarly if the wildness and monstrousness of a beast appears in human form, it must be removed from the common humanity, so to speak, of the body.' This is a duty.[102] These are Cicero's very own words, as expressed in *De Officiis*. One can imagine their influence.[†]

[†] Of course, this vindication of tyrannicide was not merely an abstract, theoretical statement of principle. In the front of his mind Cicero had one specific killing, viz. that of Caesar by, among others, Marcus Brutus. As a consequence these two men have subsequently become symbols of the principle of monarchy, and the principle of aristocracy respectively, to such an extent that when we hear either one of them praised or condemned by a writer of a later age we may with some assurance draw a conclusion as to the political views of that person. See Gundolf 1924; Clark 1981

NOTES

1. Cicero, *De Rep.*, VI.13, 'Omnibus qui patriam conservaverint, adiuverint, auxerint, certum esse in caelo definitum locum.'

2. Cicero, *De Inv.*, II.160

3. Cicero, *Orator*, 120

4. E.g. Cicero, *De Orat.*, I.68-69; See Mitchell 1991, pp.21-23

5. Cf. Cicero, *De Off.*, I.153-155

6. Cicero, *De Off.*, I.156

7. Cicero, *De Orat.*, I.33

8. Cicero, *De Orat.*, II.178

9. Cicero, *De Orat.*, II.182

10. Cicero, *De Orat.*, II.182

11. Cicero, *De Off.*, II.43-44; Cicero, *De Orat.*, II.182

12. Cicero, *De Orat.*, II.206

13. Cicero, *De Orat.*, II.209-211

14. Cicero, *De Orat.*, I.107-109; I.145-147

15. See Gelzer 1962/64, vol.I, pp.20-24. The office of military tribune was normally followed by the questorship, and then customarily by the post of aedile of tribune of the people. Only if these lower offices had been held successfully, the highest offices of praetor, consul, and censor came within one's reach.

16. Cicero, *De Off.*, I.74

17. Cicero, *De Off.*, I.74

18. Or perhaps one should say that both comprise more than a specific kind of knowledge. Hellegouarc'h 1972, pp.256-267, argues that *humanitas* is 'une notion qui englobe de la façon la plus vaste toutes celles qui constituent la *prudentia*'. The latter virtue is said to comprise both *temperantia* and *iustitia*, and *temperantia* in its turn is made up of *continentia*, *clementia*, and *modestia*. The present author believes that this picture is overly systematic. The Romans were not particularly interested in such neat and logical categorizations. But it is a fact that to their mind all of these virtues belong together.

19. This obviously harks back to the link between leadership and *beneficentia*.

20. Both of these aspects of *humanitas* are of course intimately related to the notion of *ethos* expounded above. *Clementia* as well as *decorum* are central to the presentation of the statesman's personality in public life.

21. Seneca, *De Clem.*, I.3.3

22. Seneca, *De Clem.*, I.12.3

23. Cicero, *De Off.*, I.88; Cf.Hellegouarc'h 1972, pp.261-263

24. Plutarch, *Caesar*

25. Sallust, *Bel.Cat.*, LIII-LIV

26. Sallust, *Bel.Cat.*, LIV

27. Plutarch, *Cato Maior*, c.5

28. Ramage 1973, passim

29. Cf. MacMullen 1974, p.58, who speaks of 'an almost incredible snobbery' in Tacitus, who was 'in certain respects an utter fool'.

30. Cicero, *De Off.*, I.99

31. Cicero, *De Off.*, I.99

32. Cicero, *De Off.*, I.122-130

33. Cicero, *De Off.*, I.132

34. Cicero, *De Off.*, I.135

35. Cicero, *De Off.*, I.139

36. Herodotus, *Hist.*, III.80-82

37. Thucydides, *Pelop.War*, VIII,97 The alternative translation has even stronger overtones of partisanship: 'Indeed, for the first time, at least in my life, the Athenians appear to have been well governed'. See the Penguin ed. of 1985, with notes by Finley, p.620n10

38. See only general survey of the ideal of the mixed constitution in antiquity is Aalders 1968. But see also Ryffel 1973; Fritz 1975

39. Aristotle, *Pol.*, 1279a22-1279b10

40. Aristotle, *Pol.*, 1301b39ff

41. Aristotle, *Pol.*, 1293b34-35

42. Polybius, *Hist.*, VI.3.5-6

43. Polybius, *Hist.*, VI.3.2-7

44. This famous notion is to be found in Polybius, *Hist.*, VI.9.10

45. Polybius, *Hist.*, VI.4.7-8

46. Polybius, *Hist.*, VI.5.5-8

47. Polybius, *Hist.*, VI.5.10-6.12

48. Polybius, *Hist.*, VI.4.8-11

49. Polybius, *Hist.*, VI.9.9

50. Polybius, *Hist.*, VI.7.4-8

51. Polybius, *Hist.*, VI.7.9

52. Polybius, *Hist.*, VI.8.1-2

53. Polybius, *Hist.*, VI.8.2-6

54. Polybius, *Hist.*, VI.9.2-9

55. Polybius, *Hist.*, VI.57.1

56. Polybius, *Hist.*, VI.9.12-13

57. Polybius, *Hist.*, VI,10

58. Polybius, *Hist.*, VI.11.11-12

59. Polybius, *Hist.*, VI.18.7-8

60. Polybius, *Hist.*, VI.6-17

61. Aalders 1968, ch.14

62. Aalders 1968, pp.117ff.

63. Tacitus, *Ann.*, IV.33

64. Aalders 1968, pp.112-113

65. Cicero, *De Rep.*, I.42

66. Cicero, *De Rep.*, I.43

67. Cicero, *De Rep.*, I.44

68. Cicero, *De Rep.*, I.45; I.54; I.69

69. Cicero, *De Rep.*, I.69

70. Cicero, *De Rep.*, I.58; Cf. *De Leg.*, III.24

71. Cicero, *De Rep.*, I.70

72. Polybius, *Hist.*, VI.2.3-4

73. Polybius, *Hist.*, VI.48.2-6

74. Polybius, *Hist.*, VI.50.4-5

75. Plutarch, *Lycurgus*

76. Cf. Aalders 1968, passim. This is the unmistakable drift of the discussion of mixed government by Aristotle, Polybius, and Cicero alike. Cf. e.g. Aristotle, *Pol.*, 1318b7-18 and 1309a1-4; Polybius, *Hist.*, VI.44 and VI.51.5-8; Cicero, *De Rep.*, II.56,59,61; *De Leg.*, III.6 ff., III.27-28

77. Cicero, *De Rep.*, I.69; *De Leg.*, III,30-32

78. In *De Rep.*, II.57 Cicero seems to suggest that the whole magistracy partakes in the monarchical element of the government, but in *De Leg.*, III.8 he is at one with Polybius, *Hist.*, VI.11.12 and includes only the consuls.

79. It has been asserted by Loewenstein 1973, p.175, among others, that 'factual sovereignty of the senate had no basis in the republican constitution. It developed through the clever manipulation of constitutional institutions by the senatorial managers'. It puzzles the present author how one could come to such a conclusion. The ancient sources are not particularly secretive about the factual and normative preponderance of the senate in Roman politics.

80. Cicero, *De Leg.*, III.4

81. Cicero, *De Leg.*, III.12

82. Cicero, *De Leg.*, III.37 ff.

83. Cicero, *De Leg.*, III.6-8; Cf. Polybius, *Hist.*, VI.12

84. Cicero, *De Leg.*, III.28

85. Cicero, *Pro Sest.*, 137

86. Cicero, *De Rep.*, I.39

87. Cicero, *De Leg.*, III.10,33; Cf.Polybius, *Hist.*, VI.14

88. Cicero, *De Leg.*, III.7

89. Cicero, *De Leg.*, III.10-11,27

90. Cicero, *De Leg.*, III.39

91. Cicero, *De Leg.*, III.38-39

92. Cicero, *De Leg.*, III.34,38-39

93. Cicero, *De Leg.*, III.34

94. Cicero, *De Leg.*, III.30-32

95. Cicero, *De Leg.*, III.10,28ff.

96. Polybius saw in this logic the cause of the final defeat of the Carthaginians, and one of the main explanations of Rome's success. See *Hist.*, VI.52

97. Esp. Cicero, *Pro Sest.*, 96-98

98. Plutarch, *Gaius Gracchus*; Plutarch, *Tiberius Gracchus*

99. Plutarch, *Gaius Gracchus*, c.5

100. Plutarch, *Tiberius Gracchus*, c.14, c.19; Plutarch, *Gaius Gracchus*, c.14

101. Cicero, *De Off.*, III.19

102. Cicero, *De Off.*, III.32

PART IV

THE APPEAL TO THE ANCIENTS

CHAPTER NINE

THE THÈSE NOBILIAIRE

Thus in the eighteenth century many mediocre minds were engaged in finding the only correct formula to establish a balance between the social orders, the nobility, the king, the parlements *etc., and suddenly everything -king,* parlements, *and nobility- had disappeared. The proper balance within this antagonism was the revolution of all social relations, which were the foundations of these feudal edifices and their antagonism*

Karl Marx[1]

1. Constitutionalism redivivum

More than anything, *Römertum*, as described in the previous chapter, i.e. of a literary rather than a legal kind, shaped the political and moral thought of the nobility of the ancien régime. It is the Roman notion of the good man and the good life that one encounters wherever one looks. It is true, of course, that there was disagreement over many if not most things moral and political. Other, alternative ideals vied for the heart and the head of the nobleman, most notably those of the church, whose teachings sometimes stood in glaring contrast with the notions derived from the pagans, most obviously where the latter extolled pride instead of humility, and urged to vengeance for every insult however small. However, this contradiction seemed to have bothered the theologians more than the noblemen. The condemnation of the aristocratic ethos of pride and glory was one of the principal themes of Christian moral argument in the ancien régime.[2] But the criticism did not achieve much. His honor was and remained the most important thing to the average nobleman.

This is not to say that all noblemen agreed on the exact meaning of these notions. On the contrary, throughout the ancien régime an intensive discussion took place about the moral and political significance of *vertu*, *devoir*, *honneur*, and, of course, *noblesse*. The point is that the moral and political discourse of that era centered on these notions. (It is a measure of our distance from this mental world that we do not think in terms of these notions at all.) Within limits their meaning could and did shift. Sometimes 'Spanish' pride was stressed, at other times 'Italian' elegance, but both were part of virtue and honor. The omnipresent Romans gave enough latitude for various shades of meaning, but also secured a basic unity and continuity.

By and large, this aristocratic discourse on morals and politics still awaits to be thoroughly researched. Although some work has appeared on noble thought, most of it is strongly tainted by the teleological view of history. It seems almost impossible not to give in to the temptation to link 'the aristocratic experience' to 'the origins of modern culture'.[3] In the present and the ensuing chapter we will merely give an overview of a small but important part of the aristocratic discourse of the ancien régime, viz. that which is concerned with political or governmental structure. *Römertum* is clearly present there too. For practical reasons our discussion has to be limited to this issue. The investigation of the Roman connection in the nobility's social thought at large must be left to a future work.

1.1. The ancient constitution

The history of the European theory of government is sometimes presented as the history of two competing views, the ascending and the descending thesis. The first thesis localizes original power in the people, in the community. The king is somehow chosen by the people, whom he represents and to whom he remains accountable. Consequently, a king who malfunctions can be deposed. The second thesis locates original power in God. The king derives his power from above, and is thus responsible and accountable to God alone. Due to the influence of Christianity the descending, theocratic view became an orthodoxy in the middle ages and the ascending, democratic view was driven underground. The latter reemerged in the early renaissance, however, and in the course of the following centuries gradually gained the upper hand over the former.[4]

But, while heuristically quite useful, this framework makes a teleological view of history virtually inescapable. Departing from this dichotomy every ascending theory as of, say, Marsiglio of Padua's *Defender of the Peace* (1324) will appear a democratic theory in aspiration and intent. If the 'early-modern' theorists did not draw the ultimate conclusions, it is because they were still too much caught up in pre-modern conceptions, or, alternatively, because they did not dare to spell out their results for fear of persecution. From this point of view the aristocratic political theory of the period from the renaissance to the revolution must look utterly confused, because these doctrines depend to an overwhelming degree on historical argument, whereas both the descending and the ascending thesis, strictly spoken, render the appeal to the past unnecessary.[5] The conclusion usually drawn is not surprising. Aristocratic thinking was superficial and reactionary; it is of the good-old-days type, carrying only emotional weight. To the extent that it contains anything of value, that lies buried under the historical material.

Accordingly, modern commentators of aristocratic thought are often severe, and tend to skip everything which seems merely of antiquarian interest, in search of abstract statements[6] of natural law. As a result, they bypass what is in effect the core of the argumentation.

This argumentation, the aristocratic tradition in political thought, was a product of the sixteenth century. It was developed by a few humanist jurists, whose books became the backbone of this tradition. All later authors, in the seventeenth and eighteenth century, really did nothing more than elaborate on the work of these men, specifying some points and changing minor elements, but on the whole adding little. Montesquieu is a late representative of this tradition. His magnum opus, the *Spirit of the Laws*, is undoubtedly a masterpiece, and one of the greatest products of aristocratic classicism, but its general framework and main theses can hardly be said to have been new.

The aristocratic tradition in political thought can best be seen as a protracted intellectual attempt to define the limits of the power of the central government under the head of the king. It is the reflection of a debate with royalist ideologists, the expounders of the *thèse royale*, who asserted that there ought to be no such limits. Claude de Seyssel (1450-1520), author of *La Grande Monarchie de France* (1519), Étienne Pasquier, author of *Recherches de la France* (1560), François Hotman (1524-1590), author of *Francogallia* (1573), and Phillippe du Plessis Mornay (1549-1623), the most probable author of *Vindiciae contra Tyrannos* (1579), to name only the most celebrated, were the founders of this tradition.[7] These men posed the question that remained pivotal to the political theory of the ancien régime: what is the true nature of the French monarchy? Moreover, they introduced the conceptual apparatus and the method of investigation that remained authoritative in answering that question. What makes this tradition of political theory so strange and impervious to us, is that today this question, as well as the conceptual apparatus, and the method of investigation have been completely discarded, because from a modern point of view they seem inadequate or even meaningless.

The strangeness of the political theory of the ancien régime, as devised by these men, is ultimately caused by an ontological shift, brought about by the enlightenment-thinkers and, particularly, the romantics. We will return to this in the last chapter. For now, it is sufficient to recall what has been said about this subject in the first chapter, viz. that the ontology in the ancien régime was heavily dependent upon classical example. This meant, most importantly, that reality and change are mutually exclusive, and that being therefore presupposes rest, stability, the holding on to timeless, i.e. essential features. Applied to political theory this ontology readily yields the question as to the true nature of a regime. Moreover, it readily focuses one's attention in a specific direction, towards the distant past, where the 'original or first principles' -as Machiavelli baptized them[8]- can supposedly be found.

This way of looking at these things was utterly classical. 'Original or first principles' was perhaps a new expression, but it referred to what the Romans had called the *mos maiorum*, the customs of the forefathers, and came to be known as the ancient constitution or the fundamental laws, two concepts which, implicitly or explicitly, played a tremendous role in the aristocratic political thought of the ancien régime throughout Europe. Irrespective of the exact terminology, the crux of the argument was always that one had to stick to the original principles of a regime, on pain of utter corruption and ultimate annihilation. But of course the original principles of a regime can only be determined if one possesses a typology of principles or constitutions. This is the conceptual apparatus referred to above. Not surprisingly, the constitutional scheme that came to be generally used was also derived from the ancients. It is the Aristotelian-Polybian scheme of six pure and one mixed constitution. The humanist jurists of the sixteenth century essentially applied this classical way of looking at things to their own country, and therewith set the tone for the following two centuries.

Their 'research-agenda' might be summarized as follows. The principal issue was the nature of the French regime. All agreed that it was a monarchy, but the question was what institutions characterized a monarchy. Was it a pure monarchy, or rather a mixed monarchy, containing elements of aristocracy and democracy? What was part of the monarchy's principles and what constituted a corruption? What were signs of the onset of tyranny? Was tyranny worse or to be preferred to mob-rule? What rights do the subjects of a king have, who turns into a tyrant?

To answer questions such as these our authors turned to the past, in order to determine how things had originally been arranged, and should therefore be arranged. Thus the nature of the government of the Gauls, the Romans, and the Franks -the three peoples that had inhabited the realm in the remote past, and could therefore be seen as *maiores*-, and the relationship between them, was considered of supreme importance. This issue was virtually all-decisive. For instance, if the kings were the successors of the Frankish leaders, and the latter had been elective, the former were also by nature elective. In that case, succession to the throne by any other rule constituted a corruption of the ancient constitution and a sign of (impending) tyranny, and should be canceled. In the course of time various theories were presented, but a consensus was never reached, one of the greatest sources of disunity being which contemporary institutions were part of the ancient constitution, and which were later added. Most hotly contested were the status of the estates-general, the *parlements*, the feudal law, and Roman law.

One can discern, *in abstracto*, two somewhat different positions within the aristocracy. Let us call them the position of the sword -the *thèse feodale*-, and that of the robe -the *thèse parlementaire*-; both are variants of the *thèse nobiliaire*. To these the royalists opposed the *thèse royale*. The position of the sword and of the royalists were unambiguous. The *thèse royale* was virtually the opposite of the *thèse feodale*. It was developed by a string of writers, mostly of a legal bent, strongly committed to the adoption of Roman law as the law of the land. The most influential were the three we already encountered, viz. Budé, Bodin, and Bossuet (the last of whom was not a lawyer, but a theologian), yet there were others as well. They asserted that the power of the king was absolute, because he was the legal successor of the Roman emperor. Hence, Roman law was directly applicable to the French realm, and feudal law a reprehensible corruption, due to a period of royal weakness. The estates were a merely advisory body, and the sovereign courts simple courts of law, with no legislative significance. The king was the sole legislator.

The *thèse feodale*, devised in particular by Hotman and Du Plessis Mornay, asserted that France had a mixed government, like the one the Romans had had for centuries. The origin of its political institutions lay in the German forests, and had been brought to Gaul in the fifth century by the conquering Franks. Tacitus' *Germania* was constantly quoted as a source. The Roman institutions had been wiped out by this conquest. Therefore, the French kings were the successors of the Frankish warlords, who had had limited power, and not of the Roman emperors, who had had absolute power. The estates-general was the principal limit on the royal power; it was identical to the popular assembly of the ancient Franks. The sovereign courts were a royalist innovation, with no historical legitimacy at all. Moreover, Roman law was in principle not applicable in France. The realm was wholly governed by feudal law, which was of ancient Germanic stock.

Finally, there was a distinct position associated with the *noblesse de robe*, the *thèse parlementaire*. In a sense, this position held the middle ground. Following Seyssel and Pasquier, its proponents argued that France was an absolute, but nevertheless tempered monarchy. In this tradition its institutions were traced back to ancient Gaul, as described in Caesars' *De Bello Gallico*. The writers defending this thesis sided with the royalists with regard to the estates and the legislative capacity of the king. But in contrast to them, they insisted that royal power was constitutionally limited by the sovereign courts, whom they considered the successors of the ancient popular assemblies. Hence, they ultimately agreed with the 'feudalists' that, like ancient Rome, France had a mixed government, and that a king who refused to seek *aide et conseil* was a tyrant.

Obviously, this is a simplified picture of the debate. It neglects the evolution that occurred in all three of these political positions. Nevertheless, the present writer wants to maintain that these were more or less the terms in which the political debate of the ancien régime took place, from the sixteenth century until the revolution. Because it is so different from our own debate, it is commonly ignored. The few historians who have tried to make sense of the aristocratic position have generally assimilated the *thèse nobiliaire* to the ascending thesis, mentioned above.[9] References to the estates, to ancient popular assemblies, and to elective kings seem to confirm that interpretation, and are often presented as such. On such a view, aristocratic theorizing becomes an early, as yet incomplete, instance of democratic thought.

But such a reading is evidently wrong. The *thèse nobiliaire* was not a theory of popular sovereignty, either in fact or in aspiration. First, the ancient constitution -the *mos maiorum*- limited everyone's sovereignty. Secondly, the popular assemblies were generally conceived of as a part of a mixed government, leaving substantial powers to the aristocratic and the monarchical element. Thirdly, everyone agreed that democracy was about as evil as tyranny, and more impracticable. The commons had to have a say in the government, but it had to be very limited; on that there was no quarrel between the royalists and the defenders of the aristocratic cause. The issue was mainly about the rights of the *noblesse* vis-à-vis the king, and that debate cannot be intelligibly rendered in terms of the descending versus the ascending thesis. If one wants to speak of sovereignty at all in this context, one would have to speak of the sovereignty of the dead, of the past, of the ancestors. No one -not even the king of the absolutists- was not subject to their *auctoritas*. The question was merely what the *maiores* had said.

1.2. Royal aspirations

In 987 the Carolingian king Louis V died after falling from his horse, whereupon the *grands* elected Hugh Capet as their king. At this occasion the archbishop Adalbero of Reims delivered a famous speech, in which he asserted that kingship was not a matter of hereditary right, but of mental and bodily capability. This did not have much effect, however, as for the next two centuries the Capetians were able to have their sons crowned king during their lifetime. Thus France became a hereditary monarchy in practice, long before it was one in theory. At the time of the death of Philip II -also named 'Augustus'- in 1223, the tradition of succession to the throne had acquired such durability that his son could succeed him without having been officially crowned before his father's death.

The transition from Capetian to Valois kings did not constitute a dynastic break, like the earlier transitions from the Merovingian to the Carolingian, and from the Carolingian to the Capetian dynasty. The first Valois king, Philip VI, was a direct descendent of the Capetian king Philip III (1270-1285), and given the laws of succession that had become thoroughly established by that time, he was the First Prince of the Blood and the legitimate successor. The same goes for the transition of the kingship from the House of Valois to the House of Bourbon, with the accession of Henry IV in 1589. That is why the writers of the ancien régime did not speak of a *quatrième race* and a *cinqième race*. Louis XIII, Louis XIV, Louis XV, and Louis XVI were the descendents of Hugh Capet, and therefore belonged to the *troisième race*.

The Capetian and Valois kings set out to establish a more integrated and centralized French state under one head: themselves. Understandably, this royal policy was a thorn in the flesh of the nobility, which immediately started to voice its discontent, depicting the extension of royal authority as an infringement on its ancient and well-founded rights, and complaining that 'la douce France' no longer deserved its name, now that they had been enslaved.[10] Here we have the beginnings of the political antagonism that dominated the entire ancien régime.

The medieval warrior class -the feudal lords and their noble vassals- resisted the process of royal aggrandizement of which it felt itself the victim, from the day the Capetians began to tighten and extend their grip on the French realm. By the beginning of the thirteenth century there had already been numerous protests against royal usurpation.[11] Until the second half of the sixteenth century, however, these protests were voiced mainly through violent conspirations and uprisings in times when the power of the crown was enfeebled.[12] In the end all of these uprisings and rebellions of the feudal class proved to be ineffective, although some brought the kingdom on the verge of destruction. Paradoxically, the rebellions may even have contributed to the enhancement of royal power and centralization, because they probably quickened the introduction of standing armies, country-wide taxes and a bureaucracy. With ups and downs the build-up of royal power went on year after year, decade after decade, century after century. By the sixteenth century the position of the French kings had already become quite exalted, as reflected for instance by the fact that during the reign of Francis I (1515-1547) the traditional closing formula of new royal statutes -'le roi a ordonné et établi par délibération de son conseil'- was replaced by the formula 'car tel est notre plaisir'.[13]

And yet, these monarchs were not absolute kings. Their prominence should not be exaggerated.[14] Undeniably, the power of the French kings had by this time transcended many of its medieval limits, but it was still severely circumscribed by various forces. To begin with, the particularist, feudal and clientelist fidelity to the great nobles in many places still put the allegiance of the population to the kings in the shade, setting definite limits to what the latter could do. Moreover, the bureaucracy and the army were as yet far too small to make a substantial political centralization feasible. Around 1500 there were about 12,000 royal officials on a total population of about 15 million, allowing only a very moderate degree of interference in people's life.[15] The royal army counted little more than 20,000 soldiers, many of them highly unreliable, which was clearly insufficient to enable the kings to press ahead with anything against the will of a large number of people. Also, the great nobles and the larger towns commanded considerable armies themselves. The Duc de Montmorency for example presumably had a following of eight hundred armed horsemen when he attended the council of Fontainebleau in 1560, and could have recruited an even larger army had there been any need.[16] Before new statutes and ordinances were issued the advice of the great nobles, the prelates and the major towns was still commonly invoked.[17] Possibly the most telling indication of the limitedness of the kings' power is the fact that in 1543 the annual revenue from the *taille* was about as high as it had been under Louis XI in 1481, whereas both prices and incomes had risen considerably in the intervening sixty years. To pay all their expenses, boosted by the Italian wars, the French kings of the first half of the sixteenth century had no other option than turning to expedients like selling the crown jewels and parts of the patrimonial domain, setting up a system of public credit, and creating more and more venal offices.[18]

Nevertheless, royal authority was increasing. The government centered more and more around the person of the king, who increasingly relied on a small group of professional administrators, usually from the lesser nobility, whose loyalty was secured by the fact that they owned everything they had to him. The drift towards royal authoritarianism became quite outspoken in the first half of the sixteenth century. However, a literate resistance of the feudal class failed to materialize as yet. In view of the general lack of education characteristic of the *noblesse*, as discussed in an earlier chapter, this is hardly amazing. Things changed towards the end of the century, but in the meantime opposition to royal absolutism had arisen from a different corner, that of the robe.

1.3. The mainstay of the crown

This may seem remarkable, since the robe had played a central role in the process of royal aggrandizement. Before the reign of Philip II 'Augustus' (1180-1223) France was hardly a political unity. It was divided into various duchies, counties, and other lordships, which were all quite independent even though most were theoretically held in feudal tenure of the king.[19] Some of the feudal lords wielded considerably more power than the king, whose rule was in practice restricted to the patrimonial royal domain. Philip II introduced a number of administrative and legal reforms which in the long run considerably strengthened royal authority and diminished the power of the great vassals. He for example increasingly converted feudal services into monetary payments with which he hired mercenary troops, he furthered the independence of the towns, and what is most important, he laid the foundations of a system of royal law and governmental institutions, both on the central and on the local level, manned by officials appointed and paid by the crown.

This effort in state-building is reflected very clearly in the changing character of the *curia regis*, the highest governmental council within the realm. As the successor of the Carolingian *placitum* it originally consisted of the *grands* of the realm -the crown vassals, both lay and ecclesiastical-, who met when summoned by the king and exercised advisory as well as judicial and legislative functions. Already during the reigns of Louis VI (1108-1137) and Louis VII (1137-1180), however, the *curia regis* had begun to lose its strictly feudal character, as in addition to the great vassals towns and other corporations were sometimes allowed to send their representatives to its meetings. Moreover, the influence and the power of the royal officials within the *curia regis* -the so-called *curiales*, *palatini* or *domestici*; generally lesser nobles, sometimes *roturiers*- was growing slowly but incessantly.[20] Under Philip II the financial and judicial functions of the *curia regis* were little by little separated from it and put into the hands of the *domestici* at the royal chancellery. This process was completed by Philip's son Louis VIII (1223-1226) and grandson 'Saint' Louis IX (1226-1270), who created a specialized *chambre des comptes* for financial, and a *parlement* for judicial matters.

The creation of these specialized bodies was the outflow of the growing royal influence at the local level. The Capetian kings of the twelfth and thirteenth centuries had introduced royal officials named *baillis* and *sénéchaux*, who were superimposed on the *prévôts*, the local officials of the feudal lords, and represented the king in the provinces, administering for the crown and sitting as royal judges. With the growth of the patrimonial royal domain and the extension of royal authority over the other parts of France[21] the number and the power of these officials increased, and in the middle of the thirteenth century each was assigned a fixed jurisdiction, which established a network of royal agents throughout the realm.[22] At the central level this led to a substantial increase in the number of law cases on appeal from these *baillis* and *sénéchaux* that had to be decided by the king's council. But this council had already been put under pressure by the fact that the augmented position of the king had caused an equally substantial rise in the number of cases in first instance and cases on appeal from courts of dukes, counts and other lords. Until then nothing more than the periodic judicial session of the *curia regis*, called *curia in parlemento*,[23] in which the king himself presided over the deliberations and the judges were great lords and royal officials, the need now came to be felt for separate royal courts of professional judges. This led to the creation of a permanent *parlement* and *chambre des comptes* in Paris, soon to be followed by other, similar institutions throughout the realm. Hence, the sovereign courts were born, as well as a class of men neither noble nor *roturier*, but in between, a fourth estate as it were, the *gens de robe.*

In these developments the rediscovery at the end of the eleventh century of Roman law, or rather of the sixth-century Justinian compilation of it, played a crucial role. This massive text, known as the *Corpus Iuris Civilis*, consisted of the so-called Codex,-twelve books of ordinances and decisions of the Roman emperors before Justinian-, the Novels -the laws of Justinian himself-, the Institutes -a textbook for law students-, and most importantly, the Digests, also known as the Pandects - fifty books containing extracts of the opinions of Roman jurists on all kinds of legal questions. The *Corpus Iuris* represented a system of law that was very different from the Frankish and other Germanic legal institutions that predominated when it was rediscovered at the end of the eleventh century. Yet, due to the immense prestige of the ancients and the fact that the Roman empire was generally thought still to exist, it was not regarded as an ancient system of law applicable to a different society, but as the ideal law, as the embodiment of reason.[24] Accordingly, Roman law was unhesitatingly applied to the very different political system of the medieval world.

As a consequence, from the twelfth century onwards most of the French royal officials who sat in the *curia regis*, the sovereign courts, the *baillis*, and the *sénéchaux*, were trained in Roman law. These men were the first royalist jurists. In their circle one has to look for the beginnings of the tradition of *fidélité* towards the king that was passed on from generation to generation, uninterrupted until the revolution, within a part the French nobility. It was within this tradition that the *thèse royale* was born. Fundamental to this *thèse* was the idea, derived from Roman law, of the king as a sovereign legislator.[25] In the words of a prominent thirteenth-century legist, Philip de Beaumanoir, this idea can already be discerned: 'si veut le roi, si veut la loi'. Significantly, this is a somewhat free translation of one of the most renowned phrases from Justinianus' Digests, 'quod principi placuit, leges habet vigorem'.[26]

Since this idea was clearly incompatible with the feudal view of society and the concomitant idea of law as custom, the legists began to develop different conceptions of society and law that suited better with their political theory. They gradually replaced the feudal conception of society as a pyramid without direct links between a lord and his subvassals, by a conception of society as a collection of legally equal subjects under a sovereign king, and they replaced the idea of law as custom, limiting the king's prerogative, by the idea of law as the product of royal legislation, giving shape to this prerogative. It goes without saying that this theoretical revolution did not take place overnight. For a long time, perhaps until the seventeenth century, many elements of the traditional, medieval views of government, society, and the law were retained in royalist thought. On the other hand, even in the twelfth and thirteenth century their thought already contained elements altogether foreign to the medieval mind.

As an important mainstay of the crown in those late-medieval days, the *gens de robe* used their position as royal counselors in the *curia regis*, the sovereign courts, the *baillis*, and the *sénéchaux*, to further the interests of the king. The relationship between the king and his sovereign courts was close. Major issues of legislation were usually decided in a joint session of the *curia regis*, the *parlement* and the *chambre des comptes*, overlapping membership of these councils was frequent, and the king often recruited members of the sovereign courts as advisers in matters of law and legislation.[27] In disputes between the king and his vassals or other subjects, many of which were of an utterly political nature, the sovereign courts always took the side of the crown and decided in its favor.[28] It for example assumed the right to interfere whenever a vassal's administration of justice in his fief was not in compliance with royal law; much to the distress and irritation of these vassals, many of whom were not prepared to accept more than a formal overlordship of the king over their territory.[29]

Soon after they had been separated from the *curia regis* and had become permanent courts the sovereign courts were assigned three duties, which were an integrated part of the process of legislation and gave them a *de facto* share in the legislative power. These were consecutively the duty to promulgate *arrêtes de règlement*, the duty to registrate new royal laws, and the duty to remonstrate. All of these were assigned to the sovereign courts by the king in his own interest. The duty to promulgate *arrêtes de règlement* consisted of issuing decrees overruling *coutumes* that manifestly contradicted royal laws.[30] The duty to registrate consisted of recording new royal laws[31] and notifying subordinate *baillis* and *sénéchaux*, by which way they were made known to the whole administration. The duty to remonstrate consisted of the obligation to delay registration in case of legal objections, which served to ensure that new legislation was not inconsistent with existing royal law or in some other way contradictory to the interests of the crown.[32]

1.4. The reconsideration of the robe

However, from the fifteenth century onwards the sovereign courts and the crown grew apart. The sovereign courts began to claim that the registration and the remonstrations were much more than an administrative procedure guaranteeing public notice and the uniformity of the laws. They began to expound the idea that the acceptance and registration of new laws by the sovereign courts constituted a kind of consecration of these laws, removing the flavor of arbitrariness and giving the laws the stamp of legality and legitimacy. Then, one day, they claimed that the ancient constitution of the French monarchy dictated such a consecration. Hence, the royalist party was split in two. The *robins* closest to the king remained faithful defenders of the *thèse royale*, demanding complete sovereignty for the monarch, but those associated with the sovereign courts gradually began to take a different view of the kingdom's government, developing what in effect became the *thèse parlementaire*, a variant of the *thèse nobiliaire*.

The introduction of royal *lettres de jussion* and *lits de justice* around 1400 reflect the change in the relationship between the sovereign courts and the crown. *Lettres de jussion* were issued whenever a sovereign court, after it had received the king's response to its objections, still refused to registrate new edicts, and ordered instantaneous and unconditional registration. A *lit de justice* was held whenever a sovereign court remained disobedient in spite of a *lettre de jussion*. In that case the king came to the court in person, to see to the registration.[33] Disapproving of such authoritarian measures, the magistrates started to add the phrase *lecta et publicata de expresso mandato domini regis* to edicts, in case of enforced registration.[34] Finally, the establishment of the *grand conseil* in 1497 as a separate judicial body to which the kings could evoke cases before the sovereign courts was a clear sign of the flagging relationship between the crown and the *gens de robe*.[35]

To a substantial degree increasing royal activism was the cause of this alienation. The number of royal ordinances, for instance, was rising steeply in the renaissance.[36] Under those circumstances, it was not far-fetched to conclude that old ways were put under a strain. But that is only half of the story. For the greater independence of the *gens de robe* is also a part of the explanation. The immediate cause of that was of course the proliferation of the venality of offices, which made many magistrates virtually unremovable. Yet, unremovability alone does not explain the robe's new attitude; it was accompanied by a new conception of its political role. No longer satisfied with a position as simple servants of the king, the *robins* began to conceive of themselves as royal counselors, an aspiration which was stimulated by the increasing number of ennoblements of magistrates.

2. The sources of the tradition

Claude de Seyssel, a Savoyard nobleman and a learned jurist, who spent the largest part of his active life in the service of Louis XII, as a diplomat and a royal counselor, among other things as a *maître des rêquetes*, may be credited with having opened the debate, although in some respects he belongs to the pre-history of aristocratic political thought. Most importantly, he was still a royalist in siding with Roman law against the *consuetudines feudorum*, whose authority in France he denied.[37] Moreover, in his magnum opus *La Grande Monarchie de France*, in which he gives an outline of the French constitution, it is assumed rather than explicitly expounded that the constitution is historically vindicated. But he was already a true classicist in that the ancients furnished him with his models. Browsing through the pages of this work, one encounters the ancients everywhere, on the education of princes,[38] on the importance of virtue as opposed to noble extraction,[39] on infantry and military discipline,[40] and so on.

2.1. Claude Seyssel

Seyssel translated, among others, Xenophon, Thucydides, and Appian into French.[41] For our purposes, his preface to the translation of Appian, addressing the king himself, is particularly interesting. Is opens with a summary of the discussion between some prominent Persians, recounted in the third book of Herodotus' *Histories*, about the form of state they ought to adopt.[42] Three opinions predominated. 'One among them was of the opinion that they ought to adopt a popular government (what the Greeks called a democracy) in order to avoid tyranny, which most often succeeds a monarchical regime, the rule of a single person (..) who exempts himself and is free from all law, is subject to no punishment nor to private reprimand. (..) The second speaker supported a form of government between the other two which is called "aristocracy", that is the rule of the principal men of the greatest wealth. By this means they would avoid both the tyranny of the monarch and the confusion of the multitude. (..) The third speaker was of the opinion that monarchy was better, not only than the popular regime, which there seemed no difficulty in demonstrating, but also than the aristocratic regime.'[43] From the latter 'there soon follow, because of emulation and envy, discord, partialities, hatreds, and intrigues; then seditions, mutinies, injuries, and violent acts; and finally murders, expulsions, banishments, and persecutions until there is open civil war'.[44] Hence, 'it is monarchy that is the most tolerable and most suitable, taken all in all. In addition, one sees that all the great empires which existed before that of the Romans, namely, the Assyrians, the Medes and the Persians, and the Greeks in the person of Alexander, were created and governed by a single king. One also sees that most of the world has almost always been governed (and is still governed at present) by kings and monarchs. Even in the case of Rome, they began the same way. Afterwards (..) in all their important affairs and extreme dangers they were constrained to give total authority and power for limited times to a single individual who was not subject to any law whatever. Finally, their empire by necessity reverted to a monarchy'.[45]

Yet, this vindication of monarchy was not intended by Seyssel as a defense of absolute kingship. For, he continues, even these monarchies 'suffered decay and finally came to ruin and complete alteration'.[46] The empires in the past and at present which have enjoyed the longest duration, are those in which a general concord is maintained, which is impossible 'unless the leader (is) himself ruled by good laws and the customs of society for the common good, to prevent his royal and legitimate power from being transformed into tyranny and willful domination'.[47] At this crucial point Seyssel turns to France. 'Truly, Sire, when I carefully consider the form and manner of the regime which the kings your predecessors have introduced and maintained over the French people, I find it so reasonable and so civilized that it is altogether free from tyranny. That is the reason, in my opinion, why this regime, among all others (..) has endured so long and prospered and is now at the height of its glory and prosperity. *For, looking at this French empire as a whole, it partakes of all three forms of political government.*' (emphasis added) Here we have in a nutshell what became the core of the aristocratic tradition. With an appeal, not to abstract principles of natural law but to the national past, it is argued that France possesses a mixed government. With Seyssel both elements are already there: the *mos maiorum* and the constitutional scheme. What is lacking is merely the explicit historical defense of this conception of the ancient constitution. That was to be taken up first by Pasquier in the second half of the sixteenth century.

La Grande Monarchie de France commences with a similar discussion of the forms of state, and an overview of the 'state and empire of the Romans', which is said to have been 'especially (..) long ruled and governed by the consuls and the senate under the authority of the people. During this government it fared best and went on continually expanding until it went back to monarchy. In truth this state was so arranged that it shared traits of all three forms. (..) This was the best form of government of a community and popular empire at that time or since'.[48] That it was eventually smothered in dissolution, corruption, and civil war was due to the fact that the Romans had given the people more authority than was reasonable.[49] But Seyssel does not conclude that a better mix is the solution. Instead, after a discussion of the drawbacks of aristocracy, on the basis of the Venetian example, Seyssel concludes that monarchy is the best form of state, since experience shows that it will last longer than any popular or aristocratic state.[50] The French monarchy in particular is governed by a much better order than any others now existing or known from ancient history. However, that is because it is not an ordinary monarchy: it has some 'special traits'.[51] Most importantly, 'there are several remedies to check (the kings') absolute authority if they are unrestrained and willful. (..) The royal dignity and authority remains always entire, not totally absolute nor yet too much restrained, but regulated and bridled by good laws, ordinances, and customs'.[52] Of these bridles there are three: religion, justice, and *police*. Thus, although Seyssel refrains from using the concept of a mixed government in *La Grande Monarchy*, it is clear that he had something of that kind in mind.

There is little doubt that Seyssel saw the sovereign courts as the principal check on the power of the kings.[†] They represent the bridle of justice. 'From the very outset they were staffed with such great persons in such number and of such power that the kings have always been subject to them with respect to distributive justice.'[53] 'They are a true Roman senate.'[54] Not only are they a check on the king, the insolence of the nobility is also tempered by 'fear of the system of justice'.[55] Feudal and seignorial courts do play a role in the government, but are answerable in the last resort to the sovereign courts.[56] Interestingly, Seyssel recognizes that most judicial officers belong to the third estate, since 'applying themselves more to learning than the nobility, (they) are more likely to be deserving of such responsibilities and thus obtain them by election or other means. (..) The same is true for offices of finance, accounts, secretaryships, and innumerable others which are available throughout the kingdom and which are not commonly held by members of the nobility'.[57] To the latter 'belongs the defense of the realm'.[58] Not once does Seyssel mention the estates-general by name, though he speaks of an 'occasional assembly' once, which resembles it. However, it is clear that this was not important to him.[59]

2.2. Étienne Pasquier

During the reigns of Francis I and Henry II the tendency towards royal authoritarianism became very outspoken. Little attention was paid to the sovereign courts' remonstrances, and the kings regularly resorted to evocation or enforced registration.[60] The ideas of Francis I about the constitutional role of the sovereign courts were clear almost from the day of his accession. He did not even keep up the appearance of seeking their judgement and advise.[61] It is illustrative of his opinion that when he received a delegation of the *parlement* of Paris in January 1518 he told it that France had a king and not a senate like Venice, and that the magistrates should therefore concern themselves with the administration of justice between subjects only.[62]

On the 24th of July 1527 a *lit de justice* was held at the *parlement* of Paris with the purpose of forcing the magistrates to register an edict

---

[†] Of the bridle of religion Seyssel says, on pp.53-54, that 'understanding that they must live in esteem and reputation as good Christians in order to have the love and complete obedience of the people, even though they themselves were not sufficiently dedicated to devotion to God and fear of Him, the kings of France have avoided doing outrageous and reprehensible things, if not always and in everything at least ordinarily'. *La Police*, the third bridle, consists of 'the many ordinances, made by the kings of France themselves and afterwards confirmed and approved from time to time, which tend to the conservation of the realm in general and in detail. These have been kept for such a long time that the princes never undertake to derogate from them; and if they wanted to do so, their commands would not be obeyed'. See pp.56-57

forbidding the sovereign courts to meddle with affairs of state and adding phrases expressing reservation to registrations of laws, which would affect future jurisprudence. In response to these according to the magistrates excessive royal claims, the president Guillart of the *parlement* held a speech setting out the *parlementaire* view of the nature of French kingship. After restating the traditional royalist idea of the king's unlimited authority, he asserted that the sovereign courts' constitutional role was indispensable, because it was an assembly representing the nation, a sort of estates-general.[63] In a similar situation in 1549 the first president Olivier informed Henry II that the *parlement* had originally been the king's council, in which all the important affairs of state were discussed and the royal policy was decided on. The fact that it had become a permanent body in the meantime had not changed its nature; it was still the senate of the monarchy.[64] What we witness here is the birth of the historical theory that was the linchpin of the political tradition of the robe. What Seyssel had still taken for granted, apparently became a matter of dispute in subsequent decades.

The first *parlementaire* writer to in extenso trace back this genealogy was the magistrate Étienne Pasquier. His magnum opus *Les Recherches de la France* appeared for the first time -in two volumes- in 1560 and 1565, but was revised and enlarged by him until the end of his life.[65] A very learned man indeed, his oeuvre breathes a thoroughly classicist spirit. Like Seyssel's, Pasquier's mind was filled with images from antiquity. The *Recherches* are in effect a pioneering effort to set out what were the *mos maiorum* of the French *res publica*. The ancestors, according to Pasquier, were the ancient Gauls.[66] Their institutions constitute the core of the ancient constitution of the French realm.[67] At the time, this was an entirely new view of the origins of France. The medieval chroniclers had begun their histories with the arrival of the Franks.[68] Pasquier's main source on the Gauls is Caesar's *De Bello Gallico*. Particularly book VI capita 11-20, which deal with the customs and the institutions of the Gauls, drew his attention.[69]

'Everywhere in Gaul', writes Caesar, 'there are but two classes of men who are of any account or consideration. The common people are treated almost as slaves, never venture to act on their own initiative, and are not consulted on any subject. Most of them, crushed by debt or heavy taxation or the oppression of more powerful persons, bind themselves to serve men of rank, who exercise over them all the rights that masters have over slaves. The two privileged classes are the druids and the knights. The druids officiate at the worship of the gods, regulate public and private sacrifices, and give rulings on all religious questions.(..) They are held in great honor by the people. They act as judges in practically all disputes, whether between tribes or individuals (..). All the druids are under one head, whom they hold in the highest respect. On his death, if anyone of the rest is of outstanding merit, he succeeds to the vacant place; if several have equal claims, the druids usually decide the election by voting, though sometimes they actually fight it out. On a fixed date in each year they hold a session in a consecrated spot in the country of the Carnutes, which is supposed to be the center of Gaul. (..) The druids are exempt from military service and do not pay taxes like other citizens. (..) Many present themselves of their own accord to become student of druidism, and others are sent by their parents or relatives. It is said that these pupils have to memorize a great number of verses -so many, that some of them spend twenty years at their studies. (..) The second class is that of the knights. When their services are required in some war that has broken out (..) these all take the field, surrounded by their servants and retainers, of whom each knight has a greater or smaller number according to his birth and fortune.'

Though admitting that there were differences between these ancient Gallic institutions and those of his own France, Pasquier saw in the druids the predecessors of his own social class, the robe, and in their assemblies the forerunner of the *parlements*.[70] The conclusion was that, as of old, the robe was a part of the ruling class, and the *parlements* an integrated element of the government of the realm. This explains why Pasquier went counter to the tradition and sought the social and political genealogy of France in Gaul. He knew from Caesar and Tacitus that the ancient Germans, the ancestors of the Franks, had had no druids, and spent their whole life in warlike pursuits.[71] Thus, if the French institutions were derived from the Franks the social and political position of the robe was awkward, and the *robins* could hardly claim to be members of the governing class under the ancient constitution. As we will see, the theorists of the *épée* were to draw the same conclusion at a later date, but with the opposite intention. In Pasquier's reading, the Francs were gradually 'naturalized', after their descent from the German woods, and became a part of the Gallic *chevalerie*.[72] As to Roman institutions, finally, these were by and large foreign to the ancient constitution. Gaul had been subjected by Caesar, and governed by the Romans for several centuries, but when it regained its old liberty, it resumed its ancient customs.[73] Therefore, Roman law was not applicable to the French realm. Rome was of interest only to antiquarians.[74]

Although Pasquier does not use the concept of *regimen mixtum*, he does distinguish between a monarchy and a tyranny, and asserts that in the first everyone including the king is subject to the law. This goes for France too. The kings have absolute powers, but 'render themselves voluntarily subject to the law.[75] 'Look how of old a species of aristocracy was joined to the monarchy.'[76] On this view, the stability and continuity of the monarchy depend heavily on the robe, the 'true' nobility. It is altogether crucial. 'As soon as an ordinance has been published and verified in the *parlement*, immediately the French people adhere to it without a murmur, as if this company were the link between the obedience of the subjects and the commands of the prince.'[77] Of course, in name the sovereign courts were relatively new, but as *placitum* and *champs de Mai* they were known to the government of the first and second race as well.[78] The estates-general on the other hand, Pasquier argued, have no role in government. They are an innovation, and form no part of the *mos maiorum*.[79]

Pasquier's ideas were highly influential in robe circles and seem to have been fairly representative of the *parlementaire* political thought of the late sixteenth and seventeenth century. Theorists like Du Haillan, Choppin, and the first president Harlay of the *parlement* of Paris closely followed his suit.[80] And the fact that in 1723 an edition of his collected works appeared, indicates that Pasquier's influence was anything but fleeting.

The end of the Italian wars in 1559 ushered in a period of crisis for the French monarchy, as a series of feeble rulers once again permitted the crown's authority to be challenged by the aristocracy, which felt that it had suffered a persistent encroachment on its rights under the kings of the first half of the century. To make matters worse, the spread of the reformation in France had acquired formidable dimensions by the middle of the century, which severely aggravated the crisis. Of the population as a whole never more than five percent was converted, but Protestantism proved to be particularly persuasive within the nobility. Fifty percent of it was converted to Protestantism -particularly Calvinism- in the 1560's.[81] Hence, although the huguenots, as they were called, were few in number, and eventually lost much of their support even within the aristocracy, they constituted an important political force at the time.[82] Protestantism thus added religious zeal to aristocratic malcontent about the 'despotic' behavior of French monarchs.[†83] From this powerful mixture came what were the first pronounced attempts to develop what became the *thèse feodale* in political theory.[84]

The classic texts of sixteenth-century 'feudal' political thought are written by huguenots: Hotman's *Francogallia* (1573), and the *Vindiciae*

[†] Contrary to what is still sometimes argued, by Sap 1993 for instance, there seems to be no logical, necessary link between the calvinist faith and the theories espoused by the sixteenth-century huguenots. They could and were adopted by others as well. Witness the writings of the Catholic monarchomachs. See Baumgartner 1975. Moreover, in the provincial capitals and in the councils of the remaining feudal magnates, aristocratic theorists such as Guy Coquille could be found, who also opposed royal absolutism. See Church 1941, ch.V. The truth is that the spirit of all these theories was not specifically Calvinist, but aristocratic. They did not stand for the rights of the 'chosen', but for the rights of those threatened most by the levelling effect of increasing royal power: the nobility. The religious issue was important only because it made the question of royal tyranny more pertinent.

contra Tyrannos (1579), probably written by Du Plessis Mornay, but published under the significant pseudonym of Junius Brutus.[85] Nevertheless, they contain hardly anything that is not already present in the works of Seyssel and Pasquier. They disclose the same intimacy with the classical sources, the same framework, and the same emphasis on French history. Apart from the fact that, judging by the number of citations from the Bible, Hotman and Mornay were much more religious than these earlier writers, the difference between them is first and foremost a matter of how they say it rather than what they say. The huguenots are much more radical and uncompromising in tone than Seyssel and Pasquier, but in substance their views are basically similar, although there are some significant differences in detail.

2.3. François Hotman

'For nearly twelve years', Hotman laments in the preface of his book, 'my miserable and unfortunate country has been scorched by the fires of civil war. (..) In reflecting upon these great calamities I have (..) fixed my attention on what is revealed by all the old French and German historians of our Francogallia, and from their writings I have compiled a summary of its constitution. They show that our commonwealth flourished in this form for more than a thousand years. From this review it is astonishing to find how great was the wisdom of our ancestors in constituting our commonwealth, and it does not seem possible for me to doubt in any way that the most certain remedy for our great afflictions should be sought in the constitution'.[86] One could not have wished for a more concise statement of the classicist framework.

In contrast to Pasquier, Hotman traces the origin of the French constitution back to the Franks, although he admits that 'our Gauls possessed that same form of government before they were brought under the power of the Romans'.[87] 'It is certain that the people who bore that name occupied a large part of Europe for many years and that they were German. Hence it is very surprising that no mention is made of them by Ptolemy, Strabo, and Pliny, and especially that no reference is to be found in Cornelius Tacitus.'[88] The answer must be, Hotman thinks, that 'Frank' was a title of honor later given to the Germans who had thrown off the Roman yoke.[89] They freed not only their German fatherland, but Gaul also, and added nearly the whole of Gaul to their state. The Franks intermingled with the Gauls, and became one people: hence the name of Francogallia.[90]

In view of this, it should not come as a surprise that Hotman was an outspoken opponent of the application of Roman law in France. His ideas on this issue are set out principally in another one of his tracts, the *Antitribonian* (1603).[91] In a nutshell, Hotman argues that since the laws of a state must be adapted to the form of state, and since the French state differs considerably from the Roman state, Roman law does not apply to the former.[92]

For a description of the institutions of the Germans Hotman relies heavily on Tacitus' *Germania*, a book that became staple fare in the aristocratic political tradition. This author has shown 'that kings in Germany (..) were created by suffrage only', a constitutional rule that is confirmed by later sources.[93] The Franks have always had kings, but their power is neither unlimited nor free; otherwise, they would be tyrants.[94] Whereas 'it is clear that no form of government is more remote from tyranny than this'.[95] The highest authority in the kingdom 'lay in the formal public council of the nation, which in later times was called the assembly of the three estates'.[96] This council embodies the three kinds of government, the regal, the aristocratic, and the popular type.[97] 'For such indeed was the form of government which the old philosophers (including Plato and Aristotle, whom Polybius and Cicero imitated) considered the best and most excellent, a form which was mixed and tempered from the three elements of monarchy, aristocracy and democracy. This was the form of commonwealth approved before all others by Cicero in his book of the Republic. For, since a kingly and a popular government are by nature at variance with each other, it is necessary to add some third or intermediate element common to both. Such is the role of the princes or nobles, who, because of the splendor and antiquity of their stock, approach the status of royalty, and who, because of their position as dependents (or, as is commonly put, subjects), have less dislike for those of plebeian birth'.[98] 'In constituting the kingdom of Francogallia our ancestors accepted Cicero's opinion that the best form of a commonwealth is that which is tempered by the mixture of the three kinds of government.'[99] The public council has been known by various names: as parliament or assembly of the three estates, *conventus generalis*, *curia regis*, and *placitum*.[100] 'The whole power of administering the kingdom lay with the public council.'[101] This is proved by the fact that royal laws and ordinances were concluded with the expression *quia tale est nostre placitum*, now maliciously and falsely rendered by royalist clerks as *car tel est notre plaisir*.[102]

This is a clear sign of the corruption, that according to Hotman gradually set in under the Capetian dynasty. 'As the authority of the council was supreme, the Capetians endeavored to diminish it and to substitute a number of approved judges for the council. Then they transferred the august name of parliament to that assembly of judges.'[103] Subsequently, 'all aspects of the power, dominion, and authority which we have shown to have reposed in the public council and parliament of estates throughout so many long years were entirely arrogated to itself by that spurious senate, and the kings saw that those coopted to its ranks could be depended on to be accommodating to their intentions'.[104] Hence, in Hotman's version of the ancient constitution the sovereign courts appear as usurpers of the powers of the estates-general. He hates the *robins*, calls them pettifoggers and robed vultures, and equals their rise to gangrene and the French pox.[105] They are at present the true rulers of the kingdom. Even the royal majesty itself has had to yield to their might.[106] 'The supreme assembly of lawyers in Paris (which is called the senate in purple) is so replete with wealth and dignity that, as Iugurtha is reported to have said once of the Roman senate, it seems no longer a gathering of counselors but rather one of kings and satraps.'[107] It is these people who are suffocating the nation in litigation and legal pettifoggery,[108] a complaint that is reasserted in the *Antitribonian*: 'the more laws and magistrates there are, the more wickedness and injustice there is'.[109]

2.4. Philippe du Plessis Mornay

What if the ancient constitution was overthrown by the misappropriation of more and more power by the king? At this point the aristocratic theory of history turned into a theory of resistance. Hotman did not go at length into this implication in his work, but others did.[110] Undoubtely the most famous of the books presenting such a theory of resistance against a despotic king is the *Vindiciae contra Tyrannos* by Du Plessis Mornay. He explicitly states that a king who usurps the rights of the people and does not rule in their interest becomes a tyrant and loses his title to power. From this follows the right -or indeed the duty- of resistance.

Everything depended on the distinction between a king and a tyrant, between a monarchy and a tyranny. After having described the tyrant in thoroughly classicist terms,[111] Mornay discusses the distinction between a monarchy and a tyranny, in which he in effect defines the former as a mixed government. 'As a well-constituted kingdom contains all the advantages of the other good regimes, tyranny contains all the evil of the bad ones. A kingdom resembles aristocracy in that the best men are invited to the royal council, whereas tyranny resembles oligarchy in inviting the worst and most corrupt. If the council of the first is like a gathering of kings, that of the second is a gang of tyrants. A kingdom also resembles a *politeia* in that there is an assembly of all the orders to which the best men are sent as deputies to deliberate the affairs of the commonwealth. Tyranny resembles *democratia seu ochlocratia*, because, insofar as it cannot prevent assemblies, it bends every effort, uses every device of electioneering and deception, to insure that the worst men are sent to them.'[112]

The abstract principle of resistance does not imply that things are identical for everyone. Although Mornay used abstract arguments of natural law more than Hotman, he should not be perceived as a full-fledged precursor of the eighteenth-century social-contract philosophers. In the former's treatise the historical dimension still plays a prominent role. Hence, the law that must be considered in answering the question of resistance includes the law of nature in the narrow sense, demanding self-preservation, and the *ius gentium*, but also and most importantly 'the civil law, which is the legislation that societies establish for their particular needs, so that there is one and there is another kind of government, some being ruled by one man, others by a few, and still others by all. Some people deny political authority to women, others admit them; with some, kings are chosen from a particular line, among others the choice is free; and so forth. If anyone tries to break this law through force or fraud, resistance is incumbent upon all of us, because the criminal does violence to that association to which we owe everything we have, because he subverts the foundation of the fatherland to which we are bound'.[113] Hence, the law and customs of the land are just as important or even more so, in deciding about tyranny and resistance, than universal principles and natural law.

For instance, it is clear enough, according to Mornay, that in France royal 'succession was tolerated only insofar as it was a convenient remedy for rebellions, secessions, interregna, and other dangers of election. But where succession threatened even greater dangers, where the kingdom was in jeopardy of tyranny or a tyrant had usurped the throne, a lawful assembly of the people had unquestioned authority to expel a tyrannical or incompetent king, and to install a good king in his place (..). The French took this practice over from the ancient Gauls, as is clearly indicated in Caesar, book V, where Ambiorix, king of the Eburones, avows that the powers of the kings of Gaul were such that the people lawfully assembled has no less authority over the king than the king over the people. And this is also documented by the example of Vercingetorix, who justified his plans to the assembled people'.[114]

Only those who knew the ancient constitution were therefore in the position to discern whether the king had transgressed his powers. If only for this reason, the uneducated rabble cannot ever have the right to resist. The 'many-headed multitude' does not have the right to rebel against a tyrant. 'If (..) they are not even permitted to look after themselves, they are surely not expected to look after the commonwealth.'[115] Mornay emphasized that 'when we speak of the people collectively, we mean those who receive authority from the people', that is, the magistrates below the king, to whom the people 'have given their sword'. Resistance against the tyrant was thus reserved to society's leaders, to the aristocracy.[116]

3. The guardians of the tradition

With the *Vindiciae contra Tyrannis* the aristocratic paradigm in political theory was complete. The seventeenth and eighteenth century added little or nothing truly new to the conceptions developed in the sixteenth century. Most of what was written was essentially repetitive. The debate was sometimes intense, as men quarreled over the details of the ancient constitution, the identification of the rightful heirs of the Gallic or Frankish assemblies, the limits of the royal prerogative, and other subjects, but the general framework remained the same and was shared by everyone. Hence, the tragedy of it all: for when the framework could no longer be believed in, it became almost incredible that so much intellectual (and emotional) effort had been put into what were now conceived of as non-issues.

But we are running ahead of the story, because until the end of the eighteenth century at least this tradition of aristocratic classicism in political thought was alive and well. Indeed, the book that is arguably the greatest contribution to this tradition appeared only in 1748: the *Spirit of the Laws*, by Charles Louis de Secondat, baron de la Brède et de Montesquieu, and *président à mortier* of the parlement of Bordeaux. His ideas will be the subject of the next chapter. By way of conclusion of the present chapter a short overview will be given of the main contributions to aristocratic political thought in the period between Mornay and Montesquieu.

3.1. Bernard la Roche Flavin

The single aristocratic treatise of some consequence to appear in the first half of the seventeenth century was the *Thirteen Books on the Parlements of France* (1617) by Bernard la Roche Flavin, a magistrate of the *parlement* of Toulouse.[117] He argued that the French state was a pure monarchy in which 'thus the sovereign power of the prince is a beam and a sparkle of God's omnipotence'.[118] This did not imply, however, that France had a despotic government like Turkey, in which the arbitrary will of one was law and all the others were but slaves.[119]

History proved that from the beginning of the state the French king had had a senate to stand by him and support him with *aide et conseil*.[120] Although its name changed repeatedly its essence remained untouched. It has been called, among other things, *plaids, sales, conciles, synodus, concilium*, and *placitum*, but it always remained the same senate.[121] Even the fact that the kings of the third race made it a permanent council and split it into different branches did not alter its nature.[122] It was the most exalted council of state and was to ensure the lawfulness of the king's government, preventing it from degenerating into a tyranny. Whoever said that it was established by the kings in the middle ages was wrong. 'The truth is that they were established in France at the moment of birth of the monarchy, in the time of the first kings, who held assemblies of nobles and barons at their court, to advise and consult in matters of state and justice; (..) even the ancient Gauls

(..) together had a common institution of justice and a council of state, which was held in the country of Chartres by their priests, who where named druids.'[123] And, the magistrate from Toulouse remarked, besides this general senate of druids, there were other, regional, senates. 'Caesar's account bears witness to the fact that (..) there were senates established in various places and capital cities of France.'[124]

The ancient *parlement* consisted of the princes, the great officers of the crown, the highest ecclesiastical dignitaries, and the nobility. It assembled once, twice, or thrice a year 'to discuss the affairs of state and to administer justice sovereignly over the subjects'.[125] Here, everything that was of some consequence to the kingdom was decided upon. But because of the difficulties involved in the convocation of these *parlements*, or estates-general as they were also called -many deputies travelled weeks to reach the place were the assembly was held-, the kings decided to establish 'an assembly and organization of very accomplished and capable persons, drawn from all three estates, and gave it the ancient name of *parlement*, to act as highest judge in the kingdom; and to see to the most urgent and imperative affairs of state, in anticipation of the assembly of estates-general, which was held less frequently, but to which the decision on the most serious and important things, like those concerning peace and war of the kingdom, was reserved'.[126] In other words: the sovereign courts were a kind of standing committees of the estates, guarding over its prerogatives when not assembled, and authorized to decide in its name.

La Roche Flavin indignantly disputed the royalist view that the sovereign courts were not more than courts of law, established, in the words of Louis XIII, 'to judge between master Pierre and master Jean'.[127] Since the birth of the state 'the laws had been verified there, as well as ordinances, edicts, creations of offices, peace-treaties, and other very important affairs of state, on behalf of which letters-patent were sent to them, to be deliberated on in complete freedom, to have their merits examined, and to bring forth reasonable modification'.[128] In fact, the right to remonstrate was a fundamental law of the realm, and encompassed the right to 'verify, unify, refuse, limit, or restrain' royal edicts in complete liberty.[129] This led him to the conclusion that the French monarchy was 'a composition and mixture of the three sorts of government; viz. monarchy, aristocracy, and republic: so that one serves as a bridle and check upon the other'.[130] The verification of the royal laws by the sovereign courts enhanced their legitimacy and their obeyance by the population. 'There is nothing which gives more authority to the laws and the warrants of a prince (..) than letting them be ratified by the advise of a wise council, of a senate, of a court'; when they are 'published and verified in the *parlement*, instantly the French people adhere to them *sans murmure*'.[131] We have heard that before.

3.2. The Fronde

After Richelieu's death in 1642 his centralizing policy was carried on by his pupil, the Italian cardinal Mazarin, against whom aristocratic aversion was even greater, because he was a foreigner. In 1648 things came to a head. Royal authority was at a low point. In 1643 Louis XIII had died, and had been succeeded by his four year old son Louis XIV. The minority of the king as usual increased the audacity of the aristocracy. The acquiescence in the 'despotic' government of the Italian quickly diminished. In 1648 a civil war broke out, which was to last until 1653, and came to be known as the Fronde. Exploiting the existing discontent among the population over the constantly increasing fiscal burden, which was much aggravated by the economic crisis that afflicted the country from 1647 to 1651 as a result of five subsequent harvest failures, the aristocracy rose up in rebellion in an attempt to put an end to 'ministerial despotism'.

About 5,000 political pamphlets were printed between 1648 and 1653.[132] These have been given the name of *mazarinades*, after their main target. Their writers pleaded for the reform of the state, a limitation of royal power, a convocation of the estates-general. They derived kingship from the consent of the people, linked obedience to the supremacy of the law, and gave historical 'proof' of the mixed nature of the monarchy.[133] Most of these pamphlets were rather superficial, however, and predominantly concerned with specific issues of the day. Serious theoretical treatises, in which the aristocratic position was vindicated, were conspicuously rare.[134] But the few that were published clearly breathed the spirit of sixteenth-century aristocratic political theory, preserved its heritage, and passed it on to later authors.[135] Two pamphlets in particular must be mentioned in this connection, which both appeared in 1652 and both had rather lengthy titles; an anonymous publication named *Veritable Maxims of the Government of France, Justified by the Order of Time, from the Establishment of the Monarchy up to the Present*,[136] and one named a *Collection of Veritable Maxims for the Education of the King, against the False and Pernicious Politics of Cardinal Mazarin*, written by a certain Claude Joly (1607-1700).

The anonymous *Veritable Maxims* was an utterly traditional work. Its author asserted that the Frankish assemblies in which everyone took part were continued under the name of *champs de mars* by Clovis and his successors of the first race, who respected the rights of the people. 'It is there where the laws were made, (where was) negotiated about peace, about war, alliances, and all the great affairs of the kingdom. Everything was decided by a free choice.'[137] The subsequent conquests of Charlemagne and his descendants made France so large that it was no longer possible to assemble the whole population to decide on the major affairs of state. Consequently, henceforth only the greatest lords convened to discuss these matters. 'That form of government was held on to under the third race for three hundred years. Nothing happened as yet without that public council. There wasn't any other assembly for the affairs of state and the general *police* of the kingdom. That is why the historians have called these assemblies *Judicium Francorum*. From the time of Philip Augustus, these assemblies on whose judgement everything depended, changed in name though not in authority, and one began to call them *parlement*. (..) It still represents that general assembly of the Francs. It has become sedentary, but it has preserved its dignity and powers. (..) The *parlement* has always been an *abrégé* of the three estates.'[138] The author of the *Veritable Maxims* held that the king was the image of God, and that he was the sovereign ruler whose authority was unlimited. But this did not imply that the French monarchy was despotical, in the way Turkey was. The French had not chosen a monarchical government to lose their liberty but to secure it. That is the reason why it was tempered by 'a species of aristocracy': the magistrates.[139]

The second literary outflow of the Fronde that was an important contribution to the aristocratic tradition in French political thought, was written by Claude Joly, an influential writer who associated with the highest nobility.[140] His *Collection of Veritable Maxims for the Education of the King*, also appeared in 1652.[141] It is reminiscent of Mornay, to say the least. 'The power of the kings is not absolute, without bounds and limits. (..) That is to say that the power of the kings is bounded and limited, and that they cannot dispose of their subjects according to their will and pleasure.'[142] 'It seems to some people badly informed about the position of sovereign (kings), that the people are made but for the kings; whereas on the contrary the truth is that the kings are made but for the people. For in all times there have been people without kings, but there never have been kings without a people.'[143] According to Joly the people entered into a contract, chose a king and transferred its original powers to him in return for his protection and his promise to see to it that justice was done. He insisted that when the king clearly and without a reasonable motive violated his contractual obligations the law of nature permitted the people 'de repousser la force par la force'.[144]

Unlike some of his eighteenth-century successors in the field of social-contract theory who used these abstract constructs to criticize and condemn the past, Joly regarded historical arguments as complementary and made use of them throughout his work. History proved, according to Joly, that both the estates and the sovereign courts were key parts of the ancient constitution. They assured that the kings never overstepped their boundaries, thus averting the degeneration of the monarchy into a tyranny, and a popular rebellion against the king. He could not govern without them. They were the successors of the *champs de mars* and the *placitum*, and had inherited the rights of these ancient assemblies of the people. The closing formula of the laws -'car tel est notre plaisir'-, which was regarded by the royalists as a proof that the king's authority was undivided and unlimited, was in Joly's opinion a corruption of the true formula which read 'quia tale est nostrum placitum': this is the decision taken by our assembly.[145] The estates had the right to reject new royal edicts and could propose new laws by themselves.[146] The author even spoke of a fundamental law in this context.[147] When the estates were not convened, the sovereign courts served as their substitute. These -especially the *parlement* of Paris- were the standing committees of the estates. In his view the sovereign courts had a say in 'toutes les grandes affaires du royaume'.[148]

3.3. Michel le Vassor

The Fronde was a failure, and for the next decades Louis XIV could rule without significant opposition. But the ever growing fiscal burden, the revocation of the edict of Nantes, and the example of British 'liberty' each contributed to the growth of dissenting and oppositional literature, which became a regular flood towards the end of the century. The first outspoken critics of 'the Most Christian King' were huguenot noblemen, many of whom had fled to England, the Netherlands, and Germany, after the revocation of the edict of Nantes.[149] From these countries their criticism was sent back to France in print. The most important of the many huguenot oppositional pamphlets and books that appeared in those days, was an anonymous work with a remarkable title, *Moans of France Enslaved, Aspiring to Liberty*, which dates from 1689/1690 and was probably written by the Calvinist convert and former Oratorian priest Michel le Vassor, who lived in the Netherlands.[150] This treatise circulated widely in France in the last decade of the seventeenth century, and was material in stimulating the opposition against the government.

The book begins with a denial of one of the central tenets of the royalist doctrine: the unity of crown and state, the inseparability of ruler and nation. Le Vassor asserts that this unity and inseparability may once have existed, but nowadays 'the king has taken the place of the state. It is the service of the king, it is the interest of the king (..). In sum, the king is everything and the state is nothing'.[151] The interest of the king and the needs of the nation were not identical anymore, according to Le Vassor, but completely different. Instead of the needs of the nation the interest of the king is pursued. This is wrong. The cause of this evil is the tyranny of the king, 'that arbitrary, absolute, and unlimited power, which the kings of France attribute to themselves'.[152] These despots have enslaved all of France in the centuries past as a result of which, Le Vassor contended, it now closely resembled oriental tyrannies like Turkey, Persia, and Mongolia. The king governed without consulting his natural counselors, the nobles. He regarded himself as the absolute master of the life, liberty, property, and religion of his subjects, not answerable to any of them. He exploited and ruined the population by excessive taxation, to pay for his insatiable ambitions. He had humiliated the aristocracy, and deprived it of its ancient rights. He had robbed the towns of their independence. He had turned the church into an accomplice. He disregarded customary law, and ruled by *lettres de cachet* and other forms of arbitrary legislation and jurisdiction. Etcetera, etcetera.[153]

This despotism is the cause of France's sorrowful plight. What was needed, according to Le Vassor, was the restoration of the ancient, true form of the monarchy. The *frondeurs* had already tried to bring this about, but they had unfortunately failed. Otherwise, France would have been the happiest kingdom in the world. Le Vassor asserted that French kingship had originally been, and therefore was truly elective, and that 'nothing of any importance was done in the kingdom without the advise and consent of the estates, so that the government of France was really more aristocratic than monarchic, or at least was a monarchy tempered by aristocracy, exactly like that of England'.[154] The closing formula of the laws -'car tel est notre plaisir'- which seemingly implied an absolute authority of the kings, was nothing but an adulteration of the original, real closing formula -'tale est placitum nostrum'-, in which *placitum* referred to the estates.[155] The king was *maior singulis*, but *minor universis*. It was the aristocracy's ancient right to take part in government, and a clear sign of tyranny that nowadays the government consisted exclusively of 'men of a less than mediocre extraction',[156] utterly dependent of the king, in no position to limit his powers, and inclined to think that service to the king was more important than the welfare of the country. Society was corrupted through and through. Le Vassor not only reproached the king that he had inordinately exalted his office, but also that he had levelled all others and eliminated all distinctions in society. Particularly the aristocracy had been abased. As a result, 'all people are nothing but dust under his feet'.[157] This abasement was a precondition of despotism, and had to be undone to make a return to the free society of the ancestors possible.

3.4. The Duc de Saint-Simon

The huguenot critics of Louis XIV's government were soon joined by others, the most influential of whom were two men connected to the coterie of the Duc de Bourgogne (1682-1712), the grandson of Louis XIV, and heir to the throne after the *dauphin's* decease in 1711: Saint-Simon, and Boulainvilliers.[†]

[†] A third was François de Salagnac de la Mothe-Fénelon (1651-1715), who became tutor to the Duc de Bourgogne in 1689. This writer is not included in our discussion of aristocratic political thought, because he did not publish his views on the ancient constitution of France. He wrote

Although their ideas were less hostile and combative than those of the exiles, they were much more dangerous to the government, because they were expressed at the royal court, in the immediate surroundings of the king.

Louis de Rouvroy, duc de Saint-Simon (1675-1755), is not to be confused with his nephew Claude Henri de Rouvroy, comte de Saint-Simon (1760-1825), the founder of 'modern theoretical socialism'.[158] Contrary to the latter the duke was anything but an egalitarian thinker. Scion of an ancient and distinguished noble lineages, *duc et pair de France*,[159] Saint-Simon was consumed by the idea of hierarchy, and hated the government of Louis XIV mainly for confounding all the ranks in society.[160] His pride of his lineage and the overriding importance he accorded to the genealogical background of the persons he had to deal with were common traits in the aristocracy of the ancien régime, but the duke carried it to extremes.[161] Nevertheless, his ideas seem to represent the thought of at least a part of the *haute noblesse* of the age. Although virtually his whole oeuvre remained unpublished throughout the eighteenth century, it is certain that his ideas were known and appreciated by his fellow peers, and reflected to a large extent their own thought.[162] Saint-

---

educational romances, dialogues, and travel tales for his royal pupil, the most renowned of which is *Telemachus*, which aimed to teach him the morals and politics appropriate to a king. His principal political works are the *Moral Investigation on the Duties of Kingship, Examen de Conscience sur les Devoirs de la Royauté*, which went through at least thirteen editions before the revolution, and the *Plans of Government devised with the Duc de Chevreuse to be Proposed to the Duc de Bourgogne*, also known as the *Tables de Chaulnes*. Fénelon accepts the traditional Aristotelian constitutional scheme. Besides the six pure forms of government -three virtuous and three vicious- a mixed government was possible, characterized by 'the division of sovereignty between the king, the nobles, and the people'. Fénelon complained that the monarchy had degenerated into a tyranny. The king, who should serve 'le bien public', had nothing in mind but his personal and dynastic *gloire*, for which he was willing to sacrifice the well-being of the nation. This despotic government was contrary to the true nature of the French monarchy. To suppress it, it sufficed to 'remember the true form of the kingdom'. However, Fénelon agreed with the royalists in regarding a pure monarchy as the best and most stable form of government. A mixed government is possible, he argued, but not desirable. The examples of the Roman republic and contemporary England taught him that 'such a division of sovereignty, far from establishing an equilibrium of power, often causes a perpetual fight, until one of them has subjugated the other two, and reduced everything to despotism or anarchy.' Fénelon insisted that the king's authority was absolute, implying 'the power to judge in the last resort', but not 'an arbitrary power to do whatever one wants, without any other rule and reason than the despotical will of a single person'. The king's authority was undivided and unlimited, but not arbitrary. *Salus populi* was the *suprema lex*, for which the king would be held accountable after his death by the Highest Judge. Not only was a pure monarchy the best form of government, it also was the true nature of the French constitution, which could be discovered in the past. In the first chapter of his *Examen de Conscience* Fénelon reminded his pupil to study the institutions of the past that had been illegally overthrown by his grandfather but constituted the true form of government of the kingdom. See Gallouédec-Genuys 1963

Simon may even be regarded as the spiritual father of the so-called *polysynodie*, the short-lived system of administration set up after the death of Louis XIV in 1715, that was dominated by the peers.[163] Saint-Simon owes his present fame largely to his huge *Memoirs*, which cover the last decade of the seventeenth century and the first two decades of the eighteenth century and provide an invaluable source of information on the events at the royal court in those days.[164] But a more direct, concise and elaborate exposition of Saint-Simon's political ideas can be found in the *Écrits Inédits*, published between 1880 and 1892 in eight volumes. Of the works included in that collection the *Memoir of the Renunciation*[165] is the most enlightening for our purposes.[166]

Saint-Simon's interpretative framework was the same as that of all the other aristocratic theorists. The French monarchy had an ancient constitution that could be discovered in the past and had been overthrown in the last couple of centuries by a centralizing monarch, who had usurped more and more of the ancient rights and liberties of the aristocracy, thereby corrupting the monarchy and establishing a tyranny. His scapegoats were also familiar: the ministers and the intendants. The hate of these 'vile bourgeois', who manned the governmental councils and ruled the provinces like little despots, permeated all of Saint-Simon's writings. They were 'gens de fort peu', he declared philosophically, that the king 'should plunge back into the nothing from where they were drawn'.[167] Like his fellow aristocrats, the duke was in essence opposed to the kings' policies of centralization and equalization, which led to a despotical government because they sidetracked and ruined the class that was the safeguard against this degeneration of the monarchy: the aristocracy. The centralization and the equalization should therefore be undone, and the ancient constitution of the monarchy should be restored.

Yet, not the whole aristocracy was to profit from such a restoration. Saint-Simon believed that the ancient constitution prescribed a mixed government in which political power was shared exclusively by the king and the *ducs et pairs de France*. Only the highest ranking nobles belonged to the governing elite of the realm. All the lesser nobles were excluded from it. The original constitutional constellation of the kingdom proved this. When the Franks had conquered Gaul, according to Saint-Simon, they received from their king a piece of the conquered land as a reward, the extent of which was in accordance with their rank, on the condition that they maintained some troops and led them into war at the request of the king. Those which had been given the greatest portions soon started to split them up and give them to the lesser Franks, on the condition that when requested they would follow them into war as loyal soldiers. That is how the feudal system came into existence. Those who had received their portions directly from the king were soon called *leudi* or *fidèles*. And the most considerable among them, who had received whole provinces, were called dukes or counts. Those who had received their portion from these 'premiers seigneurs' were called their vassals.[168] From these two groups, 'all of them original Francs and all conquerors of the Gauls and their kings, has emerged what we call the nobility, which long before it had that name, was but known under the generic title of *miles*, that is to say soldiers, men of war, which for a long time was the only thing that distinguished them from the common people, that is to say the indigenous Gauls who were submitted and subjected by them and hence became their serfs, that is to say like slaves, who cultivated their land and served them in all their labors and needs.'[169]

Saint-Simon admitted that in the ensuing period some of the land was given to these Gallic serfs, not as a fief, implying military service, but in return for a regular payment of rent and various other dues. 'In that way, the Gallic population of serfs was naturally divided in two: one group rested in the condition of servitude, without any property; the other group became owner of some properties, and was required to pay certain tributes. These two groups together constitute what has since then come to be called the third estate, which was divided, then as now, in a bourgeoisie and a *menu* people.[170] In addition to the nobility and the third estate the church was from the beginning part of the French monarchy, the prelates of which were also 'grands seigneurs', like the dukes and the counts, because they owned large fiefs and commanded a great number of vassals.[171]

Every year the kings convoked an assembly of the nation, under the *première race* usually in the month of March, to which all the lay and ecclesiastical *seigneurs* went with their vassals and troops. The exact nature of these assemblies was of course crucial to Saint-Simon's whole argument, because one supposedly could derive the true political rights of the different estates of the realm and the king from their proceedings. According to the duke there were two chambers, one for the ecclesiastical, and one for the lay *grands*, which convened separately. 'La foule militaire' and the king waited in the neighborhood until the two chambers had reached a decision on the proposals of the latter.[172] 'When they had come to an agreement over everything, the king declared what resolutions had been taken with regard to the matters at hand, immediately whereupon the mass of soldiers approved, or *pour mieux dire*, submitted to what had been decided and indicated its obeyance by shouts and hurrays.[173]

From this Saint-Simon drew the following conclusions. In the first place the fact that this assembly was convoked every year proved that the king was not in a position to decide on things of major importance by himself. Otherwise he would have done without it.[174] In the second place, the fact that the king did not participate in the sitting of the assembly and unquestioningly accepted whatever had been decided, proved that the *grands* were much more than simple counselors and that the authority of the king was much less than absolute. Even the etymology of the name *placita*, usually given to these assemblies, demonstrated this. The decisions reached had to please all.[175] In the third place, the fact that the 'foule militaire', 'that multitude (..) completely composed of Francs, that is to say of noblemen and warriors, which is the same thing',[176] were merely spectators standing at the sideline, proved that the lesser *gentilshommes* had no political power, to say nothing about the Gallic part of the population, which was not even present when the assemblies took place.[177]

Voilà, the type of government Saint-Simon regarded as true to the nature of the French monarchy. It is a monarchy tempered -or should one rather say dominated- by a part of the aristocracy, the *grands*: 'nothing without them, everything with them'.[178] Clovis, Charlemagne, and Hugues Capet all endorsed and upheld this type of government, according to Saint-Simon. He was well aware of the manifold differences between the governments of the first, second, and third race, but he thought these were superficial. In essence, the form of government remained the same throughout the centuries. 'Whether they had a different name, whether they included a greater or lesser number making up the assembly, they were always the same; and those who were included were always more or less powerful; whatever was the name they carried, their successors were the same, so to speak, although different men, as the first Frankish leaders and conquerors.'[179] Saint-Simon admitted that the title of *pair de France* was unknown until the commencement of the reign of the third race, but this did not mean that the peers were not part of the original constitution and thus a political nullity. It was evident, so he thought, that the peers were the successors of the first great vassals of the king. It should be recognized that 'without a name or under different names, the *pairs de France* are as ancient as the monarchy'.[180]

The final element which rounded off this constitutional theory is predictable. As we have described, Saint-Simon asserted that the French monarchy had degenerated into a tyranny in the recent past. This was the result of the centralizing and levelling policies of Louis XIV in particular, who was not prepared to share his power with the people who, as history showed, were entitled to a share in it, and instead relied on willful instruments of absolutism like the upstart ministers and intendants. And the estates? What about this medieval heritage that was cherished so much by most of the aristocratic writers? To Saint-Simon's mind they were 'but an assembly of advise and petition, without any power but that of reporting the griefs of the provinces, and without any authority but to deliberate on the means to augment and change the taxes, which was welcome to the kings and was each time permitted; and all that, without once committing the kings to conform to their advise or their requests'.[181]

3.5. Henry de Boulainvilliers

The second writer associated with the coterie of the Duc de Bourgogne, was also a man whose works exerted a major influence throughout the eighteenth century.[182] His name was Henry de Boulainvilliers, comte de Saint-Saire (1658-1722). This remarkable man, scion of an old, poor *épée* family from Normandy, wrote a number of books that were very famous before the revolution and were repeatedly reprinted, but have fallen into oblivion since. The works most important for our purposes were published after his death. These are the *History of the Ancient Government of France* (1727) and the *Essays on the Nobility of France* (1732).[183] Boulainvilliers linked up with the elder historians of the monarchy and clearly elaborated on the ideas of men like Hotman and Coquille, Le Vassor, Fénelon, and Saint-Simon about its true nature. But he was much more sophisticated then they had been, because he had a great deal more factual knowledge about the past at his disposal, amassed in the seventeenth century by *érudits* like Duchène, Du Cange, Sirmond and Baluze,[184] who had compiled and recorded many ancient chronicles without giving much thought to the interpretation of these sources.

Essential to Boulainvilliers' view of the true nature of the French monarchy is a theory we already encountered in Saint-Simon: that the Frankish army headed by Clovis conquered Gaul, and subjected its Gallo-Roman inhabitants. Thus, from its inception the French state contained two classes: the ruling nobility of Frankish origin on the one hand and the mass of the population on the other, which was of Gallo-Roman origin and had no political rights. Boulainvilliers admitted that 'it was violence that introduced the distinctions of liberty and slavery, of nobility and third estate; but even though these have vicious origins their practice has been established in the world for so long that they have acquired the force of a natural law'.[185] In other words: although men were equal in the state of nature, society, which is always caused by conquest, necessarily makes them unequal.[186] After the conquest of Roman Gaul the Franks overthrew all vestiges of Roman rule, whose name, language and customs they hated, divided the land among themselves, and held the native population as serfs.[187] 'In a word, the Gauls became subjects, while the others remained masters and free men. (..) It is certain that, since the conquest, the original Franks have been the true nobles'.[188] It is easy to grasp what all of this implies. Boulainvilliers was attacking the political aspirations of what he saw as bourgeois would-be nobles who filled the many offices of state. Like Saint-Simon and all the other aristocratic writers he regarded the nobility as the only class fitted to rule, in government as well as in society at large. The bourgeoisie lacked all the qualities needed to rule wisely and beneficently. Everyone would be better off if they sticked to their traditional role, in accordance with the true nature of the monarchy.

The true relationship between the nobility and the *roturiers* was not the only thing Boulainvilliers deduced from the Frankish conquest of Gaul. It was also intended to determine the true relationship within the nobility, and between the nobility and the king. With regard to the relationship within the nobility, Boulainvilliers was sharply critical of Saint-Simon's views. He defended the unity of the governing class, and regarded the claims of the latter as contrary to the whole aristocratic tradition.[189] The answer to the question what was the true relationship between the nobility and the king could of course be found by examining the relationship between Clovis and the Franks. Boulainvilliers was unambiguous about this. 'No one is unaware that the French, being originally free people who chose leaders for themselves called kings, to carry out the laws that they themselves had established, or to lead them in war, were far from regarding these kings as arbitrary legislators who could command anything without reason other than their own plea-sure.'[190] The conclusion was that 'it is absolutely contrary to the truth and to the spirit of the old French to imagine that the royal right was for them sovereign, monarchical or despotic'.[191] The Roman tradition of governmental absolutism had been discarded right after the invasion of Gaul, and had been supplanted by a limited monarchy. The upshot of the argument was that the royal aggrandizement that had occurred in the centuries past constituted an encroachment on the ancient liberties of the nobility and a corruption of the ancient constitution of the monarchy.

Boulainvilliers described this historical process of degeneration in detail. It set in almost immediately after the reign of Clovis, but was arrested by Charlemagne, the virtuous ruler who was 'incapable of separating his interests from those of the state',[192] as so many of his successors did. He 'believed that despotic and arbitrary government, such as his ancestor had wished to establish, being absolutely contrary to the genius of the nation and to its plain and obvious right, could not possibly endure',[193] and therefore undid the centralization that had been brought about, reinstating the assemblies of the nation -that is, of the 'Frankish' nobility- with all their ancient rights, and restoring the authority of the lords over their subjects. After the death of Charlemagne -according to Boulainvilliers the only French king entitled to the epithet 'the great'-[194] the realm repeatedly threatened to fall apart under the feeble rulership of his descendants, but the feudal system which took definite shape in the period of the second race, prevented this and conserved the rights of the aristocracy. To Boulainvilliers this system was 'le chef-d'oeuvre de l'esprit humain' in the field of constitutional theory.[195] It was the perfect embodiment of a mixed government. The rights of the aristocracy ensured 'la sûreté commune' because they established 'une barrière nécessaire' against the power of the crown, and the duties of the aristocracy with regard to their subjects ensured the welfare of the population.[196]

France would have been the happiest state in the world if this constituti-onal constellation had remained intact. But already under the Capetian kings it began to fall apart. Gradually the power of the king was increased, to the detriment of the aristocracy and the freedom of the nation. The estates lost their power, the serfs were enfranchised, an increasing number of *roturiers* was ennobled, the king and the intendants ran the central and the local government respectively. In short, the aristocracy was shut out from government and authority and shamefully abased. The nobles' ancient distinctions and honors were taken from them, putting them on the same level as ordinary mortals. According to Boulainvilliers this was what made possible and eventually led to the despotism of Louis XIV. In his eyes despotism must of necessity arise as a consequence of the equalization of all subjects in a state. The destruction of 'les puissants particulières' eliminates all barriers between the government and the subject, and gives the first the opportunity to exert an unlimited, arbitrary and therefore tyrannical power over the latter. The feudal system on the contrary is the best warrant of individual liber-ty.[197]

A reform of this despicable despotism was urgently needed, according to Boulainvilliers, but unthinkable as long as Louis XIV ruled the country. Like Fénelon and Saint-Simon he had set his hopes on the Duc de Bourgogne, who was known to be in favor of such a reform. And when in 1711 Louis XIV's son, the *grand dauphin*, died, and 'le bon Duc' became the first heir to the throne, the aristocratic party was in high spirits. The sun king was seventy-three years old and would presumably die soon, whereas the Duc de Bourgogne was a healthy young man of twenty-nine who still had many years to go. The following year, however, it was the latter who died and not the former, shattering all hopes of a near change.

NOTES

1. In a letter to P.W. Annenkow (1846), included in *Marx-Engels Werke* Vol.XXVII, p.461, 'So war im 18.Jahrhundert eine Menge mittelmäßiger Köpfe damit beschäftigt, die einzig richtige Formel zu finden, um die sozialen Stände, den Adel, den König, die Parlemente etc. ins Gleichgewicht zu bringen, und über Nacht war alles -König, Parlement und Adel- verschwunden. Das richtige Gleichgewicht in diesem Antagonismus war die Umwälzung aller gesellschaftlichen Beziehungen, die diesen Feudalgebilden und ihrem Antagonismus als Grundlage dienten.'

2. Keohane 1980, ch.6, pp.183-212 From the early seventeenth century onward the concept of *amour-propre* -the love of oneself- was central to this argument; Bénichou 1948

3. Dewald 1993, entitled *Aristocratic Experience and the Origins of Modern Culture*

4. Ullmann 1975, pp.12-13

5. Pocock 1987, pp.20-21

6. E.g. Plamenatz 1992, vol.I, esp.p.220

7. One might add Theodore Beza (1519-1605), author of *Du Droit des Magistrats* (1574), and some others as well, but because their views do no differ substantially from those of the authors mentioned, and the author has no intention of giving a complete overview of the debate, they will be left out here. See Kelley 1970, Huppert 1970, Church 1941, Lemaire 1907

8. Machiavelli, *Discorsi*, III.1

9. A recent example is Sap 1993

10. Hintze 1928, p.14 and p.491n33 and 34

11. Hintze 1928, pp.9-29

12. Jansen 1981, pp.319-320

13. This traditional closing formula of new statutes was itself a modification of an even older one. At the beginning of the fourteenth century the formula of 'adstantibus et consentientibus praelatis et baronibus' was discarded and replaced by 'le roi a ordonné et établi par délibération de son conseil', significantly shifting the emphasis to the king.

14. As Skinner, 1979, vol.II, p.255, may be doing

15. Major 1960, p.5

16. Major 1960, pp.9-10

17. Major 1960, p.130

18. Major 1960, p.127

19. The only other kingship in the Gallic lands was the kingship of Navarra, in the Pyrenees. Anderson 1979, p.85

20. Göhring 1947, p.50; Shennan 1968, p.110

21. See Hintze 1928, pp.9-47

22. Jansen 1981, p.221

23. Göhring 1947, p.62

24. Berman 1983, pp.120-128

25. The legists pictured the king as the legislator of course, but the relevant sections of the Justinianus' Digest were open to alternative interpretations. They contained the statement that the emperors' power to make law was ultimately derived from the people, that had invested him with it, and it was not clear whether this had been done unconditionally and irreversibly, or conditionally and reversibly, whether it had been a delegation or an alienation. This ambiguity left open the possibility to draw the very radical conclusions Bartolus of Saxoferrata and particularly Marsiglio of Padua were to draw from it in the fourteenth century, which came to play a major role in modern constitutionalism. See Skinner 1979, vol.I, pp.60-65 Both Bartolus and Marsiglio were steeped in Roman law. The first even wrote a commentary on the Digest, in which the limitations to be imposed on all rulers were spelled out. According to Skinner they were thinking mainly of Italian city republics, but 'it was only necessary for the same arguments to be applied in the case of a *regnum* as well as a *civitas* for a recognizable modern theory of popular sovereignty in a secular state to be fully articulated'. Alternatively, Roman law could and was regarded by many as the law of the German emperors, and as such constituted a threat to the independence of the French king. Significantly, the spread of the teaching of Roman law was initially regarded with misgivings by the latter, who even tried to prohibit it. See Shennan 1968, p.54 Only after the legists had started to equate the French king with the Roman emperor, the *Corpus Iuris* became the main theoretical cornerstone of the royalist party.

26. Quoted in Göhring 1947, p.51; Hintze 1928, p.15 But see Skinner 1979, vol.II, pp.124-134

27. Göhring 1947, pp.62-63

28. Göhring 1947, p.65

29. Jansen 1981, pp.317-328, about the role played by the *parlement* in the conflicts over the fiefs of Guyenne and Gascogne, owned by the English king.

30. Göhring 1947, p.64

31. As well as international treaties. See Göhring 1947, p.65

32. Göhring 1947, pp.63-65 At first, the duty to remonstrate was probably restricted to administrative decisions only, and did not apply to royal legislation in general. But already in the fourteenth century the *parlement* examined all royal enactments, and objected to aspects it regarded to be ill-judged. See Shennan 1968, pp.159-161

33. In the provincial sovereign courts he would be represented by the governor

34. Shennan 1968, p.161

35. Shennan 1968, p.80 and p.192 So we have a two-fold movement. While the assertivity of the kings' legislation rapidly increased in the fifteenth and sixteenth century as the hold on their minds of medieval notions with regard to the sanctity of established law waned and their self-conception as sovereign legislators gained the upper hand, at the same time the ideas of precedent, jurisprudence, and consistency in law became more and more important to the magistrates, who by that time had built up a venerated legal tradition of long standing for themselves, which inevitably made them much more respectful of customary law in general. It is undeniable that in the fifteenth and sixteenth century the sovereign courts on the whole still saw themselves as a support of the crown and not as a check. None of its members denied that the king was the ultimate source of the law. But at the same time they had gradually begun to

discard many of the legalist political ideas they had defended in the foregoing centuries. Most significantly, their dependence on Roman law diminished incessantly and they began to put more and more emphasis on the necessity for the king to act in accordance with custom and tradition. They were still far from propagating anything like a theory of a mixed constitution, like the 'feudal' aristocracy, but it is clear that by this time they no longer were compliant instruments of royal aggrandizement.

36. Lloyd 1983, p.3

37. Kelley, in: Seyssel *Monarchie*, pp.10-11

38. Seyssel, *Monarchie*, pp.68-71

39. Seyssel, *Monarchie*, pp.75, 96

40. Seyssel, *Monarchie*, third part, pp.107-128

41. Kelley, in: Seyssel, *Monarchie*, p.12

42. Herodotus, *Hist.*, III.80-83 The preface is included in Seyssel *Monarchie*, pp.170-181

43. Seyssel, *Monarchie*, pp.170-171

44. Seyssel, *Monarchie*, p.171

45. Seyssel, *Monarchie*, p.172

46. Seyssel, *Monarchie*, p.172

47. Seyssel, *Monarchie*, p.173

48. Seyssel, *Monarchie*, pp.38-41

49. Seyssel, *Monarchie*, pp.40-42

50. Seyssel, *Monarchie*, pp.42-46

51. Seyssel, *Monarchie*, pp.47-48

52. Seyssel, *Monarchie*, p.51

53. Seyssel, *Monarchie*, pp.54-56; cf. pp.174-175

54. Seyssel, *Monarchie*, p.174

55. Seyssel, *Monarchie*, pp.176-177

56. Seyssel, *Monarchie*, p.97,176

57. Seyssel, *Monarchie*, p.177; cf. p.61

58. Seyssel, *Monarchie*, p.59; cf. p.175

59. Seyssel, *Monarchie*, p.74

60. Shennan 1968, pp.192-205

61. Skinner 1979, vol.II, p.256

62. Shennan 1968, p.195

63. Shennan 1968, p.200

64. Göhring 1947, p.68

65. Pasquier *Oeuvres Complètes*, vol.I

66. Pasquier *Recherches*, col.3d

67. Pasquier, *Recherches*, col.3a

68. Huppert 1970, pp.32-35

69. Pasquier, *Recherches*, Liv.I, ch.II

70. Pasquier, *Recherches*, col.9b, col.48c

71. Caesar, *Bel.Gal.*, VI.21; Tacitus, *Germania*

72. Pasquier, *Recherches*, col.5a

73. Pasquier, *Recherches*, 16a

74. Huppert 1970, p.44

75. Pasquier, *Recherches*, col.1040d; Cf. col.66b

76. Pasquier, *Recherches*, col.1040c

77. Pasquier, *Recherches*, col.66b Quoted in Keohane 1980, p.46

78. Pasquier, *Recherches*, col.46c, col.49c

79. Keohane 1980, pp.46-47

80. Church 1941, p.75

81. Walzer 1965, pp.68-69 Most huguenot publicists and ministers were nobles. Lutheranism appealed primarily to the lower classes in France.

82. Anderson 1979, p.92 speaks of ten to twenty percent of the entire population being converted, a number which seems much too high. Cf. Skinner 1979, vol.II, p.241n1, who notes that according to the official census, which was conducted on the orders of Henry IV, when their number had reached a peak, the proportion of huguenots to the population as a whole was about one in twenty.

83. Skinner 1979, vol.II, p.241 and pp.254-255 This author argues that the fact that the huguenots were but a small minority made it impossible for them to invoke the radical Calvinist theories of resistance, which had been developed in Scotland and England a few years before, and demanded that the whole population of believers should rise up against the anti-Christ. They needed to develop an abstract ideology appealing to Catholic malcontents as well as to their co-religionists. This might have been the reason, but it seems more likely that as noblemen the huguenots had some reservations about popular uprisings.

84. Walzer 1965, p.72

85. Laski (ed.) 1924; Franklin (ed.) 1969; Giesey and Salmon (ed.) 1972; Cf. Skinner 1979, vol.II, pp.304-305

86. Hotman *Francogallia*, pp.141-143

87. Hotman *Francogallia*, p.287; Cf. pp.147-155

88. Hotman *Francogallia*, p.183

89. Hotman *Francogallia*, pp.201-205

90. Hotman *Francogallia*, pp.209-219

91. Hotman *Antitribonian*

92. Hotman *Antitribonian*, pp.1-22

93. Hotman *Francogallia*, p.221ff.

94. Hotman *Francogallia*, p.205, p.287

95. Hotman *Francogallia*, p.287

96. Hotman *Francogallia*, pp.291-293; cf. pp.231-233

97. Hotman *Francogallia*, p.293

98. Hotman *Francogallia*, pp.292-295

99. Hotman *Francogallia*, p.295 Pre-Roman Gaul had had a similar government, see p.155, p.303

100. Hotman *Francogallia*, p.323, p.329, p.419

101. Hotman *Francogallia*, p.343; cf. p.333

102. Hotman *Francogallia*, pp.345-347

103. Hotman *Francogallia*, pp.499-503 For the sake of clarity, the 1586 edition is followed at this point.

104. Hotman *Francogallia*, p.505

105. Hotman *Francogallia*, p.511, p.513, p.523

106. Hotman *Francogallia*, p.497

107. Hotman *Francogallia*, p.497

108. Hotman *Francogallia*, pp.505ff.

109. Hotman, *Antitribonian*, p.147; Cf. Cicero, *De Off.*, I.33: 'Summum ius, summa iniuria.'

110. But see Hotman *Francogallia*, ch.VII, pp.235-245

111. Laski (ed.) 1924, pp.181-188

112. Mornay, *Vindiciae*, pp.186-187

113. Mornay, *Vindiciae*, p.188

114. Mornay, *Vindiciae*, p.166 The references are to Caesar, *De Bel.Gal.*, V.27 and VII.89

115. Mornay, *Vindiciae*, p.195

116. Mornay, *Vindiciae*, pp.190-197

117. According to Ford 1968, p.223, who echoes Göhring 1947, pp.72-72, on this point, this book was 'most important of all in the parlementary past'. Moreover, Göhring, p.72, detects a 'bis zur Abhängigkeit gehende(n) Übereinstimmung' between La Roche Flavin and Montesquieu. Other authors, like Shennan 1968, pp.246-247, and Albertini 1951, p.65, on the contrary think that La Roche Flavin's contribution was rather marginal to the *parlementaire* tradition. Shennan, p.247, maintains that he 'found little response in the court, and Albertini, p.65, thinks that the *Treize Livres* were 'in den ersten Jahren nach ihrem Erscheinen (..) nicht sehr beachtet', but 'haben (..) zur Zeit der Fronde eine gewisse Rolle gespielt'. All agree, however, that La Roche Flavin was much more radical than sixteenth-century predecessors like Pasquier. Church 1941 on the other hand, p.133n38, asserts that he 'may be regarded as synthesizing the earlier, constitutional position in regard to the parlement'. To the knowledge of the present author there are no other editions of the work beside the two mentioned, which is not indicative of great popularity. On the other hand it is certain that Montesquieu knew it. It is referred to once in the *Esprit*, XXVIII,33., and Cox 1983, pp.78-79, has shown that he borrowed it from the Bibliothèque de Roi in 1748, and possibly also from other libraries. An article or a monograph about La Roche Flavin, his relationship to earlier, and his influence on later thought, would therefore be an asset.

118. La Roche Flavin, *Treize Livres*, p.690

119. Göhring 1947, pp.74-75

120. Göhring 1947, p.76

121. La Roche Flavin, *Treize Livres*, pp.4-6

122. La Roche Flavin, *Treize Livres*, pp.9-10

123. La Roche Flavin, *Treize Livres*, ed.1621, Livre I, V, p.7

124. La Roche Flavin, *Treize Livres*, p.8

125. La Roche Flavin, *Treize Livres*, p.3

126. La Roche Flavin, *Treize Livres*, livre I, VI

127. According to the Toulousian magistrate 'les Parlements n'ont esté seulement establis pour le jugement des affaires et procez entre parties privées'. Quoted in Albertini 1951, p.65

128. La Roche Flavin, *Treize Livres*, p.10 This is followed by the claim that even 'que ce qui est accordé par nos Roys aux Estats generaux, doit estre verifié en votre Cour', which seems to imply that according to La Roche Flavin the sovereign courts were in some respects more than mere standing committees of the estates.

129. Quoted in Albertini 1951, p.65

130. Quoted by Albertini, p.66.

131. Quoted in Albertini 1951, p.67

132. Jouhaud 1985, p.7 The English civil war that took place roughly at the same time, fathered twenty-two thousand pamphlets.

133. Göhring 1947, p.107

134. Keohane 1980, p.216

135. Göhring 1947, p.111

136. Carcassonne 1978, p.33; Göhring 1947, p.109

137. Quoted in Göhring 1947, p.109

138. Quoted in Göhring 1947, p.110

139. Carcassonne 1978, p.35

140. Malettke 1976, p.46

141. Of the many books Joly wrote, two more also deal with constitutional theory, the *Codicille d'Or* (1664), and the *Traité des Restitutions des Grands, précédé d'une Lettre touchant quelques Points de la Morale Chrestienne* (1665).

142. Joly *Recueil*, p.18

143. Joly *Recueil*, pp.130-131

144. Joly *Recueil*, pp.23-24 It should be noted that Joly did not concede the right to resist a tyrant to individuals. They had the duty to obey. Only the population as a whole, represented by the estates or the sovereign courts, was allowed to remove a tyrant from the throne.

145. Joly *Recueil*, pp.402-403 Hotman had of course already suggested this interpretation

146. Joly, *Recueil*, pp.287-288

147. Joly, *Recueil*, p.363 He referred to new fiscal measures in particular.

148. Joly, *Recueil*, p.376

149. The estimates regarding their number vary greatly. Keohane 1980, p.313, and Sée 1978, p.196, speak of 200,000 refugees. Williams 1970, p.164, thinks that possibly as many as 800,000 huguenots fled abroad.

150. This attribution is made by Barrière 1974, p.276, Sée 1978, p.194, and Göhring 1947, p.118; Keohane 1980, p.316n11, however, following others, thinks that Pierre Jurieu is the best guess. But this seems to be rather unlikely, since Jurieu's *Lettres Pastorales*, which appeared in the same year, are full of the language of natural law and has a definite plebeian flavor, whereas the *Soupirs* is a thoroughly aristocratic tract. See Sée 1978, pp.191-210

151. Quoted in Sée, p.195

152. Quoted in Sée, p.195

153. Göhring 1947, pp.120-121

154. Quoted in Keohane 1980, p.316

155. Göhring 1947, p.122

156. Quoted in Sée 1978, p.198

157. Quoted in Sée 1978, p.197

158. The phrase is Kolakowski's 1982, vol.I, p.187, who defines this brand of socialism as something 'conceived not merely as an ideal but as an outcome of a historical process'.

159. Bastide 1977, p.12

160. Sée 1978, p.236

161. An instance of something easily ridiculed is the enormous weight Saint-Simon attached to matters of etiquette in general, and the honorific rights of the peers in particular. The 'affaire du bonnet' which stirred up the emotions of the peerage during the regency is an example of this. It hinged on the question whether a *président* of the *parlement* of Paris should or should not remove his cap -his *mortier*- when addressing a peer, and whether the latter might keep on his when replying. Ford 1968, p.176, in his otherwise brilliant study of the French aristocracy, mistakingly regards this as evidence of the peers' obtuseness, disregarding that behind it lay important issues of social and political primacy. He even suggests that the failure of the *polysynodie* had something to do with the peers' obsession with etiquette, because 'what could be expected from a group of barely literate soldiers and pompous courtiers, who devoted more attention to deciding whether or not a subordinate official might be seated while reporting to a council than they did to the substance of his report'.

162. Ford 1968, ch.IX, pp.173-187

163. Gallouédec, p.125

164. The first edition of the *Mémoires* was published in 1788 in 2 vols., the second in 1818 in 6 vols., the third in 1829-1830 in 21 vols., the fourth in 1873-1886 in 22 vols., the fifth in 1879-1928 in 41 vols. The sixth edition is a pléiade, which is still incomplete. See Bastide 1977, pp.189-190

165. *Écrits Inédits*, vol.II, Paris 1880, pp.179-408. The complete title is *Mémoire succint sur les formalités desquelles nécessairement la renonciation du roy d'espagne tant pour luy que pour sa postérité doit estre revestue en France pour y estre justement et stabilement validée*. It was written around 1712, and is probably Saint-Simon's most systematic statement of his views on the ancient constitution of the monarchy and process of degeneration it had gone through in the recent past.

166. Two other important sources of Saint-Simon's political ideas are not included in the *Écrits Inédits*. First, an anonymous treatise entitled *Projets de Gouvernement du Duc de Bourgogne*, written by Saint-Simon in 1711, and published by P.Mesnard, Paris 1860. The manuscript is not in the handwriting of Saint-Simon, but his authorship seems to be assured. The final version of the manuscript apparently dates from 1714/1715. See Sée 1978, p.239n2 Secondly, the *Histoire de la Pairie*, written in the 1660's by the abbé le Laboureur, in commission of a group of peers including the father of Saint-Simon. It was published only in 1740, but had circulated in manuscript ever since about 1670. Since it contained essentially the same views as those later expressed by the duke, it is very likely that he read the manuscript and that his views were decisively shaped by it. See Carcassonne 1978, pp.11-14

167. Quoted in Sée 1978, p.242

168. Saint-Simon, *Renonciation*, pp.191-192

169. Saint-Simon, *Renonciation*, p.192

170. Saint-Simon, *Renonciation*, p.192

171. Saint-Simon, *Renonciation*, p.193

172. Saint-Simon, *Renonciation*, pp.193-194

173. Saint-Simon, *Renonciation*, p.194

174. Saint-Simon, *Renonciation*, pp.195-196

175. Saint-Simon, *Renonciation*, p.194

176. Saint-Simon, *Renonciation*, p.197

177. Saint-Simon, *Renonciation*, pp.197-198

178. Saint-Simon, *Renonciation*, p.205

179. Saint-Simon, *Renonciation*, p.205

180. Saint-Simon, *Renonciation*, p.202

181. Quoted in Carcassonne 1978, pp.15-16

182. A fine recent monography is Ellis 1988

183. Boulainvilliers also wrote some specifically philosophical pieces, which have been reprinted recently. See his *Oeuvres Philosophiques*, The Hague, 1973 in 2 vols. He translated Spinoza's *Ethica*. He wrote about universal and religious history, including the life and thought of Mohammed. He supposedly wrote a treatise about the meaning of hieroglyphs. And he was quite a famous astrologist in his time. See Simon 1940, pp.531-671 Mackrell 1973, p.21 notes that Boulainvilliers correctly predicted the exact hour of his own death, but was completely wrong in predicting Voltaire's death, which was used by the latter thirty years afterwards to apologize for his 'inconsiderate longevity'.

184. Carcassonne 1978, p.7

185. Quoted in Buranelli 1957, p.482

186. Buranelli 1957, pp.479-481

187. Mackrell 1973, p.22

188. Quoted in Buranelli 1957, p.483 It is amusing to note that this historical theory was used for their own purposes by some of the revolutionaries of 1789. Siéyes in his famous speech *Qu'est-ce que le Tiers-Etat?* asked the rhetorical question 'pourquoi ne renverrait-il pas dans les forêts de Franconie toutes ces familles qui conservant la folle prétention d'être issues de la race des conquérants, et d'avoir succédé à leurs droits?' Quoted in Simon 1940, p.128

189. Ford 1968, pp.184-185

190. Quoted in Buranelli 1957, p.485

191. Quoted in Buranelli 1957, p.484

192. Quoted in Buranelli 1957, p.486

193. Quoted in Buranelli 1957, p.486

194. Carcassonne 1978, p.19 It is clear at which other French king this pun is directed.

195. Quoted by Simon 1940, p.151

196. Simon 1949, p.151; Buranelli 1957, p.486

197. Carcassonne 1978, p.24

CHAPTER TEN

MONTESQUIEU'S LINEAGE

*To know well the era of the moderns, one must
know well the era of the ancients*

Montesquieu[1]

*In monarchical and moderate states, power is
limited by that which is its spring; I mean honor,
which reigns like a monarch over the prince and
the people. One will not cite the laws of religion
there; a courtier would consider himself ridiculous: one will cite without interruption the laws of
honor*

Montesquieu[2]

1. Father of modernity

Few men have suffered more from the attempt of posterity to subject them to
its own concerns and categories, than Charles Louis de Secondat, baron de la
Brède et de Montesquieu, the author of the *Spirit of the Laws* (1748).

1.1. Interpretation and appropriation

The two most commonly expressed ideas about Montesquieu are first, that he
was a founding father and secondly, that he was inconsistent in his thought.
He is declared to be the founder of political science,[3] the originator of the
liberal tradition,[4] the precursor of sociology,[5] an early functionalist,[6] a
precursor of historicist individualism and developmentalism,[7] one of the
inventors of the separation of powers,[8] and so on. In short, Montesquieu is
hailed as the intellectual father of many a modern creed. Most commentators
accordingly assume a tone of respectful admiration. Montesquieu is
unfailingly judged to be a 'great thinker', the *Spirit* a 'masterpiece'. 'The
scope of (his) science of society', it is generally agreed, 'was without parallel
in the eighteenth century.'[9]

The thing is that with equal predictability these acclaims are followed by
the chastisement of inconsistency, ambiguity, and confusion. Montesquieu's
magnum opus in particular is said to lack a 'logical structure',[10] is argued to
contain a 'potpourri' of different subjects.[11] The author seems to vacillate
between Cartesian rationalism and Newtonian empiricism,[12] between moral

absolutism and moral relativism,[13] between description and prescription.[14] Particularly the last chapters of the *Spirit*, which deal with the early history of the French monarchy, are considered enigmatic. Montesquieu here seems to lapse into 'the confined sphere of aristocratic ideology', that he had successfully transcended in the other parts of the book.[15] The views he vindicates in those chapters are 'fanciful', 'self-serving', and 'inaccurate'. They are 'bad history and bad law, a transparent defense of privilege in the guise of constitutional principles'.[16] Consequently, the issue is commonly given only slight attention, and is never seen as a vital part of what Montesquieu had to say.[17]

On closer consideration, the paradox of simultaneous praise and blame is easily explained. For both praise and blame are contained in the concept of a precursor itself. A precursor is someone who is already on the right track, so to speak, who has discovered part of the truth. He is thus ahead of his time, he has made more progress than his contemporaries, and that is laudable. But at the same time, his views are still tainted by myth and falsehood. The precursor has not yet succeeded in discarding all the old-time beliefs. Now and then, he gets off the track. Hence, his ambiguity and confusion. Montesquieu neatly fits into this picture. Indeed, his case seems to be an indisputable piece of evidence for it.

Nevertheless, we should ask ourselves if we do justice to Montesquieu if we insist on treating him as a precursor to our own concerns and categories. Maybe we give him both too much and too little credit in doing so. Too much, in viewing him as a precursor who has seen further than others in his day, and too little in viewing him as ambiguous and confused. Maybe Montesquieu is not at all, or not primarily at least, a precursor of modernity, but first and foremost an epigone of antiquity. If, departing from such a framework, the supposed ambiguity and confusion disappear, a strong case can indeed be made for the view that our mixed feelings about Montesquieu are the result not of his shortcomings, but of our lack of reflexivity about the nature of the historical enterprise. In considering Montesquieu as a precursor we in fact treat him as one of us, as taking part in our discussion. We approach him teleologically: he leads up to us, as it were. In sum, the standard view of Montesquieu seems to be greatly affected by the disposition to look for the present in the past, i.e. by the teleological approach to history.

The present author does not want to deny that Montesquieu was in effect in many ways a precursor of later creeds, but his being a source of inspiration to successive generations does not mean that he already tried to say, albeit rather clumsily, what they achieved to express with greater clarity and consistency. Instead, the relation between Montesquieu and those inspired by him seems to be largely a relation of selective reading and creative misunderstanding. One can only see Montesquieu as a precursor of modernity *malgré-*

lui. But in that case one should not accuse him of being ambiguous and inconsistent.

1.2. The first rate

A correct and complete understanding of Montesquieu presupposes that we see him not as a predecessor of a new tradition, not as the harbinger of the new in the old, but as a participant in the discourse of his own day, elaborating on a tradition lying even further back in time. Admittedly, Montesquieu himself seems to deny this. Presumably in order to stress the ingenuity of the work, the *Spirit* was preceded by an epigram taken from Ovid's *Metamorphoses*, stating that *prolem sine matre creatam*: this child was created without a mother. Many have taken the claim at face value. And the conventional reading of the history of political and moral thought, focussing on the 'all-time greats', seems to confirm it. But this is of course a mistaken idea. As was to be expected, the historians who have taken the trouble to study second-rate figures have come up with plenty of sources that have exerted an influence on Montesquieu's thought.[18] This has led them to the conclusion that, speaking of his work as 'motherless', Montesquieu was not being fair to his contemporaries and predecessors.[19]

Yet, although closer to the truth than the belief in his novelty, this view doesn't seem to do justice to Montesquieu either. It is evident that the author was not bluffing, but was really convinced to have achieved something out of the ordinary. And his contemporaries, sympathetic or not, acknowledged it, if only, like Voltaire, by their apparent lack of understanding.[20] The *Spirit* was not just another contribution to a long-standing tradition, which could be readily recognized and categorized. It was highly idiosyncratic, both in style and in content. On the other hand, one must not jump to the conclusion that Montesquieu was 'beyond tradition'. What distinguishes him, and other first rate minds, from the second rate is that, in the interplay between *langue* and *parole*, their *parole* stands out and is material to the transformation of the *langue*, whereas in lesser mortals the *langue* is more in control of the *parole*. In a very real sense, therefore, the first rate is upsetting and destructive of the tradition, whereas the second rate is its guardian and upholder. But that does not mean that the first rate is not part of a tradition, or can radically break with it. Outside of a *langue* there is no *parole*.

Montesquieu is part of the aristocratic tradition in the political and moral thought of the ancien régime. Both the man and his oeuvre bear witness to that. As to the man: he once addressed his son with the words 'my son, (..) you are a man of both the robe and the sword. How you want to give an account of your position, is up to you.[21] It was true. Montesquieu's great-grandfather was of the *noblesse d'épée*, a huguenot whose lordship of Montesquieu had been raised to a barony by Henry IV in 1606. Both of his grandfathers had been *présidents* of the parlement at Bordeaux. His father was a soldier. And Montesquieu himself had been *président* in the same *parlement* as his grandfathers.[22] His education was typical of the *haute robe*: first the *collège de Juilly*, and then the university of Bordeaux, where he studied law.[23]

As to Montesquieu's oeuvre, the framework of his thought is unquestionably of classicist origin and design. The central concern of Montesquieu's work is the analysis of the nature and the causes of tyranny or despotism, the cure he proposes is a form of mixed government, conceived of as the ancient constitution of the realm. More generally, the *mos maiorum*, the virtues of the ancestors, must be respected on pain of utter corruption, i.e. the loss of liberty and the onset of servitude. Moreover, both the virtues and the vices are those of the Romans.

It has frequently been suggested that Montesquieu improved on the ancients by considering the relation between 'political superstructure and the social foundations'. 'In classical political philosophy no one bothered to examine (that) relationship. (..) Montesquieu's decisive contribution was precisely to combine the analysis of forms of government with the study of social organizations in such a way that each regime was also seen as a certain type of society.'[24] On this view, Montesquieu substituted the moralism *cum* voluntarism of the ancients by a modern naturalism *cum* determinism; despotism is no longer seen as an effect of vice, but of the climate, the nature of the terrain, and so on.[25] However, this antithesis is strained, because both the Romans and Montesquieu believed that moral and physical causes operate in concurrence, and that virtue can subdue natural temptations or obstacles.[26] The difference is one of degree rather than kind. All in all, the judgement that Montesquieu 'cast in his lot with the ancients against the moderns' seems to be the correct reading.[27]

1.3. The forms of state

The linchpin of the political analysis in the whole of Montesquieu's work is the classical Aristotelian-Polybian constitutional scheme. True, at a first glance he appears to deviate from the tradition in the *Spirit*. For in the first sentence of book II the reader is told that 'there are three kinds of government: republican, monarchical, and despotic'.[28] But a few lines further on, the republican form of government is divided into a democratic and an aristocratic species, a distinction which is preserved throughout the *Spirit*. That makes four forms of government. In book VIII, which is entitled 'Of the corruption of the principles of the three governments', the number is extended to six, three good and three degenerated forms of government.

'The principle of democracy is corrupted (..) when the spirit of extreme equality is taken up and each one wants to be the equal of those chosen to command. So the people, finding intolerable even the power they entrust to others, want to do everything themselves.'[29] Instead of seeking one's equals for masters, which is the true spirit of equality, the people seek to have no master at all.[30] However, 'the more the people appear to take advantage of their liberty, the nearer they approach the moment they are to lose it. Petty tyrants are formed, having all the vices of a single one. What remains of liberty soon becomes intolerable. A single tyrant rises up, and the people lose everything, even the advantages of their corruption'.[31] As to aristocracy, Montesquieu argues that it 'is corrupted when the power of the nobles becomes arbitrary'.[32] It has then changed into an oligarchy.[33] It is the despotism of the few. The corruption of the monarchy, finally, is 'the despotism of one alone'. 'The monarchy is ruined when the prince, referring everything to himself exclusively, reduces the state to its capital, the capital to the court, and the court to his person alone.'[34] In effect, all men are reduced to slavery, who obey because they fear.[35] In monarchy too, 'the prince is the source of all political and civil power', but there his power flows through intermediate powers, such as the nobility, the clergy, and the *dépots de lois*, which temper and moderate the power of the prince, and make it more constant.[36]

When he was done with his exposition of the principal features of the six pure types, Montesquieu was ready to introduce the seventh and best form of government, the *regimen mixtum*. It is the subject of book XI. Chapter six of this book, undoubtedly the most famous chapter in the *Spirit*, entitled 'Of the constitution of England', is plainly a description of the principles of a mixed government, in which power is shared by the people, the nobility, and the prince. But the English are not the only ones with such a government. As is set out in the second half of book XI, the ancient Romans also possessed it, both under the kings and during the republic. And the French? Although Montesquieu avoids the use of the term, it is clear that he believes his fatherland to have a mixed government as well, different in detail but not in principle from the English constitution.[37] As a matter of fact, the distinction between a monarchy and a mixed government is blurred by Montesquieu. But as we have seen, that was customary in the aristocratic political thought of the ancien régime.

The thread that runs through all of Montesquieu's writings is his abiding ambition to go to the core of these different forms of government and understand what makes them work and what effects their decline. As a classicist he believed that this involved the discovery of the few essential, universal features hidden behind the veil of empirical multiplicity. And precisely because these features were regarded as universal, i.e. transcending the particularity of time and place, history nor geography set boundaries to the investigation of and the evidence pertaining to the forms of government mentioned. Ancient Carthage and distant China, Nero and Richelieu, the *Leges Langobardorum* and the establishments among the Egyptians, all were relevant, all were pieces of the puzzle. Nevertheless, one source unquestionably stands out as the most important *Fundgrube*: ancient Rome.

It is true that he published only one relatively short treatise wholly devoted to the Romans, the *Considerations on the Causes of the Grandeur of the Romans and of their Decadence* (1734), but the *Spirit* depends heavily on them, and many of his unpublished manuscripts are at least in part concerned with the Romans. This sense of significance is well captured by the *cri de coeur* noted down in the *Considerations* that 'I can let nothing pass that serves to get to know the genius of the Roman people'.[38] It is repeated, in different words, in the *Spirit*: 'one can never quit the Romans.' To know the causes of the grandeur and decline of the Romans is to know the past, the present and the future of France. For the Romans had had a mixed government, which eventually changed into a malign despotism. And the French were on the same road to serfdom. The onset of tyranny could only be prevented if one understood what had happened to the Romans, so that one was able to avoid repeating the mistakes that they had made.

1.4. Considerations on the Romans

The *Considerations* are clearly the product of a classicist mind. It begins with an enumeration of the principles on which the Roman republic was based. Then it explains the success of the Romans in building an empire as an outflow of these principles. Subsequently, corruption sets in and the republic is lost. It concludes with an overview of the principles of the despotic state which resulted. 'Here we have in a word the history of the Romans: they vanquished all the peoples by their maxims; but once they had arrived there, their republic could not survive, they had to change the government, and the maximes emplyed by this new government, which were contrary to the first, effected the loss of their grandeur.'[39] It is a framework that recurs in the *Persian Letters* and the *Spirit*. If only because of this, it is impossible to call Montesquieu a modern. Modern thought begins with the disposal of this framework.

But Montesquieu's classicism goes deeper than this. In the 'maximes' themselves one also recognizes the Roman way of thinking. The citizens of the republic were wholly warlike and patriotic. They gladly sacrificed themselves for the *res publica*. Their military discipline was outstanding. They were poor by choice and always worked hard. Everyone owned a piece of land, giving him both a source of livelihood and a personal interest in the defense of the realm. There was little commerce and no luxury. As a consequence, avarice was unknown, as were vanity, and effeminacy. Political power, finally, was divided between the people, the senate, and the magistrates, as a result of which all abuse of power could be corrected.[40]

Corruption eventually set in, however. As the legions passed the Alps the army of citizen-warriors became an army of professional soldiers, who were loyal to their general more then to the *res publica*. The Asian conquests introduced the Romans to eastern luxuries. The newly enfranchised citizens did not have the same patriotic spirit, the same love of liberty, the same hatred of tyranny as the old Romans. A civil war broke out, and several generals tried to establish a one-man rule. Finally Augustus established a durable servitude.[41]

If the principle of the republic was war, the principle of the empire was peace. It became dangerous to do great deeds in the service of the state, because the emperor might be envious. One better stayed out of sight. Public business was henceforth conducted in the household of the emperor: everything became secret. All the great men depended for their employment and income on him; hence flattery, infamy, and crime became necessary means to arrive. Eventually even the fighting spirit was lost. 'The Romans came to command all peoples, not only by the art of war, but also by their prudence, their wisdom, their constancy, their love of glory and of the fatherland. When, under the emperors, all their virtues evaporated, the art of war endured with them, with which, notwithstanding the feebleness of the tyranny of their princes, they conserved what they had acquired. But when corruption established itself even in the army, they became prey to all the peoples.'[42] No longer prepared to defend themselves the Romans had to pay for their defense. But peace cannot be bought in this way, for those who are hired for that purpose, sooner or later make themselves master of everything.[43]

We may conclude that, whatever may have been Montesquieu's originality and idiosyncracy in detail, in general this sketch of the rise and decline of the Romans was wholly in line with classicist tradition. But it is a classicism of a Livian rather than a Polybian/Aristotelian style. Little concerned with constitutional design in the narrow sense of the word -only one chapter is devoted to legal issues- it concentrated on matters of moral fiber and their relation with the social system.

1.5. The tradition of Hotman

In the *Spirit of the Laws* we encounter the opposite approach. Polybius and Aristotle have taken the place of Livy; almost everything seems to be a question of law now. The reader is still confronted with the Romans roughly on every other page, but most remarks now deal with their legal institutions. However, this does not mean that Montesquieu has abandoned the classicist framework. On the contrary, the empirical multiplicity of the laws is consistently aligned to a small number of universal principles: the forms of government. Different laws are said to be appropriate under different forms of government. For instance, democracies need other laws than monarchies. If the lawgiver does not take heed of that, the state is bound to corrupt and change its form of government.

This idea was anything but original to Montesquieu. It had been expressed many times before, and is in fact a thoroughly classical notion. Hotman for example had argued along the same lines in the *Antitribonian*. 'The laws of the country must be accommodated to the state and the form of the republic, and not the republic to the law. This is what Aristotle has written in the third book of his *Politics*. Because the laws are given to preserve the republic in its essence, form and attributes. That can be learned from the three forms of republic the Greeks have of old named monarchy, aristocracy, and democracy; that is to say the government of one, of the notable men, and of the community. For the laws which are proper to a popular state, which is governed by the community, are accommodated to its essence and form, and are mostly not useful in a kingdom, just like the cloths of a humpback misfit an upright man. In the same way, each time a change in the essence of a republic has occurred, one immediately changed the laws, statutes, and political ordinances. The history of Rome provides an example. As soon as the kings had been abolished and the popular state established, for one hundred and fifty years one spoke of nothing but the fashioning of new laws, appropriate to a democracy, to prevent infinite troubles and *nouvelletés* appearing by default of good laws, and thus keeping the community content. They had to send ambassadors to the free cities of Greece, such as Athens and Sparta, to inform themselves about their statutes and *police*, and to bring copies with them that could serve as an example for the new republic. Immediately after the overthrow of the popular state and the introduction of tyranny by the Caesars, the ancient royal law was reinstalled, containing a succinct declaration of the power and sovereign authority of the monarch. The magistracy of the tribunes, that conserved the popular state, the *comitiae* and popular assemblies, the provocations, the authority of the senate, and other things were quickly nullified. Previously, the people gave law, governed the magistrates, and decided about peace, war, and alliances. All of this was now put into the hands of the emperor. As a consequence, all the magistracies and offices, military as well as judicial, were altered again, to accommodate them to the new form the republic had then acquired. This brought about a change in the laws as well, since the magistracy and the law are corresponding things. As the ancients said: the law is a mute magistrate, and the magistrate is a speaking law.'[44]

All of this, including the magistracy as the *bouche de la loi* returns in the *Spirit*, and is derived *linea recta* from the Romans. That is the *langue* Montesquieu shared with Hotman. There is no denying that the *Spirit* is a remarkable work, for it is probably the most idiosyncratic examination of the various forms of government written in the ancien régime. But although it is a highly personal *patois* in its use of the traditional concepts and categories, it is still well within the bounds of the classicist *langue*.

2. Son of antiquity

The ancients associated virtue with reason, reason with law, and law with the good forms of government. Conversely, vice was associated with the passions, the passions with lawlessness, and lawlessness with the corrupted forms of government.

2.1. Virtue, honor, and the laws

Montesquieu agreed that good aristocratic and good democratic government are grounded in virtue, defined as love of the homeland and of equality.[45] But 'this love, requiring a continuous preference of the public interest over one's own, produces the individual virtues'.[46] Hence, it also involves a 'desire for true glory, self-renunciation, and sacrifice of one's dearest interests'.[47] And 'when that virtue ceases, ambition enters those hearts that can admit it, and avarice enters them all. Desires change their objects. (..) What was a *maxim* is now called *severity*; what was *rule* is now called *constraint*; what was *vigilance* is now called *fear*. There, frugality, not the desire to possess, is avarice. Formerly, the goods of individuals made up the public treasury; the public treasury has now become the patrimony of individuals'.[48] 'The natural place of virtue is with liberty, but virtue can no more be found with extreme liberty than with servitude.'[49] Virtue and liberty presuppose courage and continence, moderation and prudence.[50] This is unequivocally the *langue* of classicism.

And what about Montesquieu's discussion of monarchy? The ancients of course held that virtue was necessary in this form of government as well, especially in the prince. Not surprisingly then, a genre of advise-books of princes developed within the classicist tradition, the so-called mirrors-for-princes, exhorting them to be virtuous.[51] However, this genre was mainly the offspring of royalist authors; as has been set out, the defenders of the *thèse nobiliaire* had more faith in a limitation of the king's constitutional powers. Nevertheless, it should be noted that, wholly in line with the tradition, Montesquieu explicitly mentions magnanimity and clemency as the distinctive qualities of monarchs.[52]

This is not to say that only the prince must be virtuous in a monarchy. Tradition had it that at least the greatest of his subjects should possess a measure of virtue. If the people are vicious, they are 'ready for slavery', as Tacitus had remarked, and despotism will ensue.[53] It is at this point that

Montesquieu appears to deviate from classicism, arguing that 'in monarchies politics accomplishes great things with as little virtue as it can',[54] which was obviously a provocative thing to say at the time.[55] The author was clearly aware of this, for he continued in a conciliatory tone, 'I hasten and lengthen my steps, so that none will believe I satirize monarchical government.' That virtue is lacking in a monarchy, does not mean that a monarchy is vicious. For honor takes its place 'and represents it everywhere'.[56] Since honor was intimately linked to virtue in the classicist tradition, this was a soothing explanation.

Yet, honor was customarily regarded as the crown of the virtues, whereas Montesquieu here introduces honor as their substitute. What does that mean? Honor is defined by him as concerned with those virtues (!) which 'are always less what one owes to others than what one owes to oneself; they are not what calls to our fellow citizens as what distinguishes us from them'.[57] 'One judges men's actions here not as good but as fine, not as just but as great; not as reasonable, but as extraordinary.'[58] Honor invokes the things associated with the idea of conquest, of greatness of spirit, of daringness and frankness.[59] Honor depends on the doing of admirable deeds. Honor 'obliges men to do all the difficult actions (..) which require force, with no reward other than the renown'.[60] Hence, 'the nature of honor is to have the whole universe as a censor'.[61] 'Shame comes from all sides.'[62] A breach of honor is a disgrace, and 'disgrace (..) is equivalent to a penalty'.[63] Indeed, 'the greatest penalty for a bad action will be to be convicted of it'.[64]

There is nothing really uncommon about this analysis of honor, apart from the fact that this would traditionally have been called false honor, for its lack of direction towards the common good. In particular, it is strongly reminiscent of Cicero's remarks on Caesar in De Officiis. Interestingly, Montesquieu admits in one place that what he calls by the name of honor is 'philosophically speaking (..) false honor', presumably because it is driven by the love of self instead of the love of homeland.[65] Hence, it seems that, on a closer view, Montesquieu's analysis is by and large in agreement with the classicist tradition.

There is one fundamental difference, nonetheless. As we have seen, the ancients believed that all was lost if virtue and honor were to grow apart. A false honor, like Caesar's, was a menace to society, precisely because he possessed all the virtues except the one that turned them to a social use. Montesquieu in contrast argues that this lack is inconsequential. 'Honor makes all the parts of the body politic move; its very actions binds them, and each person works for the common good, believing he works for his individual interests.'[66] What we have here is a notion of the 'invisible hand', of the intention-repercussion paradox. Although not a discovery of Montesquieu,[67] this aspect of his thought was not indebted to the ancients, whose mind was closed to that notion.

Nevertheless, the contradiction should not be exaggerated. The ancient conception of the legislator as the fountainhead of the social order was not at all rejected by Montesquieu. Spontaneous order was feasible only when 'joined with the force of laws'.[68] That is to say, the legislator must give laws that regulate the working of the principle of a constitution.[69] Romulus, Solon, and Lycurgus are the models.[70] The Romans had regarded especially the first lawgivers as important to a state. They are the authors of the laws and institutions that determine the fate of the state.[71] Montesquieu shared that view. 'In the days of birth of republics, the chiefs are the ones who found the custom, thereafter the custom is what forms the chiefs of republics.'[72] In line with the above, he asserted that the lawgiver of a democracy (and an aristocracy) must install virtue, whereas the lawgiver of a monarchy must stimulate honor. The former is the most difficult thing in the world, since it runs counter to all the passions. The latter is somewhat easier, since honor 'is favored by the passions and favors them in turn'.[73] If nothing at all is done a despotic government will develop. Good government 'is a masterpiece of legislation that chance rarely produces and prudence is rarely allowed to produce. By contrast, a despotic government leaps to view, so to speak; (..) as only passions are needed to establish it, everyone is good enough for that'.[74]

Montesquieu had interesting things to say about the laws and institutions needed in a democracy, which have been an important source of inspiration for Rousseau and other eighteenth-century radicals. But too much has been made of this element of his thought. It should be remembered that democracy was not his real concern. It is in a sense a side-issue, discussed mainly to let the principal features of a monarchy come to the fore with greater clarity. For that was Montesquieu's real interest: the monarchy and its corrupt counterpart despotism. As the modern state, though commonly called a democracy, is the heir of Montesquieu's monarchy rather than of his democracy, this should interest us. Let us therefore turn to the laws necessary to uphold a monarchy.

2.2. Monarchy and aristocracy

'Since honor is the principle of this government, the laws should relate to it.' That means first of all that 'in a monarchy they must work to sustain that nobility for whom honor is, so to speak, both child and father'.[75] Honor is the aristocratic principle -a traditional view. The implication is that the nobility stands between the monarchy and its corruption into a tyranny -also a traditional view. Montesquieu is unusually explicit about this. 'In a way, the nobility is the essence of monarchy, whose fundamental maxim is, *no monarch, no nobility; no nobility no monarch*; rather, one has a despot.' (author's emphasis)[76] The nobility is a *pouvoir intermediaire* that functions as a check upon the arbitrary power of the prince.[77] 'There is nothing in a monarchy that laws, religion, and honor prescribe so much as obedience to the will of the prince, but this honor dictates to us that the prince should never prescribe an action that dishonors us because it would make us incapable of serving him.'[78]

Montesquieu defines the nobility as 'altogether warlike'.[79] 'For the nobility, honor prescribes nothing more than serving the prince in war.'[80] But the robe is not ignored. 'The ignorance natural to the nobility, its laxity, and its scorn for civil government require a body that constantly brings the laws out of the dust in which they would be buried': the depository of the laws.[81] It is evident that the sovereign courts are meant here. This body is the preserve of the robe, 'that estate (..) lying between the great nobility and the people'.[82] They too are a check upon royal power. 'The bodies that are the depository of the laws never obey better than when they drag their feet and bring into the prince's business the reflection that one can hardly expect from the absence of enlightenment in the court concerning the laws of state and the haste of the prince's councils. What would have become of the finest monarchy in the world if the magistrates, by their slowness, their complaints, and their prayers, had not checked the course of even the virtues of its kings (..)?'[83] Hence, the sword and the robe each have their own assignment, and should stick to it. 'In monarchies, the object of men of war is only glory, or at least honor or fortune. One should be very careful not to give civil employment to such men; they must, on the contrary, be contained by civil magistrates.'[84]

That these magistracies are sold is no problem. 'Venality is good in a monarchical state, because it provides for performing as a family vocation what one would not want to undertake from virtue, and because it destines each to his duty and renders the orders of the state more permanent.'[85] Thus, cleverly rendering to all what is due to them, Montesquieu avoids taking sides in the constitutional debate between robe and sword. On his view both partake in the constitution. Nevertheless, he ultimately seems to take the side of the robe. It is the robe that has to contain the sword, and it is only the robe that plays a distinctly positive role in the central government of the realm. Of the estates-general little or nothing is heard.[86]

And the people, the democratic element in the constitution? In a monarchy the people have no direct interference with the government. Instead, 'the people (..) have tribunes': the nobility, the robe, and also the clergy.[87] 'The people, led by themselves, always carry things as far as they can go; all the disorder they commit is extreme; whereas in monarchies, things are very rarely carried to excess.' There 'people of wisdom and authority intervene; temperings are proposed, agreements are reached, corrections are made'.[88] Montesquieu has little faith in the common people, 'whose nature is to act from passion'.[89] Even in a democracy they have to be kept under a tight reign by a senate 'to which age, virtue, gravity, and service give entrance', and whose members 'are seen by the people as simulacra of gods'.[90] In a monarchy, the intermediary powers, who in a sense represent the people, at the same time 'do not want the people to have the upper hand too much'.[91] In other words, the aristocratic element in the constitution is a check not only on the monarchical element, but also on the democratic element. This is in all respects a Roman view of good government.

2.3. Liberty and commerce

Montesquieu's debt to the ancients goes much beyond his discussion of the forms of government and his vindication of a mixed constitution. The whole book is permeated by the spirit of classicism. In the standard interpretation of the *Spirit*, which takes the book as a major source of modern thought, much is made of Montesquieu's treatment of freedom and commerce in particular.[92] Both are said to be given a typically modern definition, an undertaking explained as a part of a wholesale attempt to replace the political ideas of the ancients with a new, modern political science.[93] On this view, Montesquieu is in the vanguard of modernity. However, such a reading is not borne out by the text. It is based on two mistakes: a selective reading and a false view of the ancients.

The first mistake, a selective reading of the text, is very common. Most commentators concentrate on the books and the chapters which appear to be modern, and simply ignore the rest. Other, more sophisticated commentators resort to what might be called the inconsistency-thesis. Being a precursor of modernity, Montesquieu was not yet completely consistent in his ideas, they argue. Still other, even more sophisticated commentators resort to a theory of disguise. Montesquieu hid his true meaning, it is asserted, he was voluntarily obscure, so that only the few capable of dealing with the truth would understand, and the vast majority of unwise would not be confused and upset.[94] But, although this theory is certainly not pointless, the difficulty with it is that one can always argue that every piece of text that contradicts the secret meaning is part of the disguise and therefore meaningless, a loophole which is sure to effect grave errors of interpretation.

The second mistake, which makes Montesquieu appear as a precursor of modernity, is a false understanding of antiquity, that is to say, a false understanding in respect to Montesquieu. The novelty of the latter depends crucially on what he is presumed to be reacting against. Take liberty for instance. 'Political liberty consists in security or at least in the opinion one has of one's security', according to Montesquieu.[95] This opinion is then contrasted with that of the ancients, who allegedly defined political liberty as the right to participate in the government of the state. But a closer examination reveals that the antithesis is largely based on a false opposition. The ancient concept of liberty generally has a different meaning than here suggested, both to the Greeks and the Romans.[96] Admittedly, the Greek concept of *eleutheria* is sometimes used in this sense, but not so the Roman concept of *libertas*. And for Montesquieu the ancients were the Romans. A comparison of his use of the concept of liberty with that of the Romans makes clear that, like them, he places it in opposition to *servitus* on the one hand, and *licentia* on the other, and aligns it to *civitas*. The primary meaning of liberty to both the Romans and Montesquieu was thus 'not being a slave' but a *liber*, a juridically free(born) man, with full legal rights. When Paulus told the soldier that he was a Roman citizen he was not referring to his right to take office.

The same goes more or less for Montesquieu's supposed break with the ancients over commerce, discussed principally in book XX of the *Spirit*. The question is to what extent Montesquieu is really 'at odds with traditional morality' on this issue.[97] Let us see what he has to say about it. 'Commerce cures destructive prejudices, and it is an almost general rule that whereever there are gentle mores, there is commerce and that whereever there is commerce, there are gentle mores. (..) One can say that the laws of commerce perfect mores for the same reason that these same laws ruin mores. Commerce corrupts pure mores and this was the subject of Plato's complaints; it polishes and softens barbarous mores, as we see every day.'[98]

As an analysis of a factual relation, this judgement is hardly new, although the ancients spoke of *luxuria* and *avaritia* rather than commerce. But they were well aware that the two were related. Statements to this effect can be found in Caesar, Tacitus, Petronius, Juvenal and many others. It is true that Montesquieu's appraisal of commerce seems to be somewhat more positive than that of the ancients, but the difference between them can easily be exaggerated. On the one hand, Montesquieu was evidently aware of and concerned with the relation between gentleness of mores and vices like effeminacy, cowardice, and mean-spiritedness, a connection also stressed by the ancients.[99] On the other hand, the ancients' opposition against commerce was far from absolute. What they opposed was not commerce *per se*, but the involvement of the commercial interest in the government of the state. The spirit of commerce was considered contrary to the spirit of political leadership. It must therefore be kept in its rightful place; there is no suggestion that it must be exterminated. Montesquieu agreed with this. In a monarchy 'the laws must favor all the commerce that the constitution of this government can allow',[100] but 'it is against the spirit of monarchy for the nobility to engage in commerce'.[101]

2.4. The ancient constitution

If the hypothesis vindicated by the present author is correct, and Montesquieu should be understood as a classicist rather than a modern author, the last five books of the *Spirit*, together making up part VI, lose their enigmatic character. Usually depicted as an appendix, a historical *Exkurs*, an afterthought, or an atavistic flinch, but little integrated with the main body of the work, from our perspective the last chapters are securely bound up with the general account. Part I to V give us Montesquieu's variant of the classicist *maior* -the abstract political science-, part VI gives us his view of the *minor*: the place of France in the abstract scheme. Tradition had it that this place depended on the *mos maiorum*, the ancient constitution, and Montesquieu wholeheartedly concurred. In the whole of the *Spirit* there is not a flicker of doubt about this framework. Hence, every interpretation of this work must come to grips with it, and relate it to the general tenets of his thinking. But if that is true, it is no longer possible to see Montesquieu as a precursor of modernity.

'In the old French laws one surely finds the spirit of monarchy.'[102] In other words: the ancient constitution of France is monarchical. It can be found in the works of Caesar and Tacitus, dealing with the *mores* of the Germans.[103] For the French constitution was brought to Gaul by *nos pères*, the Franks and the other Germanic peoples, who conquered the Roman empire and overthrew the Roman institutions.[104] Significantly, this is where the English constitution comes from as well. 'If one wants to read the admirable work by Tacitus on the customs of the Germans one will see that the English have taken their idea of political government from the Germans. This fine system was found in the forests.'[105] Indeed, all the European monarchies seem to have been found in the German forests. 'Here is how the plan for the monarchies that we know was formed. The Germanic nations who conquered the Roman empire were very free, as is known. On the subject one has only to see Tacitus on *the mores of the Germans* (author's emphasis). The conquerors spread out across the country (..). When they were in Germany, the whole nation could be assembled. When they dispersed during the conquest, they could no longer assemble. Nevertheless, the nation had to deliberate on its business as it had done before the conquest; it did so by representatives. Here is the origin of Gothic government among us. It was first a mixture of aristocracy and monarchy. Its drawback was that the common people were slaves; it was a good government that had within itself the capacity to become better. Giving letters of emancipation became the custom, and soon the civil liberties of the people, the prerogatives of the nobility and of the clergy, and the power of the kings, were in such concert that there has never been, I believe, a government on earth as well tempered as that of each part of Europe during the time that this government continued to exist.'[106] The implicit suggestion is of course that the ancient constitution had later come under attack as the kings and the ministers tried to usurp more and more powers of the nobility and the people, and transform the monarchy into a tyranny.[107] Hence Montesquieu's political agenda: the preservation, and where necessary restoration, of the ancient constitution.

The *bête noire* of the last chapters of the *Spirit* is a certain abbé Dubos, who had published a voluminous *Critical History of the Establishment of the French Monarchy* in 1734, in which the royalist view of the ancient constitution was set out with unprecedented learning and in great detail.[108] 'The abbé Dubos wants to remove any idea that the Franks entered Gaul as conquerors; according to him our kings, summoned by the peoples, did nothing but take the place and succeed to the rights of the Roman emperors.'[109] Strange as it may seem today, this was the core of the argument between the king's party and the aristocracy. For, given the classicist framework, the truth of the claim would imply that the kings, as successors of the Roman emperors, possessed absolute political power in the realm. The medieval participation of the nobility in the government would then be a corruption of the ancient constitution, and the process of centralization that had been going on for several centuries merely a restoration of that constitution.

Montesquieu takes great pains to show that the origin of the constitution must be sought in the usages and the customs of the Germans, and not in those of the Romans. 'Clovis, near the end of his reign, was made consul by the emperor Anastasius, but what right could a simple one-year authority give him? It is likely, says the abbé Dubos, that in the same document the emperor Anastasius made Clovis proconsul. And I for myself, I shall say that it is likely that he did not. Concerning a fact that is founded on nothing, the authority of the one who denies it is equal to the authority of the one who alleges it. I even have a reason for this. Gregory of Tours, who speaks of the consulate, says nothing about the proconsulate. This proconsulate would have been for only about six month. Clovis died a year and a half after being made consul; it is not possible to make the proconsulate a hereditary post. Finally, when the consulate and, if one wants, the proconsulate, were given to him, he was already master of the monarchy and all his rights were established. The second proof alleged by the abbé Dubos is the emperor Justinian's assignment to the children and grandchildren of Clovis of all the rights of dominion over Gaul. (..) Justinian did not possess an inch of land there (..). The Frankish monarchy was already founded; the regulation of its establishment was complete; the reciprocal rights of persons and of the various nations living under the monarchy were agreed upon.'[110]

In addition to this direct refutation Montesquieu also provided one a little bit more roundabout. It centered on the so-called Salic law, the law of inheritance which was generally considered a fundamental law of the realm.[111] Montesquieu devoted a whole chapter of the *Spirit* to the Roman laws on inheritance, to show that these differed substantially from French law.[112] The point was obviously to prove that French law was of Germanic and not of Roman stock, and Roman law not the law of the land.[113]

All that remained for him to do was the assessment of the customs the Franks had brought with them from the German woods, and to trace through time their survival, under various names and in different forms, or their corruption. 'It is impossible to inquire (..) into our political right if one does not know perfectly the laws and the *mores* of the German peoples.'[114] In this Montesquieu on the whole follows Boulainvilliers. He disagrees with the latter only in his belief that the Franks, upon their conquest of Gaul, had put the indigenous people into a kind of servitude.[115] For the rest, his views are similar if not the same. His attention goes almost exclusively to the feudal system, and although he did not say it explicitly, it is clear that he agreed with Boulainvilliers that this system was 'le chef-d'oeuvre de l'esprit humain'.

NOTES

1. Montesquieu, *Pensées*, nr.399 'Pour bien connaître les temps modernes, il faut bien connaître les temps anciens.'

2. Montesquieu, *Esprit*, III.10 'Dans les Etats monarchiques et modérés, la puissance est bornée par ce qui en est le ressort; je veux dire l'honneur, qui règne, comme un monarque, sur le prince et sur le peuple. On n'ira point lui alléguer les lois de la religion; un courtisan se croirait ridicule: on lui alléguera sans cesse celles de l'honneur.'

3. Althusser 1981, p.11 'C'est une verité de déclarer Montesquieu *le fondateur de la science politique*. (author's emphasis) Auguste Comte l'a dit, Durkheim l'a redit, et personne n'a sérieusement contesté cet arrêt.'

4. Pangle 1989, p.4

5. Aron 1971, p.17; Gay 1977. vol.II, p.323

6. Thompson et al. 1990, p.109

7. Meinecke 1965, p.178

8. Vile 1967, p.76

9. Haddock 1980, p.83

10. Haddock 1980, p.83

11. Gay 1977, vol.II, p.324

12. Haddock 1980, pp.83-84; Gay 1977, vol.II, p.326

13. Berlin 1981, pp.130-161

14. Gay 1977, vol.II, pp.330-332, who, condescendingly, finds this ambiguity 'touching'.

15. Gay 1977, vol.II, p.467

16. Gay 1977, vol.II, p.466

17. E.g. Aron 1971, pp.58-59, in whose discussion of Montesquieu the issue is brought up almost as an afterthought.

18. Esp. Carcassonne 1978; Dedieu 1909; Keohane 1980

19. Keohane 1980, p.393, who mentions only 'contemporaries'.

20. Gay 1977, vol.II, p.324

21. Montesquieu, *Pensées*, nr.69

22. Shackleton 1963, pp.1-2

23. Shackleton, pp.5-8

24. Aron 1971, p.25

25. Pangle 1989, p.34, pp.162-163; The Straussians are much too rigid in their use of the dichotomy of ancients and moderns. Every writer as of Machiavelli is regarded as modern, i.e. a determinist and a materialist, reducing ultimate human motivation to mere bodily self-preservation. This betrays a teleological view of history. Cf. Hirschmann 1981, whose book suffers from the same shortcoming. Significantly, it commences with a -very short- chapter entitled 'The idea of glory and its downfall'. Furthermore, Montesquieu is presented, p.73, as a 'crown witness for the thesis of this essay'. But surely it cannot have escaped Hirschmann that to Montesquieu the conception of honor -intimately related to the notion of glory- was still very much alive?

26. Montesquieu, *Esprit*, XIV,5

27. Keohane 1980, p.419; Chaimowicz 1985, pp.11-16

28. Montesquieu, *Esprit*, II.1

29. Montesquieu, *Esprit*, VIII.2

30. Montesquieu, *Esprit*, VIII.3

31. Montesquieu, *Esprit*, VIII.2

32. Montesquieu, *Esprit*, VIII.5

33. Montesquieu, *Esprit*, VIII.5 note a

34. Montesquieu, *Esprit*, VIII.6

35. Montesquieu, *Esprit*, III.9-10

36. Montesquieu, *Esprit*, II.4; III.10; V.11

37. Montesquieu, *Lettres Persanes*, CXXXI; *Esprit*, XI.8

38. Montesquieu, *Considérations sur les Causes de la Grandeur des Romains et de leur Décadence*, XIV

39. Montesquieu, *Considérations*, XVIII

40. Montesquieu, *Considérations*, I-VIII

41. Montesuieu, *Considérations*, IX-XII

42. Montesquieu, *Considérations*, XVIII

43. Montesquieu, *Considérations*, XIII-XVIII

44. Hotman, *Antitribonian*, II; Cf. Cicero, *De Leg.*, III.2 'magistratum legem esse loquentem'

45. Montesquieu, *Esprit*, Avertissement; cf. III.5 where it is called 'love of the homeland'; IV.5 'love of the laws and the homeland'; V.2 'love of the republic'

46. Montesquieu, *Esprit*, IV.5

47. Montesquieu, *Esprit*, III.5

48. Montesquieu, *Esprit*, III.3

49. Montesquieu, *Esprit*, VIII.3

50. Montesquieu, *Esprit*, V.3; XVII.2; XII.5, and passim

51. Skinner 1979, vol.I, pp.118-128

52. Montesquieu, *Esprit*, V.12; VI.21

53. Montesquieu, *Esprit*, XIV-XVII

54. Montesquieu, *Esprit*, III.5

55. The apologetic *avertissement*, first included in the revised 1757 edition, is devoted to this issue.

56. Montesquieu, *Esprit*, III.6

57. Montesquieu, *Esprit*, IV.2

58. Montesquieu, *Esprit*, IV.2

59. Montesquieu, *Esprit*, IV.2

60. Montesquieu, *Esprit*, III.7

61. Montesquieu, *Esprit*, V.19

62. Montesquieu, *Esprit*, VI.21; cf.VI.12

63. Montesquieu, *Esprit*, VI.21

64. Montesquieu, *Esprit*, VI.9

65. Montesquieu, *Esprit*, III.7-8

66. Montesquieu, *Esprit*, III.7

67. Keohane 1980, pp.283-311

68. Montesquieu, *Esprit*, III.6

69. Montesquieu, *Esprit*, V.1

70. Montesquieu, *Esprit*, V.5

71. Cf. Cicero, *De Rep.*, II.1.ff.

72. Montesquieu, *Considérations*, I 'Dans la naissance des sociétés, ce sont les chefs des républiques qui font l'institution, et c'est ensuite l'institution qui forme les chefs des répubiques.'

73. Montesquieu, *Esprit*, IV.5

74. Montesquieu, *Esprit*, V.14

75. Montesquieu, *Esprit*, V.9; cf.XIII.20 'Glory and honor are for that nobility which knows, sees, and feels no real good except honor and glory.'

76. Montesquieu, *Esprit*, II.4

77. Montesquieu, *Esprit*, II.4

78. Montesquieu, *Esprit*, IV.2

79. Montesquieu, *Esprit*, XX.22

80. Montesquieu, *Esprit*, IV.2

81. Montesquieu, *Esprit*, II.4

82. Montesquieu, *Esprit*, XX.22

83. Montesquieu, *Esprit*, V.10

84. Montesquieu, *Esprit*, V.19

85. Montesquieu, *Esprit*, V.19

86. Cf. Montesquieu, *Esprit*, XXVII.9

87. Montesquieu, *Esprit*, II.4; V.11

88. Montesquieu, *Esprit*, V.11

89. Montesquieu, *Esprit*, II.2

90. Montesquieu, *Esprit*, V.7

91. Montesquieu, *Esprit*, V.11

92. Pangle 1989; Rahe 1992

93. Hirschmann 1981; Pangle 1989; Rahe 1992

94. Pangle 1989, pp.11-19

95. Montesquieu, *Esprit*, XII.2; cf. XI.6

96. Raaflaub 1985; Kloesel 1983

97. Pangle 1989, p.202

98. Montesquieu, *Esprit*, XX.1

99. Montesquieu, *Esprit*, XX.2; XX.14

100. Montesquieu, *Esprit*, V.9

101. Montesquieu, *Esprit*, XX.21

102. Montesquieu, *Esprit*, VI.10

103. Montesquieu, *Esprit*, XXX.2

104. Montesquieu, *Esprit*, VI.18; X.3

105. Montesquieu, *Esprit*, XI.6

106. Montesquieu, *Esprit*, XI.8

107. Keohane 1980, p.397

108. Montesquieu, *Esprit*, esp.XXX

109. Montesquieu, *Esprit*, XXX.24

110. Montesquieu, *Esprit*, XXX.24

111. Montesquieu, *Esprit*, XVIII.22; XXVIII.1

112. Montesquieu, *Esprit*, XVII

113. Montesquieu, *Esprit*, XVIII.4

114. Montesquieu, *Esprit*, XXX.19

115. Montesquieu, *Esprit*, XXX.10-11

PART V

THE ANCIENTS AND THE MODERNS

CHAPTER ELEVEN

CLASSICISM, ROMANTICISM, AND MODERNITY

> *Romanticism is the art of presenting to people
> literary works which, in the present state of their
> habits and beliefs, is capable of giving them the
> greatest pleasure possible. Classicism on the
> contrary presents them with a literature giving the
> greatest possible pleasure to their great-grandpar-
> ents*
>
> *Stendhal[1]*

> *Gentlemen, we are neither Persians subjected to a
> despot, nor Egyptians subjugated by priests, nor
> Gauls who can be sacrificed by their druids, nor
> finally Greeks or Romans, whose share in social
> authority consoled them for their private enslave-
> ment. We are modern men, who wish each to enjoy
> our own rights, each to develop our own faculties
> as we like best, without harming anyone; (..)
> needing the authorities only to give us the general
> means of instruction which they can supply, as
> travellers accept from them the main roads without
> being told by them which route to take*
>
> *Constant[2]*

1. The modern

'One can never quit the Romans', wrote Montesquieu.[3] We know that this
was a judgement he shared with most of his contemporaries. What we also
know is that it is not shared by our contemporaries. What has happened?
What has made us lose our interest in the Romans? Why do we believe that
they have nothing to tell us, whereas the educated elite of the ancien régime
thought that life could not be lived well without them? What has caused our
alienation? The answer probably lies in that most complex of notions:
modernity. If there is one thing that makes them foreign to us, it is that we
think we are modern, and they were still quite self-consciously ancient.

Arguably, the subject of modernity is the paramount theme of nine-

teenth- and twentieth-century social and political philosophy. As has been set
out in the first chapter, the teleological approach to history is closely linked
to the moderns' preoccupation with their roots. In a way typical of the
parvenu, we have been deeply concerned with the creation of a counterfeit
lineage, reaching back over the centuries, proclaiming as ancestors many who
have nothing to do with us, and inflating the importance of those who are
truly our forebears, but were in reality of little significance. But if that is the
case, and our genealogy as moderns is much less glorious than we tend to
pride ourselves on, the question is raised how modern the moderns really are.
This final chapter offers some reflections on this issue. Being a subject
probably even less well investigated than that discussed in the main body of
this book, the reader should not expect anything very definitive. Moreover, the
validity of the general story is in no way dependent upon the suggestions
made in the present chapter. It is more the synopsis and preface to a sequel,
than a summary and conclusion of this work.

1.1. Aufklärungsdenken

What is modernity? Sociologically, modernity refers to industry as opposed
to agriculture, to the city as opposed to the village, to the secular as opposed
to the religious, to equality as opposed to hierarchy, to cosmopolitanism as
opposed to localism, to science as opposed to belief, and so on. But behind
these great transformations lies something that is at the root of them all, viz.
a new way of thinking about the world and man, a new ontology. This new
ontology is commonly referred to as *Aufklärungsdenken*, enlightenment
thought. More specifically, on this view modernity is associated with the
'project' of the enlightenment thinkers to extend the method of the natural
science of Copernicus, Galilei, and Newton to the sphere of man and society.
The philosophical language in which this 'project' is expressed has various
'vernaculars', such as utilitarianism, naturalism, and positivism, but these are
ontologically identical. Most importantly, perhaps, the underlying concept of
knowledge is technological or instrumental. As will be remembered, the
ancients regarded this as the lowest type of knowledge, which was associated
with the sphere of production and reproduction, with ordinary life, as opposed
to the higher, i.e. political and philosophical life. Writers like Bacon, Hobbes,
and Locke, who promoted the technological conception of knowledge were
well aware of this. Their stance was, in part at least, inspired by social
motives. Knowledge had to contribute to the improvement of the general
condition of all man, including the meanest.[4] Obviously, this was an
inversion of classicist beliefs.

Technological knowledge takes the ends of man for granted, in the sense
that knowledge concentrates on the ways and means to achieve these ends,
and not on the ends themselves. It is therefore non- or even anti-normative in

intention. Classicist *prudentia* on the other hand is normative knowledge of man's ends. It is concerned with his *telos*. Its basic norm is the need to transcend the passions to realize the good life. Conversely, the enlightenment self-consciously takes the passions as its point of departure. Moral transcendence is declared impossible. As a consequence, the qualitative distinction between for instance cowardice and courage is lost: they are merely different passions. Horizontality thus replaces verticality, the knowledge how to achieve an end replaces the knowledge what ends to achieve, and a gap is opened between 'is' and 'ought'.

Classicist *prudentia* presupposes voluntarism, since it is essentially concerned with choice. Technological knowledge on the contrary is necessarily of a determinist type, and strictly causal. It is a catalogue of means, which are valuable only if they are effective in bringing about, in causing, the wanted end. But the determinism is of a specific kind: it is repeatable, it is universal. Hence, like classicist knowledge, this modern knowledge is independent of time and place. Newton's laws are not only operative in Britain, even though that is where they were discovered. Had it not been repeatable, it would not have been useful; and that was after all the criterion. Like the classicist view, the enlightenment view thus presumes that behind the phenomenological diversity hides a similarity, a homogeneity. However, the homogeneity is different. For the classicist it is a matter of identity, for the *Aufklärungsdenker* a matter of cause and effect. The first beliefs that the world contains universal entities, the second that it contains universal laws of motion. (In the thought of the most consistent enlightenment thinkers identity is altogether discarded, i.e reduced to motion.) The first is an anatomy of the cosmos, the second a physiology. The first considers stability and rest the normal state of being, the second perpetual change and transformation. The first sees change as a jump from one identity to another, the second as infinitesimal by necessity: nature does not make jumps, *natura non facit saltus*.

The utilitarian 'vernacular', that is widespread in social thought today, particularly in economics, is probably the most distinct of modern languages. It is in virtually every respect opposite to classicism. Utilitarianism takes the passions -rebaptized as preferences- as given. Preference-formation, a key issue in classicism, is regarded as irrelevant. Every preference is as good as any other. The question is merely how these preferences can be satisfied to as great as possible an extent. Knowledge is knowledge how to achieve that. It is essentially a matter of knowing and combining various (infinitesimal) utility-curves, which are shaped according to a small number of simple universal laws, such as the law of diminishing marginal utility. Social institutions -including the law- are judged according to their contribution to the realization of preferences. They have to be useful. The argument that they have existed for ages, has no force whatsoever, unless of course their longevity is taken as evidence of their usefulness. But that is a minority viewpoint, and somewhat hybrid. The general idea is that institutions should continuously adapt to ever changing circumstances. Hence, an appeal to the *mos maiorum* is bound to fall on deaf ears. As a matter of fact, from a utilitarian perspective the fact that something has existed for a long time is cause for suspicion. Taking all this into consideration, one can hardly remain amazed that we have quitted the Romans. If this is really how we as moderns look upon ourselves and the world, the Romans have little to say to us indeed.

And yet, something is lacking in this sketch of the *condition moderne*. For, since its inception, or even its conception, modernity, as depicted above, has been accompanied by critics. Modernity has produced its own *Apokalyptiker*. These critics are sometimes labelled *Gegenaufklärer*, anti-enlightenment thinkers. But these are merely negative descriptions. Stated affirmatively, they are most accurately called romantics. It is sometimes argued, particularly by these critics themselves, that they somehow stand outside of modernity. But that judgement is basically wrong. The romantic tradition is itself a child of modernity. In fact, romanticism is as much a reaction to the classicism of the ancien régime, as to the thought of the enlightenment, something the German founders of this tradition were well aware of. Moreover, it shares some important features with the enlightenment tradition. It is thus as modern as the latter. Nevertheless, there is something to the view of romanticism as alien to modernity. For, though a part of modernity, it is at the same time a new classicism, a return to the ancients. Albeit in many ways sharply critical of classicism, romanticism strives to preserve some central aspects of that heritage for the modern world, which is threatened by annihilation by the *Glückseligkeitslehre* of the enlightenment thinkers. Significantly, the founders of romanticism returned to the ancients, but even more significantly these were not the same ancients as those of the ancien régime. Instead of to Rome, they turned to Greece. Let us dwell somewhat longer on this topic, because it seems that if anything has been left of what connects us with the ancients, it must be looked for here in the first place.

1.2. Anti-classicism

Romanticism is often, and rightly, contrasted with classicism. In many significant ways romantic thought is at odds with the tenets of classicism. As a matter of fact, originally romanticism was in part at least a self-conscious revolt against this earlier way of thinking.[5] Romanticism is one of those concepts that defies definition.[6] Nevertheless, it seems to possess an underlying, fundamental unity, or at least some key characteristics.[7] First and foremost, the romantics shared a specific concept of being. As we have seen, the classicist mind equated reality with universality and eternity, with the invariable as opposed to the merely local and temporary. This was the predominant view of reality within the cultural elite of the seventeenth and eighteenth century. It decisively structured the political thought of the age. Truth could be found in the essential, in the general, in that which transcends time and space, is of all times and places. That explains among other things why seventeenth- and eighteenth-century historians were so 'unhistorical' in the eyes of their nineteenth- and twentieth-century successors: they showed no regard for the particularity, the uniqueness, the incommensurability of past times and places, and freely and frequently compared every time and place to all others. To them Roman history was not only and not even primarily the history of a small city-state in middle Italy that developed into the hugest empire the world had as yet seen, but the most illustrious and instructive *exemplum* of the general laws governing the history of all nations of all times.[8]

Romanticism changed all this, for it was at bottom a radical reinterpretation of the concept of reality or nature, as comes to the fore in Sir Walter Scott's dictum of the 'general variety which Nature seems to have adopted as a principle through all her works, (..) anxious to avoid (..) anything like an approach to absolute uniformity'.[9] As is readily apparent from these lines the romantic notion of reality was the exact antipode of the one prevalent in the ancien régime. Now, peculiarity, singularity, uniqueness, incomparability, originality became the defining marks of being, and uniformity, invariability, universality, timelessness, its opposite, its denial. Truth could still be found, but it was no longer the one and only everlasting truth, valid irrespective of time and place. The truth was historicized, individualized, subjectivized.[10]

One of the effects was, as we have seen, that the idea of history -and historiography- acquired an entirely novel meaning. Instead of assuming that *l'histoire se repète*, because historical development was governed by general laws, the uniqueness and singularity of every past event was now stressed. Differences came to be considered as more important than similarities. As a result the idea that historical causality could be studied on a macro-level came under suspicion, and was replaced by explanation on a micro-level, if not by an outright rejection of the possibility of drawing causal inferences and the recommendation to stick to (detailed) description. The fall of the Roman republic, for example, used to be explained as the corollary of, among other things, the influx of luxury from the east in the aftermath of the Macedonian wars, undermining civic virtue. The inverse relation between luxury and civic virtue was regarded as a general law, applying equally to the Romans of the second and the first century B.C. and to eighteenth-century Frenchmen. In contrast to this universalist approach in explaining the fall of the Roman republic romantic authors tended to emphasize the particularities of the republic, and the specificity of the constellation of factors which contributed to its downfall, as for instance the character of Cicero and Caesar.

The change from the previous emphasis on Rome to that on Greece had much to do with this new romantic perspective. What the romantics admired in the ancient Greeks was their 'originality'. If traditionally the Greeks had been judged as somewhat primitive precursors of the Romans, who were considered to have built on the experience of the first, to have incorporated the knowledge and skills of the Greeks in their own culture, and reached a much higher standard of refinement and taste, the romantics introduced the view, which is still predominant, that Roman art and literature was but an imitation of the achievements of the Greeks, and hence possessing little merit.[11] To the romantics the creative act, the *inventio*, was the true mark of brilliance, of genius as they would have called it, whereas linking up with predecessors, learning from tradition, *imitatio* was only secondary, and to the more extreme among them even suspect, because curtailing the imagination. The Greeks were the inventors and the Romans the imitators, therefore the romantics extolled the first, and were much less enthusiastic about the second. Gradually, this view became a commonplace. As a contemporary scholar expresses it, 'in the ancient world it was the Greeks who were the *originators* (emphasis added); the Romans did little more than reproduce Greek ideas in a different language and with at most a slightly different tone and accent. It is not until St.Augustine that we find a Latin-speaking thinker of undoubted originality, who has a place in the history of thought on his own merits. It is therefore understandable that the history of Roman thought should be neglected'.[12] In other words, merit depends on 'originality'. Roman thought is not interesting, because it is not original.

1.3. Man as a creator

Romantic man is first and foremost a creator, *ein Schöpfer*. He is a genius, not because of his intelligence, but because of his originality. He thinks of new things, unthought of before. In this he is almost divine, much more than a mere creature, *ein Geschöpf*. He is not only part of the creation, but takes part in it. He shapes the world according to his image.[13] Ontologically, this entails that the self has a transcendental status. It is something active, primal, a native growth, determining rather than being determined by the outside world, molding man's experience, rather than being molded by it. Kant was of course one of the first to draw this conclusion, but his conclusions did not even nearly exhaust all the new vista's made possible by the notion of man as a creator.

Because creativity is the core of the romantic idea of man it is easily understandable that the artist is regarded as the paragon of humanity by many romantics. The sculptor, architect, the painter, the poet, the composer, they are the heroes of romanticism, because they most clearly reflect the idea of man as a creative being. As a result the artist, his art, and the aesthetic in general acquired a status incomparably higher than they had in earlier times. Traditionally, art was regarded an adornment, as luxury. The aristocracy of the ancien régime appreciated art in all its forms. The nobles were the ones who commissioned and collected art, thus doing most to further its production. But, although art was taken seriously, that was nothing as compared to the decisiveness it was credited with by the romantics. To the aristocracy of the ancien régime art was an enrichment of its life, something that could be enjoyed, relished, even loved, but it was not crucial. Art enlivened, but was not really an indispensable part of the good life. Consequently, the artist was seen -and treated-, by others as well as himself, as a supplier of graceful ornaments, of exquisite decoration. To the romantics on the other hand art was the most exalted expression of humanity, the point of contact of man with the divine. Art was greatly upgraded. From being a mere ornament it turned into something vital, overriding all other human interests. The status of the artist boomed proportionately. As the embodiment of the idea of creativity he was transformed from a servant into a hero raised above other man.

There is a telling difference for instance in both the social position and self-perception of Mozart and Beethoven. The first still belonged to the ancien régime, in which musicians were lower or middle-ranking servants in the houses of the great, or minor cathedral functionaries. In 1781 Mozart was placed below the valets in the household of the archbishop of Salzburg.[14] Beethoven would have none of this. He saw himself as a higher species of man. In *The Birth of the Modern*, Johnson recounts the anecdote that once, when walking with Goethe in the public gardens at Teplitz, and the empress of Austria and various dukes approached with all their attendants, Beethoven turned to Goethe, saying: 'Now keep your arm linked in mine, they must make way for us, not us for them'. Goethe, who was a founder of romanticism but still belonged to the old world, in bewilderment and embarrassment withdrew his arm, stepped aside and took off his hat. Beethoven, his arms crossed, walked straight through the crowd of dukes, only moving his hat a little. The dukes parted to make room for him and all greeted him kindly. At the end of the path Beethoven waited for Goethe, who had been bowing deeply. 'I have waited for you', he said, 'because I honor and revere you as you deserve. But you have done too much honor to those there'.[15]

In general, it can be said that with the rise of romanticism aesthetic categories moved into the spotlights of the intellectual stage. Their aestheticism was probably the principle reason why the romantics felt attracted to the Greeks. To them ancient Greece signified principally 'natural beauty' in art and life. None so much as this people valued beauty. In the most famous of all Greek myths, the story of the Trojan war, beauty played a decisive role. When the world's *handsomest* man, Paris, is asked to decide which one is the *fairest* goddess, Hera, Athena, or Aphrodite, and the first promises to make him ruler of the world, the second to make him always victorious in war, and the third the love of the world's most *beautiful* woman, he does not hesitate to appoint Aphrodite as the fairest. Beauty meant much more to the Greeks than to the Romans. The Greek concept of beauty -*to kallon*- refers to a cardinal virtue, and has strong overtones of excellence and nobility, whereas the Roman concept of *pulchritudo* refers to a qualification of secondary importance, which has no such connotations. Beauty is a prime feature of the Greek man of excellence -*ho kaloskagathos*-, a feature which seems to be impertinent to the Roman idea of what it meant to be a *bonus* or an *optimus*.[16]

This is not to say that beauty became the measuring rod of everything, the ultimate criterion of value, but that certain ideas which are related to the view of man as a creative being came to the fore. In the romantic mind the ancient Greeks were linked to beauty, beauty to art, and art to creativity, which to them was paramount. When man is pictured as a creator, not a creature, he is looked upon in a specific way: instead of being made he makes, instead of being acted upon he acts, instead of being ruled he rules, instead of obeying he wills, instead of being determined he determines. What we have here is the romantic notion of individual freedom: *autonomy*. Its tremendous influence in our days stands in no need of further proof, yet it was quite unknown before the end of the eighteenth century.[17] To be sure, the idea of autonomy goes back to the ancient Greeks. But they used it to denote what they called a free political community, i.e. an independent polis where the people had an important share in the government. The classical idea of autonomy thus refers to the political freedom of a collectivity. The romantics individualized and spiritualized it. They argued that man is free to the extent that he is a creator, spiritually independent of external forces, and thus self-determined in the most literal sense. It follows that he is unfree to the extent that he is not the ultimate creator of his own acts, determined by something beyond the self, a *heteronomous* being. Hence, he not only derives little benefit from listening to others, including the 'others inside of him', but could be positively harmed by it. What he should concentrate on is his 'authentic inner voice', his own will, the signs of life of his real self. It is the historical merit of Winckelmann's writings to have introduced the novel, romantic view on art and on the relation between art and society.

In classicist thought the question of art was an issue of secondary importance, a derivative of other questions. The question Rousseau posed to himself in his first *Discourse* (1750), for instance, still reflected a typically classicist concern: 'Whether the restoration of the sciences and the arts has contributed to a purification or a corruption of morals?'[18] The effect of art on society is what interested the classicist. Winckelmann reversed the question, focusing on the effect of society on art.[19] The Athenians of the classical age, that opened with the fall of the tyrants, he regarded as most laudable; there art was protected and encouraged to the utmost, and art inspired a whole people. 'The Athenians elevated themselves over all other cities by that victory (near Marathon, AK). They were the first of the Greeks to become *gesitteter* and to lay down their weapons, without which in the most ancient times no Greek even in peace appeared in public; likewise, its prestige and increasing power turned this city into the most important center of the arts and the sciences in Greece. That is why one said that the Greeks had most things in common, but only the Athenians knew the road to immortality'.[20] Winckelmann's interest in the effect of society on art must have seemed rather frivolous from a classicist point of view, because it mistakes a mediate for an ultimate concern, a judgement which in its turn must have seemed a misunderstanding from a romantic perspective, which takes the flourishing of art as the prototypical form of creation, which is of man's essence. (Note Winckelmann's -unclassical- suggestion that *Sittlichkeit* is linked to going about unarmed.)

On this view, man is more than a mere blender of existing components. He literally generates out of nothing. Hence, what counts in art is not that it is a good reflection of the world outside, but an authentic, original expression of the man within. Imitation is the negation of creation, and therefore has no value as art. The corollary of this is that art cannot be bound by any rules other than those made by the artist himself. The artist who is willing to compromise, for instance by embroidering on a successful theme, in order to please the public, is at best a bore and at worst an opportunistic imitator prostituting himself, and betraying the essence of art, even if he imitates only his own earlier creations. A finished work of art has the melancholy effect of a calendar whose year has expired. It is realized and therefore a thing of the past, whose remaining value lies entirely in the fact that it was once original. What apparently matters most in this view is the quality of the vision, the state of mind of the artist, not the quality of the product. What really counts is the input, not the outcome, why something is done, not what is done, the motives, not the consequences, the content, not the form.

1.4. Romantic ethics and politics

This was a truly revolutionary theory of art, running counter to most if not all classicist rules. But only when the romantics applied it to the realms of ethics and politics did all of its implications become fully visible. If to act morally right one must, above all, act and not be acted upon, only the impulses of the authentic will are to be taken into account, not what others will, and not what 'the other inside of' the agent wills. That is what constitutes integrity, sincerity, truthfulness. These concepts are obviously much older, but their meaning shifted fundamentally. Whereas truthfulness etc. used to denote accordance with objectivity, it now began to signify accordance with subjectivity, i.e. with the self.[21] This interestingly suggests that truthfulness does not depend on the question whether a statement fits 'the facts', but whether the person who utters it 'really means' what he says. The question whether it is really his view thus replaces the question whether his view is a correct view. Hence, *prudentia, doctrina, consilium* and other classicist virtues, which are meant to assure that a man knows the way of the world and therefore does the right thing, now all seem insignificant and secondary. What counts most is that man is really 'committed' to his expressed views. Otherwise he is an 'opportunist'. More generally, what counts is 'to be oneself', i.e. to let only the self determine one's acts. That is the meaning of authenticity. To be yourself in this sense, *bei sich selbst sein*, as Hegel put it, constitutes autonomy, independence, true freedom. Only the acts of a free man are creative acts, are genuinely human acts. A man whose acts are not means of self-expression, but ways to please others -'inside or outside'- is a hypocrite, a philistine, a slave. So much for *urbanitas* and *decorum*, obligingness and proper forms, benevolence and deference, convention and *mos maiorum*. They are all looked upon with contempt, because they must be bought at the cost of betraying one's authenticity.

The conception of politics also changed in the wake of these romantic ideas. In this realm a similar shift occurred from representation or reflection of objectivity to expression of subjectivity, from adaption to creation. This effected a new conception of a superior politician. If he had formerly been a man with an astute knowledge of human nature, a high capability of realistically assessing the facts, and masterly self-control, a *homo humanissimus*, whose virtues enabled him to master any situation, the idea of a superior politician now became that of a *visionary*, the creator of a new social order as a work of art.[22] The relationship between the politician and the world is like the relationship between an artist and his material. Politics becomes an expression of the politician's self. Again, the intentions overshadow the consequences, the activity outshines the product. The latter are nothing in themselves. Their significance depends entirely upon what the politician put into them. Hence, politics becomes a goal in itself, a constant, never ending, restless pursuit of the new, a feature romantic politics shares with romantic art, love, and all other possible human pursuits that lend themselves to a romantic interpretation.[23]

1.5. Inspiration

In the popular picture of romanticism one of its most salient features is the espousal of feeling, sensitivity, emotion. In fact, this is often regarded as its primary characteristic, but that is a half-truth at most. As far as emotion really was more heavily emphasized, that was an outflow of the idea of creativity. On this view, emotions are thought of as a specific kind of extra-rational experience from which human creativity is derived. Reason can only analyze on the basis of premises that are already known, and cannot come up with something really new and original. For that the extra-rational powers of the imagination -of 'inspiration'- are needed and reason is merely a hindrance. This concept of inspiration is central to romanticism. It is thoroughly 'unreasonable' in the sense that it is neither reasonableness, nor calculation or reflection, but a flash of insight coming out of the blue, without any effort. A moment of inspiration is a spontaneous occurrence, it cannot be invoked, cannot be controlled. At most, it can be conjured up, like a spirit. It suddenly gives birth to something which wasn't there a moment ago and is hence truly a moment of creation. This is why the romantics tend to associate emotion with inspiration. In addition to being 'unreasonable' both have, phenomenologically at least, many identical characteristics. Like inspiration an emotion can hardly be invoked or controlled and is suddenly there. It is little wonder therefore that, once the idea found acceptance that innovation was a matter of spontaneous flashes of insight, emotions began to be regarded as a fountain of knowledge as well. Like classicism, romanticism thus regards reason as a restriction of emotion, but whereas the first praise such restraint as a sign of virtue, the latter condemn it as obstruction of spontaneity. The classicist and the romantic views of the relation between reason and feeling are structurally identical. They differ only in the valuation of the restraint exerted by reason. (The enlightenment view on the other hand is entirely different. It considers, as Hume expressed it, reason 'the slave of the passions'. Hence, by definition reason can't act as a restraint on feeling.) The idea behind the classicist view is that emotion, which is associated with impulsiveness, is generally an insufficiently trustworthy compass to steer by, and often positively dangerous. Accordingly, politeness and good manners are esteemed as effective ways to discipline what was seen as the darker side of human nature. Feelings were suspect, strong feelings condemned. In the romantic view on the other hand anything that can block or stand in the way of creativity should be mistrusted, anything that promotes it should be given free rein, or at least the benefit of the doubt. For in restraining one's own emotions and those of others one represses man's most valuable asset, his creativity.

The upgrading by the romantics of the emotions as a source of knowledge has some remarkable effects, particularly with regard to the issue of self-knowledge. Once the 'heart' was envisaged as a fountainhead of knowledge, it was no great distance to the view of the 'heart' as a source of self-knowledge as well. Consequently, the seeming spontaneity of the emotions is taken as a proof that they are untainted by 'foreign' i.e. 'outer' influences. They are thus the expressions of man's true self. It follows that in restraining one's emotions one gives others a false, dishonest picture of oneself, one is being hypocritical. Moreover, it follows that refusing to listen to or resisting one's emotions, not to lose one's *continentia*, amounts to hiding from oneself, and thus stands in the way of autonomy. Obviously, this is a complete inversion of the classicist view, which holds that self-control is one of the cardinal virtues, and that being governed by one's emotions is a sign of weakness and effeminacy.

1.6. Alienation once again

Yet another implication of the romantic idea that creativity is central to humanity is that man is profoundly different from his fellow man. His originality makes him *unique*. The *locus classicus* of this creed are the first sentences of the *Confessions* of that great precursor of romanticism, Jean-Jacques Rousseau[24]: 'I am made unlike any one I have ever met; I will even venture to say that I am like no one in the whole world. I may be no better, but at least I am different'.[25] The fact that he is unique makes romantic man irreplaceable and of incalculable value. Innovations of supreme importance may be lost irretrievably if he is not given the opportunity to express his self completely, to develop and use its potential to the utmost. In finding out what he must do romantic man cannot let himself be driven by external forces. He derives little benefit from the experience of others. *Exempla* are serviceable only to similar beings, but he is not similar to anyone. To know what to do he can only look inside, study and examine himself, listen to his inner voice. Learning from others, imitating the experienced, obeying the rules incorporating the collective wisdom of generations are all secondary. What really counts is introspection. His unique self makes romantic man supremely important, but also separates him spiritually from all other human beings, as a result of the fact that it is impossible for others to really understand him. Alienation is the word for it.

At this point the romantic idea of man splits in two. The first accepts and even glories in his separateness and incomprehensibility. He is spiritually self-sufficient, he needs no understanding, he is the ultimate *Einzelgänger*, the lone hero, *sich selbst genug*, either of a positive-adventurous or of a negative-nihilistic sort. His alienation makes him 'cool', i.e. *ironical*. He is never totally committed, never completely here, always somewhat detached, remote. Irony is an expedient with which romantic man keeps the world at a distance.[26] It includes everything and makes him incapable of taking anything seriously. The only thing the romantic hero cannot be ironical about is his own self. That would involve an objectification of the self, which shatters its sovereignty, its final authority, and hence romanticism itself.[27] His 'twin brother' bears no likeness to him at all in this respect. He is a sufferer. His alienation expresses itself in *Weltschmerz*. The price this second romantic man has to pay for his uniqueness is a deep loneliness, a tragic feeling of separateness and incompleteness, experienced particularly when not alone. He longs passionately for the elimination of his loneliness, for complete companionship, vitreous visibility, utter unity. Failing that he feels a void that makes him desperate, sometimes desperate enough to take his own life to end the agony.[28] But his longing, his quest for re-integration, can also turn him into a rebel who rises against the existing social order, which is blamed for the troubled state of his mind, or into a seeker of true love, that will put an end to his loneliness.[29] In the eyes of the romantic sufferer present society, present human relations are insufficient and fraudulent and slowly suffocating him.

Particularly the romantic rebel is an interesting figure. Yearning for a radical break with current conditions, he is either a revolutionary or a reactionary of a new kind, unlike any the world had seen before. He is a *Schwärmer*. With regard to the revolutionary it can be said that compared to him his predecessors, from Caesar to Washington, had aims that were limited and down-to-earth. They aspired to replace rulers, or at the most to modify and correct the political system, whereas he envisions a completely new type of -unalienated- man in a new society that is a true community. At this point romanticism merges with radical democratic ideas, hence transforming almost beyond recognition this ancient tradition, which was not romantic at all. Rousseau -he again!- was father to this merger. When he speaks, in the *Contrat Social*, of the social contract as 'the total alienation of each associate with all his rights to the whole community', receiving 'each member as an indivisible part of the whole', thereby producing 'a collective moral body', a 'common *moi*' (author's emphasis), a 'public person', he is speaking the language of a romantic.[30] The incorporation of the self into the community implies of course that the individual mind is dethroned as creator of the world, but this does not bring romanticism to an end. On the contrary, the self now returns as a superhuman collective 'individual', shaping the world, and using concrete persons as its instruments. Here, what began as individualism turns into collectivism.

The romantic reactionary on the other hand, who hates the present with equal intensity, looks upon the past -often the middle ages- as a paradise lost, in which neither urbanization, nor industrialization, mechanization, bourgeois philistinism, capitalism, secularization, specialization, or some other countenance of modernity had yet deformed the world and spiritually torn apart its inhabitants. He is not the first *laudator temporis acti* of course; praising the past was, as we have seen, a favorite pastime of the French aristocracy throughout the ancien régime, and of the ancient Romans as well. But the nature of his praise is of a very different order. Preromantic reactionaries, like Montesquieu, were essentialists. They lacked the notion of individual uniqueness. Their intellectual activity was tuned to the idea that behind all variety unchanging features and principles of being lay hidden, the discovery of which was their job. Hence, they regarded human nature as basically the same everywhere (which of course was not to deny the existence of profound differences between individuals and between societies). All humans are different variations on the same theme. They can be meaningfully held against the same measuring-rod. Individuals may be unknown to others in fact, but they are not unknowable in principle. And the same goes for political systems. These too could be held against a single measuring-rod, and could in effect all be compared with each other. The romantic reactionary's point of departure is the notion of uniqueness that all romantics share. He believes that this uniqueness is the product of historical growth, a perspective which evidently fits in ill with an outspoken individualism. Speaking of unique products of historical growth the romantic reactionary refers to collectivities, not to individuals. Unique here applies to a people, a culture, a nation, not to a person. Hence, the feeling of separateness and alienation applies to relations between such collectivities, not between persons. True understanding is perfectly feasible within a collectivity, but utterly impossible between persons from different collectivities. Only time, if anything, can change this. In the meantime one should refrain from copying institutions on a grand scale from other collectivities, because these would be *Fremdkörper*, which evolved and are successful within a specific setting, which is completely different from the setting they are transposed to. That virtually ensures failure, from the viewpoint of the romantic reactionary, upsetting the grown equilibrium within the collectivity, thereby impeding its performance and possibly endangering its flourishing or even its survival. Hence, the importance of long duration and stability. In this view the creative power is not inherent in the individual or the community, but in historical growth. Therefore, all things enhancing the continuity of the collectivity, like religion and aristocratic lineages, deserve support.

2. The ancient

If this analysis of romanticism contains some truth, it is clear why it is commonly regarded as antithetical to classicism. Most of the classical/classicist virtues are discarded, some are even considered pernicious. The two moral languages therefore seem to have little or nothing in common. And yet, a closer consideration reveals that such a conclusion is premature. The romantics' return to classical antiquity is in itself an indication that they feel aligned to the ancients, although, of course, the fact that it was *Griechentum* rather than *Römertum* that attracted them, should remind us that theirs wasn't a return to the ancients in the traditional style. The question must therefore be posed what the romantics found so important in antiquity.

2.1. A new classicism

At the beginning of this chapter it was argued that romanticism should be contrasted with classicism, that in fact romanticism was originally a self-conscious revolt against this earlier way of thinking. However, that is only one side of the coin. The other side is that romanticism was also, and in the same measure, a self-conscious reaction against *Aufklärungsdenken*: against naturalism, positivism, and utilitarianism. It is presumably in this context that one must situate the romantics' new classicism.

As we have seen, the enlightenment view takes the passions i.e. preferences as its point of departure. It has no preference as to specific preferences. If some preferences are discouraged or even prohibited, it is because they interfere too much with the realization of other preferences, not because they are *an sich* objectionable. *Jeder soll nach seiner Façon selig werden.* Those standing in this tradition have thus concentrated on the question how preferences -whatever they may be- can best be realized. This is of course the question of instrumental rationality, of how ends and means can best be met. Moreover, they have argued that this is the only question that can rationally be dealt with, since in the formation of the preferences themselves reason has no leading part: reason is the slave of the passions. As a consequence of this view, the classical/classicist notion of moral choice becomes redundant and devoid of meaning. Choice, like reason, becomes instrumental or technological. Choice involves means rather than ends; the only reason to reject ends is because of a lack of means. That implies a rejection of what the classical/classicist mind regarded as the fundamental distinction between man and beast, viz. the capacity of a moral choice. Hence, man becomes a mammal, and naturalism is born. The only difference between ourselves and the other animals is that we have a greater technical proficiency in achieving our ends.

It is against this reductionism that romanticism comes up. It reintroduces the question of preference-formation, and therewith reintroduces the *telos*, that has no place in the enlightenment view. According to the romantics some preferences should be rejected, or at least subdued. In this they were at one with the classicists. But they were no longer able to use classical virtue and vice as a criterion. Instead they proposed the self, man's unique personality, the fountainhead of creativity. If preferences emanated from the self they were to be approved, otherwise they should be spurned.

As has already been said above, there is a structural similarity between this romantic view and the Roman model of the mind, in that both see the mind as something inherently conflicting, and both discern a hero and a villain in the inner conflict. Of course, the hero and the villain are not the same in the two models of the mind. In the romantic view the 'self' is the hero, and 'internalized society' or 'die wechselnde Neigung'[31] is the villain, in the Roman view 'virtue' is the hero, and 'vice' is the villain. In the romantic view a choice should ideally be a faithful reflection or an authentic emanation of the self, i.e. a man's personality. He should resist that part of himself which is nothing but society 'inside his head' or his ever changing animal inclinations. But in a sense, Xenophon's story of Heracles and the two paths of life also applies to the romantic view. To live true to oneself is a very difficult thing to do. It is in many ways much less complicated and therefore tempting to conform to society's expectations and standards and the immediate impulses. The first is a hard and long path, the second an easy and pleasant one. The analogy with Roman thought is obvious. In this there is a clear link between the Roman and the romantic view of the mind. The latter is evidently indebted to the former. Admittedly, the difference between the two views is great. The romantic ideal of 'going your own way' would have been inconceivable to the Roman mind. In contrast to the romantic demand to listen to the voice of the self, which speaks of different things and maybe even in a different language to every self, and therefore entails endless variety, the Roman called on to virtue, which was uniform at all times and in all places and was learned by imitation. Nevertheless, the affinity of the romantic distinction between self and other, autonomy and heteronomy on the one hand and the Roman distinction between virtue and vice on the other can scarcely be overlooked.

Might it really be the case then that romanticism should in the end be conceived of as a new classicism, irrespective of all the differences with the old classicism? It surely looks like it. But does this also mean that romanticism is the only link left between the moderns and the ancients? Or do we also have other, perhaps closer, ties to our ancestors? It seems an appropriate conclusion to both this chapter and this book to end with some remarks on this issue.

2.2. The old classicism

In essence, aristocratic classicism was not a unique phenomenon. Although perhaps unparalleled in sophistication, and singular in its minutiae, it is recognizably the conception of ethics and politics common to all, or almost all, governing classes in every traditional society. Central to each of these conceptions are notions of virtue and honor, not much unlike those of the Romans we discussed in this book. Let us refer to them as variants of the honor ethic. The key-words of this ethic are: pride, reputation, glory, respect, dignity, composure, courage, continence, recognition, seemliness, loyalty, liberality, and on the other hand shame, humiliation, treason, insult, effeminacy, avarice, and so on.

This is a genuinely universal ethic, much more so than the views derived from the enlightenment or from romanticism. Certainly, there have always and everywhere been critics of the honor ethic; in our own history we have had the Platonists, who teach that it is truth that matters, and not what other people think is the truth, the cynics, who teach that pride is vanity, the skeptics, who teach that glory is the most ephemeral of things, the epicureans, who teach that the pains of (public) life outweigh the pleasures, the priests, who teach that God must be honored and man must be humble, and so on. However, although these critics of the honor ethic might have won a battle now and then, they always lost the war. Indeed, it seems that the honor ethic is one of the constants of human life. In view of this, it is remarkable how little one hears of it today. Has modernity brought about the demise of the honor ethic?

It is a fact that 'official' moral and political discourse in the modern world is monopolized by various strands of enlightenment and romantic thought. It interprets the world in terms of either contract, utility-maximization, right, cost and benefit, property, ownership, investment and consumption, pain and pleasure, rational choice, revealed preference, exchange, and the like, or in term of authenticity, self-realization, alienation, originality, individuality etc. Conspicuously absent from these moral and political languages are the key-words of the honor ethic. They do not seem to fit in anywhere, and are in general rejected by both traditions. For enlightenment thinkers honor is incompatible with interest or even rationality-foolish pride!-, for romantics it is contrary to authenticity. But does this mean that the honor ethic has withered away, or should one rather say that it has been driven underground?

On closer examination, there can be no doubt that the honor ethic is still very much a part of our life, although it is almost never acknowledged. The moral order existing among soccer fans, boy scouts, and soldiers are obvious instances of this morality, but the idea of honor turns up in all sorts of contexts, diffused through society. Indeed, it seems to be an important part of the moral cement of our society, although perhaps not as important as in traditional societies. But if that is the case, the question arises why this is not recognized? It seems rather strange that a morality we apparently still live by, at least partially, is ostracized. How can we understand ourselves if we refuse to take into consideration that we to a large degree think in terms of the honor ethic?

The answer is simple but profound. Our forgetfulness of this ethic is due to the very framework we use in thinking about these matters, viz. the ancient versus the modern. Through this framework we have apriori defined ourselves as moderns and the ancients as what we no longer are, as the world we have lost. In trying to understand modernity, we concentrate on what is new, using the old merely by way of contrast. Because we do not look for it, the presence of the old is overlooked. And when its presence is so obvious that we have to acknowledge it, we shrug it off as a rudiment of earlier, more primitive times, that is bound to disappear sooner or later. For we know that this cannot be us, since we are -by definition- modern. Yet, if we want to find out how modern we really are, we will have to drop this assumption, and trace the remnants of the ancient in ourselves.

NOTES

1. From: *Racine et Shakespeare*, quoted in Furst 1969, p.20 Significantly, Henri Beyle derived his pseudonym Stendhal from Winckelmann's place of birth in Germany, the village of Stendal. See Pfeiffer 1982, p.207n5: 'Le Romantisme est l'art de présenter aux peuples les oeuvres littéraires qui, dans l'état actuel de leurs habitudes et de leurs croyances, sont susceptibles de leur donner le plus de plaisir possible. Le classicisme, au contraire, leur présente la littérature qui donnait le plus grand plaisir possible à leurs arrière-grands-pères.'

2. Constant, *De la Liberté des Anciens et des Modernes*, p.323

3. Montesquieu, *Esprit*, XI.13

4. Taylor 1989, part III

5. Schenk 1979

6. Literally hundreds of different meanings have been identified. In an article in 1924, 'On the discrimination of romanticism', Lovejoy already concluded that it is impossible to find a definition of romanticism that covers all its aspects. See Lovejoy 1955, pp.228-253

7. Furst 1969, introduction, pp.13-26; Hoffmeister 1990, pp.10-11

8. Chaimowicz 1985, p.11

9. Scott, quoted in Schenk 1979, p.15

10. Berlin, preface in Schenk 1979, pp.xiii-xviii

11. Pfeiffer 1982, p.210

12. Clarke 1956, p.v.

13. Jones 1974, ch.9

14. Johnson 1991, p.117

15. Johnson 1991, pp.117-118

16. Cf. Meister, ' Die Tugenden der Römer', in: Oppermann (ed.) 1967, p.13

17. Berlin 1990, pp.207-237

18. Rousseau, *Discours si le Rétablissement des Sciences et des Arts a Contribué a Épurer les Moeurs*, beginning

19. Winckelmann *Geschichte der Kunst des Altertums*, ch.4.1

20. Winckelmann, *Geschichte*, p.305

21. Trilling 1971

22. Berlin, 1990, p.231

23. With regard to love and the consequences of viewing love romantically, see in particular De Rougemont 1956, p.319, who is very pessimistic and believes romanticism poses a threat to civilization. We can only hope, he argues, that 'the very excesses of passion will excite a reaction in the guise of new *formal modes*, and there will thus be set up a new classical age'.

24. Of course, in many respects Rousseau is still a son of the classicist era, particularly in his political thought. It is perhaps most accurate to see him as the great-grandfather of romanticism, Kant and Herder as its grandfathers, and Fichte as its real father. It seems likely by the way that both grandfathers would not have been very fond of their offspring, if they had lived to see it grow up. Cf. Berlin 1990, pp.207-237, esp.220-225.

25. Rousseau, *Confessions*

26. Schmitt 1986, p.72

27. Schmitt 1986, p.73 The man who is both ironical and self-ironical has two options. Either he becomes a nihilist, denying that anything is valuable, or he consciously refuses to be ironical and self-ironical and is, as Nietzsche said of the ancient Greeks, *oberflächlich aus Tiefe.*

28. Cf. Rousseau, *Confessions*, bk.IX

29. Schenk 1979, p.22, title of the chapter

30. Rousseau, *Contrat Social*, bk.I, Ch.VI

31. Humboldt, *Ideen zu einem Versuch die Grenzen der Wirksamkeit des Staats zu Bestimmen*, ch.II

PRIMARY SOURCES

A. CLASSICAL SOURCES

Ammianus Marcellinus, *Roman History (Rerum Gestarum)*, J.C.Rolfe (ed.), 3 vols., Cambridge Mass. and London

Appian, *Roman History*, H.White (ed.), 4 vols., Cambridge Mass. and London

Aristotle, *Nicomachean Ethics (Ethica Nicomachea)*, J.A.K.Thomson & H.Tredennick, J.Barnes (eds.), Harmondsworth 1986

Aristotle, *Politics (Politica)*, H.Rackam (ed.), Cambridge Mass. and London 1977; T.Sinclair & T.J.Saunders (eds.), Harmondsworth 1983; W.D.Ross & B.Jowett (eds.), in: *Works*, vol. X, Oxford 1952

Aristotle (apoc.), *Economics (Oeconomica)*, W.D.Ross & E.S.Forster (eds.), in: *Works*, vol. X, Oxford 1952

St.Augustine, *City of God (De Civitate Dei)*, in Dutch translation, *De Stad Gods*, G.Wijdeveld (ed.), Baarn and Amsterdam 1984

Caesar, *Commentaries on the Gallic War (De Bello Gallico)*, S.A.Handford & J.F.Gardner (eds.), Harmondsworth 1982

Caesar, *Commentaries on the Civil War (De Bello Civilis)*, J.F.Gardner (ed.), New York 1985

Cato, *On Agriculture (De Re Rustica)*, W.D.Hooper & H.B.Ash (eds.), Cambridge Mass. and London 1960

Cicero, *Tusculan Disputations (Tusculanae Disputationes)*, J.E.King (ed.), Cambridge Mass. and London 1971

Cicero, *On Duties (De Officiis)*, W.Miller (ed.), Cambridge Mass. and London 1973; M.T.Griffin & E.M.Atkins (eds.), Cambridge etc. 1991

Cicero, *On Invention (De Inventione)*, H.M.Hubbell (ed.), Cambridge Mass. and London 1976

Cicero, *Orator*, G.L.Hendrickson (ed.), Cambridge Mass. and London 1988

Cicero, *On the Orator (De Oratore)*, E.W.Sutton & H.Rackam (eds.), 2 vols., Cambridge Mass. and London 1979/92; in Dutch translation, *Drie Gesprekken over de Redenaarskunst*, H.W.A. van Rooijen-Dijkman & A.D.Leeman (eds.), Amsterdam 1989

Cicero, *On Laws (De Legibus)*, C.W.Keyes (ed.), Cambridge Mass. and London 1988

Cicero, *Cato, on Old Age (Cato, de Senectute)*, W.A.Falconer (ed.), Cambridge Mass. and London 1992

Cicero, *On the Republic (De Re Publica)*, C.W.Keyes (ed.), Cambridge Mass. and London 1988

Cicero, *In Defense of Sestius (Pro Sestio)*, R.Gardner (ed.), Cambridge Mass. and London 1966

Cicero, *On Ends (De Finibus Bonorum et Malorum)*, H.Rackam (ed.), Cambridge Mass. and London 1961

Cicero, *Laelius, on Friendship (Laelius, de Amicitia)*, W.A.Falconer (ed.), Cambridge Mass. and London 1992; M.Grant (ed.), in: *Cicero; on the good life*, Harmondsworth 1982

Cicero, *In Defense of Flaccus (Pro Flacco)*, C.MacDonald (ed.), Cambridge Mass. and London

Cicero, *In Defense of Plancius (Pro Plancio)*, N.H.Watts (ed.), Cambridge Mass. and London

Cicero, *The Divisions of Oratory (De Partitione Oratoria)*, H.Rackam (ed.), Cambridge Mass. and London 1992

Cicero, *Brutus*, H.M.Hubbell (ed.), Cambridge Mass. and London 1988

Dio Cassius, *Roman History*, E.Cary & H.B.Forster (eds.), 9 vols., Cambridge Mass. and London

Dionysius of Halicarnassus, *Roman Antiquities*, E.Cary (ed.), 7 vols., Cambridge Mass. and London

Hesiod, *Works and Days*, D.Wender (ed.), Harmondsworth 1985

Herodotus, *Histories*, in Dutch translation, *Historiën*, O.Damsté (ed.), Houten 1987

Horace, *Odes and Epodes*, C.E.Bennett (ed.), Cambridge Mass. and London 1968; C.J.Kraemer Jr. (ed.), in: *Complete Works*, New York 1936

Juvenal, *Sixteen Satires*, P.Green (ed.), Harmondsworth 1967; in German translation, *Satiren*, H.C.Schnur (ed.), Stuttgart 1978

Livy, *History of Rome from its Foundation (Ab Urbe Condita)*, 4 vols., vol.I (books I-V): *Early History of Rome*, A. de Sélincourt & R.M.Ogilvie (eds.), Harmondsworth 1986; vol.II (books VI-X): *Rome and Italy*, B.Radice & R.M.Ogilvie (eds.), Harmondsworth 1986; vol.III (books XXI-XXX), *War with Hannibal*, A. de Sélincourt & B.Radice (eds.), Harmondsworth 1987; vol.IV (books XXXI-XLV), *Rome and the Mediterranean*, H.Bettenson & A.H.McDonald (eds.), Harmondsworth 1986

Lucan, *Pharsalia*, J.D.Duff (ed.), Cambridge Mass. and London 1977

Petronius, *Satyricon*, M.Heseltine & E.H.Warmington (eds.), Cambridge Mass. and London 1987

Plato, *Republic (Politeia)*, D.Lee (ed.), Harmondsworth 1980; A.Bloom (ed.), New York 1991

Pliny the younger, *Panegyricus*, B.Radice (ed.), Cambridge Mass. and London 1976

Plutarch, *Parallel Lives (Vitae)*, Dryden transl., A.H.Clough (ed.), 2 vols., New York 1992; *Makers of Rome* (contains the biographies of Coriolanus, Fabius Maximus, Marcellus, Cato the Elder, Tiberius Gracchus, Gaius Gracchus, Sertorius, Brutus, and Mark Anthony), I.Scott-Kilvert (ed.), New York 1985; *Fall of the Roman Republic* (contains the biographies of Marius, Sulla, Crassus, Pompey, Caesar, and Cicero), R.Warner, R.Seager (eds.), Harmondsworth 1988

Plutarch, *Moral Essays (Moralia)*, H.N.Fowler (ed.), 15 vols., Cambridge Mass. and London

Polybius, *Histories*, W.R.Paton (ed.), 6 vols., Cambridge Mass. and London 1972, vol.III contains book V

Sallust, *War with Catiline (Bellum Catilinae)*, J.C.Rolfe (ed.), Cambridge Mass. and London 1985

Sallust, *War with Iugurtha (Bellum Iugurthinum)*, J.C.Rolfe (ed.), Cambridge Mass. and London 1985

Sciptores Historiae Augustae, D.Magie (ed.), 3 vols., Cambridge Mass. and London, vol.II contains the biography of Alexander Severus

Seneca, *Letters to Lucilius (Epistulae ad Lucilium)*, R.M.Gummere (ed.), 3 vols., Cambridge Mass. and London

Seneca, *Moral Essays*, J.W.Basore (ed.), 3 vols., Cambridge Mass. and London, vol.I contains *De Ira* and *De Clementia*

Suetonius, *Lives of the Caesars (De Vita Caesarum)*, J.C.Rolfe (ed.), 2 vols., Cambridge Mass. and London

Tacitus, *On Germany (Germania)*, H.Mattingly & S.A.Handford (eds.), Harmondsworth 1988

Tacitus, *Annals (Annales)*, M.Grant (ed.), New York 1984

Tacitus, *Agricola*, H.Mattingly & S.A.Handford (eds.), Harmondsworth 1988

Thucydides, *History of the Peloponnesian War*, R.Warner & M.I.Finley (eds.), Harmondsworth 1985

Varro, *On Agriculture (Rerum Rusticarum)*, W.D.Hooper & H.B.Ash (eds.), Cambridge Mass. and London 1960

Virgil, *Georgics (Georgica)*, H.R.Fairclough (ed.), Cambridge Mass. and London

Xenophon, *Memories of Socrates (Memorabilia)*, E.C.Marchant (ed.), Cambridge Mass. and London 1979

Xenophon, *On Estate Management (Oeconomicus)*, E.C.Marchant (ed.), Cambridge Mass. and London 1979

B. SOURCES OF THE 16th-19th CENTURY

Anonymous, *Les Véritables Maximes du Gouvernement de la France, justifiées par l'Ordre des Temps depuis l'Establissement de la Monarchie jusques à Présent*, Paris 1652

Bodin, Jean, *Les Six Livres de la République*, 1576; Aalen 1977 (reprint of the Paris edition of 1583); in German translation: P.C. Mayer-Tasch and B.Wimmer (eds.), *Sechs Bücher über den Staat*, München 1981
Bossuet, Jacques-Bénigne, *Discours sur l'Histoire Universelle*, 1681; Paris 1876, in English translation: O.Ranum and E.Forster (ed.), *Discourse on Universal History*, Chicago and London 1976
Bossuet, Jacques-Bénigne, *Politique tirée des Propres Paroles de l'Escriture Sainte*, 1709; J. Le Brun (ed.), Geneva 1967; in English translation, P.Riley (ed.), *Politics drawn from the Very Words of the Holy Scripture*, Cambridge 1990
Boulainvilliers, Henri de, *Histoire de l'Ancien Gouvernement de la France, avec XIV Lettres Historiques sur les Parlements ou Etats Généraux*, The Hague 1727
Boulainvilliers, Henri de, *Essais sur la Noblesse de France, Contenant une Dissertation sur son Origine et Abaissement*, Amsterdam 1732
Budé, Guillaume, *L'Institution du Prince*, 1547; included in C. Bontemps et al., *Le Prince dans la France des XVIe et XVIIe Siècles*, Paris 1965

Constant, Benjamin, *Troisième leçon à l'Athénée royal: 'De la Liberté des Anciens et des Modernes'*, 1820; in English translation: B.Fontana (ed.), *Political Writings*, Cambridge 1988

Diderot, Denis and Jean d'Alembert (eds.), *Encyclopédie ou Dictionnaire Raisonné des Sciences, des Arts, et des Métiers*, photomechanic reprint of the 'compact edition', 5 vols., New York and Paris, n.d.
Digests and other sources of Roman law (selections), in: L.Huchthausen (ed.), *Römisches Recht*, Berlin and Weimar 1991

Fénelon, François, *Examen de Conscience sur les Devoirs de la Royauté*, Paris
Fénelon, François, *Plans de Gouvernement concertés avec le Duc de Chevreuse pour être proposés au Duc de Bourgogne*, also known as the *Tables de Chaulnes*, Paris 1711
Filmer, Robert, *Patriarcha* 1680; included in: J.P. Sommerville (ed.), *Patriarcha and other Writings*, Cambridge 1991

Hobbes, *Leviathan*, 1651; M.Oakeshott (ed.) Oxford n.d.; K.R.Minogue (ed.), London etc. 1979

Hotman, François, *Antitribonian*, 1603; H. Duranton (ed.), Saint-Etienne 1980

Hotman, François, *Francogallia*, 1575; R.F.Giesey and J.H.M.Salmon (eds.), Cambridge 1972; also, abridged, in J.Franklin (ed.), *Constitutionalism and Resistance in the Sixteenth Century*, New York 1969

Humboldt, Wilhelm von, *Ideen zu einem Versuch die Grenzen der Wirksamkeit des Staats zu Bestimmen*, 1851; H.Klenner (ed.), Leipzig 1985

Hume, David, *Treatise of Human Nature*, 1739/40; L.A.Selby-Bigge & P.H.Niddich (eds.), Oxford 1987

Joly, Claude, *Recueil des Maximes Véritables et Importantes pour l'Institution du Roy contre la Fausse et Pernicieuze politique du Cardinal Mazarin, Prétendu Sur-intendant de l'Éducation de sa Majesté*, Paris 1652

Machiavelli, Niccolo, *Discourses on the First Ten Books of Livy*, M.Lerner (ed.), New York 1940

Marx, Karl and Friedrich Engels, *Marx-Engels Werke*, Berlin, vols. XXI and XXVII

Mill, John Stuart, *On Liberty*, 1859; H.B.Acton (ed.), London etc. 1980

Montaigne, *Essais*, 1580; in: R.Barral and P.Michel (ed.), *Oeuvres Complètes*, Paris 1967; in English translation: M.A. Screech (ed.), *Complete Essays*, Harmondsworth 1991

Montesquieu, Charles Louis de, *Considérations sur les Causes de la Grandeur des Romains et et de leur Décadence*, 1734; J.Ehrard (ed.), Paris 1968

Montesquieu, Charles Louis de, *De l'Esprit des Lois*, 1748; V.Goldschmidt (ed.), 2 vols. Paris 1979; in English translation: A. Cohler et al. (ed.), *The Spirit of the Laws*, Cambridge 1989

Montesquieu, Charles Louis de, *Oeuvres Complètes*, D.Oster (ed.), Paris 1964

Nietzsche, *Zur Genealogie der Moral*, 1887; in: *Werke in Drei Bänden*, K.Schlechta (ed.), Darmstadt 1994

Pasquier, Étienne, *Les Recherches de la France*, 1560; in: *Oeuvres Complètes*, 2 vols., Geneva 1971 (1723)

Plessis Mornay, Philippe du, *Vindiciae contra Tyrannos*, Edinburgh 1579; in English translation: H.J. Laski (ed.) *Defence of Liberty against Tyrants*, London 1924; also, abridged, in: J. Franklin (ed.), *Constitutionalism and Resistance in the Sixteenth Century*, New York 1969

Roche Flavin, Bernard la, *Treize Livres sur les Parlemens*, Geneva 1621 (1618)

Rousseau, Jean-Jacques, *Discours si le Rétablissement des Sciences et des Arts a Contribué a Épurer les Moeurs*, 1750; Paris n.d.

Rousseau, Jean-Jacques, *Contrat Social*, 1762; Paris n.d.

Rousseau, Jean-Jacques, *Confessions*, 1781; A. van Bever (ed.), 3 vols., Paris

Saint-Simon, Louis de Rouvroy, Duc de, *Mémoire Succint sur les Formalités desquelles Nécessairement la Renonciation du Roy d'Espagne tant pour Luy que pour sa Postérité doit estre Revestue en France pour y estre Justement et Stabilement Validée*, in: M.P.Faugère (ed.), *Écrits Inedits de Saint-Simon*, 8 vols. Paris 1880/1892

Schlegel, Friedrich, *Werke in Einem Band*, Vienna and Munich 1982

Seyssel, Claude de, *La Grande Monarchie de France*, 1519; Jacques Poujol (ed.) Paris 1961; in English translation: J.H. Hexter et al. (ed.), The Monarchy of France, New Haven and London 1981

Smith, Adam, *Theory of Moral Sentiments*, 1759; D.D.Raphael & A.L.Macfie (eds.), Indianapolis 1982

Smith, Adam, *Lectures on Jurisprudence*, Report of 1762/63 and of 1766; R.L.Meek et al. (eds.), Indianapolis 1982

Tocqueville, Alexis de, *L'Ancien Régime et la Revolution*, 1856; in: J.C. Lamberti and F. Mélonio (eds.), *Oeuvres*, Paris 1986; in English translation: H.Brogan and S.Gilbert (eds.), *The Ancien Regime and the French Revolution*, London 1974

Vassor, Michel le, *Soupirs de la France Esclave, qui Aspire après la Liberté*, Amsterdam 1690

Winckelmann, Johannes, *Geschichte der Kunst des Altertums*, 1764; ed. Vienna 1934

SECONDARY SOURCES

Aalbers, J. & M.Prak (eds.), 1987, *De Bloem der Natie, Adel en Patriciaat in de Noordelijke Nederlanden*, Meppel en Amsterdam

Aalders H.Wzn, G.J.D., 1968, *Die Theorie der Gemischten Verfassung im Altertum*, Amsterdam

Aalders H.Wzn, G.J.D., 1982, *Plutarch's Political Thought*, Amsterdam etc.

Adam, T., 1970, *Clementia Principis, der Einfluß Hellenistischer Fürstenspiegel auf den Versuch einer Rechtlichen Fundierung des Principats durch Seneca*, Stuttgart

Adkins, A.W.H., 1975, *Merit and Responsibility, a Study in Greek Values*, Chicago and London (1960)

Albertini, R. von, 1951, *Das Politische Denken in Frankreich zur Zeit Richelieus*, Marburg

Althusser, L., 1981, *Montesquieu, la Politique et l'Histoire*, Paris (1959)

Anderson, P., 1979, *Lineages of the Absolutist State*, London (1974)

Antoine, M., 1970, *Le Conseil du Roi sous Louis XV*, Paris et Geneva

Arendt, H., 1990, *On Revolution*, Harmondsworth, (1963)

Arendt, H., 1977, *Between Past and Future*, Harmondsworth (1968)

Arnheim, M.T.W., 1977, *Aristocracy in Greek Society*, Thames and Hudson

Aron, R., 1971, *Main Currents in Sociological Thought,* vol.I, Harmondsworth (1965)

Baldick, R., 1970, *The Duel, a History of Duelling*, London etc. (1965)

Barber, E.G., 1955, *The Bourgeoisie of 18th Century France*, Princeton

Barber, R., 1974, *The Knight and Chivalry*, London (1970)

Barrière, P., 1974, *La Vie Intellectuelle en France du 16e Siècle à l'Époque Contemporaine*, Paris (1961)

Bastide, F.R., 1977, *Saint-Simon*, Paris (1953)

Baum, A., 1979, *Montesquieu and Social Theory*, Oxford etc.

Baumgartner, F., 1976, *Radical Reactionaries, the Political Thought of the French Catholic League*, Geneva

Beard, M. and M.Crawford, 1985, *Rome in the Late Republic*, Ithaca

Beckett, J.V., 1986, *The Aristocracy in England 1660-1914*, Oxford

Behrens, C.B.A., 1985, *Society, Government, and the Enlightenment: the Experiences of Eighteenth-Century France and Prussia*, Thames and Hudson

Bénichou, P., 1948, *Morales du Grand Siècle*, 6th ed., Paris

Berlin, I., 1979, *Four Essays on Liberty*, Oxford etc. (1969)

Berlin, I., 1981, *Against the Current*, Oxford etc. (1979)

Berlin, I., 1990, *The Crooked Timber of Humanity*, London

Berman, H.J., 1983, *Law and Revolution, the Formation of the Western Legal Tradition*, Cambridge Mass.

Best, G., 1982, *Honour among Nations, Transformations of an Idea*, Toronto

Billacois, F., 1986, *Le Duel dans la Société Française des XVIe au XVIIe Siècles*, Paris

Bitton, D., 1969, *The French Nobility in Crisis 1560-1640*, Stanford

Blanning, J.C.W., 1987, *The French Revolution, Aristocrats versus Bourgeois?*, London etc.

Bloch, M., 1968, *La Société Féodale*, Paris (1939)

Bluche, F., 1986, *Les Magistrats du Parlement de Paris au XVIIIe Siècle 1715-1771*, Besançon (1960)

Bluche, F., 1973, *La Vie Quotidienne de la Noblesse Française au XVIIIe Siècle*, Paris

Bluche, F., 1986, *Louis XVI*, Paris

Bolgar, R.R.,1977, *The Classical Heritage and its Beneficiaries*, Cambridge etc. (1954)

Bolgar, R.R. (ed.), 1976, *Classical Influences on European Culture A.D.1500-1700*, Cambridge etc.

Bolgar, R.R. (ed.), 1979, *Classical Influences on Western Thought A.D.1650-1870*, Cambridge etc.

Bontems, C. et al., 1965, *Le Prince dans la France des XVIe et XVIIe Siècles*, Paris

Brunt, P.A., 1982, 'Nobilitas and Novitas', in: *Journal of Roman Studies*, LXXII, pp.1-17

Buranelli, V., 1957, 'The Historical and Political Thought of Boulainvilliers', in: *Journal of the History of Ideas*, XVIII, pp.475-494

Burke, P., 'A Survey of the Popularity of Ancient Historians 1450-1700', in: *Theory and History*, V 1966, pp.135-152

Bush, M.L., 1984, *The English Aristocracy*, Manchester

Bush, M.L., *Rich Noble, Poor Noble*, Manchester and New York 1988

Butterfield, H., 1959, *The Whig Interpretation of History*, London (1931)

Butterfield, H., 1988, *Georg III and the Historians*, London (1957)

Cairns, D.L., 1993, *Aidos, the Psychology and Ethics of Honour and Shame in Ancient Greek Literature*, Oxford

Campbell, C., 1987, *The Romantic Ethic and the Spirit of Modern Consumerism*, Oxford

Campbell, P.R., 1988, *The Ancien Régime in France*, Oxford and New York

Cannadine, D., 1990, *The Decline and Fall of the British Aristocracy*, New Haven and London

Cannon, J., 1987, *Aristocratic Century, the Peerage of Eighteenth-Century England*, Cambridge (1984)

Carcassonne, E., 1978, *Montesquieu et le Problème de la Constitution Française au XVIIIe Siècle*, Geneva (1927)

Carré, H., 1920, *La Noblesse Française et l'Opinion Publique au XVIIIe Siècle*, Paris

Cary, M., 1957, *History of Rome, down to the Reign of Constantine*, 2nd ed. London (1954)

Casey, J., 1991, *Pagan Virtue*, Oxford (1990)

Cauer, F., 1903, *Ciceros Politisches Denken*, Berlin

Chaimowicz, Th., 1985, *Freiheit und Gleichgewicht im Denken Montesquieus und Burkes*, Vienna & New York

Chartier, R. et al., 1976, *l'Éducation en France du XVIe au XVIIIe Siècle*, Paris

Chaussinand-Nogaret, G., 1984, *La Noblesse au XVIIIe Siècle, de la Féodalité au Lumières*, Brussels (1976)

Chaussinand-Nogaret, G. (ed.), 1991, *Histoire de Élites en France du XVIe au XXe Siècle*, Paris

Chevalier, R. (ed.), 1987, *L'Antiquité Gréco-Romaine vue par le Siècle des Lumières*, Tours

Christ, K., 1972, *Von Gibbon bis Rostovtzeff, Leben und Werk Führender Althistoriker der Neuzeit*, Darmstadt

Christ, K., 1990, *Neue Profile der Alten Geschichte*, Darmstadt

Church, W.F., 1941, *Constitutional Thought in Sixteenth-Century France, a Study in the Evolution of Ideas*, Cambridge Mass.

Clarke, M.L., 1956, *The Roman Mind, Studies in the History of Thought from Cicero to Marcus Aurelius*, London

Clarke, M.L., 1981, *The Noblest Roman, Marcus Brutus and his Reputation*, London

Cobban, A., 1973, 'The Myth of the French Revolution', in: Schmitt (ed.) 1973, pp.170-194, originally published as inaugural lecture, London 1955

Cobban, A., 1964, *The Social Interpretation of the French Revolution*, Cambridge

Coing, H., 1979, 'Roman Law and the National Legal Systems', in: Bolgar (ed.) 1979

Cox, I., 1983, *Montesquieu and the History of French Laws*, Oxford

Cragg, G.R., 1976, *The Church in the Age of Reason*, Harmondsworth (1960)

Cuénin, M., 1982, *Le Duel sous l'Ancien Régime*, Paris

Curzon, A., 1920, *l'Enseignement du Droit Français dans les Universités de France aux XVIIe et XVIIIe Siècles*, Paris

Dakin, D., 1972, *Turgot and the Ancien Régime in France*, New York (1939)

Davies, J.K., 1978, *Democracy and Classical Greece*, Hassocks, Sussex

Dedieu, J., 1909, *Montesquieu et la Tradition Politique Anglaise en France*, Paris

Delbrück, H., 1900/20, *Geschichte der Kriegskunst im Rahmen der Politischen Geschichte*, 4 vols. Berlin

Desgraves, L. (ed.), 1954, *Catalogue de la Bibliothèque de Montesquieu*, Geneva

Devyver, A., 1973, *Le Sang Épuré, les Préjugés de Race chez lez Gentilshommes Français de l'Ancien Régime 1560-1720*, Brussels

Dewald, J., 1993, *Aristocratic Experience and the Origins of Modern Culture*, Berkeley etc.

Dorey, T.A. (ed.) 1966, *Latin Historians*, London

Dorey, T.A. (ed.), 1971, *Livy*, London

Doyle, W., 1978, *The Old European Order 1660-1800*, Oxford

Doyle, W., 1980, *Origins of the French Revolution*, Oxford

Doyle, W., 1990, *The Oxford History of the French Revolution*, Oxford and New York (1989)

Duby, G., 1980, *The Three Orders*, Chicago and London, (1978)

Earl, D., 1970, *The Moral and Political Tradition of Rome*, London (1967)

Earl, D., 1961, *The Political Thought of Sallust*, Cambridge

Egret, J., 1970, *Louis XV et l'Opposition Parlementaire 1715-1774*, Paris

Ehrenberg, V., 1964, *The Greek State*, New York (1960)

Ehrenberg, V., 1975, *From Solon to Socrates*, London (1968)

Ellis, H.E., 1988, *Boulainvilliers and the French Monarchy*, Ithaca and London

Etter, E.L., 1966, *Tacitus in der Geistesgeschichte des 16. und 17. Jahrhunderts*, Basel and Stuttgart

Farrar, C., 1989, *The Origins of Democratic Thinking, the Invention of Politics in Classical Athens*, Cambridge (1988)

Feenstra, R., 1992, 'Law', in: Jenkyns (ed.) 1992

Ferguson, J., *Moral Values in the Ancient World*, London 1958

Finley, M.I., 1973, *Democracy Ancient and Modern*, New Brunswick and London

Finley, M.I., 1980, *Ancient Slavery and Modern Ideology*, London

Fisher, N.R.E., 1992, *Hybris, a Study in the Values of Honour and Shame in Ancient Greece*, Warminster

Floquet, P.A., 1864, *Bossuet, Précepteur du Dauphin*, Paris

Ford, F.L., 1968, *Robe and Sword; the Regrouping of the French Aristocracy after Louis XIV*, Cambridge Mass. (1953)

Forster R. and E. (eds.), 1969, *European Society in the Eighteenth Century*, New York

Foucault, M., 1984, *Histoire de la Sexualité*, vol.III: *Le Souci de Soi*, Paris

Franklin, J., 1966, *Jean Bodin and the Sixteenth-Century Revolution in the Methodology of Law and History*, New York and London (1963)

Franklin, J., 1973, *Jean Bodin and the Rise of Absolutist Theory*, New York and Cambridge

Friedrich, C.J., 1972, *Tradition and Authority*, London and Basingstroke

Friedrich, H., 1991, *Montaigne*, Berkeley etc. (1949)

Frijhoff, W. and D.Julia, 1975, *École et Société dans la France d'Ancien Régime*, Paris

Fritz, K. von, 1975, *The Theory of the Mixed Constitution in Antiquity*, New York (1954)

Furet, F., 1981, *Interpreting the French Revolution*, Cambridge

Furst, L.R., 1969, *Romanticism in Perspective*, London etc.

Gadamer, H.G., 1990, *Wahrheit und Methode*, Tübingen (1960)

Gallouédec-Genuys, F., 1963, *La Conception du Prince dans l'Oeuvre de Fénélon*, Paris

Ganshof, F.L., 1976, *Feudalism*, London (1944)

Garnsey, P., 1970, *Social Status and Legal Privilege in the Roman Empire*, Oxford

Gay, P., 1977, *The Enlightenment, an Interpretation*, 2 vols., New York and London, (1969)

Gelzer, M., 1962/64, *Kleine Schriften*, 3 vols., Wiesbaden

Giardina, A. (ed.), 1993, *The Romans*, Chicago and London (1989)

Gilmore, M.P., 1941, *The Argument from Roman Law in Political Thought 1200-1600*, Cambridge Mass.

Göhring, M., 1965, *Ämterkäuflichkeit im Ancien Régime*, Vaduz (1938)

Göhring, M., 1947, *Weg und Sieg der Modernen Staatsidee in Frankreich*, Tübingen (1946)

Goodwin, A. (ed.), 1953, *European Nobility in the Eighteenth Century*, London

Goodwin A., 1965, 'The Social Structure and Economic and Political Attitude of the French Nobility in the Eighteenth Century', in: *Rapports du XIIe Congrès International des Sciences Historiques*, Vol.I, Vienna

Goubert, P. and D.Roche, 1984, *Les Français et l'Ancien Régime*, 2 vols., Paris

Goyet, Th., 1965, *L'Humanisme de Bossuet*, 2 vols., Paris

Grant, M., 1974, *The Climax of Rome, the Final Achievement of the Ancient World A.D. 161-337*, London (1968)

Grellet-Dumazeau, A., 1913, *L'Affaire du Bonnet et les Mémoires de Saint-Simon*, Paris

Groethuysen, B., 1978, *Die Entstehung der Bürgerlichen Welt- und Lebensanschauuung*, 2 vols. Frankfurt a.M. (1927)

Gundolf, F., 1924, *Caesar, Geschichte seines Ruhmes*, Berlin

Habbakkuk, H.J., 1953, 'England', in: Goodwin (ed.) 1953

Haddock, B., 1980, *An Introduction to Historical Thought*, London

Hahlweg, W., 1941, *Die Heeresreform der Oranier und die Antike*, Berlin

Hamel, Ch., 1867, *Histoire de l'Abbaye et du Collège de Juilly*, Paris

Hamscher A.N., 1976, *The Parlement of Paris after the Fronde 1653-1673*, Pittsburgh

Hamscher, A.N., 1987, *The Conseil Privé and the Parlements in the Age of Louis XIV, a Study of French Absolutism*, Philadelphia

Hayek, F.A., 1979, *The Counterrevolution of Science*, Indianapolis (1952)

Heinze, R., 1960, *Vom Geist des Römertums*, Stuttgart (1938)

Hellegouarc'h, J., 1972, *Le Vocabulaire Latin de Relations et des Partis Politique sous la République*, Paris (1963)

Hensel, P., 1928, 'Montaigne und die Antike', in: F.Saxl (ed.), *Vorträge der Bibliothek Warburg 1925/26*, Leipzig and Berlin

Hexter, J.H., 1976, *Reappraisals in History*, London (1961)

Hexter, J.H., 1973, *The Vision of Politics on the Eve of the Reformation: More, Machiavelli and Seyssel*, New York

Hexter, J.H., 1971, *Doing History*, Bloomington and London

Highet, G., 1985, *The Classical Tradition, Greek and Roman Influences on Western Literature*, New York and Oxford (1949)

Hintze, H., 1928, *Staatseinheit und Föderalismus im alten Frankreich und in der Revolution*, Berlin and Leipzig

Hirschmann, A.O., 1981, *The Passions and the Interests, Political Arguments for Capitalism before its Triumph*, Princeton (1977)

Höfer, A. and R.Reichardt, 1986, 'Honnête homme, honnêteté, honnêtes gens' in: *Handbuch Politisch-sozialer Grundbegriffe in Frankreich 1680-1820*, vol.VII, München

Hoffmeister, G., 1990, *Deutsche und Europäische Romantik*, 2nd edition, Stuttgart

Homo, L., 1941, *Nouvelle Histoire Romaine*, Paris

Howard, M. 1976, *War in European History*, London etc.

Howard, M.W., 1970, *The Influence of Plutarch in the Major European Literatures of the Eighteenth Century*, Chapel Hill

Huizinga, J., 1955, *The Waning of the Middle Ages*, Harmondsworth (1924)

Huppert, G., 1970, *The Idea of Perfect History, Historical Erudition and Historical Philosophy in Renaissance France*, Urbana Illinois

Huppert, G, 1977, *Les Bourgeois Gentilshommes*, Chicago and London

Huppert, G., 1984, *Public Schools in Renaissance France*, Urbana and Chicago

Jaeger, W., 1973, *Paideia*, 3 vols., New York and Oxford (1939-43)

Jansen, H.P.H., 1981, *Geschiedenis van de Middeleeuwen*, Utrecht and Antwerp (1978)

Jenkyns, R. (ed.), 1992, *The Legacy of Rome, a New Appraisal*, Oxford

Johnson, P., 1991, *The Birth of the Modern*, London

Jones, H.M., 1974, *Revolution and Romanticism*, Cambridge Mass.

Jong, J. de, 1987, *Een Deftig Bestaan*, Utrecht and Antwerp

Jouanna, A., 1976, *L'Idée de Race en France au XVIe Siècle et au Début du XVIIe Siècle 1498-1614*, 3 vols. Paris

Jouanna, A., 1989, *Le Devoir de Révolte, la Noblesse Française et la Gestation de l'État Moderne 1559-1661*, Paris

Jouhaud, Ch., 1985, *Mazarinades, la Fronde des Mots*, Paris

Kaser, M., 1986, *Römisches Privatrecht*, München (1960)

Keen, M., 1984, *Chivalry*, New Haven and London

Kelley, D.R., 1970, *Foundations of Modern Historical Scholarship: Language, Law, and History in the French Renaissance*, New York and London

Kelsen, H., 1945, *General Theory of Law and State*, Cambridge Mass.

Keohane, N.O., 1980, *Philosophy and the State in France, the Renaissance to the Enlightenment*, Princeton

Keppie, L., 1984, *The Making of the Roman Army, from Republic to Empire*, London

Kiernan, V.G., 1988, *The Duel in European History, Honour and the Reign of the Aristocracy*, Oxford

Klein, R. (ed.), 1966, *Das Staatsdenken der Römer*, Darmstadt

Klein R. (ed.), 1969, *Prinzipat und Freiheit*, Darmstadt

Klingner, F., 1984, *Römische Geisteswelt*, Stuttgart 1965

Kloesel, H., 1983, 'Libertas', in: Oppermann (ed.) 1983

Knauss, B., 1964, *Staat und Mensch in Hellas*, Darmstadt (1940)

Knoche, U., 1983, 'Der Römische Ruhmesgedanke', in: Oppermann (ed.) 1983

Kolakowski, L., 1982, *Main Currents of Marxism*, 3 vols., Oxford and New York (1978)

Kopp, A., 1969, *Staatsdenken und Politisches Handeln bei Seneca und Lucan*, Heidelberg

Koschaker, P., 1953, *Europa und das Römische Recht*, München and Berlin
Kossmann, E.H., 1960, *Politieke Theorie in het Zeventiende-Eeuwse Neder land*, Verhandelingen der Koninklijke Nederlandse Academie van Weten-schappen, Afd. Letterkunde, Nieuwe Reeks, dl.LXVII, nr.2, Amsterdam
Kunkel, W., 1982, *Geschiedenis van het Romeinse Recht*, Utrecht and Antwerp, 6th ed. (1972)

Lakebrink, M., 1967, *Montesquieus Cicero-Rezeption*, Freiburg
Lassaigne, J.D., 1965, *Les Assemblées de la Noblesse de France aux XVIIe et XVIIIe Siècles*, Paris
Lemaire, A., 1907, *Les Lois Fondamentales de la Monarchie Française d'après les Théoreticiens de l'Ancien Régime*, Paris
Lemaitre J., 1910, *Fénelon*, Paris
Levantal, Ch., 1987, *La Robe contre l'Épée?*, n.p.
Levin, L.M., 1973, *The Political Doctrine of Montesquieu's Esprit des Lois, its Classical Background*, Westport Connecticut (1936)
Levin, W.R., 1933, *Claude de Seyssel*, Heidelberg
Lieven, D., 1992, *The Aristocracy in Europe 1815-1914*, London
Livingstone, R.W., 1932, 'The Position and Function of Classical Studies in Modern English Education', in, F.Saxl. (ed.), *Vorträge der Bibliothek Warburg 1930/31*, Leipzig and Berlin
Lloyd, H.A., 1983, *The State, France, and the Sixteenth Century*, London
Loewenstein, K., 1973, *The Governance of Rome*, The Hague
Lovejoy, A., 1955, *Essays in the History of Ideas*, New York (1948)
Lovejoy, A., 1968, *Reflections on Human Nature*, Baltimore (1961)
Lovejoy, A., 1964, *The Great Chain of Being*, Cambridge Mass, and London (1936)
Lukes, S., 1973, *Individualism*, Oxford
Lütcke, K.H., 1968, *Auctoritas bei Augustin*, Stuttgart etc.

Mackrell, J.Q.C., 1973, *The Attack on 'Feudalism' in Eighteenth-Century France*, London and Toronto
MacMullen, R., 1974, *Roman Social Relations*, New Haven and London
Major, J.R., 1960, *Representative Institutions in Renaissance France 1421-1559*, Madison
Malettke, K., 1976, *Opposition und Konspiration unter Ludwig XIV*, Göttingen
Mat-Hasquin, M., 1981, *Voltaire et l'Antiquité Greque*, Oxford
Maurach, G., 1991, *Seneca, Leben und Werk*, Darmstadt
Mayer, A.J., 1981, *The Persistence of the Old Regime; Europe to the Great War*, New York
McManners, J., 'France', in: Goodwin (ed.) 1953

Megill, A., 1987 *Prophets of Extremity* Berkeley etc. (1985)

Meinecke, F., *Die Entstehung des Historismus*, München (1959)

Mettam, R., 1988, *Power and Faction in Louis XIV's France*, Oxford and New York

Meyer, E., 1948, *Römischer Staat und Staatsgedanke*, Zürich

Meyer, J., 1973, *Noblesse et Pouvoirs dans l'Europe d'Ancien Régime*, Paris

Meyer, J., 1991, *La Noblesse Française à l'Époque Moderne, XVIe-XVIIIe Siècle*, Paris

Mingay, G.E., 1963, *English Landed Society in the Eighteenth Century*, London and Toronto

Mitchell, Th., 1979, *Cicero, the Ascending Years*, New Haven and London

Mitchell, Th., 1991, *Cicero, the Senior Statesman*, New Haven and London

Momigliano, A., 1969, 'Seneca between Political and Contemplative Life', in: Momigliano, A., *Quarto Contributo alla Storia degli Studi Classici e del Mondo Antico*, Roma

Momigliano, A., 1977, *Essays in Ancient and Modern Historiography*, Oxford

Momigliano, A., 1990, *Classical Foundations of Modern Historiography*, Berkeley

Mommsen, Th., 1932, *Römische Geschichte*, Vienna, abridged ed.

Mommsen, Th., 1871/88, *Römisches Staatsrecht*, 5 vols., Leipzig

Mommsen, Th., 1899, *Römisches Strafrecht*, Leipzig

Moore Jr., B., 1984, *Privacy*, New York and London

Mossé, C., 1989, *L'Antiquité dans la Révolution Française*, Paris

Mousnier, R., 1971, *La Vénalité des Offices sous Henri IV et Louis XIII*, Paris (1947)

Mousnier, R., 1979, *The Institutions of France under the Absolute Monarchy 1598-1789*, Chicago and London

Neumann, F., 1949, 'Editor's introduction', in: Montesquieu, *The Spirit of the Laws*, Th.Nugent (transl.), New York and London

Neuschel, K., 1989, *Word of Honor, Interpreting Noble Culture in Sixteenth-Century France*

Nicolet, C., 1988, *The World of the Citizen in Republican Rome*, Berkeley and Los Angeles (1976)

Nierop, H.F.K. van, 1990, *Van Ridders tot Regenten, de Hollandse Adel in de Zestiende en de Eerste Helft van de Zeventiende Eeuw*, Amsterdam (1984)

Oestreich, G., 1969, *Geist und Gestalt des Frühmodernen Staates*, Berlin

Oksenberg-Rorty, A., 1976, 'A literary postscript: characters, persons, selves, individuals', in: Amélie Oksenberg Rorty (ed.), *The Identities of Persons*, Berkeley etc.

Oppermann, H. (ed.), 1983, *Römische Wertbegriffe*, Darmstadt (1967)
Ossowska, M., 1972, *Social Determinants of Moral Ideas*, Philadelphia (1970)

Painter, S., 1977, *French Chivalry, Chivalric Ideas and Practices in Mediaeval France*, Ithaca and London (1957)
Palmer, R.R., 1959/1964, *The Age of Democratic Revolution*, 2 vols., Princeton
Pangle, Th., 1989, *Montesquieu's Philosophy of Liberalism*, Chicago and London (1973)
Parker, D., 1983, *The Making of French Absolutism*, London
Parker, H.T., 1937, *The Cult of Antiquity and the French Revolution*, Chicago
Pfeiffer, R., 1982, *Die Klassische Philologie von Petrarca bis Mommsen*, München
Plamenatz, J., 1992, *Man and Society*, 3 vols., London and New York (1963)
Pocock, J.G.A., 1989, *Politics, Language, and Time*, Chicago and London (1971)
Pocock, J.G.A., 1985, *Virtue, Commerce, and History*, Cambridge
Pocock, J.G.A., 1987, *The Ancient Constitution and the Feudal Law*, Cambridge (1957)
Pöschl, V., 1936, *Römischer Staat und Griechisches Staatsdenken bei Cicero, Untersuchungen zu Ciceros Schrift De Republica*, Berlin
Powis, J., 1984, *Aristocracy*, Oxford
Prang, H. (ed.), 1968, *Begriffsbestimmung der Romantik*, Darmstadt
Praz, M., 1970, *The Romantic Agony*, London and New York (1933)
Preston, R.A. and S.F.Wise, 1970, *Man in Arms, a History of Warfare and its Interrelations with Western Society*, 2nd edition, New York and Washington

Raaflaub, K., 1985, *Die Entdeckung der Freiheit*, München
Rahe, P.A., 1992, *Republics, Ancient and Modern*, Chapel Hill and London
Ramage, E.S., 1973, *Urbanitas; Ancient Sophistication and Refinement*, Norman Oklahoma
Ravitch, N., 1966, *Sword and Mitre, Government and Episcopate in France and England in the Age of Aristocracy*, The Hague and Paris
Rawson, E., 1975, *Cicero, a Portrait*, London
Rawson, E., 1991, *The Spartan Tradition in European Thought*, Oxford (1969)
Rébelliau, A., 1905, *Bossuet*, Paris 2nd ed.
Rehm, W., 1952, *Griechentum und Goethezeit*, 3rd ed.
Reichardt, R. and E.Schmitt (eds.), *Handbuch Politisch-Sozialer Grundbegriffe in Frankreich 1680-1820*, München

Reynolds, L.D. (ed.), 1983, *Texts and Transmission, a Survey of the Latin Classics*, Oxford

Roberts, M., 1967, 'The Military Revolution 1560-1660', in: M.Roberts, *Essays in Swedish History*, London

Roche, D., 1988, *Les Républicains des Lettres, Gens de Culture et Lumières au XVIIIe Siècle*, Paris

Rolfe, J.C., 1963, *Cicero and his Influence*, New York

Roloff, H., 1983, 'Maiores bei Cicero', in: Oppermann, (ed.) 1983

Rorty, R. et al. (eds.), 1984, *Philosophy in History*, Cambridge

Rougemont, D. de, 1956, *Passion and Society*, 2nd ed. London

Russell, B., 1979, *History of Western Philosophy*, London etc. (1946)

Ryffel, H., 1973, *Metabolè Politeión*, New York (1949)

Salmon, J.H.M., 1975, *Society in Crisis, France in the Sixteenth Century*, London and Tonbridge

Sap, J.W., 1993, *Wegbereiders der Revolutie*, Groningen

Shackleton, R., 1963, *Montesquieu, a Critical Biography*, Oxford (1961)

Schalk, E., 1986, *From Valor to Pedigree, Ideas of Nobility in France in the Sixteenth and Seventeenth Century*, Princeton

Schenk, H.G., 1979, *The Mind of the European Romantics*, Oxford (1966)

Schmitt, C., 1986, *Political Romanticism*, Cambridge Mass. and London (1919)

Schmitt, E. (ed.), 1973, *Die Französische Revolution*, Darmstadt

Schnur, Roman (ed.), 1986, *Die Rolle der Juristen bei der Entstehung des Modernen Staates*, Berlin

Scott, H.M., 1995, *The European Nobilities in the Seventeenth and Eighteenth Centuries*, 2 vols., London and New York

Schulz, F., 1963, *History of Roman Legal Science*, Oxford (1949)

Schumpeter, J., 1951, *Imperialism and Social Classes*, New York

Sée, H., 1978, *Les Idées Politiques en France au XVIIe Siècle*, Geneva (1923)

Shellabarger, S., 1935, *Lord Chesterfield*, New York

Shennan, J.H., 1968, *The Parlement of Paris*, Ithaca

Sherwin-White, A.N., 1987, *The Roman Citizenship*, Oxford, 2nd ed. (1973)

Sicard, A., 1970, *Les Études Classiques avant la Révolution*, Geneva (1887)

Simon, R., 1940, *Henry de Boulainviller: Historien, Politicien, Philosophe, Astrologe 1658-1722*, Gap

Skinner, Q., 1979, *The Foundations of Modern Political Thought*, 2 vols., Cambridge etc. (1978)

Stone, B., 1981, *The Parlement of Paris 1774-1789*, Chapell Hill

Süss, W., 1966, *Cicero, eine Einführung in seine Philosophischen Schriften*, Wiesbaden

Swart, K.W., 1949, *Sale of Offices in the Seventeenth Century*, The Hague
Syme, R., 1989, *The Roman Revolution*, Oxford and New York (1939)
Syme, R., 1958, *Tacitus*, 2 vols., Oxford

Tarkiainen, T., 1966, *Die Athenische Demokratie*, Zürich and Stuttgart
Taylor, A.J. (ed.), 1975, *The Standard of Living in Britain in the Industrial Revolution*, London and New York
Taylor, Ch., 1989, *Sources of the Self*, Cambridge
Taylor, G.V., 1973, 'Noncapitalist Wealth and the Origins of the French Revolution', in: Schmitt (ed.) 1973, originally in: The American Historical Review LXXII, 1967, pp.469-496
Thompson, M. et al., 1990, *Cultural Theory*, Boulder etc.
Trilling, L., 1971, *Sincerity and Authenticity*, Cambridge Mass.
Tuck, R., 1979, *Natural Right Theories, their Origin and Development*, Cambridge
Tully, J. (ed.), 1988, *Meaning and Context*, Oxford
Turner, F.M., 1981, *The Greek Heritage in Victorian Britain*, New Haven and London

Ullmann, W., 1975, *Medieval Political Thought*, Harmondsworth (1965)

Veyne, P., 1990, *Bread and Circuses*, Harmondsworth, abridged transl. of: *Le Pain et le Cirque*, Paris 1976
Veyne, P., 1992, 'The Roman Empire', in: P.Veyne (ed.), *The History of Private Life*, vol.I, Cambridge Mass. and London (1987)
Vierhaus, R. (ed.), 1971, *Der Adel vor der Revolution*, Göttingen
Vile, M., 1967, *Constitutionalism and the Separation of Powers*, Oxford
Vinogradoff, P., 1929, *Roman Law in Medieval Europe*, 2nd edition, Oxford
Vogt, J., 1974, *Ancient Slavery and the Ideal of Man*, Oxford

Walsh, P.G., 1967, *Livy, his Historical Aims and Methods*, Cambridge
Walzer, M., 1965, *The Revolution of the Saints, a Study of the Origins of Radical Politics*, Cambridge Mass. and London
Wardman, A., 1974, *Plutarch's Lives*, London
Weis, E., 'Der Französische Adel im 18.Jahrhundert', in: Vierhaus (ed.) 1971
Weiss, R., 1969, *The Renaissance Discovery of Classical Antiquity*, Oxford
Williams, B., 1993, *Shame and Necessity*, Berkeley etc.
Williams, E.N., 1970, *The Ancien Régime in Europe, Government and Society in the Major States 1648-1789*, London etc.
Wirszubski, Ch., 1950, *Libertas as a Political Idea at Rome during the Late Republic and Early Principate*, Cambridge

Wood, N., 1991, *Cicero's Social and Political Thought*, Berkeley etc. (1988)

Zielinski, Th., 1912, *Cicero im Wandel der Jahrhunderte*, 3rd ed. Leipzig and Berlin

Zimmern, A., 1969, *The Greek Commonwealth*, London etc. (1911)

INDEX

ABOUT THE AUTHOR

Andreas A.M. Kinneging studied political science at the Catholic University of Nijmegen. In 1990 he was appointed professor of political science at the University of Leiden. He is the author of various works (in Dutch), including *Liberalism and Political Economy, Philosophical Foundations of Liberalism,* and briefer writings in the periodical literature, and is the editor of *The Philosophers of Classical Liberalism.*